Clemes

# COLLINS

# ITALIAN

# PHRASE BOOK

D1221846

HarperCollins*Publishers*

first published in this edition 1995

© HarperCollins Publishers 1995

**first reprint 1996**

ISBN 0 00 470867-9

*Typeset by Morton Word Processing Ltd, Scarborough*
*Printed and bound in Great Britain by*
*Caledonian International Book Manufacturing Ltd, Glasgow, G64*

## Introduction

Your **Collins Phrase Book** is designed to give you instant access to all the words and phrases you will want while travelling abroad on business or for pleasure.

Unlike other phrase books it is arranged in A-Z order to take you straight to the word you want without having to search through different topics. And its simple, easy-to-use pronunciation guide to every word and phrase will ensure you communicate with confidence.

At the bottom of each page there is a list of ABSOLUTE ESSENTIALS – the key phrases and expressions you will need in any situation. And between the two sides of your **Phrase Book** you will find further explanations of pronunciation, charts showing how to convert from metric to imperial measures and easy reference lists of *Car Parts, Colours, Countries, Drinks, Fish and Seafood, Fruit and Nuts, Meats, Shops*, and *Vegetables*. These pages have a grey border to help you find them easily and to show you where one side of the **Phrase Book** ends and the other begins.

And finally, in the comprehensive glossary at the end of your **Phrase Book** you will find over 4,000 foreign-language words and phrases clearly translated. So in one complete package you have all the benefits of a dictionary with the simplicity of a phrase book. We hope you will enjoy using it.

## Abbreviations used in the text

| | |
|---|---|
| *adj* | adjective |
| *adv* | adverb |
| *Anat* | anatomical |
| *cm* | centimetre(s) |
| *conj* | conjunction |
| *equiv* | equivalent |
| *etc* | etcetera |
| *f* | feminine noun |
| *fpl* | feminine plural noun |
| *g* | gram(s) |
| *kg* | kilogram(s) |
| *km* | kilometre(s) |
| *l* | litre(s) |
| *m* | masculine noun; metre(s) |
| *m/f* | masculine or feminine noun |
| *mpl* | masculine plural noun |
| *n* | noun |
| *pl* | plural noun |
| *prep* | preposition |
| ® | registered trade mark |
| *sing* | singular |
| *vb* | verb |

# ENGLISH–ITALIAN

| | | |
|---|---|---|
| **a** | un | "oon" |
| | una | "oona" |
| ▷ a man | un uomo | "oon womo" |
| ▷ a woman | una donna | "oona donna" |
| **abbey** | l'abbazia (f) | "abbatseea" |
| **about** | su | "soo" |
| (*approximately*) | circa | "cheerka" |
| ▷ a book about Venice | un libro su Venezia | "oon leebro soo vaynaytsya" |
| ▷ about ten o'clock | circa le dieci | "cheerka lay deeechee" |
| **above** | sopra | "sopra" |
| **abseiling** | la discesa a corda doppia | "la deeschayza a korda doppya" |
| **access:** | | |
| ▷ is there access for the disabled? | è reso possibile l'accesso ai portatori di handicap? | "e rayzo poseebeelay lachaysso ayee portatohree dee andeekap" |
| **accident** | l'incidente (m) | "eencheedentay" |
| ▷ I've had an accident | ho avuto un incidente | "o avooto oon eencheedentay" |
| ▷ there's been an accident | c'è stato un incidente | "che stahto oon eencheedentay" |
| **accommodation** | l'alloggio (m) | "allodjo" |
| ▷ I need 3 nights' accommodation | cerco alloggio per tre notti | "cherkoh allodjo per tray nottee" |
| **to ache** | fare male | "fahray mahlay" |
| ▷ I've got a stomach ache | ho mal di stomaco | "o mal dee stohmako" |
| **activities:** | | |
| ▷ do you have activities for children? | organizzate delle attività per bambini? | "organeedzzahtay daylay atteeveeta payr bambeenee" |

|  |  |  |
|---|---|---|
| ▷ what indoor/outdoor activities are there? | quali attività ricreative al chiuso/all'aperto si possono fare? | "kwalee atteeveeta reekrayateevay al keeoozo/allahpayrto see possohno fahray" |
| **adaptor** (electrical) | il riduttore | "reedoottohray" |
| **address** | l'indirizzo (m) | "eendeereetsso" |
| ▷ my address is ... | il mio indirizzo è... | "eel meeo eendeereetsso e" |
| ▷ take me to this address | mi porti a quest'indirizzo | "mee portee a kwaysteendeereetsso" |
| ▷ will you write down the address please? | può scrivermi l'indirizzo, per cortesia? | "pwo skreevermee leendeereetsso payr kortayzeea" |
| **adhesive tape** | il nastro adesivo | "nastro adayzeevo" |
| ▷ I need some adhesive tape | ho bisogno di nastro adesivo | "o beezohnyo dee nastro adayzeevo" |
| **admission charge** | il prezzo del biglietto d'ingresso | "pretsso dayl beelyaytto deengresso" |
| **adult** | l'adulto (m) | "adoolto" |
| **advance:** | | |
| ▷ in advance | in anticipo | "een anteecheepo" |
| ▷ do I pay in advance? | pago in anticipo? | "pahgo een anteecheepo" |
| ▷ do I need to book in advance? | devo prenotare in anticipo? | "dayvo praynohtahray een anteecheepo" |
| **aerobics** | l'aerobica (f) | "ayrohbeeka" |
| **after** | dopo | "dopo" |
| **afternoon** | il pomeriggio | "pomayreedjo" |
| **aftershave** | il dopobarba | "dopobahrba" |
| **again** | di nuovo | "dee nwovo" |
| ▷ can you try again? | può provare di nuovo? | "pwo provahray dee nwovo" |
| **agent** | l'agente (m/f) | "ajentay" |

**ago:**

| ▷ long ago | tanto tempo fa | "tanto taympo fa" |
| ▷ a week ago | una settimana fa | "oona saytteemahna fa" |

| **AIDS** | l'AIDS (*m*) | "aeedeeayssay" |

| **air conditioning** | l'aria (*f*) condizionata | "ahreea kondeetsyonahta" |
| ▷ the air conditioning is not working | l'aria condizionata non funziona | "lahreea kondeetsyonahta nohn foontsyohna" |

| **air hostess** | l'hostess (*f*) | "ohstess" |

| **air line** (*in garage*) | il tubo dell'aria | "toobo dayllahreea" |

| **airline** | la linea aerea | "leenaya aayraya" |

| **air mail** | via aerea | "veea aayraya" |
| ▷ by air mail | per via aerea | "payr veea aayraya" |

| **air mattress** | il materassino gonfiabile | "matayrasseeno gonfeeahbeelay" |

| **airport** | l'aeroporto (*m*) | "aayroporto" |
| ▷ to the airport, please | all'aeroporto, per favore | "allaayroporto payr fahvohray" |

| **aisle** (*of church*) | la navata | "nahvahtah" |
| (*in train*) | il corridoio | "korreedohyo" |
| ▷ I'd like an aisle seat | vorrei un posto centrale | "vorreee oon posto chayntrahlay" |

| **alarm** | l'allarme (*m*) | "allahrmay" |

**alarm call:**

| ▷ an alarm call at 7 a.m. please | vorrei essere svegliato alle 7 di mattina, per favore | "vorreee essayray zvaylyahto allay settay dee mahteena payr fahvohray" |

| **alarm clock** | la sveglia | "zvaylya" |

| **alcohol** | l'alcool (*m*) | "alkool" |

| **alcoholic** | alcolico | "alkoleeko" |
| | alcolica | "alkoleeka" |

*ABSOLUTE ESSENTIALS*

| I don't understand | non capisco | "nohn kapeesko" |
| I don't speak Italian | non parlo l'italiano | "nohn parloh leetalyahno" |
| do you speak English? | parla inglese? | "parla eenglayzay" |
| could you help me? | può aiutarmi? | "pwo ayootarmee" |

| **all** | tutto | "tootto" |
| | tutta | "tootta" |
| **allergic** | allergico | "al**layr**jeeko" |
| | allergica | "al**layr**jeeka" |
| ▷ **I'm allergic to penicillin** | sono allergico alla penicillina | "sohnoh al**layr**jeeko alla payneecheel**lee**na" |
| **allowance** (*customs*) | la quantità consentita | "kwantee**ta** konsayn**tee**ta" |
| ▷ **I have the usual allowances of alcohol/ tobacco to declare** | ho la quantità consentita di alcool/ tabacco | "o la kwantee**ta** konsayn**tee**ta dee alkool/ta**bak**ko" |
| **all right** (*agreed*) | va bene | "va benay" |
| ▷ **are you all right?** | stai bene? | "staee benay" |
| **almond** | la mandorla | "**man**dorla" |
| **almost** | quasi | "kwahzee" |
| **also** | anche | "ankay" |
| **always** | sempre | "saympray" |
| **am:** | | |
| ▷ **I am** | sono | "sohnoh" |
| ▷ **I am not ready** | non sono pronto | "nohn sohnoh pronto" |
| **ambulance** | l'ambulanza (*f*) | "amboo**lant**sa" |
| ▷ **call an ambulance** | chiamate un'ambulanza | "keea**mah**tay oonamboo**lant**sa" |
| **America** | l'America (*f*) | "a**may**reeka" |
| **American** | americano | "amayree**kah**no" |
| | americana | "amayree**kah**na" |
| **amusement park** | il luna park | "loona park" |
| **anaesthetic** | l'anestetico (*m*) | "anay**ste**teeko" |
| **anchovy** | l'acciuga (*f*) | "ah**choo**ga" |
| **and** | e | "ay" |

| ABSOLUTE ESSENTIALS | | |
| --- | --- | --- |
| **I would like ...** | vorrei... | "vo**reee**" |
| **I need ...** | ho bisogno di... | "o bee**zohn**yo dee" |
| **where is ...?** | dov'è...? | "do**veh**" |
| **I'm looking for ...** | sto cercando... | "sto chayr**kan**do" |

| | | |
|---|---|---|
| **anorak** | la giacca a vento | "jakka a vento" |
| **another** | un altro | "oon altro" |
| | un'altra | "oon altra" |
| ▷ **another beer?** | ancora una birra? | "an**koh**ra oona beerra" |
| **antibiotic** | l'antibiotico (*m*) | "anteebee**o**teeko" |
| **antifreeze** | l'antigelo (*m*) | "antee**jay**lo" |
| **antihistamine** | l'antistaminico (*m*) | "anteestah**mee**neeko" |
| **antiseptic** | l'antisettico (*m*) | "antee**set**teeko" |
| **any:** | | |
| ▷ **I haven't any money** | non ho soldi | "nohn o soldee" |
| **apartment** | l'appartamento (*m*) | "apparta**mayn**to" |
| ▷ **we've booked an apartment in the name of ...** | abbiamo prenotato un appartamento a nome di... | "ab**yah**mo prayno**tah**to oon apparta**mayn**to a nohmay dee" |
| **apéritif** | l'aperitivo (*m*) | "apayree**tee**vo" |
| ▷ **we'd like an apéritif** | vorremmo un aperitivo | "vor**raym**mo oon apayree**tee**vo" |
| **apple** | la mela | "mayla" |
| **appointment** | l'appuntamento (*m*) | "appoonta**mayn**to" |
| ▷ **I'd like to make an appointment** | vorrei prendere un appuntamento | "vor**reee pren**dayray oon appoonta**mayn**to" |
| ▷ **can I please have an appointment?** | posso fissare un appuntamento, per favore? | "pohsso fees**sah**ray oon appoonta**mayn**to payr fa**voh**ray" |
| ▷ **I have an appointment with ...** | ho un appuntamento con... | "o oon appoonta**mayn**to kohn" |
| **apricot** | l'albicocca (*f*) | "albee**kok**ka" |
| **April** | aprile (*m*) | "ah**pree**lay" |
| **are:** | | |
| ▷ **you are** | sei | "say" |
| (*plural*) | siete | "see**ay**tay" |

| | | |
|---|---|---|
| (*polite form*) | è | "ay" |
| ▷ **we are** | siamo | "see**yah**mo" |
| ▷ **they are** | sono | "sohnoh" |
| **arm** | il braccio | "bratcho" |
| ▷ **in my arms** | nelle mie braccia | "nayllay meeay bratcha" |
| **armbands** (*for swimming*) | i bracciali | "brat**chah**lee" |
| **arrivals** | gli arrivi | "ar**ree**vee" |
| to **arrive** | arrivare | "arree**vah**ray" |
| ▷ **what time does the bus/train arrive?** | a che ora arriva l'autobus/il treno? | "ah kay ohra ahr**ree**va **low**toboos/eel traynoh" |
| ▷ **we arrived early/late** | siamo arrivati presto/tardi | "see**ah**mo arree**vah**tee presto/tardee" |
| **art gallery** | la galleria d'arte | "gallay**ree**a dartay" |
| **artichoke** | il carciofo | "kar**choh**fo" |
| **ascent:** | | |
| ▷ **when is the last ascent?** | quand'è l'ultima salita? | "kwande **lool**teema sa**lee**ta" |
| **ashore:** | | |
| ▷ **can we go ashore now?** | possiamo tornare a riva adesso? | "pohs**syah**mo tohr**nah**ray ah reeva a**days**so" |
| **ashtray** | il portacenere | "portachaynayray" |
| ▷ **may I have an ashtray?** | posso avere un portacenere? | "posso a**vay**ray oon porta**chay**nayray" |
| **asparagus** | gli asparagi | "a**spa**rajee" |
| **aspirin** | l'aspirina (*f*) | "aspee**ree**na" |
| **asthma** | l'asma (*f*) | "azma" |
| ▷ **I suffer from asthma** | soffro di asma | "sohffro dee azma" |
| **at** | a | "a" |
| ▷ **at home** | a casa | "a kahsa" |

| | | |
|---|---|---|
| **Athens** | Atene (f) | "atay nay" |
| **aubergine** | la melanzana | "maylant**sah**na" |
| **August** | agosto | "a**goh**sto" |
| **Australia** | l'Australia (f) | "ow**strah**lya" |
| **Australian** | australiano | "owstral**yah**no" |
| | australiana | "owstral**yah**na" |
| **Austria** | l'Austria (f) | "**ows**treeya" |
| **Austrian** | austriaco | "ows**tree**yako" |
| | austriaca | "ows**tree**yaka" |
| **automatic** | automatico | "owto**ma**teeko" |
| | automatica | "owto**ma**teeka" |
| ▷ **is it an automatic (car)?** | è un'automatica? | "ay oonowto**ma**teeka" |
| **autumn** | l'autunno (m) | "ow**toon**no" |
| **avalanche** | la valanga | "va**lan**ga" |
| ▷ **is there danger of avalanches?** | c'è pericolo di valanghe? | "che pay**ree**kolo dee va**lan**gay" |
| **avocado** | l'avocado (m) | "avo**kah**do" |
| **baby** | il bambino | "bam**bee**no" |
| **baby food** | gli alimenti per bambini | "alee**mayn**tee payr bam**bee**nee" |
| **baby seat** (in car) | il seggiolino per bebè | "sayjoh**lee**no payr baybay" |
| **baby-sitter** | il/la baby-sitter | "babysitter" |
| **baby-sitting:** | | |
| ▷ **is there a baby-sitting service?** | c'è un servizio di babysitter? | "che oon sayr**veets**yo dee babysitter" |
| **back**¹ n (of body) | la schiena | "ske**ee**na" |
| ▷ **I've got a bad back** | ho mal di schiena | "oh mal dee ske**ee**na" |

| *ABSOLUTE ESSENTIALS* | | |
|---|---|---|
| **I don't understand** | non capisco | "nohn ka**pee**sko" |
| **I don't speak Italian** | non parlo l'italiano | "nohn parloh leetal**yah**no" |
| **do you speak English?** | parla inglese? | "parla eeng**lay**zay" |
| **could you help me?** | può aiutarmi? | "pwo ayoo**tar**mee" |

| | | |
|---|---|---|
| ▷ **I've hurt my back** | mi sono fatto male alla schiena | "mee sohnoh fahttoh mahlay ahlla skeeena" |
| **back**[2] *adv:* | | |
| ▷ **we must be back at the hotel before six o'clock** | dobbiamo tornare in albergo prima delle sei | "dobyahmo tornahray een albayrgo preema dayllay sayee" |
| **backpack** | lo zaino | "**dza**eeno" |
| **bacon** | la pancetta | "pan**chayt**ta" |
| **bad** (*food*) | guasto | "gwasto" |
| | guasta | "gwasta" |
| (*weather, news*) | brutto | "brootto" |
| | brutta | "brootta" |
| **badminton** | il badminton | "badmeenton" |
| **bag** | la borsa | "borsa" |
| (*suitcase*) | la valigia | "va**lee**ja" |
| **baggage** | i bagagli | "ba**gal**yee" |
| **baggage allowance:** | | |
| ▷ **what is the baggage allowance?** | qual è il peso massimo consentito per il bagaglio? | "kwal ay eel payzo **mahs**seemo kohnsayn**tee**to payr eel ba**gal**yo" |
| **baggage reclaim** | il ritiro bagagli | "ree**tee**ro ba**gal**yee" |
| **baker's** | la panetteria | "panayttay**ree**a" |
| **balcony** | il balcone | "bal**koh**nay" |
| ▷ **do you have a room with a balcony?** | avete una camera con balcone? | "ah**vay**tay oona **ka**mayra con bal**koh**nay" |
| **ball** | la palla | "palla" |
| **ball game** | il gioco della palla | "johko dayla palla" |
| **banana** | la banana | "ba**na**na" |
| **band** (*musical*) | la banda | "banda" |

| ABSOLUTE ESSENTIALS | | |
|---|---|---|
| I would like ... | vorrei... | "vor**eee**" |
| I need ... | ho bisogno di... | "o bee**zohn**yo dee" |
| where is ...? | dov'è...? | "do**veh**" |
| I'm looking for ... | sto cercando... | "sto chayr**kan**do" |

| | | |
|---|---|---|
| **bandage** | la benda | "benda" |
| **bank** | la banca | "banka" |
| ▷ **is there a bank nearby?** | c'è una banca qui vicino? | "chay oona banka kwee vee**chee**no" |
| **bar** | il bar | "bar" |
| **barber** | il barbiere | "barb**yer**ay" |
| **basket** | il cestino | "chay**stee**no" |
| **bath** | il bagno | "banyo" |
| ▷ **to take a bath** | fare il bagno | "fahray eel banyo" |
| **bathing cap** | la cuffia | "koofya" |
| **bathroom** | il bagno | "banyo" |
| **battery** | la batteria | "battay**ree**a" |
| **to be** | essere | "**ay**ssayray" |

| | | |
|---|---|---|
| I am | sono | "sohnoh" |
| you are (*informal singular*) | sei | "say" |
| (*formal singular*) | è | "ay" |
| he/she/it is | è | "ay" |
| we are | siamo | "see**yah**mo" |
| you are (*plural*) | siete | "see**yay**tay" |
| they are | sono | "sono" |

| | | |
|---|---|---|
| **beach** | la spiaggia | "spee**ad**ja" |
| **beach ball** | il pallone da spiaggia | "pah**loh**nay da spee**ad**ja" |
| **beach umbrella** | l'ombrellone (*m*) | "ombray**loh**nay" |
| **beans** | i fagioli | "fa**jo**lee" |
| **beautiful** | bello | "bello" |
| | bella | "bella" |

| ABSOLUTE ESSENTIALS | | |
|---|---|---|
| **do you have ...?** | avete...? | "avaytay" |
| **is there ...?** | c'è...? | "che" |
| **are there ...?** | ci sono...? | "chee sohno" |
| **how much is ...?** | quanto costa...? | "kwanto kosta" |

| | | |
|---|---|---|
| **bed** | il letto | "letto" |
| **bedding:** | | |
| ▷ **is there any spare bedding?** | ci sono altre lenzuola e coperte? | "chee sohnoh altray layntswola ay kopayrtay" |
| **bedroom** | la camera da letto | "kamayra da letto" |
| **beef** | il manzo | "mandzo" |
| **beefburger** | l'hamburger (m) | "amboorgayr" |
| **beer** | la birra | "beerra" |
| ▷ **a draught beer, please** | una birra alla spina, per favore | "oona beerra alla speena payr favohray" |
| **beetroot** | la barbabietola | "bahrbabyetola" |
| **before** | prima di | "preema dee" |
| to **begin** | cominciare | "komeenchahray" |
| **behind** | dietro (di) | "deeetro (dee)" |
| **below** | sotto | "sotto" |
| **belt** | la cintura | "cheentoora" |
| **Berlin** | Berlino (f) | "bayrleeno" |
| **beside** | accanto a | "akkanto a" |
| **best:** | | |
| ▷ **the best** | il/la migliore | "eel/la meelyohray" |
| **better (than)** | meglio (di) | "melyo (dee)" |
| **between** | fra | "fra" |
| **bicycle** | la bicicletta | "beecheeklaytta" |
| **big** | grande | "granday" |
| ▷ **it's too big** | è troppo grande | "ay troppo granday" |
| **bigger** | più grande | "peeoo granday" |

| | | |
|---|---|---|
| ▷ do you have a bigger one? | ne avete uno più grande? | "nay ah**vay**tay oono peeoo granday" |
| **bikini** | il bikini | "bee**kee**nee" |
| **bill** | il conto | "kontoh" |
| ▷ put it on my bill | lo metta sul mio conto | "lo maytta sool meeo kontoh" |
| ▷ the bill, please | il conto, per favore | "eel kontoh payr fa**voh**ray" |
| ▷ can I have an itemized bill? | è possibile avere un conto dettagliato? | "ay po**ssee**beelay ah**vay**ray oon kontoh daytah**lya**to" |
| **bin** | il bidone | "bee**doh**nay" |
| **binoculars** | il binocolo | "bee**no**kolo" |
| **bird** | l'uccello (*m*) | "oot**chel**lo" |
| **birthday** | il compleanno | "komplay**an**no" |
| ▷ Happy Birthday! | Buon compleanno! | "bwon komplay**an**no" |
| **birthday card** | il biglietto di auguri di buon compleanno | "beel**yayt**to dee ow**goo**ree dee bwon komplay**an**no" |
| **bit:** | | |
| ▷ a bit of | un po' di | "oon po dee" |
| to **bite** | mordere | "**mohr**dayray" |
| (*insect*) | pungere | "**poon**jayray" |
| **bitten** | morso | "morso" |
| | morsa | "morsa" |
| (*by insect*) | punto | "poonto" |
| | punta | "poonta" |
| **bitter** | amaro | "a**mah**ro" |
| | amara | "a**mah**ra" |
| **black** | nero | "nayro" |
| | nera | "nayra" |
| **blackcurrant** | il ribes nero | "reebes nayro" |

*ABSOLUTE ESSENTIALS*

| | | |
|---|---|---|
| I don't understand | non capisco | "nohn ka**pees**ko" |
| I don't speak Italian | non parlo l'italiano | "nohn parloh leetal**yah**no" |
| do you speak English? | parla inglese? | "parla eeng**lay**zay" |
| could you help me? | può aiutarmi? | "pwo ayoo**tar**mee" |

| **blanket** | la coperta | "ko**payr**ta" |
| **bleach** | la candeggina | "kanday**jee**na" |
| **blister** (*on skin*) | la vescica | "**vay**sheeka" |
| **blocked** | bloccato | "blok**kah**to" |
| | bloccata | "blok**kah**ta" |
| ▷ **the drain is blocked** | sono bloccate le condutture | "sohnoh blok**kah**tay lay kohndoot**too**ray" |
| **blood group** | il gruppo sanguigno | "**groo**ppo san**gween**yo" |
| ▷ **my blood group is ...** | il mio gruppo sanguigno è... | "eel meeo **groo**ppo san**gween**yo e" |
| **blouse** | la camicetta | "kamee**chayt**ta" |
| to **blow-dry** | asciugare con il föhn | "ashoo**gah**ray kohn eel fon" |
| ▷ **a cut and blow-dry, please** | taglio e messa in piega, con il föhn, per favore | "talyo ay mayssa een pyega kohn eel fon payr fa**voh**ray" |
| **blue** | blu | "bloo" |
| **boarding card** | la carta d'imbarco | "karta deem**bar**ko" |
| **boarding house** | la pensione | "paynsee**oh**nay" |
| **boat** | la barca | "barka" |
| **boat trip** | la gita in barca | "jeeta een barka" |
| ▷ **are there any boat trips on the river/lake?** | ci sono delle gite in barca sul fiume/lago? | "chee sohnoh dayllay jeetay een barka sool fee**oo**may/lahgo" |
| **boiled** | bollito | "bol**lee**ta" |
| | bollita | "bol**lee**to" |
| **Bonn** | Bonn (*f*) | "bon" |
| **book**[1] *n* | il libro | "**lee**bro" |
| ▷ **a book of tickets** | un blocchetto di biglietti | "oon blok**kayt**to dee beely**ayt**tee" |

ABSOLUTE ESSENTIALS

| **I would like ...** | vorrei... | "vo**reee**" |
| **I need ...** | ho bisogno di... | "o bee**zohn**yo dee" |
| **where is ...?** | dov'è...? | "do**veh**" |
| **I'm looking for ...** | sto cercando... | "sto chayr**kan**do" |

| | | |
|---|---|---|
| to **book**[2] *vb* | prenotare | "prayno**tah**ray" |
| ▷ **can you book me into a hotel?** | può prenotarmi un posto in albergo? | "pwo prayno**tahr**mee oon pohstoh een al**bayr**go" |
| ▷ **should I book in advance?** | devo prenotare in anticipo? | "dayvo prayno**tah**ray een an**tee**cheepo" |
| ▷ **the table is booked for eight o'clock this evening** | il tavolo è riservato per le otto di questa sera | "eel **tah**volo e reezayr**vah**to payr lay otto dee **kway**sta sayra" |
| **booking** | la prenotazione | "praynotats**yoh**nay" |
| ▷ **can I change my booking?** | posso cambiare la mia prenotazione? | "posso kamb**yah**ray la meea praynotats**yoh**nay" |
| ▷ **I confirmed my booking by letter** | ho confermato la prenotazione per lettera | "o konfayr**mah**to la praynotats**yoh**nay payr **let**tayra" |
| ▷ **is there a booking fee?** | bisogna pagare la prenotazione? | "bee**zoh**nya **pa**gahray la praynotats**yoh**nay" |
| **booking office** | la biglietteria | "beelyaytttay**ree**a" |
| **bookshop** | la libreria | "leebray**ree**a" |
| **boot** (*shoe*) | lo stivale | "stee**vah**lay" |
| (*of car*) | il portabagagli | "portahba**gal**yee" |
| ▷ **a pair of boots** | un paio di stivali | "oon pahyo dee stee**vah**lee" |
| **border** | la frontiera | "front**ye**ra" |
| **botanic gardens** | i giardini botanici | "jar**dee**nee boh**tah**neechee" |
| **both** | tutti e due | "toottee ay dooay" |
| **bottle** | la bottiglia | "bot**teel**ya" |
| ▷ **a bottle of mineral water, please** | una bottiglia di acqua minerale, per favore | "oona bot**teel**ya dee akwa meenay**rah**lay payr fa**voh**ray" |
| ▷ **a bottle of gas** | una bombola (di gas) | "**bom**bohla (dee gaz)" |
| **bottle opener** | l'apribottiglie (*m*) | "apreebot**teel**yay" |

| | | |
|---|---|---|
| **do you have ...?** | avete...? | "avaytay" |
| **is there ...?** | c'è...? | "che" |
| **are there ...?** | ci sono...? | "chee sohnoh" |
| **how much is ...?** | quanto costa...? | "kwanto kosta" |

## box

14

| | | |
|---|---|---|
| box | la scatola | "**skah**tola" |
| box office | il botteghino | "bottay**gee**no" |
| boy | il ragazzo | "ra**gats**so" |
| boyfriend | il ragazzo | "ra**gats**so" |
| bra | il reggiseno | "raydjee**say**no" |
| bracelet | il braccialetto | "bratcha**layt**to" |
| brake fluid | l'olio (*m*) per i freni | "olyo payr ee fraynee" |
| brakes | i freni | "fraynee" |
| brandy | brandy | "brandy" |
| ▷ I'll have a brandy | prendo un brandy | "prendo oon brandy" |
| bread | il pane | "pahnay" |
| ▷ could we have some more bread? | ci porta ancora pane, per favore? | "chee pohrta an**koh**ra pahnay payr fa**voh**ray" |
| breakable | fragile | "**fra**jeelay" |
| breakdown | il guasto | "gwasto" |
| breakdown van | il carro attrezzi | "karro at**trayts**see" |
| ▷ can you send a breakdown van? | può mandare un carro attrezzi? | "pwo man**dah**ray oon karro at**trayts**see" |
| breakfast | la colazione | "kolats**yoh**nay" |
| ▷ what time is breakfast? | a che ora è la colazione? | "a kay ohra e la kolats**yoh**nay" |
| ▷ can we have breakfast in our room? | ci può portare la colazione nella nostra stanza? | "chee pwo por**tah**ray la kolats**yoh**nay nella nostra stantsa" |
| breast (*of woman*) | il seno | "sayno" |
| (*chest*) | il petto | "paytto" |
| (*of chicken*) | il petto | "paytto" |
| to breast-feed | allattare (al seno) | "allat**tah**ray (al sayno)" |
| to breathe | respirare | "rayspee**rah**ray" |

ABSOLUTE ESSENTIALS

| | | |
|---|---|---|
| yes (please) | sì (grazie) | "see (gratsyay)" |
| no (thank you) | no (grazie) | "no (gratsyay)" |
| hello | salve | "salvay" |
| goodbye | arrivederci | "arreevay**dayr**chee" |

| ▷ he can't breathe | non può respirare | "nohn pwo rayspee**rah**ray" |
|---|---|---|
| **briefcase** | la cartella | "kartella" |
| to **bring** | portare | "porta**hr**ay" |
| **Britain** | La Gran Bretagna | "gran bray**tan**ya" |
| ▷ have you ever been to Britain? | è mai stato in Gran Bretagna? | "e maee stahto een gran bray**tan**ya" |
| **British** | britannico britannica | "breet**an**neeko" "breet**an**neeka" |
| **broccoli** | i broccoli | "**broh**kohlee" |
| **brochure** | il dépliant | "daypleeon" |
| **broken** | rotto rotta | "rohtto" "rohtta" |
| ▷ I have broken the window | ho rotto un vetro | "o rohtto oon vaytro" |
| ▷ the lock is broken | la serratura è rotta | "la sayrra**too**ra e rohtta" |
| **broken down** | guasto guasta | "gwasto" "gwasta" |
| ▷ my car has broken down | la mia macchina si è rotta | "la meea **mak**keena see e rohtta" |
| **broken into:** | | |
| ▷ my car has been broken into | mi hanno aperto la macchina | "mee anno a**payr**to la **mak**keena" |
| **brooch** | la spilla | "speella" |
| **broom** | la scopa | "skopa" |
| **brother** | il fratello | "fratello" |
| **brown** | marrone | "mar**roh**nay" |
| **brush** | la spazzola | "**spats**sola" |
| **Brussels** | Bruxelles (f) | "brooksel" |

ABSOLUTE ESSENTIALS

| I don't understand | non capisco | "nohn ka**pee**sko" |
|---|---|---|
| I don't speak Italian | non parlo l'italiano | "nohn parloh leetal**yah**no" |
| do you speak English? | parla inglese? | "parla eeng**lay**zay" |
| could you help me? | può aiutarmi? | "pwo ayoo**tar**mee" |

| | | |
|---|---|---|
| **Brussels sprouts** | i cavoletti di Bruxelles | "kahvo**layt**tee dee brooksel" |
| **bucket** | il secchiello | "sek**yayl**lo" |
| **buffet** | il buffet | "boo**fe**" |
| **buffet car** | la carrozza ristorante | "karro**tss**a reesto**ran**tay" |
| **bulb** | la lampadina | "lampa**dee**na" |
| **bum bag** | il marsupio | "mar**soo**pyo" |
| **bun** | il panino dolce | "pa**nee**no dohlchay" |
| **bungee jumping:** | | |
| ▷ **where can I go bungee jumping?** | dove si può fare bungee jumping? | "dohvay see pwo fahray **ban**djee **jam**peeng" |
| **bureau de change** | l'ufficio (m) di cambio | "oo**ffee**cho dee **kam**byo" |
| **burst:** | | |
| ▷ **a burst tyre** | una gomma a terra | "**goh**mma a tayrra" |
| **bus** | l'autobus (m) | "**ow**toboos" |
| ▷ **where do I get the bus to town?** | dove posso prendere l'autobus per la città? | "dohvay posso **pren**dayray **low**toboos payr la cheetta" |
| ▷ **does this bus go to ...?** | quest'autobus va a...? | "kway**stow**toboos va a" |
| ▷ **where do I get a bus for the cathedral?** | da dove parte l'autobus per il duomo? | "da dohvay partay **low**toboos payr eel dwomo" |
| ▷ **which bus do I take for the museum?** | quale autobus devo prendere per andare al museo? | "kwalay **ow**toboos dayvo **pren**dayray payr an**dah**ray al moo**zay**o" |
| ▷ **how frequent are the buses to town?** | ogni quanto ci sono gli autobus per la città? | "onyee kwanto chee sohnoh lyee **ow**toboos payr la cheetta" |
| ▷ **what time is the last bus?** | quando parte l'ultimo autobus? | "kwando partay **lool**teemo **ow**toboos" |
| ▷ **when does the bus leave?** | a che ora parte l'autobus? | "a kay ohra partay **low**toboos" |

| | | |
|---|---|---|
| ▷ what time does the bus arrive? | a che ora arriva l'autobus? | "a kay ohra arreeva **low**toboos" |
| **business** | gli affari | "af**fah**ree" |
| ▷ I am here on business | sono qui per affari | "sohnoh kwee payr af**fah**ree" |
| ▷ a business trip | un viaggio d'affari | "vee**adj**o daf**fah**ree" |
| **bus station** | la stazione degli autobus | "stats**yoh**nay dayllay **ow**toboos" |
| **bus stop** | la fermata (dell'autobus) | "fayr**mah**ta (dayl**low**toboos)" |
| **bus tour** | la gita in pullman | "jeeta een poolman" |
| **busy** | occupato occupata | "okkoo**pah**to" "okkoo**pah**ta" |
| ▷ the line is busy | la linea è occupata | "la leenya e okoo**pah**ta" |
| **but** | ma | "ma" |
| **butcher** | il macellaio | "machayl**la**yo" |
| **butter** | il burro | "boorro" |
| **button** | il bottone | "bot**toh**nay" |
| to **buy** | comprare | "kom**prah**ray" |
| ▷ where do we buy our tickets? | dove si comprano i biglietti? | "dohvay see **kohm**prano ee beely**ayt**tee" |
| ▷ where can I buy some postcards? | dove posso comprare delle cartoline? | "dohvay posso kom**prah**ray dayllay karto**lee**nay" |
| **by** *(close to)* *(via)* *(beside)* | vicino a via accanto a | "vee**chee**no a" "veea" "ak**kan**to a" |
| **bypass** | la strada di circonvallazione | "strahda dee cherkonvallats**yoh**nay" |
| **cabaret** | il cabaret | "kaba**re**" |

ABSOLUTE ESSENTIALS

| | | |
|---|---|---|
| do you have ...? | avete...? | "avaytay" |
| is there ...? | c'è...? | "che" |
| are there ...? | ci sono...? | "chee sohnoh" |
| how much is ...? | quanto costa...? | "kwanto kosta" |

| | | |
|---|---|---|
| ▷ where can we go to see a cabaret? | dove possiamo andare per vedere un cabaret? | "dohvay posyahmo andahray payr vaydayray oon kabare" |
| **cabbage** | il cavolo | "kahvolo" |
| **cabin** (*hut*) | la capanna | "kapanna" |
| (*on ship*) | la cabina | "kabeena" |
| ▷ a first/second class cabin | una cabina di prima/ seconda classe | "oona kabeena dee preema/saykohnda klassay" |
| **cable car** | la funivia | "fooneeveea" |
| **café** | il caffè | "kaffe" |
| **cagoule** | la giacca a vento | "jakka a vento" |
| **cake** | la torta | "torta" |
| **calculator** | la calcolatrice | "kahlkohlahtreechay" |
| **call**[1] *n* (*on telephone*) | la chiamata | "keeamahta" |
| ▷ a long-distance call | una chiamata interurbana | "keeamahta eentayroorbahna" |
| ▷ an international call | una chiamata internazionale | "oona keeamahta eentayrnatsyonahlay" |
| ▷ I want to make a phone call | voglio fare una telefonata | "volyo fahray oona taylayfonahta" |
| to **call**[2] *vb* | chiamare | "keeamahray" |
| ▷ may I call you tomorrow? | la posso chiamare domani? | "la posso keeamahray dohmahnee" |
| ▷ please call me back | la prego di richiamare | "la praygo dee reekeeamahray" |
| **call box** | la cabina telefonica | "kabeena taylayfohneeka" |
| **calm** | calmo | "kalmo" |
| | calma | "kalma" |
| ▷ keep calm! | calma! | "kalma" |
| **camcorder** | il camcorder | "kamkohrdayr" |

| **camera** | la macchina fotografica | "**mak**keena foto**gra**feeka" |
|---|---|---|
| to **camp** | campeggiare | "kampayd**jah**ray" |
| ▷ **may we camp here?** | possiamo campeggiare qui? | "pos**yah**mo kampayd**jah**ray kwee" |
| **camp bed** | il lettino da campeggio | "let**tee**no da kam**payd**jo" |
| **camp site** | il campeggio | "kam**payd**jo" |
| ▷ **we're looking for a camp site** | stiamo cercando un campeggio | "stee**ah**mo chayr**kan**do oon kam**payd**jo" |
| **can**[1] *n* | il barattolo | "ba**rat**tolo" |
| **can**[2] *vb* | potere | "po**tay**ray" |

| **I can** | posso | "posso" |
|---|---|---|
| **you can** (*informal singular*) | puoi | "pwoy" |
| (*formal singular*) | può | "pwo" |
| **he/she/it can** | può | "pwo" |
| **we can** | possiamo | "pos**yah**mo" |
| **you can** (*plural*) | potete | "po**tay**tay" |
| **they can** | possono | "**pos**sohno" |

| ▷ **can I ...?** | posso...? | "posso" |
|---|---|---|
| ▷ **we can't come** | non possiamo venire | "nohn pos**yah**mo vay**nee**ray" |
| **Canada** | il Canada | "kana**da**" |
| **Canadian** | canadese | "kana**day**zay" |
| **canal** | il canale | "ka**nah**lay" |
| to **cancel**: | | |
| ▷ **I want to cancel my booking** | vorrei disdire la prenotazione | "vor**reee** dis**dee**ray la praynotats**yoh**nay" |

*ABSOLUTE ESSENTIALS*

| **I don't understand** | non capisco | "nohn ka**pee**sko" |
|---|---|---|
| **I don't speak Italian** | non parlo l'italiano | "nohn parloh leetal**yah**no" |
| **do you speak English?** | parla inglese? | "parla eeng**lay**zay" |
| **could you help me?** | può aiutarmi? | "pwo ayoo**tar**mee" |

**cancellation:**

| | | |
|---|---|---|
| ▷ **are there any cancellations?** | sono state disdette delle prenotazioni? | "sohnoh stahtay dees**day**tay daylay praynotats**yoh**nee" |
| **canoe** | la canoa | "kan**oa**" |
| **canoeing:** | | |
| ▷ **where can we go canoeing?** | dove possiamo andare a fare canoa? | "dohvay pos**syah**mo an**dah**ray a fahray kan**oa**" |
| **can-opener** | l'apriscatole (m) | "apree**skat**ohlay" |
| **car** | la macchina | "**mak**keena" |
| ▷ **I want to hire a car** | voglio noleggiare una macchina | "volyo nolaydj**ah**ray oona **mak**keena" |
| ▷ **my car has been broken into** | mi hanno aperto la macchina | "mee anno a**payr**to la **mak**keena" |
| ▷ **my car has broken down** | la mia macchina si è rotta | "la meea **mak**keena see e rohtta" |
| **carafe** | la caraffa | "ka**raf**fa" |
| ▷ **a carafe of house wine please** | una caraffa di vino della casa, per favore | "oona ka**raf**fa dee veeno dayla kaza payr fa**voh**ray" |
| **caravan** | la roulotte | "roo**lot**" |
| ▷ **can we park our caravan there?** | possiamo mettere là la nostra roulotte? | "pos**yah**mo **mayt**tayray la la nostra roo**lot**" |
| **caravan site** | il campeggio per roulotte | "kam**payd**jo payr roo**lot**" |
| **carburettor** | il carburatore | "kahrboora**toh**ray" |
| **card** (greetings) (playing) | la cartolina la carta da gioco | "karto**lee**na" "karta da joko" |
| ▷ **birthday card** | il biglietto di auguri di buon compleanno | "beel**yay**to dee ow**goo**ree dee bwon komplay**an**no" |
| **cardigan** | il cardigan | "cardigan" |

| ABSOLUTE ESSENTIALS | | |
|---|---|---|
| I would like ... | vorrei... | "vor**eee**" |
| I need ... | ho bisogno di... | "o bee**zoh**nyo dee" |
| where is ...? | dov'è...? | "do**veh**" |
| I'm looking for ... | sto cercando... | "sto chayr**kan**do" |

## cash desk

| | | |
|---|---|---|
| **careful** | attento | "at**tayn**to" |
| | attenta | "at**tayn**ta" |
| ▷ **be careful!** | stia attento! | "**stee**a at**tayn**to" |
| **car ferry** | il traghetto | "tra**gayt**to" |
| **car number** | il numero di targa | "eel **noo**mayroh dee **tahr**ga" |
| **car park** | il parcheggio | "par**kayd**jo" |
| ▷ **is there a car park near here?** | c'è un parcheggio qui vicino? | "chay oon par**kayd**jo kwee vee**chee**no" |
| **carpet** | il tappeto | "tap**pay**to" |
| **carriage** (*railway*) | la carrozza | "kar**rots**sa" |
| **carrier bag** | la busta di plastica | "**boos**ta dee **plas**teeka" |
| ▷ **could I have a carrier bag?** | potrei avere una busta di plastica? | "po**tray** a**vay**ray **oo**na **boos**ta dee **plas**teeka" |
| **carrots** | le carote | "ka**ro**tay" |
| to **carry** | portare | "por**tah**ray" |
| **car wash** | il lavaggio auto | "la**vad**jo **ow**to" |
| ▷ **how do I use the car wash?** | come funziona il lavaggio auto? | "**koh**may foonts**yoh**na eel la**vad**jo **ow**to" |
| **case** (*suitcase*) | la valigia | "va**lee**ja" |
| **cash**[1] *n* | i contanti | "kon**tan**tee" |
| ▷ **I haven't any cash** | non ho contanti | "nohn o kon**tan**tee" |
| ▷ **can I get a cash advance with my credit card?** | posso avere un anticipo con la mia carta di credito? | "**posso** a**vay**ray oon an**tee**cheepo kohn la **mee**a **kar**ta dee **kray**deeto" |
| to **cash**[2] *vt* (*cheque*) | incassare | "eenkas**sah**ray" |
| ▷ **can I cash a cheque?** | posso incassare un assegno? | "**posso** eenkas**sah**ray oon as**sayn**yo" |
| **cash desk** | la cassa | "**kas**sa" |

| | | |
|---|---|---|
| **cash dispenser** | lo sportello automatico | "sport**ay**llo owtoh**mah**teeko" |
| **cashier** | il cassiere | "kas**ye**ray" |
| **casino** | il casinò | "kazee**no**" |
| **cassette** | la cassetta | "ka**sayt**ta" |
| **cassette player** | il mangiacassette | "mandjahkas**say**tay" |
| **castle** | il castello | "ka**stel**lo" |
| ▷ **is the castle open to the public?** | il castello è aperto al pubblico? | "eel ka**stel**lo e a**payr**to al **poob**bleeko" |
| **Catacombs** | le Catacombe | "kata**kom**bay" |
| **to catch** | prendere | "**pren**dayray" |
| ▷ **where do we catch the ferry to ...** | dove si prende il traghetto per... | "dohvay see prenday eel tra**gayt**to payr" |
| **cathedral** | il duomo | "dwomo" |
| ▷ **excuse me, how do I get to the cathedral?** | scusi, come faccio per andare al duomo? | "skoozee kohmay fatcho payr an**dah**ray al dwomo" |
| **Catholic** | cattolico cattolica | "kat**to**leeko" "kat**to**leeka" |
| **cauliflower** | il cavolfiore | "kahvolf**yoh**ray" |
| **cave** | la grotta | "grotta" |
| **caviar** | il caviale | "ka**vya**lay" |
| **CD** | il CD | "cheedee" |
| **celery** | il sedano | "**se**dano" |
| **cemetery** | il cimitero | "cheemee**tay**ro" |
| **centimetre** | il centimetro | "chayn**tee**maytro" |
| **central** | centrale | "chayn**trah**lay" |

| | | |
|---|---|---|
| **yes (please)** | sì (grazie) | "see (gratsyay)" |
| **no (thank you)** | no (grazie) | "no (gratsyay)" |
| **hello** | salve | "salvay" |
| **goodbye** | arrivederci | "arreevay**dayr**chee" |

| **central station** | la stazione centrale | "stats**yoh**nay chayn**trah**lay" |
| ▷ **where is the central station?** | dov'è la stazione centrale? | "dohveh la stats**yoh**nay chayn**trah**lay" |
| **centre** | il centro | "**chen**tro" |
| ▷ **how far are we from the town centre?** | quanto dista il centro da qui? | "kwanto deesta eel **chen**tro da kwee" |
| **cereal** (*for breakfast*) | i fiocchi di cereali | "fee**ok**kee dee chayray**ah**lee" |
| **certain** (*sure*) | certo | "**chayr**to" |
| | certa | "**chayr**ta" |
| **certificate** | il certificato | "chayrteefee**kah**to" |
| ▷ **an insurance certificate** | un certificato di assicurazione | "oon chayrteefee**kah**to dee asseekoorats**yoh**nay" |
| **chain** | la catena | "ka**tay**na" |
| ▷ **do I need chains?** | c'è bisogno di catene? | "che bee**zohn**yo dee ka**tay**nay" |
| **chair** | la sedia | "**sed**ya" |
| **chairlift** | la seggiovia | "saydjo**vee**a" |
| **chalet** | lo chalet | "sha**le**" |
| **champagne** | lo champagne | "shang**pan**ye" |
| **change**[1] *n* | il cambio | "**kamb**yo" |
| (*small coins*) | gli spiccioli | "**speet**cholee" |
| (*money returned*) | il resto | "**res**to" |
| ▷ **could you give me change of ...?** | mi può dare... in moneta? | "mee pwo dahray ... een mo**nay**ta" |
| ▷ **sorry, I don't have any change** | mi dispiace, non ho spiccioli | "mee deespee**a**chay nohn o **speet**cholee" |
| ▷ **keep the change** | tenga pure il resto | "tenga pooray eel **res**to" |
| ▷ **have you any change?** | avete da cambiare? | "a**vay**tay da kamb**yah**ray" |
| **to change**[2] *vb* | cambiare | "kamb**yah**ray" |

*ABSOLUTE ESSENTIALS*

| **I don't understand** | non capisco | "nohn ka**pees**ko" |
| **I don't speak Italian** | non parlo l'italiano | "nohn parloh leetal**yah**no" |
| **do you speak English?** | parla inglese? | "parla eeng**lay**zay" |
| **could you help me?** | può aiutarmi? | "pwo ayoo**tar**mee" |

| | | |
|---|---|---|
| ▷ where can I change some money? | dove posso cambiare i soldi? | "dohvay posso kambyahray ee soldee" |
| ▷ I'd like to change these traveller's cheques | vorrei cambiare questi traveller's cheque | "vorreee kambyahray kwaystee travellers cheque" |
| ▷ I want to change some pounds into lire | vorrei cambiare delle sterline in lire | "vorreee kambyahray dayllay stayrleenay een leeray" |
| ▷ where can I change the baby? | dove posso cambiare il bambino? | "dohvay posso kambyahray eel bambeeno" |
| ▷ where do I change? (bus etc) | dove devo cambiare? | "dohvay dayvo kambyahray" |
| ▷ where do we change? (clothes) | dove sono gli spogliatoi? | "dohvay sohnoh lyee spolyatoee" |
| ▷ is the weather going to change? | il tempo cambierà? | "eel tempo kambyayra" |
| ▷ can I change my booking? | posso cambiare la mia prenotazione? | "posso kambyahray la meea praynotatsyohnay" |
| **changing room** | lo spogliatoio | "spolyatoyo" |
| **Channel tunnel** | il tunnel sotto la Manica | "toonel sohttoh la maneeka" |
| **chapel** | la cappella | "kappella" |
| **charge¹** n: | | |
| ▷ is there a charge per kilometre? | bisogna pagare secondo il chilometraggio? | "beezohnya pagahray saykohndoh eel keelomaytradjo" |
| ▷ I want to reverse the charges | voglio addebitare la spesa al ricevente | "volyo addaybeetahray la spayza al reechayventay" |
| ▷ is there a charge? | bisogna pagare? | "beezohnya pahgahray" |
| **to charge²** vb: | | |
| ▷ how much do you charge? | quanto vuole? | "kwanto vwohlay" |

ABSOLUTE ESSENTIALS

| | | |
|---|---|---|
| I would like ... | vorrei... | "voreee" |
| I need ... | ho bisogno di... | "o beezohnyo dee" |
| where is ...? | dov'è...? | "doveh" |
| I'm looking for ... | sto cercando... | "sto chayrkando" |

| ▷ please charge it to my room | lo metta sul conto della camera, per favore | "lo maytta sool kohnto dayla kamayra payr favohray" |
|---|---|---|
| **cheap** | economico economica | "aykonomeeko" "aykonomeeka" |
| **cheaper** | meno costoso meno costosa | "mayno kohstohzo" "mayno kohstohza" |
| ▷ have you anything cheaper? | c'è niente di meno costoso? | "chay neeayntay dee mayno kohstohzo" |
| to **check** | controllare | "kontrollahray" |
| to **check in** (*at airport*) (*at hotel*) | fare il check-in firmare il registro | "fahray eel checkin" "feermahray eel rayjeestro" |
| ▷ where do I check in for the flight to Milan? | dov'è il check-in del volo per Milano? | "dohvay eel checkin del vohloh payr meelahno" |
| ▷ when do I have to check in? | quando devo fare il check-in? | "kwando dayvo fahray eel checkin" |
| ▷ where do I check in my luggage? | dove si fa il check-in? | "dohvay see fah eel checkin" |
| **check-in desk** | l'accettazione (*f*) bagagli | "atchayttatsyohnay bagalyee" |
| **cheerio** | ciao | "chao" |
| **cheers!** | salute! | "salootay" |
| **cheese** | il formaggio | "formadjo" |
| **cheeseburger** | il cheeseburger | "cheezboorgayr" |
| **chemist's** | la farmacia | "farmacheea" |
| **cheque** | l'assegno (*m*) | "assaynyo" |
| ▷ can I pay by cheque? | posso pagare con un assegno? | "posso pagahray kohn oon assaynyo" |
| ▷ I want to cash a cheque, please | vorrei incassare un assegno, per favore | "vorreee eenkassahray oon assaynyo payr favohray" |

*ABSOLUTE ESSENTIALS*

| do you have ...? | avete...? | "avaytay" |
|---|---|---|
| is there ...? | c'è...? | "che" |
| are there ...? | ci sono...? | "chee sohnoh" |
| how much is ...? | quanto costa...? | "kwanto kosta" |

| | | |
|---|---|---|
| **cheque book** | il libretto degli assegni | "lee**brayt**to dayllyee as**sayn**yee" |
| ▷ **I've lost my cheque book** | ho perso il libretto degli assegni | "o payrso eel lee**brayt**to dayllyee as**sayn**yee" |
| **cheque card** | la carta assegni | "karta as**sayn**yee" |
| **cherries** | le ciliegie | "cheel**ye**jay" |
| **chess** | gli scacchi | "s**kah**kee" |
| ▷ **to play chess** | giocare a scacchi | "jo**kah**ray a s**kah**kee" |
| **chest** | il petto | "petto" |
| ▷ **I have a pain in my chest** | ho un dolore al petto | "o oon doh**loh**ray al petto" |
| **chestnut** | la castagna | "ka**stan**ya" |
| **chewing gum** | la gomma da masticare | "**goh**mma da mastee**kah**ray" |
| **chicken** | il pollo | "**poh**llo" |
| **chickenpox** | la varicella | "varee**chel**la" |
| **chicken soup** | la minestra di pollo | "mee**nay**stra dee **poh**llo" |
| **child** | il bambino | "bam**bee**no" |
| | la bambina | "bam**bee**na" |
| **child minder** | la bambinaia | "bambee**nay**a" |
| **children** (*infants*) | i bambini | "bam**bee**nee" |
| (*older children*) | i ragazzi | "ra**gats**see" |
| ▷ **is there a children's pool?** | c'è una piscina per bambini? | "che oona pee**shee**na payr bam**bee**nee" |
| ▷ **is there a paddling pool for the children?** | c'è una piscina per bambini? | "chay oona pee**shee**na payr bam**bee**nee" |
| **chi(l)li** | il peperoncino | "paypayron**chee**no" |
| **chips** | le patatine fritte | "pata**tee**nay freettay" |
| **chives** | l'erba (*f*) cipollina | "ayrba cheepoh**lee**na" |

| | | |
|---|---|---|
| **chocolate** | la cioccolata | "chokko**lah**ta" |
| ▷ **I'd like a bar of chocolate, please** | una tavoletta di cioccolata, per favore | "oona tavoh**layt**ta dee chokko**lah**ta payr fa**voh**ray" |
| **chocolates** | i cioccolatini | "chokkola**tee**nee" |
| **chop:** | | |
| ▷ **a pork/lamb chop** | una costoletta di maiale/agnello | "oona kostoh**layt**ta dee mayalay/ah**nyayl**lo" |
| **Christmas** | il Natale | "na**tah**lay" |
| ▷ **Merry Christmas!** | buon Natale! | "bwon na**tah**lay" |
| **church** | la chiesa | "kee**ee**za" |
| ▷ **where is the nearest church?** | dov'è la chiesa più vicina? | "doh**ve** la kee**ee**za peeoo vee**chee**na" |
| ▷ **where is there a Protestant/Catholic church?** | dove posso trovare una chiesa protestante/cattolica? | "dohvay posso tro**vah**ray oona kee**ee**za **pro**taystantay/ kat**toh**leeka" |
| **cider** | il sidro | "**see**dro" |
| **cigar** | il sigaro | "**see**garo" |
| **cigarette papers** | le cartine per sigarette | "kar**tee**nay payr seega**rayt**tay" |
| **cigarettes** | le sigarette | "seega**rayt**tay" |
| ▷ **a packet of cigarettes, please** | un pacchetto di sigarette, per favore | "oon pak**kayt**to dee seega**rayt**tay payr fa**voh**ray" |
| **cinema** | il cinema | "**chee**nayma" |
| ▷ **what's on at the cinema?** | cosa danno al cinema? | "koza danno al **chee**nayma" |
| **circus** | il circo | "**cheer**ko" |
| **cities** | le città | "chee**ta** " |
| **city** | la città | "chee**ta** " |

| | | |
|---|---|---|
| **clean¹** *adj* | pulito | "pooleeto" |
| | pulita | "pooleeta" |
| ▷ the room isn't clean | la stanza non è pulita | "la stantsa nohn ay pooleeta" |
| ▷ could I have a clean spoon/a clean fork please? | potrei avere un cucchiaio pulito/una forchetta pulita, per favore? | "potray **ah**vayray oon koo**kya**yo poo**lee**to/oona for**kayt**ta poo**lee**ta payr fa**voh**ray" |
| to **clean²** *vb* | pulire | "pooleeray" |
| ▷ where can I get this skirt cleaned? | dove posso far pulire questa gonna? | "dohvay posso fahr pooleeray kwaysta gonna" |
| **cleaner** | l'addetto/a alle pulizie | "ad**dayt**to/a allay pooleetseeay" |
| ▷ which day does the cleaner come? | in che giorno vengono a fare le pulizie? | "een kay jorno **ven**gohno a fahray lay pooleetseeay" |
| **cleansing cream** | la crema detergente | "krema daytayr**jen**tay" |
| **cleansing solution for contact lenses** | il liquido per la pulizia delle lenti a contatto | "**lee**kweedo payr la pooleetseea dayllay layntee a kon**tat**to" |
| **client** | il/la cliente | "klee**en**tay" |
| **cliff** (*sea cliff*) | la scogliera | "sko**lyay**ra" |
| (*of mountain*) | il dirupo | "dee**roo**po" |
| **climbing** | l'alpinismo (*m*) | "alpee**neez**mo" |
| **climbing boots** | gli scarponi da montagna | "skar**poh**nee da mon**tan**ya" |
| **cloakroom** | il guardaroba | "gwarda**roh**ba" |
| **clock** | l'orologio (*m*) | "oro**lo**jo" |
| ▷ 5 o'clock | le 5 | "lay **cheen**kway" |
| **close¹** *adj* (*near*) | vicino a | "vee**chee**no a" |
| | vicina a | "vee**chee**na a" |

| to **close**² *vb* | chiudere | "kee**oo**dayray" |
| ▷ what time do you close? | a che ora chiudete? | "a kay ohra kee**oo**day**tay**" |
| ▷ the door will not close | la porta non si chiude | "la porta nohn see kee**oo**day" |
| **closed** | chiuso | "kee**oo**zo" |
| | chiusa | "kee**oo**za" |
| **cloth** | lo straccio | "stratcho" |
| **clothes** | i vestiti | "vay**stee**tee" |
| **clothes peg** | la molletta | "mol**layt**ta" |
| **cloudy** | nuvoloso | "noovo**loh**zo" |
| | nuvolosa | "noovo**loh**za" |
| **clove** | il chiodo | "kee**o**do" |
| **club** | il club | "kloob" |
| ▷ a night club | un night-club | "oon nayt kloob" |
| ▷ a set of golf clubs | un set di mazze da golf | "oon set dee matsay da golf" |
| **coach** (*bus*) | il pullman | "poolman" |
| (*train*) | la carrozza | "kar**rots**sa" |
| ▷ when does the coach leave in the morning? | a che ora parte il pullman alla mattina? | "a kay ohra partay eel poolman alla mat**tee**na" |
| **coach station** | la stazione delle autocorriere | "stats**yoh**nay daylay owtohkohr**ryay**ray" |
| **coach trip** | la gita in pullman | "jeeta een poolman" |
| **coast** | la costa | "kosta" |
| **coastguard** | il guardacoste | "gwarda**kos**tay" |
| **coat** | il cappotto | "kap**pot**to" |
| **coat hanger** | la gruccia | "grootcha" |
| **cockroaches** | gli scarafaggi | "skara**fah**djee" |
| **cocktail** | il cocktail | "cocktail" |

| | | |
|---|---|---|
| **cocoa** | il cacao | "ka**ka**o" |
| **coconut** | la noce di cocco | "**noh**chay dee **kok**ko" |
| **cod** | il merluzzo | "mayr**loot**so" |
| **coffee** | il caffè | "kaf**fe**" |
| ▷ **white coffee** | il caffellatte | "kaffay**laht**tay" |
| ▷ **black coffee** | il caffè nero | "kaf**fe** nayro" |
| **coin** | la moneta | "mo**nay**ta" |
| ▷ **what coins do I need?** | che monete mi servono? | "kay moh**nay**tay mee **sayr**vohno" |
| ▷ **a 100 lire coin** | una moneta da cento lire | "oona mo**nay**ta da **chay**nto **lee**ray" |
| **Coke**® | la coca | "**ko**ka" |
| **colander** | lo scolapasta | "skola**pas**ta" |
| **cold**[1] *n* | il raffreddore | "raffrayd**doh**ray" |
| ▷ **I have a cold** | ho il raffreddore | "o eel raffrayd**doh**ray" |
| **cold**[2] *adj* | freddo | "fray**ddo**" |
| | fredda | "fray**dda**" |
| ▷ **I'm cold** | ho freddo | "o fray**ddo**" |
| ▷ **will it be cold tonight?** | farà freddo stasera? | "fara freddo sta**say**ra" |
| **cold meat** | gli affettati | "affayt**tah**tee" |
| **Colosseum** | il Colosseo | "kolos**say**o" |
| **colour** | il colore | "ko**loh**ray" |
| ▷ **I don't like the colour** | non mi piace il colore | "nohn mee peea**chay** eel koh**loh**ray" |
| ▷ **I need a colour film** | ho bisogno di un rullino a colori | "o bee**zohn**yo dee oon rool**lee**no a koh**loh**ree" |
| ▷ **do you have it in another colour?** | l'avete in un diverso colore? | "lah**vay**tay een oon dee**vayr**so ko**loh**ray" |
| ▷ **a colour TV** | un televisore a colori | "oon taylayvee**zoh**ray a ko**loh**ree" |
| **comb** | il pettine | "**pet**teenay" |

*compulsory*

| | | |
|---|---|---|
| to **come** | venire | "vay**nee**ray" |
| (*arrive*) | arrivare | "arree**vah**ray" |
| ▷ **what does that come to?** | quanto fa in tutto? | "kwanto fa een tootto" |
| to **come back** | tornare | "tor**nah**ray" |
| to **come in** | entrare | "ayn**trah**ray" |
| ▷ **come in!** | avanti! | "a**van**tee" |
| **comfortable** | comodo | "**ko**modo" |
| | comoda | "**ko**moda" |
| **commission** | la commissione | "kohmees**syoh**nay" |
| ▷ **how much commission do you charge?** | quanto chiedete di commissione? | "kwanto kyay**day**tay dee kohmees**syoh**nay" |
| **compact disc** | il compact disc | "**kom**pakt deesk" |
| **compact disc player** | il lettore CD | "layt**toh**ray cheedee" |
| **company** | la compagnia | "kompan**yee**a" |
| **compartment** | lo scompartimento | "skompartee**mayn**to" |
| ▷ **I want to book a seat in a non-smoking compartment** | voglio prenotare un posto in uno scompartimento per non fumatori | "volyo prayno**tah**ray oon posto een oono skompartee**mayn**to payr nohn fooma**toh**ree" |
| to **complain** | fare un reclamo | "**fah**ray oon ray**klah**mo" |
| ▷ **I want to complain about the service** (*in shop etc*) | ho un reclamo da fare riguardo il servizio | "o oon ray**klah**mo da **fah**ray ree**gwar**do eel sayr**vee**tsyo" |
| **comprehensive insurance cover** | la polizza casco | "poh**leet**sa kasko" |
| ▷ **how much extra is comprehensive insurance cover?** | quant'è il supplemento per la polizza casco? | "kwan**te** eel sooplay**mayn**to payr la poh**leet**sa kasko" |
| **compulsory** | obbligatorio | "obbleega**tor**yo" |
| | obbligatoria | "obbleega**tor**ya" |

ABSOLUTE ESSENTIALS

| | | |
|---|---|---|
| I don't understand | non capisco | "nohn ka**pees**ko" |
| I don't speak Italian | non parlo l'italiano | "nohn parloh leetal**yah**no" |
| do you speak English? | parla inglese? | "parla eeng**lay**zay" |
| could you help me? | può aiutarmi? | "pwo ayoo**tar**mee" |

| | | |
|---|---|---|
| **computer** | il computer | "komputer" |
| **concert** | il concerto | "kon**chayr**to" |
| **condensed milk** | il latte condensato | "lahttay kondayn**sah**to" |
| **conditioner** | il balsamo | "**bal**samo" |
| **condom** | il preservativo | "praysayrvah**tee**vo" |
| ▷ **a packet of condoms** | un pacchetto di preservativi | "oon pak**kay**to dee praysayrvah**tee**vee" |
| **conductor** | il bigliettaio | "beelyaytt**tay**o" |
| **conference** | il congresso | "kon**gres**so" |
| **confession** | la confessione | "konfays**yoh**nay" |
| ▷ **I want to go to confession** | voglio andare a confessarmi | "volyo an**dah**ray a konfays**sahr**mee" |
| to **confirm** | confermare | "konfayr**mah**ray" |
| **congratulations** | le congratulazioni | "kongratoolats**yoh**nee" |
| to **connect** | collegare | "kohlay**gah**ray" |
| **connection** (*flight, train*) | la coincidenza | "koeenchee**dayn**tsa" |
| ▷ **I missed my connection** | ho perso la coincidenza | "o payrso la koeenchee**dayn**tsa" |
| **constipated** | stitico<br>stitica | "**stee**teeko"<br>"**stee**teeka" |
| **constipation** | la stitichezza | "steetee**kayt**sa" |
| **consulate** | il consolato | "konso**lah**to" |
| ▷ **where is the British consulate?** | dov'è il consolato britannico? | "doh**ve** eel konso**lah**to bree**tan**neeko" |
| to **contact** | contattare | "kontatt**tah**ray" |
| ▷ **where can I contact you?** | dove la posso contattare? | "dohvay la posso kontatt**tah**ray" |
| **contact lenses** | le lenti a contatto | "lentee a kon**tat**to" |

| | | |
|---|---|---|
| ▷ **contact lens cleaner** | il liquido per lenti a contatto | "eel **lee**kweedo payr lentee a kon**tatt**o" |
| ▷ **hard contact lenses** | le lenti a contatto rigide | "lay lentee a kon**tatt**o **ree**jeeday" |
| ▷ **soft contact lenses** | le lenti a contatto morbide | "lay lentee a kon**tatt**o **mor**beeday" |
| **continental breakfast** | la colazione all'europea | "kolats**yoh**nay allayooro**paya**" |
| **contraceptive** | il contraccettivo | "kontratchayt**tee**vo" |
| **controls** | i comandi | "ko**man**dee" |
| ▷ **how do I operate the controls?** | come funzionano i comandi? | "**koh**may foontsy**oh**nano ee ko**man**dee" |
| to **cook** | cucinare | "koochee**nah**ray" |
| **cooker** | la cucina | "koo**chee**na" |
| ▷ **how does the cooker work?** | come funziona la cucina? | "**ko**may foonts**yoh**na la koo**chee**na" |
| **cool** | fresco | "**fray**sko" |
| | fresca | "**fray**ska" |
| **copy**[1] *n* | la copia | "**kop**ya" |
| ▷ **four copies please** | quattro copie, per favore | "**kwa**tro **kop**yay payr fa**voh**ray" |
| to **copy**[2] *vb*: | | |
| ▷ **I want to copy this document** | voglio fare una copia di questo documento | "**vol**yo **fah**ray oona **kop**ya dee **kwaysto** dokoo**maynt**o" |
| **corkscrew** | il cavatappi | "kava**tapp**ee" |
| **corner** | l'angolo (*m*) | "**ang**olo" |
| ▷ **it's round the corner** | è dietro l'angolo | "e dee**ee**tro **lang**ohlo" |
| **cornflakes** | i cornflakes | "cornflakes" |
| **cortisone** | il cortisone | "kortee**zoh**nay" |
| **cosmetics** | i cosmetici | "koz**may**teechee" |

ABSOLUTE ESSENTIALS

| | | |
|---|---|---|
| **do you have ...?** | avete...? | "a**vay**tay" |
| **is there ...?** | c'è...? | "che" |
| **are there ...?** | ci sono...? | "chee **soh**noh" |
| **how much is ...?** | quanto costa...? | "**kwanto kosta**" |

| to cost | costare | "kostahray" |
|---|---|---|
| ▷ **how much does it cost to get in?** | quanto costa il biglietto di entrata? | "kwanto kosta eel beelyaytto dee ayntrahta" |
| ▷ **how much does it do/they cost?** | quanto costa/costano? | "kwanto kosta/kostano" |
| **cot** | il lettino | "laytteeno" |
| ▷ **have you got a cot for the baby?** | avete un lettino per il bambino? | "avaytay oon laytteeno payr eel bambeeno" |
| **cotton** | il cotone | "kotohnay" |
| **cotton wool** | il cotone idrofilo | "kotohnay eedrofeelo" |
| **couchette** | la cuccetta | "kootchaytta" |
| ▷ **I want to reserve a couchette** | voglio prenotare una cuccetta | "volyo praynotahray oona kootchaytta" |
| **cough** | la tosse | "tohssay" |
| ▷ **I have a cough** | ho la tosse | "o la tohssay" |

**could:**

| I could | potrei | "potray" |
|---|---|---|
| you could (*informal singular*) | potresti | "potraystee" |
| (*formal singular*) | potrebbe | "potraybbay" |
| he/she/it could | potrebbe | "potraybbay" |
| we could | potremmo | "potraymmo" |
| you could (*plural*) | potreste | "potraystay" |
| they could | potrebbero | "potraybbayro" |

| **country** (*not town*) | la campagna | "kampanya" |
|---|---|---|
| (*nation*) | il paese | "paayzay" |
| **couple** (*two people*) | la coppia | "kopya" |
| **courgettes** | gli zucchini | "tsookkeenee" |
| **courier** | il corriere | "korreeeray" |

ABSOLUTE ESSENTIALS

| yes (please) | sì (grazie) | "see (gratsyay)" |
|---|---|---|
| no (thank you) | no (grazie) | "no (gratsyay)" |
| hello | salve | "salvay" |
| goodbye | arrivederci | "arreevaydayrchee" |

| | | |
|---|---|---|
| ▷ **I want to send this by courier** | voglio spedire questo tramite corriere | "volyo spay**dee**ray kwaysto **tra**meetay korree**e**ray" |
| **course** (*of meal*) | il piatto | "pee**att**o" |
| **cover charge** | il coperto | "ko**payr**to" |
| **crab** | il granchio | "grankyo" |
| **cramp:** | | |
| ▷ **I've got cramp (in my leg)** | ho un crampo alla gamba | "o oon krampo alla gamba" |
| **crash:** | | |
| ▷ **there's been a crash** | c'è stato un incidente | "chay stahto oon eenchee**dayn**tay" |
| ▷ **I've crashed my car** | ho avuto un incidente con la macchina | "o ah**voo**to oon eenchee**dayn**tay kohn la **mak**keena" |
| **crash helmet** | il casco (di protezione) | "kasko (dee protayts**yoh**nay)" |
| **cream** (*lotion*) (*on milk*) | la crema la panna | "krema" "panna" |
| **credit card** | la carta di credito | "karta dee **kray**deeto" |
| ▷ **can I pay by credit card?** | posso pagare con la carta di credito? | "posso pa**gah**ray kohn la karta dee **kray**deeto" |
| ▷ **I've lost my credit card** | ho perso la carta di credito | "o payrso la karta dee **kray**deeto" |
| **crisps** | le patatine | "pata**tee**nay" |
| **croissant** | il croissant | "krwa**san**" |
| to **cross** (*road*) | attraversare | "attravayr**sah**ray" |
| **cross-country skiing:** | | |
| ▷ **is it possible to go cross-country skiing?** | è possibile fare sci di fondo? | "e pos**see**beelay fahray shee dee fondo" |

*ABSOLUTE ESSENTIALS*

| | | |
|---|---|---|
| **I don't understand** | non capisco | "nohn ka**pees**ko" |
| **I don't speak Italian** | non parlo l'italiano | "nohn parloh leetal**yah**no" |
| **do you speak English?** | parla inglese? | "parla eeng**lay**zay" |
| **could you help me?** | può aiutarmi? | "pwo ayoo**tar**mee" |

| | | |
|---|---|---|
| **crossed line** | l'interferenza (f) | "eentayrfay**rent**sa" |
| **crossing** | la traversata | "travayr**sah**ta" |
| ▷ **how long does the crossing take?** | quanto dura la traversata? | "kwanto doora la travayr**sah**ta" |
| **crossroads** | l'incrocio (m) | "een**kroh**cho" |
| **crowded** | affollato affollata | "affol**lah**to" "affol**lah**ta" |
| **cruise** | la crociera | "kro**che**ra" |
| **cucumber** | il cetriolo | "chaytree**o**lo" |
| **cup** | la tazza | "**tat**sa" |
| ▷ **could we have another cup of coffee, please** | ancora una tazza di caffè, per favore | "an**koh**ra oona tatsa dee kaffe payr fa**voh**ray" |
| **cupboard** | l'armadio (m) | "ar**mah**dyo" |
| **curler** | il bigodino | "beego**dee**no" |
| **currant** | l'uva sultanina (f) | "oovah soolta**nee**na" |
| **current** | la corrente | "kor**rayn**tay" |
| ▷ **are there strong currents?** | ci sono correnti forti? | "chee sohnoh kor**rayn**tee fortee" |
| **cushion** | il cuscino | "koo**shee**no" |
| **custard** | la crema pasticcera | "krema pasteet**che**ra" |
| **customs** | la dogana | "do**gah**na" |
| **cut¹** n | il taglio | "**tal**yo" |
| ▷ **a cut and blow-dry, please** | taglio e messa in piega con il föhn, per favore | "**tal**yo ay mayssa een pyega kohn eel fon payr fa**voh**ray" |
| to **cut²** vb | tagliare | "tal**yah**ray" |

| | | |
|---|---|---|
| ▷ **he has cut himself** | si è tagliato | "see e talyahto" |
| ▷ **I've been cut off** | è caduta la linea | "ay cahdootah lah leenaya" |
| **cutlery** | le posate | "pozahtay" |
| **cycle** | la bicicletta | "beecheeklaytta" |
| **cycle path** | la pista ciclabile | "peesta cheeklahbeelay" |
| **cycle helmet** | il casco per ciclista | "kasko payr cheekleesta" |
| **cycling:** | | |
| ▷ **we would like to go cycling** | vorremmo andare in bicicletta | "vorraymmo andahray een beecheeklaytta" |
| **daily** (*each day*) | ogni giorno | "onyee jorno" |
| **dairy products** | i latticini | "latteecheenee" |
| **damage** | il danno | "danno" |
| **damp** | umido | "oomeedo" |
| | umida | "oomeeda" |
| ▷ **my clothes are damp** | i miei vestiti sono umidi | "ee myay vaysteetee sohnoh oomeedee" |
| **dance**[1] *n* | il ballo | "ballo" |
| **to dance**[2] *vb* | ballare | "ballahray" |
| **dangerous** | pericoloso | "payreekolohzo" |
| | pericolosa | "payreekolohza" |
| **dark** | scuro | "skooro" |
| | scura | "skoora" |
| **date** | la data | "dahta" |
| ▷ **what is the date today?** | che giorno è oggi? | "kay jorno e odjee" |
| **date of birth** | la data di nascita | "dahta dee nasheeta" |
| **daughter** | la figlia | "feelya" |
| **day** | il giorno | "jorno" |

*ABSOLUTE ESSENTIALS*

| | | |
|---|---|---|
| **do you have ...?** | avete...? | "avaytay" |
| **is there ...?** | c'è...? | "che" |
| **are there ...?** | ci sono...? | "chee sohnoh" |
| **how much is ...?** | quanto costa...? | "kwanto kosta" |

| | | |
|---|---|---|
| **day trip** | la gita (in giornata) | "jeeta (een jornahta)" |
| **dear** | caro | "kahro" |
| | cara | "kahra" |
| **decaffeinated coffee** | il caffè decaffeinato | "kaffe daykaffayeenahto" |
| **December** | dicembre | "deechaymbray" |
| **deck** | il ponte | "pohntay" |
| ▷ **can we go out on deck?** | possiamo andare sul ponte? | "posyahmo andahray sool pohntay" |
| **deck chair** | la sedia a sdraio | "sedya a zdrayo" |
| **to declare** | dichiarare | "deekyarahray" |
| ▷ **I have nothing to declare** | non ho niente da dichiarare | "nohn o neeentay da deekyarahray" |
| ▷ **I have a bottle of spirits to declare** | ho una bottiglia di liquore da dichiarare | "o oona botteelya dee leekwohray da deekyarahray" |
| **deep** | profondo | "profohndo" |
| | profonda | "profohnda" |
| ▷ **how deep is the water?** | quanto è profonda l'acqua? | "kwanto e profohnda lakwa" |
| **deep freeze** | il surgelatore | "soorjaylatohray" |
| **to defrost** | scongelare | "skonjaylahray" |
| **to de-ice** | liberare dal ghiaccio | "leebayrahray dal geeatcho" |
| **delay** | il ritardo | "reetahrdo" |
| ▷ **the flight has been delayed (by 6 hours)** | il volo ha subito un ritardo (di 6 ore) | "eel vohloh a soobeeto oon reetahrdo (dee say ohray)" |
| **delicious** | delizioso | "dayleetsyohzo" |
| | deliziosa | "dayleetsyohza" |
| **dentist** | il/la dentista | "daynteesta" |

| | | |
|---|---|---|
| ▷ **I need to see the dentist (urgently)** | devo farmi vedere dal dentista (urgentemente) | "dayvo fahrmee vay**day**ray dal dayn**tee**sta (oorjayntay**mayn**tay)" |
| **dentures** | la dentiera | "dayn**tye**ra" |
| ▷ **my dentures need repairing** | devo far riparare la dentiera | "dayvo fahr reepah**rah**ray la dayn**tye**ra" |
| **deodorant** | il deodorante | "dayohdoh**ran**tay" |
| **department store** | il grande magazzino | "granday magadz**zee**no" |
| **departure lounge** | la sala d'attesa | "sahla dat**tay**za" |
| **departures** | le partenze | "par**tent**say" |
| **deposit** | la cauzione | "kowts**yoh**nay" |
| ▷ **what is the deposit?** | quant'è la cauzione? | "kwante la kowts**yoh**nay" |
| **dessert** | il dolce | "dohlchay" |
| ▷ **we'd like a dessert** | vorremmo un dolce | "vor**raym**mo oon dohlchay" |
| ▷ **the dessert menu please** | la lista dei dolci, per favore | "la leesta day dohlchee payr fa**voh**ray" |
| **details** | i dettagli | "dayt**tal**yee" |
| **detergent** | il detersivo | "daytayr**see**vo" |
| **detour** | la deviazione | "dayveeats**yoh**nay" |
| to **develop** | sviluppare | "sveeloop**pah**ray" |
| **diabetic** | diabetico | "deea**be**teeko" |
| | diabetica | "deea**be**teeka" |
| ▷ **I am diabetic** | sono diabetico | "sohnoh deea**be**teeko" |
| **dialling code** | il prefisso (telefonico) | "pray**fees**so taylay**fo**neeko" |
| ▷ **what is the dialling code for the UK?** | qual'è il prefisso per la Gran Bretagna? | "kwale eel pray**fees**so payr la gran bray**tan**ya" |
| **diamond** | il diamante | "deea**man**tay" |

| | | |
|---|---|---|
| **diarrhoea** | la diarrea | "deear**ray**a" |
| ▷ **I need something for diarrhoea** | ho bisogno di qualcosa contro la diarrea | "o bee**zohn**yo dee kwal**ko**za kohntro la deear**ray**a" |
| **diary** | l'agenda (*f*) | "a**jen**da" |
| **dictionary** | il dizionario | "deetsyo**nahr**yo" |
| **diesel** | il gasolio | "ga**zol**yo" |
| **diet** | la dieta | "dee**ee**ta" |
| **different** | diverso | "dee**vayr**so" |
| | diversa | "dee**vayr**sa" |
| ▷ **I would like something different** | vorrei qualcosa di diverso | "vor**eee** kwal**ko**za dee dee**vayr**so" |
| **difficult** | difficile | "deef**fee**cheelay" |
| **dinghy** | il canotto | "ka**not**to" |
| **dining car** | il vagone ristorante | "va**goh**nay reestoh**ran**tay" |
| **dining room** | la sala da pranzo | "**sah**la da **prant**so" |
| **dinner** | la cena | "**chay**na" |
| **direct** (*train etc*) | diretto | "dee**ret**to" |
| | diretta | "dee**ret**ta" |
| **directory** | l'elenco (*m*) telefonico | "ay**len**ko taylay**fo**neeko" |
| **directory enquiries** | il servizio informazioni elenco abbonati | "sayr**vee**tsyo eenformats**yoh**nay ay**len**ko abbo**nah**tee" |
| ▷ **what is the number for directory enquiries?** | qual è il numero del servizio informazioni elenco abbonati? | "kwa**lay** eel **noo**mayroh dayl sayr**vee**tsyo eenformats**yoh**nay ay**len**ko abbo**nah**tee" |
| **dirty** | sporco | "**spor**ko" |
| | sporca | "**spor**ka" |
| ▷ **the wash basin is dirty** | il lavandino è sporco | "eel lavan**dee**no e **spor**ko" |

*ABSOLUTE ESSENTIALS*

| | | |
|---|---|---|
| **I would like ...** | vorrei... | "vor**eee**" |
| **I need ...** | ho bisogno di... | "o bee**zohn**yo dee" |
| **where is ...?** | dov'è...? | "do**veh**" |
| **I'm looking for ...** | sto cercando... | "sto chayr**kan**do" |

| **disabled** | portatore di handicap | "portah**toh**ray dee **an**deekap" |
| | portatrice di handicap | "portah**tree**chay dee **an**deekap" |
| ▷ **is there a toilet for the disabled?** | c'è una toilette per portatori di handicap? | "che oona twa**let** payr portah**toh**ray dee **an**deekap" |
| ▷ **do you have facilities for the disabled?** | avete strutture per portatori di handicap? | "ah**vay**tay stroot**too**ray payr portah**toh**ray dee **an**deekap" |
| ▷ **do you provide access for the disabled?** | è reso possibile l'accesso ai portatori di handicap? | "e rayzo pos**see**beelay la**chays**so ayee portah**toh**ray dee **an**deekap" |
| **disco** | la discoteca | "deesko**te**ka" |
| **discount** | lo sconto | "skontoh" |
| ▷ **do you offer a discount for cash?** | fate sconti per pagamenti in contanti? | "**fah**tay skontee payr paga**mayn**tee een kon**tan**tee" |
| ▷ **are there discounts for students?** | ci sono sconti per studenti? | "chee **soh**noh skontee payr stoo**dayn**tee" |
| **dish** | il piatto | "pee**at**to" |
| ▷ **how is this dish cooked?** | come viene cucinato questo piatto? | "**koh**may **vyay**nay koochee**nah**to kwesto pee**at**to" |
| ▷ **how is this dish served?** | com'è servito questo piatto? | "koh**may** sayr**vee**to kwesto pee**at**to" |
| ▷ **what is in this dish?** | che ingredienti ci sono in questo piatto? | "kay eengraydee**ayn**tee chee **soh**noh een kwesto pee**at**to" |
| **dishtowel** | lo strofinaccio | "strofee**nat**cho" |
| **dishwasher** | la lavastoviglie | "lavasto**veel**yay" |
| **disinfectant** | il disinfettante | "deezeenfayt**tan**tay" |
| **distilled water** | l'acqua (f) distillata | "akwa deestee**llah**ta" |

---

**ABSOLUTE ESSENTIALS**

| **do you have ...?** | avete...? | "a**vay**tay" |
| **is there ...?** | c'è...? | "che" |
| **are there ...?** | ci sono...? | "chee **soh**noh" |
| **how much is ...?** | quanto costa...? | "**kwan**to kosta" |

## *dive*

### to **dive**:

| | | |
|---|---|---|
| ▷ **where is the best place to dive?** | dov'è il posto migliore per fare immersione subacquea? | "do**veh** eel pohsto meel**yoh**ray payr fahray eemayrs**yoh**nay soo**bak**waya" |
| **diversion** | la deviazione | "dayveeats**yoh**nay" |
| ▷ **is there a diversion?** | c'è una deviazione? | "chay oona dayveeats**yoh**nay" |
| **diving** | l'immersione (*f*) subacquea | "eemayrs**yoh**nay soo**bak**waya" |
| ▷ **I'd like to go diving** | vorrei fare immersione subacquea | "vor**reee** fahray eemayrs**yoh**nay soo**bak**waya" |
| **divorced** | divorziato<br>divorziata | "deevorts**yah**to"<br>"deevorts**yah**ta" |
| **dizzy** | stordito<br>stordita | "stor**dee**to"<br>"stor**dee**ta" |
| ▷ **I feel dizzy** | ho il capogiro | "o eel kapo**jee**ro" |
| to **do** | fare | "fahray" |

| | | |
|---|---|---|
| **I do** | faccio | "fatcho" |
| **you do** (*informal singular*) | fai | "fayee" |
| (*formal singular*) | fa | "fa" |
| **he/she/it does** | fa | "fa" |
| **we do** | facciamo | "fatch**ah**mo" |
| **you do** (*plural*) | fate | "fahtay" |
| **they do** | fanno | "fanno" |

| | | |
|---|---|---|
| **dock** (*wharf*) | il molo | "mohloh" |
| **doctor** | il medico | "**me**deeko" |
| ▷ **can I make an appointment with the doctor?** | posso prendere appuntamento con il medico? | "posso **prayn**dayray appoonta**mayn**to kohn eel **me**deeko" |

ABSOLUTE ESSENTIALS

| | | |
|---|---|---|
| **yes (please)** | sì (grazie) | "see (gratsyay)" |
| **no (thank you)** | no (grazie) | "no (gratsyay)" |
| **hello** | salve | "salvay" |
| **goodbye** | arrivederci | "arreevay**dayr**chee" |

| | | |
|---|---|---|
| ▷ **I need a doctor** | ho bisogno di un medico | "o bee**zohn**yo dee oon **me**deeko" |
| ▷ **call a doctor** | chiamate un medico | "keea**mah**tay oon **me**deeko" |
| **documents** | i documenti | "dokoo**mayn**tee" |
| **doll** | la bambola | "**bam**bola" |
| **dollars** | i dollari | "**dol**laree" |
| **door** | la porta | "porta" |
| **double** | doppio | "dopyo" |
| | doppia | "dopya" |
| **double bed** | il letto matrimoniale | "letto matreemon**yah**lay" |
| **double room** | la camera matrimoniale | "**ka**mayra matreemon**yah**lay" |
| ▷ **I want to reserve a double room** | vorrei prenotare una camera matrimoniale | "vor**reee** prayno**tah**ray oona **ka**mayra matreemohn**yah**lay" |
| **doughnut** | il krapfen | "krafen" |
| **down** | giù | "joo" |
| ▷ **to go down** (*downstairs*) | scendere | "**shayn**dayray" |
| **downstairs:** | | |
| ▷ **they live downstairs** | abitano al piano di sotto | "a**bee**tahno al pee**ah**no dee sohtoh" |
| **drain:** | | |
| ▷ **the drain is blocked** | sono bloccate le condutture | "sohnoh blok**kah**tay lay kohndoot**too**ray" |
| **draught** | la corrente (d'aria) | "kor**ren**tay (dahrya)" |
| **draught beer** | la birra alla spina | "beerra alla speena" |
| ▷ **a draught beer** | una birra alla spina | "oona beerra alla speena" |
| **dress¹** *n* | il vestito | "vay**stee**to" |

*ABSOLUTE ESSENTIALS*

| | | |
|---|---|---|
| **I don't understand** | non capisco | "nohn ka**pee**sko" |
| **I don't speak Italian** | non parlo l'italiano | "nohn parloh leetal**yah**no" |
| **do you speak English?** | parla inglese? | "parla eeng**lay**zay" |
| **could you help me?** | può aiutarmi? | "pwo ayoo**tar**mee" |

| | | |
|---|---|---|
| to **dress**[2] vb: | | |
| ▷ **to get dressed** | vestirsi | "vay**steer**see" |
| **dressing** (for food) | il condimento | "kondee**mayn**to" |
| **drink**[1] n | la bibita | "**bee**beeta" |
| ▷ **a cold/hot drink** | una bibita calda/fredda | "oona **bee**beeta kalda/<br>**fray**dda" |
| ▷ **would you like a drink?** | gradice qualcosa da<br>bere? | "gra**dee**shay kwal**ko**za da<br>**bay**ray" |
| to **drink**[2] vb | bere | "**bay**ray" |
| ▷ **what would you like to<br>drink?** | cosa beve? | "**ko**za **bay**vay" |
| **drinking chocolate** | la cioccolata calda | "chokko**lah**ta kalda" |
| **drinking water** | l'acqua (f) potabile | "akwa po**tah**beelay" |
| to **drive** | guidare | "gwee**dah**ray" |
| ▷ **he was driving too fast** | andava troppo veloce | "an**dah**va troppo<br>vay**loh**chay" |
| **driver** (of car) | l'autista (m/f) | "ow**tee**sta" |
| **driving licence** | la patente | "pa**ten**tay" |
| ▷ **my driving licence<br>number is ...** | il numero della mia<br>patente è... | "eel **noo**mayro **day**lla<br>**mee**a pa**ten**tay e" |
| ▷ **I don't have my<br>driving licence on me** | non ho la patente con<br>me | "nohn o la pa**ten**tay kohn<br>may" |
| to **drown**: | | |
| ▷ **someone is drowning!** | qualcuno sta affogando! | "kwal**koo**no sta<br>affoh**gan**do" |
| **drunk** | ubriaco<br>ubriaca | "oobree**a**ko"<br>"oobree**a**ka" |
| **dry**[1] adj | secco<br>secca | "**say**kko"<br>"**say**kka" |
| to **dry**[2] vb | asciugare | "ashoo**gah**ray" |

| ▷ where can I dry my clothes? | dove posso far asciugare i vestiti? | "dohvay posso fahr ashoo**gah**ray ee vay**stee**tee" |

to **dry-clean**:

| ▷ I need this dry-cleaned | devo far pulire a secco questo capo | "dayvo fahr poo**lee**ray a saykko kwesto kapo" |

| **dry-cleaner's** | la tintoria | "teento**ree**a" |
| **duck** | l'anatra (*f*) | "anatra" |

**due**:

| ▷ when is the train due? | quando dovrebbe arrivare il treno? | "kwando dov**rayb**bay arree**vah**ray eel treno" |

| **dummy** | la tettarella | "taytta**rel**la" |
| **dune** | la duna | "doona" |
| **during** | durante | "doo**ran**tay" |
| **duty-free** | esente da dogana | "ay**zen**tay da do**gah**na" |
| **duty-free shop** | il duty free | "duty free" |
| **duvet** | il piumino | "peeoo**mee**no" |
| **dynamo** | la dinamo | "**dee**namo" |
| **each** | ogni | "onyee" |
| **ear** | l'orecchio (*m*) | "o**rayk**yo" |
| **earache** | il mal d'orecchi | "mal do**rayk**yee" |

**earlier**:

| ▷ I would prefer an earlier flight | preferirei prendere un volo che parte prima | "prayfay**ree**ray **prayn**dayray oon volo kay partay preema" |

| **early** | presto | "presto" |
| **earrings** | gli orecchini | "orayk**kee**nee" |
| **east** | l'est (*m*) | "est" |
| **Easter** | la Pasqua | "paskwa" |

| easy | facile | "**fa**cheelay" |
| to eat | mangiare | "man**jah**ray" |
| ▷ I don't eat meat | non mangio carne | "nohn manjo karnay" |
| ▷ would you like something to eat? | vuole mangiare qualcosa? | "vwolay man**jah**ray kwal**ko**za" |
| ▷ have you eaten? | ha mangiato? | "a man**jah**to" |
| EC | la CEE | "cheh" |
| eel | l'anguilla (f) | "an**gwee**lla" |
| egg | l'uovo (m) | "wovo" |
| ▷ two eggs | due uova | "dooay wova" |
| ▷ fried egg | uovo fritto | "wovo freetto" |
| ▷ hard-boiled egg | uovo sodo | "wovo sodo" |
| ▷ scrambled eggs | uova strapazzate | "wova strapats**sah**tay" |
| eight | otto | "ohtto" |
| eighteen | diciotto | "dee**choht**to" |
| eighty | ottanta | "oht**tan**ta" |
| either: | | |
| ▷ either one | l'uno o l'altro | "loono o laltro" |
| elastic | l'elastico (m) | "ay**las**teeko" |
| elastic band | l'elastico (m) | "ay**las**teeko" |
| electric | elettrico | "ay**let**treeko" |
| | elettrica | "ay**let**treeka" |
| electrician | l'elettricista (m) | "aylettree**chee**sta" |
| electricity | l'elettricità (f) | "aylettreechee**ta**" |
| ▷ is the cost of electricity included in the rental? | nell'affitto è compresa la luce? | "nellaf**feet**to e kom**pray**za la loochay" |
| electricity meter | il contatore dell'elettricità | "konta**toh**ray dayllaylettreechee**ta**" |
| electric razor | il rasoio elettrico | "ra**zo**yo ay**let**treeko" |

| **eleven** | undici | "**oon**deechee" |
|---|---|---|
| **to embark**: | | |
| ▷ **when do we embark?** | quando ci imbarchiamo? | "kwando chee eembark**yah**mo" |
| **embassy** | l'ambasciata (f) | "amba**shah**ta" |
| **emergency** | l'emergenza (f) | "aymayr**jen**tsa" |
| **empty** | vuoto | "**vwo**to" |
| | vuota | "**vwo**ta" |
| **end** | la fine | "**fee**nay" |
| **engaged** (*to be married*) | fidanzato | "feedant**sah**to" |
| | fidanzata | "feedant**sah**ta" |
| (*phone, toilet*) | occupato | "okkoo**pah**to" |
| ▷ **the line's engaged** | la linea è occupata | "la **lee**naya e okkoo**pah**ta" |
| **engine** | il motore | "mo**toh**ray" |
| **England** | l'Inghilterra (f) | "eengeel**terra**" |
| **English** | inglese | "eeng**lay**zay" |
| ▷ **I'm English** | sono inglese | "**soh**noh eeng**lay**zay" |
| ▷ **do you speak English?** | parla inglese? | "**parla** eeng**lay**zay" |
| ▷ **do you have any English books/ newpapers?** | avete libri/giornali inglesi? | "a**vay**tay leebree/jor**nal**ee eeng**lay**zee" |
| **to enjoy**: | | |
| ▷ **I enjoyed the tour** | la visita mi è piaciuta | "la **vee**zeeta mee e peea**choo**ta" |
| ▷ **I enjoy swimming** | mi piace nuotare | "mee peea**chay** nwo**tah**ray" |
| ▷ **enjoy your meal!** | buon appetito! | "bwon appay**tee**to" |
| **enough** | abbastanza | "abba**stan**tsa" |
| ▷ **that's enough, thank you** | basta così, grazie | "**bah**stah ko**see** grah**tsyay**" |

| **enquiry desk** | il banco delle informazioni | "banko dayllay eenformats**yoh**nay" |
| **entertainment:** | | |
| ▷ **what entertainment is there?** | quali locali o spettacoli ci sono? | "kwalee lo**kah**lee o spayt**tah**kolee chee sohnoh" |
| **entrance** | l'ingresso (m) | "een**gres**so" |
| **entrance fee** | il prezzo d'ingresso | "pretsso deen**gres**so" |
| **entry visa** | il visto d'ingresso | "veesto deen**gres**so" |
| ▷ **I have an entry visa** | ho un visto d'ingresso | "o oon veesto deen**gres**so" |
| **envelope** | la busta | "boosta" |
| **epileptic** | epilettico epilettica | "epee**layt**teeko" "epee**layt**teeka" |
| **equipment** | l'attrezzatura (f) | "attraytssa**too**ra" |
| ▷ **can we hire the equipment?** | possiamo noleggiare l'attrezzatura? | "pos**yah**mo nolayd**jah**ray lattraytssa**too**ra" |
| **escalator** | la scala mobile | "skahla **mo**beelay" |
| **especially** | specialmente | "spaychal**mayn**tay" |
| **essential** | essenziale | "ayssaynts**yah**lay" |
| **Eurocheque** | l'eurocheque (m) | "**ayoo**rochek" |
| ▷ **do you take Eurocheques?** | accettate eurocheque? | "achayt**tah**tay **ayoo**rochek" |
| **Europe** | l'Europa (f) | "ayoo**ro**pa" |
| **European** | europeo europea | "ayooro**pay**o" "ayooro**pay**a" |
| **European Community** | la Comunità Europea | "komoonee**ta** ayooro**pay**a" |
| **evening** | la sera | "sayra" |
| ▷ **in the evening** | di sera | "dee sayra" |

ABSOLUTE ESSENTIALS

| I would like ... | vorrei... | "vo**reee**" |
| I need ... | ho bisogno di... | "o bee**zohn**yo dee" |
| where is ...? | dov'è...? | "do**veh**" |
| I'm looking for ... | sto cercando... | "sto chayr**kan**do" |

| | | |
|---|---|---|
| ▷ **what is there to do in the evenings?** | che cosa si può fare di sera? | "kay koza see pwo fahray dee sayra" |
| ▷ **what are you doing this evening?** | cosa fa questa sera? | "koza fah kwesta sayra" |
| **evening meal** | la cena | "chayna" |
| **every** | ogni | "onyee" |
| **everyone** | tutti | "toottee" |
| **everything** | tutto | "tootto" |
| **excellent** | ottimo | "**ot**teemo" |
| | ottima | "**ot**teema" |
| ▷ **the lunch was excellent** | il pranzo era ottimo | "eel prantso ayra **ot**teemo" |
| **except** | eccetto | "ayt**chet**to" |
| **excess luggage** | il bagaglio in eccedenza | "ba**gal**yo een aytchay**den**tsa" |
| **exchange¹** *n* | lo scambio | "skambyo" |
| **to exchange²** *vb* | cambiare | "kamb**yah**ray" |
| ▷ **could I exchange this please?** | posso cambiarlo, per favore? | "posso kamb**yahr**lo payr fa**voh**ray" |
| **exchange rate** | il cambio | "kambyo" |
| ▷ **what is the exchange rate?** | a quanto è il cambio? | "a kwanto e eel kambyo" |
| **excursion** | l'escursione (*f*) | "ayskoors**yoh**nay" |
| ▷ **what excursions are there?** | che escursioni ci sono? | "kay ayskoors**yoh**nee chee sohnoh" |
| **to excuse** | scusare | "skoo**zah**ray" |
| ▷ **excuse me!** (*sorry*) | mi scusi! | "mee skoozee" |
| (*when passing*) | permesso! | "payr**mays**so" |
| **exhaust pipe** | il tubo di scappamento | "toobo dee skappa**mayn**to" |

ABSOLUTE ESSENTIALS

| | | |
|---|---|---|
| **do you have ...?** | avete...? | "avaytay" |
| **is there ...?** | c'è...? | "che" |
| **are there ...?** | ci sono...? | "chee sohnoh" |
| **how much is ...?** | quanto costa...? | "kwanto kosta" |

| | | |
|---|---|---|
| **exhibition** | la mostra | "mostra" |
| **exit** | l'uscita (f) | "oosheeta" |
| ▷ where is the exit? | dov'è l'uscita? | "dohveh loosheeta" |
| ▷ which exit for ...? | qual è l'uscita per...? | "kwal e loosheeta payr" |
| **expensive** | costoso | "kohstohzo" |
| | costosa | "kohstohza" |
| ▷ I want something more expensive | voglio qualcosa di più costoso | "volyo kwalkoza dee peeoo kohstohzoh" |
| ▷ it's too expensive | è troppo caro | "e trohppo karo" |
| **expert** | l'esperto (m) | "ayspayrto" |
| | l'esperta (f) | "ayspayrta" |
| **to expire** (ticket, passport) | scadere | "skadayray" |
| **express**[1] n (train) | l'espresso (m) | "ayspraysso" |
| **express**[2] adj (parcel etc) | espresso | "ayspraysso" |
| **extra** (spare) | in più | "een peeoo" |
| (more) | supplementare | "soopplaymayntahray" |
| **eye** | l'occhio (m) | "okyo" |
| ▷ I have something in my eye | ho qualcosa nell'occhio | "o kwalkoza nellokyo" |
| **eye liner** | la matita per occhi | "mateeta payr okkee" |
| **eye shadow** | l'ombretto (m) | "ombraytto" |
| **face** | il viso | "eel veezo" |
| **face cream** | la crema per il viso | "krayma payr eel veezo" |
| **facilities** | i servizi | "sayrveetsee" |
| ▷ do you have any facilities for the disabled? | avete strutture per portatori di handicap? | "avaytay stroottooray payr portatohree dee andeekap" |
| ▷ what facilities do you have here? | che servizi avete qui? | "kay sayrveetsee avaytay kwee" |

ABSOLUTE ESSENTIALS

| yes (please) | sì (grazie) | "see (gratsyay)" |
|---|---|---|
| no (thank you) | no (grazie) | "no (gratsyay)" |
| hello | salve | "salvay" |
| goodbye | arrivederci | "arreevaydayrchee" |

| ▷ do you have facilities for children? | avete dei servizi particolari per i bambini? | "a**vay**tay dayee sayr**veet**see parteeko**lah**ree payr ee bam**bee**nee" |
| ▷ are there facilities for mothers with babies? | ci sono dei servizi per madri con bambini? | "chee sohnoh dayee sayr**veet**see payr madree kohn bam**bee**nee" |
| ▷ what sports facilities are there? | che sport si possono fare? | "kay sport see **pos**sono fahray" |
| **factor:** | | |
| ▷ factor 8/15 suntan lotion | la lozione solare fattore 8/15 | "lots**yoh**nay so**lah**ray fat**toh**ray ohtto/**kween**deechee" |
| **factory** | la fabbrica | "**fab**breeka" |
| ▷ I work in a factory | lavoro in una fabbrica | "la**voh**ro een oona **fab**breeka" |
| to **faint** | svenire | "svay**nee**ray" |
| **fainted** | svenuto svenuta | "zvay**noo**to" "zvay**noo**ta" |
| **fair** (*fun fair*) | il luna park | "**loona** park" |
| to **fall** | cadere | "ka**day**ray" |
| **family** | la famiglia | "fa**meel**ya" |
| **famous** | famoso famosa | "fa**moh**zo" "fa**moh**za" |
| **fan** (*electric*) | il ventilatore | "vaynteela**toh**ray" |
| **fan belt** | la cinghia del ventilatore | "**cheen**gya dayl vaynteela**toh**ray" |
| **far** | lontano lontana | "lon**tah**no" "lon**tah**na" |
| ▷ is it far? | è lontano? | "e lon**tah**no" |
| ▷ how far is it to ...? | quanto dista...? | "**kwanto** deesta" |

ABSOLUTE ESSENTIALS

| I don't understand | non capisco | "nohn ka**pee**sko" |
| I don't speak Italian | non parlo l'italiano | "nohn parloh leetal**yah**no" |
| do you speak English? | parla inglese? | "parla eeng**lay**zay" |
| could you help me? | può aiutarmi? | "pwo ayoo**tar**mee" |

| | | |
|---|---|---|
| **fare** | la tariffa | "ta**reef**fa" |
| ▷ **what is the fare to the town centre?** | qual è la tariffa per andare in centro? | "kwal e la ta**reef**fa payr an**dah**ray een chentro" |
| **farm** | la fattoria | "fatto**ree**a" |
| **farmhouse** | la cascina | "ka**shee**na" |
| **fast** | veloce | "vay**lo**chay" |
| ▷ **he was driving too fast** | guidava troppo veloce | "gwee**dah**va troppo vay**lo**chay" |
| **fast food** | il fast food | "fast food" |
| **fat** | grasso | "grasso" |
| | grassa | "grassa" |
| **father** | il padre | "padray" |
| **fault** (*defect*) | il difetto | "dee**fet**to" |
| ▷ **it's not my fault** | non è colpa mia | "nohn e kohlpa meea" |
| **favourite** | preferito | "prayfay**ree**to" |
| | preferita | "prayfay**ree**ta" |
| ▷ **what's your favourite drink?** | qual è la sua bibita preferita? | "kwal e la sooa **bee**beeta prayfay**ree**ta" |
| **fax** | il fax | "faks" |
| ▷ **can I send a fax from here?** | posso mandare un fax da qui? | "posso man**dah**ray oon faks da kwee" |
| ▷ **what is the fax number?** | qual è il numero di fax? | "kwal e eel **noo**mayro dee faks" |
| **February** | febbraio | " fayb**bra**yo" |
| **to feed** | dare da mangiare a | "dahray da man**jah**ray a" |
| ▷ **where can I feed the baby?** | dove posso dare da mangiare al bambino? | "dohvay posso dahray da man**jah**ray al bam**bee**no" |
| **to feel** | sentirsi | "sayn**teer**see" |
| ▷ **I don't feel well** | non mi sento bene | "nohn mee saynto benay" |
| ▷ **I feel sick** | mi sento male | "mee saynto mahlay" |

ABSOLUTE ESSENTIALS

| | | |
|---|---|---|
| **I would like ...** | vorrei... | "vo**reee**" |
| **I need ...** | ho bisogno di... | "o bee**zohn**yo dee" |
| **where is ...?** | dov'è...? | "do**veh**" |
| **I'm looking for ...** | sto cercando... | "sto chayr**kan**do" |

| | | |
|---|---|---|
| **ferry** | il traghetto | "tra**gayt**to" |
| **festival** | la festa | "festa" |
| to **fetch** (*bring*) | portare | "por**tah**ray" |
| (*go and get*) | andare a prendere | "an**dah**ray a **pren**dayray" |
| **fever** | la febbre | "**febb**ray" |
| ▷ **he has a fever** | ha la febbre | "a la **febb**ray" |
| **few** | pochi | "**pok**ee" |
| | poche | "**pok**ay" |
| ▷ **a few** | alcuni | "al**koo**nee" |
| | alcune | "al**koo**nay" |
| ▷ **there are few left** | ne restano pochi | "nay **ray**stahno pokee" |
| **fiancé(e)** | il fidanzato | "feedant**sah**to" |
| | la fidanzata | "feedant**sah**ta" |
| **field** | il campo | "**kamp**o" |
| **fifteen** | quindici | "**kween**deechee" |
| **fifty** | cinquanta | "cheen**kwan**ta" |
| to **fill** | riempire | "reeaym**pee**ray" |
| to **fill up** (*container*) | riempire | "reeaym**pee**ray" |
| ▷ **fill it up, please** | il pieno, per favore | "eel pee**e**no payr fa**voh**ray" |
| **fillet** | il filetto | "fee**layt**to" |
| **filling** | l'otturazione (*f*) | "ottoorats**yoh**nay" |
| ▷ **a filling has come out** | mi è uscita l'otturazione | "mee e oo**shee**ta lottoorats**yoh**nay" |
| ▷ **could you do a temporary filling?** | può farmi una otturazione provvisoria? | "pwo **fahr**mee oona ottoorats**yoh**nay provvee**zoh**reea" |
| **film** (*in cinema*) | il film | "feelm" |
| (*for camera*) | la pellicola | "payl**lee**kola" |
| | il rullino | "rool**lee**no" |

| | | |
|---|---|---|
| **do you have ...?** | avete...? | "a**vay**tay" |
| **is there ...?** | c'è...? | "che" |
| **are there ...?** | ci sono...? | "che **soh**noh" |
| **how much is ...?** | quanto costa...? | "**kwan**to **kos**ta" |

| | | |
|---|---|---|
| ▷ **which film is on at the cinema?** | che film danno al cinema? | "kay feelm danno al **chee**nayma" |
| ▷ **I need a colour/black and white film** | ho bisogno di un rullino a colori/in bianco e nero | "o bee**zohn**yo dee oon roo**lee**no a koh**loh**ree/een bee**an**ko ay nayro" |
| ▷ **can you develop this film?** | può sviluppare questo rullino? | "pwo zveeloop**pah**ray kwaysto roo**lee**no" |
| ▷ **the film has jammed** | il rullino si è bloccato | "eel roo**lee**no see e blok**kah**to" |
| ▷ **am I allowed to film here?** | è permesso usare la cinepresa qui? | "e payr**mays**so oo**zah**ray la cheenay**pray**za kwee" |
| **filter** | il filtro | "**feel**tro" |
| **filter coffee** | il caffè da passare al filtro | "kaffe da pas**sah**ray al **feel**tro" |
| **filter-tipped** | con filtro | "kohn **feel**tro" |
| **fine**¹ *n (Law)* | la multa | "**mool**ta" |
| ▷ **how much is the fine?** | quant'è la multa? | "kwan**te** la **mool**ta" |
| **fine**² *adj (good)* | bello bella | "bello" "bella" |
| ▷ **is it going to be fine?** (*weather*) | sarà una bella giornata? | "sa**ra** oona bella jor**nah**ta" |
| **to finish** | finire | "feenee**ray**" |
| ▷ **when does the show finish?** | quando finisce lo spettacolo? | "kwando fee**nee**shay lo spayt**tah**kohlo" |
| ▷ **when will you have finished?** | quando finirà? | "kwando feenee**ra**" |
| **fire** | il fuoco | "**fwo**ko" |
| ▷ **fire!** | al fuoco! | "al **fwo**ko" |
| **fire brigade** | i vigili del fuoco | "**vee**jeelee dayl **fwo**ko" |
| **fire extinguisher** | l'estintore (*m*) | "aysteen**toh**ray" |
| **fireworks** | i fuochi d'artificio | "**fwo**kee dahrtee**fee**cho" |

| | | |
|---|---|---|
| **firework display** | lo spettacolo di fuochi d'artificio | "spay**tta**hkohlo dee fwokee dahrtee**fee**cho" |
| **first** | primo | "**pree**mo" |
| | prima | "**pree**ma" |
| **first aid** | il pronto soccorso | "pronto sok**kor**so" |
| **first class** | la prima classe | "**pree**ma klassay" |
| ▷ **a first class return to ...** | un biglietto di andata e ritorno in prima classe per... | "oon beel**yayt**to dee an**dah**ta ay ree**tohr**no een preema klassay payr" |
| **first floor** | il primo piano | "**pree**mo pee**ah**no" |
| **first name** | il nome di battesimo | "nohmay dee bat**tay**zeemo" |
| **fish¹** *n* | il pesce | "**pay**shay" |
| to **fish²** *vb* | pescare | "pay**skah**ray" |
| ▷ **can we fish here?** | possiamo pescare qui? | "pos**yah**mo pay**skah**ray kwee" |
| ▷ **can I go fishing?** | posso andare a pescare? | "posso an**dah**ray a pay**skah**ray" |
| ▷ **where can I go fishing?** | dove posso andare a pescare? | "dohvay posso an**dah**ray a pay**skah**ray" |
| **fishing rod** | la canna da pesca | "kanna da payska" |
| **fit¹** *n (medical)* | l'attacco *(m)* | "at**tak**ko" |
| **fit²** *adj:* | | |
| ▷ **to be fit** | essere in forma | "**ays**sayray een forma" |
| to **fit³** *vb (clothes)* | andare (bene) | "an**dah**ray (benay)" |
| ▷ **it doesn't fit** | non mi va | "nohn mee va" |
| **five** | cinque | "**cheen**kway" |
| to **fix** | riparare | "reepa**rah**ray" |

*ABSOLUTE ESSENTIALS*

| | | |
|---|---|---|
| **I don't understand** | non capisco | "nohn ka**pees**ko" |
| **I don't speak Italian** | non parlo l'italiano | "nohn parloh leetal**yah**no" |
| **do you speak English?** | parla inglese? | "parla eeng**lay**zay" |
| **could you help me?** | può aiutarmi? | "pwo ayoo**tar**mee" |

| | | |
|---|---|---|
| ▷ **where can I get this fixed?** | dove lo posso portare a riparare? | "dohvay loh posso portahray a reeparahray" |
| **fizzy** | frizzante | "freedzzantay" |
| ▷ **a fizzy drink** | una bibita frizzante | "beebeeta freedzzantay" |
| **flash** | il flash | "flash" |
| ▷ **the flash is not working** | non funziona il flash | "nohn foontsyohna eel flash" |
| **flask** | il thermos | "termos" |
| ▷ **a flask of coffee** | un thermos di caffè | "oon termos dee kaffe" |
| **flat** (*apartment*) | l'appartamento (*m*) | "appartamaynto" |
| **flat tyre** | la foratura | "foratoora" |
| **flavour** | il gusto | "goosto" |
| ▷ **what flavours do you have?** | che gusti avete? | "kay goostee avaytay" |
| **flight** | il volo | "vohloh" |
| ▷ **are there any cheap flights?** | ci sono voli a poco prezzo? | "chee sohnoh vohlee a pohko pretsso" |
| ▷ **I've missed my flight** | ho perso il volo | "o payrso eel vohloh" |
| ▷ **my flight has been delayed** | il mio volo ha subìto un ritardo | "eel meeo vohloh a soobeeto oon reetardo" |
| **flint** | la pietrina | "peeaytreena" |
| **flippers** | le pinne | "peennay" |
| **flooded:** | | |
| ▷ **the bathroom is flooded** | si è allagato il bagno | "see e allagahto eel banyo" |
| **floor** (*of building*) | il piano | "peeahno" |
| (*of room*) | il pavimento | "paveemaynto" |
| ▷ **what floor is it on?** | a che piano è? | "a kay peeahno e" |
| ▷ **on the top floor** | all'ultimo piano | "alloolteemo peeahno" |
| **Florence** | Firenze (*f*) | "feerentsay" |

| **flour** | la farina | "fareena" |
|---|---|---|
| ▷ **plain flour** | la farina | "fareena" |
| ▷ **self-raising flour** | la miscela di farina e lievito | "mee**shay**la dee fa**ree**na ay **lee**ay**vee**to" |
| ▷ **wholemeal flour** | la farina integrale | "fareena eentay**grah**lay" |
| **flowers** | i fiori | "fee**o**ree" |
| ▷ **a bunch/bouquet of flowers** | un mazzo/bouquet di fiori | "oon matsoh/boo**ke** dee fee**o**ree" |
| **flu** | l'influenza (f) | "eenfloo**ent**sa" |
| ▷ **I've got flu** | ho l'influenza | "o leenfloo**ent**sa" |
| **to flush:** | | |
| ▷ **the toilet won't flush** | non si può tirare l'acqua | "nohn see pwo tee**rah**ray lakwa" |
| **fly** (*insect*) | la mosca | "moska" |
| **flying:** | | |
| ▷ **I hate flying** | odio volare | "**oh**dyo voh**lah**ray" |
| **fly sheet** | il soprattetto | "soprat**tayt**to" |
| **foggy:** | | |
| ▷ **it's foggy** | c'è nebbia | "che **nayb**bya" |
| **to follow** | seguire | "say**gwee**ray" |
| ▷ **follow me** | mi segua | "mee saygwa" |
| **food** | il cibo | "cheebo" |
| ▷ **where is the food department?** | dov'è il reparto alimentari? | "doh**veh** eel ray**par**to aleemayn**tah**ree" |
| **food poisoning** | l'intossicazione (f) alimentare | "eentosseekats**yoh**nay aleemayn**tah**ray" |
| **foot** (*metric equiv = 0.30m*) | il piede il piede | "pee**e**day" "pee**e**day" |
| **football** (*game*) (*ball*) | il calcio il pallone | "kalcho" "pal**loh**nay" |
| ▷ **let's play football** | giochiamo a calcio | "jok**yah**mo a kalcho" |

| **for** | per | "payr" |
|---|---|---|
| **foreign** | straniero | "stran**ye**ro" |
| | straniera | "stran**ye**ra" |
| **forest** | la foresta | "fo**re**sta" |
| to **forget** | dimenticare | "deemayntee**kah**ray" |
| ▷ **I've forgotten my passport/the key** | ho dimenticato il passaporto/la chiave | "o deemaynteekahto eel passa**por**to/la kee**a**vay" |
| **fork** | la forchetta | "for**kayt**ta" |
| (*in road*) | la biforcazione | "beeforkats**yoh**nay" |
| **fortnight** | quindici giorni | "**kween**deechee jornee" |
| **forty** | quaranta | "kwa**ran**ta" |
| **fountain** | la fontana | "fon**tah**na" |
| **four** | quattro | "**kwat**tro" |
| **fourteen** | quattordici | "kwat**tor**deechee" |
| **France** | la Francia | "**fran**cha" |
| **free** (*not occupied*) | libero | "**lee**bayro" |
| | libera | "**lee**bayra" |
| (*costing nothing*) | gratis | "**gra**tees" |
| ▷ **I am free tomorrow morning/for lunch** | sono libero domani mattina/per pranzo | "sohnoh **lee**bayro do**mah**nee mat**tee**na/payr prantso" |
| ▷ **is this seat free?** | è libero questo posto? | "e **lee**bayro kwaysto posto" |
| **freezer** | il congelatore | "konjayla**toh**ray" |
| **French** | francese | "fran**chay**zay" |
| **French beans** | i fagiolini | "fajo**lee**nee" |
| **frequent** | frequente | "fray**kwen**tay" |
| ▷ **how frequent are the buses?** | quanto frequenti sono gli autobus? | "kwanto fray**kwen**tee sohnoh lee **ow**toboos" |

| | | |
|---|---|---|
| **fresh** | fresco | "fresko" |
| | fresca | "freska" |
| ▷ **are the vegetables fresh or frozen?** | la verdura è fresca o surgelata? | "la vayrdoora e freska o soorjaylahta" |
| **fresh air** | l'aria (f) fresca | "areea freska" |
| **fresh vegetables** | la verdura fresca | "vayrdoora freska" |
| **Friday** | il venerdì | "vaynayrdee" |
| **fridge** | il frigorifero | "freegoreefayro" |
| **fried** | fritto | "freetto" |
| | fritta | "freetta" |
| **friend** | l'amico (m) | "ameeko" |
| | l'amica (f) | "ameeka" |
| **from** | da | "da" |
| ▷ **I want to stay three nights from ... till ...** | voglio restare per tre notti dal... fino al... | "volyo raystahray payr tray nottee dal... feeno al" |
| **front** | davanti | "davantee" |
| **frozen** (*food*) | surgelato | "soorjaylahto" |
| | surgelata | "soorjaylahta" |
| **fruit** | la frutta | "frootta" |
| **fruit juice** | il succo di frutta | "sookko dee frootta" |
| **fruit salad** | la macedonia | "machaydonya" |
| **frying pan** | la padella | "padella" |
| **fuel** | il combustibile | "komboosteebeelay" |
| **fuel pump** | la pompa di benzina | "pompa dee baynzeena" |
| **full** (*hotel, petrol tank*) | pieno | "peeeno" |
| | piena | "peeena" |
| ▷ **I'm full (up)** | sono sazio | "sohnoh satsyo" |
| **full board** | la pensione completa | "paynseeohnay kompleta" |
| **funny** (*amusing*) | divertente | "deevayrtentay" |

| (*strange*) | strano | "strahno" |
| | strana | "strahna" |
| **fur** | la pelliccia | "pay**lleet**cha" |
| **fuse** | il fusibile | "foo**zee**beelay" |
| ▷ **a fuse has blown** | è saltato un fusibile | "e sal**tah**to oon foo**zee**beelay" |
| ▷ **can you mend a fuse?** | può riparare un fusibile? | "pwo reepa**rah**ray oon foo**zee**beelay" |
| **gallery** | la galleria | "gallay**ree**a" |
| **gallon** (*metric equiv = 4.55 litres*) | il gallone | "gal**loh**nay" |
| **gambling** | il gioco d'azzardo | "joko dad**zza**rdo" |
| **game** | il gioco | "joko" |
| ▷ **a game of chess** | una partita a scacchi | "oona par**tee**ta a skakkee" |
| **gammon** | il prosciutto | "pro**shoot**to" |
| **garage** | l'officina (*f*) | "offee**chee**na" |
| ▷ **can you tow me to a garage?** | può trainarmi fino a un'officina? | "pwo tryee**nar**mee feeno a oonoffee**chee**na" |
| **garden** | il giardino | "jar**dee**no" |
| ▷ **can we visit the gardens?** | possiamo visitare i giardini? | "poss**yah**mo veezee**tah**ray ee jar**dee**nee" |
| **garlic** | l'aglio (*m*) | "alyo" |
| ▷ **is there any garlic in it?** | c'è aglio? | "che alyo" |
| **gas** | il gas | "gaz" |
| ▷ **I can smell gas** | sento odore di gas | "saynto o**doh**ray dee gaz" |
| **gas cylinder** | la bombola di gas | "**bom**bola dee gas" |
| **gear:** | | |
| ▷ **first/third gear** | la prima/terza marcia | "preema/tayrtsa mahrcha" |

| | | |
|---|---|---|
| **gears** | le marce | "**mah**rchay" |
| **Genoa** | Genova (f) | "**je**nova" |
| **gentleman** | il signore | "seen**yoh**ray" |
| **gents** | la toilette (per signori) | "twa**let** (payr seen**yoh**ree)" |
| ▷ **where is the gents?** | dov'è la toilette per signori? | "doh**veh** la twa**let** payr seen**yoh**ree" |
| **genuine** (*leather, silver*) | vero | "**vay**ro" |
| | vera | "**vay**ra" |
| (*antique, picture*) | autentico | "ow**ten**teeko" |
| | autentica | "ow**ten**teeka" |
| **German** | tedesco | "tay**day**sko" |
| | tedesca | "tay**day**ska" |
| **German measles** | la rosolia | "rozo**lee**a" |
| **Germany** | la Germania | "jayr**mah**nya" |
| **to get** (*obtain*) | ottenere | "otta**nay**ray" |
| (*receive*) | ricevere | "ree**chay**vayray" |
| (*fetch*) | prendere | "**pren**dayray" |
| ▷ **please tell me when we get to ...** | per favore mi dica quando arriviamo a... | "payr fa**voh**ray mee **dee**ka kwando arree**vyah**mo a" |
| ▷ **I must get there by 8 o'clock** | devo essere là entro le 8 | "**day**vo **ays**sayray la **ayn**tro lay **oht**to" |
| ▷ **please get me a taxi** | mi chiami un taxi, per favore | "mee kee**a**mee oon tak**see** payr fa**voh**ray" |
| **to get back:** | | |
| ▷ **when do we get back?** | quando ritorniamo? | "kwando retorn**yah**mo" |
| **to get into** (*house, clothes*) | entrare in | "ayn**trah**ray een" |
| (*vehicle*) | salire in | "sa**lee**ray een" |
| **to get off** (*bus etc*) | scendere da | "**shayn**dayray da" |
| ▷ **where do I get off?** | dove devo scendere? | "**doh**vay **day**vo **shayn**dayray" |

ABSOLUTE ESSENTIALS

| | | |
|---|---|---|
| **do you have ...?** | avete...? | "a**vay**tay" |
| **is there ...?** | c'è...? | "che" |
| **are there ...?** | ci sono...? | "chee **soh**noh" |
| **how much is ...?** | quanto costa...? | "**kwan**to **kos**ta" |

| | | |
|---|---|---|
| ▷ **will you tell me where to get off?** | mi può dire quando devo scendere? | "mee pwo deeray kwando dayvo **shayn**dayray" |
| **gift** | il regalo | "ray**gah**lo" |
| **gift shop** | il negozio di articoli da regalo | "nay**gots**yo dee ar**tee**kolee daray**gah**lo" |
| **to giftwrap:** | | |
| ▷ **please giftwrap it** | me lo incarta, per favore? | "may lo een**kar**ta payr fa**voh**ray" |
| **gin** | il gin | "gin" |
| ▷ **I'll have a gin and tonic** | prendo un gin tonic | "prendo oon jeen **to**neek" |
| **ginger** | lo zenzero | "**dzaynd**zayro" |
| **girl** | la ragazza | "ra**gats**sa" |
| **girlfriend** | la ragazza | "ra**gats**sa" |
| **to give** | dare | "**dah**ray" |
| **to give back** | restituire | "raysteetoo**ee**ray" |
| **to give way:** | | |
| ▷ **he did not give way** | non ha dato la precedenza | "nohn a dahto la praychay**dent**sa" |
| **glass** (*for drinking*) | il bicchiere | "beek**ye**ray" |
| (*substance*) | il vetro | "**vay**tro" |
| ▷ **a glass of lemonade** | un bicchiere di limonata | "oon beek**ye**ray dee leemo**nah**ta" |
| ▷ **broken glass** | i vetri rotti | "**vay**tree **roht**tee" |
| **glasses** | gli occhiali | "ok**yah**lee" |
| ▷ **can you repair my glasses?** | mi può riparare gli occhiali? | "mee pwo repa**rah**ray lyee ok**yah**lee" |
| **gloves** | i guanti | "**gwan**tee" |
| **glue** | la colla | "**kol**la" |
| **gluten** | il glutine | "**gloo**teenay" |

| to **go** | andare | "an**dah**ray" |

| I go | vado | "vahdoh" |
| you go (*informal singular*) | vai | "vay" |
| (*formal singular*) | va | "vah" |
| he/she/it goes | va | "vah" |
| we go | andiamo | "andy**ah**mo" |
| you go (*plural*) | andate | "an**dah**tay" |
| they go | vanno | "vahnno" |

▷ **I'm going to the beach** vado in spiaggia "vahdoh een speeadja"

▷ **I must go back now** adesso devo ritornare "a**days**so dayvo reetor**nah**ray"

▷ **you go on ahead** vada avanti lei "vahda a**van**tee layee"

| to **go back** | ritornare | "reetor**nah**ray" |
| to **go down** (*stairs etc*) | scendere | "**shayn**dayray" |
| to **go in** | entrare | "ayn**trah**ray" |
| to **go out** (*leave*) | uscire | "oo**shee**ray" |

| **goggles** (*for swimming*) | gli occhiali | "o**kyah**lee" |
| (*for skiing*) | gli occhiali da sci | "o**kyah**lee da shee" |

| **gold** | d'oro | "doroh" |

| **gold-plated** | placcato oro | "plak**kah**to oroh" |
| | placcata oro | "plak**kah**ta oroh" |

| **golf** | il golf | "golf" |

▷ **where can we play golf?** dove possiamo giocare a golf? "dohvay pos**syah**mo jo**kah**ray a golf"

| **golf ball** | la pallina da golf | "pal**lee**na da golf" |

| **golf club** (*stick*) | la mazza da golf | "mattsa da golf" |
| (*association*) | il golf club | "golf kloob" |

| **golf course** | il campo di golf | "kampo dee golf" |

*ABSOLUTE ESSENTIALS*

| I don't understand | non capisco | "nohn ka**pee**sko" |
| I don't speak Italian | non parlo l'italiano | "nohn parloh leetaly**ah**no" |
| do you speak English? | parla inglese? | "parla eeng**lay**zay" |
| could you help me? | può aiutarmi? | "pwo ayoo**tar**mee" |

| | | |
|---|---|---|
| ▷ is there a public golf course near here? | c'è un campo di golf aperto al pubblico qui vicino? | "che oon kampo dee golf apayrto al poobleeko kwee veecheeno" |
| good | buono | "bwono" |
| | buona | "bwona" |
| (pleasant) | bello | "bello" |
| | bella | "bella" |
| good afternoon | | |
| (early) | buon giorno | "bwon jorno" |
| (later) | buona sera | "bwona sayra" |
| goodbye | arrivederci | "arreevaydayrchee" |
| good evening | buona sera | "bwona sayra" |
| Good Friday | il Venerdì Santo | "vaynayrdee santo" |
| good-looking | attraente | "attraayntay" |
| good morning | buon giorno | "bwon jorno" |
| good night | buona notte | "bwona nottay" |
| gram | il grammo | "grammo" |
| ▷ 500 grams of mince meat | 5 etti di carne macinata | "cheenkway aytee dee karnay macheenahta" |
| granddaughter | la nipote | "neepotay" |
| grandfather | il nonno | "nonno" |
| grandmother | la nonna | "nonna" |
| grandson | il nipote | "neepotay" |
| grapefruit | il pompelmo | "pompelmo" |
| grapefruit juice | il succo di pompelmo | "sookko dee pompelmo" |
| grapes | l'uva (f) | "oova" |
| ▷ seedless grapes | l'uva senza semi | "loova saynza saymee" |
| grass | l'erba (f) | "ayrba" |
| gravy | il sugo | "soogo" |

ABSOLUTE ESSENTIALS

| | | |
|---|---|---|
| I would like ... | vorrei... | "voreee" |
| I need ... | ho bisogno di... | "o beezohnyo dee" |
| where is ...? | dov'è...? | "doveh" |
| I'm looking for ... | sto cercando... | "sto chayrkando" |

| greasy | grasso<br>grassa | "grasso"<br>"grassa" |
| ▷ the food is very greasy | il cibo è molto grasso | "eel cheebo e molto grasso" |
| ▷ shampoo for greasy hair | lo shampoo per capelli grassi | "lo shampoh payr kapayllee grassee" |
| **Greece** | la Grecia | "graycha" |
| **Greek** | greco<br>greca | "grayko"<br>"grayka" |
| **green** | verde | "vayrday" |
| **green card** | la carta verde | "karta vayrday" |
| **green pepper** | il peperone verde | "paypayrohnay vayrday" |
| **grey** | grigio<br>grigia | "greejo"<br>"greeja" |
| **grilled** | alla griglia | "alla greelya" |
| **grocer's** | il negozio di alimentari | "naygotsyo dee aleemayntahree" |
| **ground** | la terra | "terra" |
| **ground floor** | il pianterreno | "peeanterrayno" |
| ▷ could I have a room on the ground floor? | potrei avere una stanza al pianterreno? | "potray avayray oona stantsa al peeantayrrayno" |
| **groundsheet** | il telone impermeabile | "taylohnay eempayrmayahbeelay" |
| **group**<br>(of tourists) | il gruppo<br>la comitiva | "grooppo"<br>"komeeteeva" |
| ▷ do you give discounts for groups? | fate sconti per comitive? | "fatay skontee payr komeeteevay" |
| **group passport** | il passaporto collettivo | "passaporto kollaytteevo" |
| **guarantee** | la garanzia | "garantseea" |

*ABSOLUTE ESSENTIALS*

| do you have ...? | avete...? | "avaytay" |
| is there ...? | c'è...? | "che" |
| are there ...? | ci sono...? | "chee sohnoh" |
| how much is ...? | quanto costa...? | "kwanto kosta" |

| | | |
|---|---|---|
| ▷ it's still under guarantee | è ancora sotto garanzia | "e an**koh**ra sotto garant**see**a" |
| ▷ a five-year guarantee | una garanzia di cinque anni | "oona garant**see**a dee cheenkway annee" |
| **guard** (on train) | il capotreno | "kapo**tray**no" |
| ▷ have you seen the guard? | ha visto il capotreno? | "a veesto eel kapo**tray**no" |
| **guest** (house guest) (in hotel) | l'ospite (m/f) il/la cliente | "**os**peetay" "klee**en**tay" |
| **guesthouse** | la pensione familiare | "paynsee**oh**nay famee**lyah**ray" |
| **guide** | la guida | "**gweeda**" |
| ▷ is there an English-speaking guide? | c'è una guida che parla inglese? | "che oona gweeda kay parla een**glay**zay" |
| **guidebook** | la guida | "**gweeda**" |
| ▷ do you have a guidebook in English? | avete una guida in inglese? | "a**vay**tay oona gweeda een een**glay**zay" |
| ▷ do you have a guidebook to the cathedral? | avete una guida sulla cattedrale? | "a**vay**tay oona gweeda soolla kattay**drah**lay" |
| **guided tour** | la visita guidata | "**vee**zeeta gwee**dah**ta" |
| ▷ what time does the guided tour begin? | a che ora comincia la visita guidata? | "a kay ohra koh**meen**cha la **vee**zeeta gwee**dah**ta" |
| **gums** | le gengive | "jayn**jee**vay" |
| ▷ my gums are bleeding | mi sanguinano le gengive | "mee san**gwee**nano lay jayn**jee**vay" |
| ▷ my gums are sore | mi fanno male le gengive | "mee fanno mahlay lay jayn**jee**vay" |
| **gym** | la palestra | "pa**lay**stra" |
| **gym shoes** | le scarpe da ginnastica | "skarpay da jeen**nas**teeka" |
| **haemorrhoids** | le emorroidi | "aymor**ro**eedee" |

|  |  |  |
|---|---|---|
| ▷ I need something for haemorrhoids | ho bisogno di qualcosa contro le emorroidi | "o bee**zohn**yo dee kwal**ko**za kontro lay aymor**ro**eedee" |
| **hair** | i capelli | "ka**payl**lee" |
| ▷ my hair is naturally curly/straight | i miei capelli sono mossi/dritti al naturale | "ee myayee ka**payl**lee sohnoh mossee/dreettee al natoo**rah**lay" |
| ▷ I have greasy/dry hair | ho capelli grassi/secchi | "o ka**payl**lee grassee/ saykkee" |
| **hairbrush** | la spazzola per capelli | "**spats**sola payr ka**payl**lee" |
| **haircut** | il taglio di capelli | "talyo dee ka**payl**lee" |
| **hairdresser** | il parrucchiere la parrucchiera | "parrook**ye**ray" "parrook**ye**ra" |
| **hairdryer** | il föhn | "fon" |
| **hairgrip** | il fermacapelli | "fayrmaka**payl**lee" |
| **hair spray** | la lacca per capelli | "lakka payr ka**payl**lee" |
| **hake** | il nasello | "na**zayl**lo" |
| **half** | la metà | "may**ta**" |
| ▷ a half bottle of ... | una mezza bottiglia di... | "oona medzza bot**teel**ya dee" |
| ▷ half past two | le due e mezza | "lay dooay ay medzza" |
| **half board** | la mezza pensione | "medzza paynsee**oh**nay" |
| **half fare** | metà prezzo | "may**ta** pretsso" |
| **half-price** | a metà prezzo | "a may**ta** pretsso" |
| **ham** | il prosciutto | "pro**shoot**to" |
| **hamburger** | l'hamburger (*m*) | "am**boor**gayr" |
| **hand** | la mano | "**mah**no" |
| **handbag** | la borsetta | "bor**sayt**ta" |

| | | |
|---|---|---|
| ▷ my handbag's been stolen | mi hanno rubato la borsetta | "mee anno roo**bah**to la bor**sayt**ta" |
| **handbrake** | il freno a mano | "**frayno** a **mahno**" |
| **handicap:** | | |
| ▷ my handicap is ... | il mio handicap è... | "eel **mee**o **an**deekap e" |
| ▷ what's your handicap? | qual è il suo handicap? | "kwal eh eel **soo**o **an**deekap" |
| **handicapped** | handicappato handicappata | "andeekap**pah**to" "andeekap**pah**ta" |
| **handkerchief** | il fazzoletto | "fatsso**layt**to" |
| **handle** | la maniglia | "ma**neel**ya" |
| ▷ the handle has come off | si è staccata la maniglia | "see ay stak**kah**ta la ma**neel**ya" |
| **hand luggage** | il bagaglio a mano | "ba**gal**yo a **mahno**" |
| **handmade** | fatto a mano | "fatto a **mahno**" |
| ▷ is this handmade? | è fatto a mano? | "e fatto a **mahno**" |
| **hang-glider** | il deltaplano | "delta**plah**no" |
| **hang-gliding:** | | |
| ▷ I'd like to go hang-gliding | vorrei uscire col deltaplano | "vor**eee** oo**shee**ray kohl delta**plah**no" |
| **hangover** | i postumi d'una sbornia | "po**stoo**mee doona **zbor**nya" |
| **Hanover** | Hanover (*f*) | "a**noh**vayr" |
| **to happen** | succedere | "soot**che**dayray" |
| ▷ what happened? | cos'è successo? | "ko**ze** soot**ches**so" |
| ▷ when did it happen? | quando è successo? | "kwando e soot**ches**so" |
| **happy** | felice | "fay**lee**chay" |
| ▷ I'm not happy with ... | non sono soddisfatto di... | "nohn sohnoh sohdees**faht**to dee" |
| **harbour** | il porto | "porto" |

| ABSOLUTE ESSENTIALS | | |
|---|---|---|
| I would like ... | vorrei... | "vor**eee**" |
| I need ... | ho bisogno di... | "o bee**zohn**yo dee" |
| where is ...? | dov'è...? | "do**veh**" |
| I'm looking for ... | sto cercando... | "sto chayr**kando**" |

| hard | duro | "dooro" |
| | dura | "doora" |
| hat | il cappello | "kappello" |
| to **have** | avere | "avayray" |

| | | |
|---|---|---|
| **I have** | ho | "o" |
| **you have** (*informal singular*) | hai | "ayee" |
| (*formal singular*) | ha | "ah" |
| **he/she/it has** | ha | "ah" |
| **we have** | abbiamo | "abbyahmo" |
| **you have** (*plural*) | avete | "avaytay" |
| **they have** | hanno | "anno" |

| ▷ **do you have ...?** | avete...? | "avaytay" |
| **hay fever** | la febbre da fieno | "febbray da feeeno" |
| **hazelnut** | la nocciola | "notchola" |
| **he** | lui | "looee" |
| **head** | la testa | "testa" |
| **headache** | il mal di testa | "mal dee testa" |
| ▷ **I want something for a headache** | voglio qualcosa per il mal di testa | "volyo kwalkoza payr eel mal dee testa" |
| ▷ **I have a headache** | ho mal di testa | "o mal dee testa" |
| **headlights** | i fari | "fahree" |
| **head waiter** | il capocameriere | "kapokamayrryeray" |
| **health food shop** | il negozio di prodotti dietetici | "naygotsyo dee prodohttee deeaytayteechee" |
| to **hear** | sentire | "saynteeray" |
| **heart** | il cuore | "kworay" |
| **heart attack** | l'infarto (*m*) | "eenfarto" |

ABSOLUTE ESSENTIALS

| **do you have ...?** | avete...? | "avaytay" |
| **is there ...?** | c'è...? | "che" |
| **are there ...?** | ci sono...? | "chee sohnoh" |
| **how much is ...?** | quanto costa...? | "kwanto kosta" |

**heart condition:**

▷ **I have a heart condition** — soffro di mal di cuore — "sohffro dee mal dee kworay"

**heater** — la stufa — "stoofa"

▷ **the heater isn't working** — non funziona la stufa — "nohn foontsyohna la stoofa"

**heating** — il riscaldamento — "reeskaldamaynto"

▷ **I can't turn the heating off/on** — non riesco a spegnere/ ad accendere il riscaldamento — "nohn reeesko a spaynyayray/ad atchendayray eel reeskaldamaynto"

**heavy** — pesante — "payzantay"

▷ **this is too heavy** — è troppo pesante — "e trohppo payzantay"

**hello** — ciao — "chao"
  (on telephone) — pronto — "pronto"

**help¹** n — l'aiuto (m) — "ayooto"

▷ **help!** — aiuto! — "ayooto"

▷ **fetch help quickly!** — andate a chiedere aiuto, presto! — "andahtay a keeedayray ayooto presto"

**to help²** vb — aiutare — "ayootahray"

▷ **can you help me?** — può aiutarmi? — "pwo ayootahrmee"

▷ **help yourself!** — prego, si serva! — "praygoh see sayrva"

**her:**

▷ **her hat** — il suo capello — "eel sooo kappello"

▷ **her car** — la sua macchina — "la sooa makkeena"

▷ **her books** — i suoi libri — "ee swoyee leebree"

▷ **her shoes** — le sue scarpe — "lay sooay skarpay"

**hers** — (il) suo — "sooo"
  (la) sua — "sooa"
  (i) suoi — "swoyee"
  (le) sue — "sooay"

**herb** — l'erba (f) aromatica — "ayrba aromahteeka"

| | | |
|---|---|---|
| **here** | qui | "kwee" |
| ▷ here you are! | eccoti qui! | "**ayk**kohtee kwee" |
| **herring** | l'aringa (*f*) | "a**reen**ga" |
| **high** (*price, number etc*) | alto | "alto" |
| | alta | "alta" |
| (*speed*) | forte | "fortay" |
| ▷ how high is it? | quant'è alto? | "kwan**te** alto" |
| ▷ 200 metres high | alto 200 metri | "alto dooay chento maytree" |
| **high blood pressure** | la pressione alta | "praysee**oh**nay alta" |
| **high chair** | il seggiolone | "saydjo**loh**nay" |
| **highlights** (*in hair*) | i colpi di sole | "kohlpee dee sohlay" |
| **high tide** | l'alta marea (*f*) | "alta ma**ray**a" |
| ▷ when is high tide? | quando c'è l'alta marea? | "kwando che lalta ma**ray**a" |
| **hill** | la collina | "kol**lee**na" |
| **hill walking:** | | |
| ▷ I'd like to go hill walking | vorrei andare a fare una camminata in montagna | "vor**reee** ahn**dah**ray a fahray oona kammee**nah**ta een mon**tan**ya" |
| **to hire** | noleggiare | "nolayd**jah**ray" |
| ▷ I want to hire a car | vorrei noleggiare una macchina | "vor**reee** nolayd**jah**ray oona **mak**keena" |
| ▷ can I hire a deck chair? | posso noleggiare una sedia a sdraio? | "posso nolayd**jah**ray oona sedya a zdrayo" |
| **his¹** *adj*: | | |
| ▷ his hat | il suo capello | "eel **soo**o kap**pel**lo" |
| ▷ his car | la sua macchina | "la **soo**a **mak**keena" |
| ▷ his books | i suoi libri | "ee swoyee leebree" |
| ▷ his shoes | le sue scarpe | "lay sooay skarpay" |
| **his²** *pron* | (il) suo | "**soo**o" |
| | (la) sua | "**soo**a" |

ABSOLUTE ESSENTIALS

| | | |
|---|---|---|
| I don't understand | non capisco | "nohn ka**pees**ko" |
| I don't speak Italian | non parlo l'italiano | "nohn parloh leetal**yah**no" |
| do you speak English? | parla inglese? | "parla eeng**lay**zay" |
| could you help me? | può aiutarmi? | "pwo ayoo**tar**mee" |

| | (i) suoi | "swoyee" |
| | (le) sue | "**soo**ay" |
| to **hit** | colpire | "kol**pee**ray" |
| to **hitchhike** | fare l'autostop | "fahray lowto**stop**" |
| **HIV-negative** | sieronegativo | "seeayrohnaygah**tee**vo" |
| | sieronegativa | "seeayrohnaygah**tee**va" |
| **HIV-positive** | sieropositivo | "seeayrohposee**tee**vo" |
| | sieropositiva | "seeayrohposee**tee**va" |
| to **hold** | tenere | "tay**nay**ray" |
| (*contain*) | contenere | "kontay**nay**ray" |
| ▷ **could you hold this for me?** | me lo può tenere? | "may lo pwo tay**nay**ray" |
| **hold-up** (*traffic jam*) | l'ingorgo (*m*) | "een**gor**go" |
| ▷ **what is causing this hold-up?** | perché c'è questo ingorgo? | "payr**kay** che kwaysto een**gor**go" |
| **hole** | il buco | "**boo**ko" |
| **holiday** (*day off*) | la festa | "**festa**" |
| ▷ **on holiday** | in vacanza | "een va**kant**sa" |
| ▷ **I'm on holiday here** | sono qui in vacanza | "sohnoh kwee een va**kant**sa" |
| **holiday resort** | la località turistica | "lokal**ee**ta too**rees**teeka" |
| **holiday romance** | la storia d'amore nata in vacanza | "**stor**reeah d'a**moh**ray nata een vah**kahn**tsa" |
| **home** | la casa | "**kasa**" |
| ▷ **when do you go home?** | quando torna a casa? | "kwando torna a **kasa**" |
| ▷ **I'm going home tomorrow/on Tuesday** | torno a casa domani/ martedì | "torno a kasa do**mah**nee/ martay**dee**" |
| ▷ **I want to go home** | voglio tornare a casa | "volyo tor**nah**ray a **kasa**" |

**homesick:**

| ABSOLUTE ESSENTIALS | | |
|---|---|---|
| **I would like ...** | vorrei... | "vo**reee**" |
| **I need ...** | ho bisogno di... | "o bee**zohn**yo dee" |
| **where is ...?** | dov'è...? | "**doveh**" |
| **I'm looking for ...** | sto cercando... | "sto chayr**kando**" |

| ▷ **to be homesick** | avere nostalgia di casa | "a**vay**ray nostal**jee**a dee kasa" |
| **honey** | il miele | "mee**ee**lay" |
| **honeymoon** | la luna di miele | "loona dee mee**ee**lay" |
| ▷ **we are on (our) honeymoon** | siamo in luna di miele | "see**yah**mo een loona dee mee**ee**lay" |
| **to hope** | sperare | "spay**rah**ray" |
| ▷ **I hope so/not** | spero di sì/no | "**spay**ro dee see/no" |
| **hors d'oeuvre** | l'antipasto (*m*) | "antee**pas**to" |
| **horse** | il cavallo | "ka**val**lo" |
| **horse riding:** | | |
| ▷ **to go horse riding** | andare a cavalcare | "an**dah**ray a kaval**kah**ray" |
| **hose** | il manicotto | "manee**kot**to" |
| **hospital** | l'ospedale (*m*) | "ospay**dah**lay" |
| ▷ **we must get him to hospital** | dobbiamo portarlo all'ospedale | "do**byah**mo por**tar**lo allospay**dah**lay" |
| ▷ **where's the nearest hospital?** | dov'è l'ospedale più vicino? | "doh**ve** lospay**dah**lay pee**oo** vee**chee**no" |
| **hot** | caldo | "**kal**do" |
| | calda | "**kal**da" |
| (*spicy*) | piccante | "peek**kan**tay" |
| ▷ **I'm hot** | ho caldo | "o **kal**do" |
| ▷ **it's hot** (*weather*) | fa caldo | "fa **kal**do" |
| ▷ **it's a bit too hot** (*food*) | è un po' troppo piccante | "e oon poh troppo peek**kan**tay" |
| **hotel** | l'albergo (*m*) | "al**bayr**go" |
| ▷ **can you recommend a (cheap) hotel?** | mi può consigliare un albergo (poco costoso)? | "mee pwo kohnseel**yah**ray oon al**bayr**go (poko ko**stoh**zo)" |
| **hour** | l'ora (*f*) | "**oh**ra" |
| ▷ **an hour ago** | un'ora fa | "oon**oh**ra fa" |

ABSOLUTE ESSENTIALS

| **do you have ...?** | avete...? | "a**vay**tay" |
| **is there ...?** | c'è...? | "che" |
| **are there ...?** | ci sono...? | "chee **soh**noh" |
| **how much is ...?** | quanto costa...? | "**kwan**to **kos**ta" |

| | | |
|---|---|---|
| ▷ in two hours time | tra due ore | "tra dooay ohray" |
| ▷ the journey takes 2 hours | è un viaggio di 2 ore | "e oon veeadjo dee dooay ohray" |
| **house** | la casa | "kasa" |
| **house wine** | il vino della casa | "veeno daylla kasa" |
| ▷ a bottle/carafe of house wine | una bottiglia/caraffa di vino della casa | "oona botteelya/karaffa dee veeno daylla kasa" |
| **hovercraft** | l'hovercraft (m) | "**oh**vayrkraft" |
| ▷ we came by hovercraft | abbiamo preso l'hovercraft | "ab**byah**mo prayzo **loh**vayrkraft" |
| **how** (in what way) | come | "kohmay" |
| ▷ how much? | quanto? | "kwanto" |
| | quanta? | "kwanta" |
| ▷ how many? | quanti? | "kwantee" |
| | quante? | "kwantay" |
| ▷ how are you? | come sta? | "kohmay sta" |
| ▷ how are you feeling now? | come si sente ora? | "kohmay see sayntay ohra" |
| **hundred** | cento | "chaynto" |
| ▷ about a hundred people | un centinaio di persone | "oon chaynteenayo dee payr**soh**nay" |
| **hungry:** | | |
| ▷ I am hungry | ho fame | "o **fah**may" |
| ▷ I am not hungry | non ho fame | "nohn o **fah**may" |
| **hurry:** | | |
| ▷ I'm in a hurry | ho fretta | "o fraytta" |
| **to hurt** | fare male | "fahray mahlay" |
| ▷ he is hurt | si è fatto male | "see e fahtto mahlay" |
| ▷ he has hurt himself | si è fatto male | "see e fahtto mahlay" |
| ▷ my back hurts | mi fa male la schiena | "mee fa mahlay la skee**e**ena" |
| ▷ he has hurt his leg/arm | si è fatto male alla gamba/al braccio | "see e fahtto mahlay alla gamba/al braccho" |

ABSOLUTE ESSENTIALS

| | | |
|---|---|---|
| yes (please) | sì (grazie) | "see (gratsyay)" |
| no (thank you) | no (grazie) | "no (gratsyay)" |
| hello | salve | "salvay" |
| goodbye | arrivederci | "arreevay**dayr**chee" |

| | | |
|---|---|---|
| husband | il marito | "mareeto" |
| hydrofoil | l'aliscafo (*m*) | "aleeskahfo" |
| I | io | "**ee**o" |
| ice | il ghiaccio | "gee**at**cho" |
| ice cream | il gelato | "jay**lah**to" |
| iced (*drink*) | ghiacciato | "geeat**chah**to" |
| | ghiacciata | "geeat**chah**ta" |
| (*coffee, tea*) | freddo | "frayddo" |
| | fredda | "fraydda" |
| ice lolly | il ghiacciolo | "geeat**cho**lo" |
| ice rink | la pista di pattinaggio su ghiaccio | "peesta dee patteena**dj**o soo gee**at**cho" |
| ice skates | i pattini da ghiaccio | "**patt**eenee da gee**at**cho" |
| ice skating | il pattinaggio sul ghiaccio | "eel patteena**dj**o sool gee**at**cho" |
| ▷ can we go ice skating? | possiamo andare a pattinare sul ghiaccio? | "pos**yah**mo an**dah**ray a patteena**hray** sool gee**at**cho" |
| icy | ghiacciato | "geeat**chah**to" |
| | ghiacciata | "geeat**chah**ta" |
| ▷ icy roads | le strade ghiacciate | "lay straday geeat**chah**tay" |
| if | se | "say" |
| ignition | l'accensione (*f*) | "atchayns**yoh**nay" |
| ill | malato | "ma**lah**to" |
| | malata | "ma**lah**ta" |
| immediately | subito | "**soo**beeto" |
| important | importante | "eempor**tan**tay" |
| impossible | impossibile | "eempos**see**beelay" |
| in | in | "een" |

| | | |
|---|---|---|
| **inch** (*metric equiv =* 2.54cm) | il pollice | "**pol**leechay" |
| **included** | compreso<br>compresa | "kom**pray**zo"<br>"kom**pray**za" |
| ▷ **is service included?** | il servizio è compreso? | "eel sayr**veet**syo e kom**pray**zo" |
| **indicator** (*on car*) | la freccia | "fraycha" |
| ▷ **the indicator isn't working** | la freccia non funziona | "la fraycha nohn foontz**yoh**na" |
| **indigestion:** | | |
| ▷ **I have indigestion** | non ho digerito | "nohn o deejay**ree**to" |
| **indoor:** | | |
| ▷ **indoor swimming pool** | la piscina coperta | "lah pee**shee**na ko**payr**ta" |
| ▷ **indoor tennis** | il tennis al coperto | "eel tennees al ko**payr**to" |
| **indoors**<br>(*at home*) | dentro<br>a casa | "dayntro"<br>"a kasa" |
| **infectious** | contagioso<br>contagiosa | "konta**joh**zo"<br>"konta**joh**za" |
| ▷ **is it infectious?** | è contagioso? | "e konta**joh**zo" |
| **information** | le informazioni | "eenformats**yoh**nee" |
| ▷ **I'd like some information about ...** | vorrei delle informazioni su... | "vor**reee** dayllay eenformats**yoh**nee soo" |
| **information office** | l'ufficio (*m*) informazioni | "oof**fee**cho eenformats**yoh**nee" |
| **injection** | l'iniezione (*f*) | "eenyeyts**yoh**nay" |
| ▷ **please give me an injection** | mi faccia un'iniezione, per favore | "mee fatcha ooneenyet**syoh**nay payr fa**voh**ray" |
| **injured** | ferito<br>ferita | "fay**ree**to"<br>"fay**ree**ta" |
| ▷ **he is seriously injured** | è ferito gravemente | "e fay**ree**to grahvay**mayn**tay" |

| **ink** | l'inchiostro (*m*) | "eenkyostro" |
| **insect** | l'insetto (*m*) | "eensetto" |
| **insect bite** | la puntura d'insetto | "poontoora deensetto" |
| **insect repellent** | l'insettifugo (*m*) | "eensetteefoogo" |
| **inside** | dentro | "dayntro" |
| ▷ **let's go inside** | andiamo dentro | "andyahmo dayntro" |
| **instant coffee** | il caffè solubile | "kaffe soloobeelay" |
| **instead** | invece | "eenvaychay" |
| **instructor** | l'istruttore (*m*) | "eestroottohray" |
| **insulin** | l'insulina (*f*) | "eensooleena" |
| **insurance** | l'assicurazione (*f*) | "asseekooratsyohnay" |
| ▷ **will the insurance pay for it?** | l'assicurazione lo rimborsa? | "lasseekooratsyohnay loh reemborsa" |
| **insurance certificate** | il certificato di assicurazione | "chayrteefeekahto dee asseekooratsyohnay" |
| ▷ **can I see your insurance certificate, please** | posso vedere la sua assicurazione per favore? | "posso vaydayray la sooa asseekooratsyohnay payr favohray" |
| **to insure:** | | |
| ▷ **can I insure my luggage?** | posso assicurare il bagaglio? | "posso asseekoorahray eel bagalyo" |
| **interesting** | interessante | "eentayraysantay" |
| ▷ **can you suggest somewhere interesting to go?** | può consigliarmi qualche luogo interessante da visitare? | "pwo konseelyarmee kwalkay lwohgoh eentayraysantay da veezeetahray" |
| **international** | internazionale | "eentayrnatsyonahlay" |
| **interpreter** | l'interprete (*m/f*) | "eentayrpraytay" |

*ABSOLUTE ESSENTIALS*

| do you have ...? | avete...? | "avaytay" |
| is there ...? | c'è...? | "che" |
| are there ...? | ci sono...? | "chee sohnoh" |
| how much is ...? | quanto costa...? | "kwanto kosta" |

| | | |
|---|---|---|
| ▷ **could you act as an interpreter for us please?** | ci potrebbe fare da interprete, per favore? | "chee po**trayb**bay fahray da een**tayr**praytay payr fa**voh**ray" |
| **into** | in | "een" |
| **invitation** | l'invito (m) | "een**vee**to" |
| **to invite** | invitare | "eenvee**tah**ray" |
| ▷ **it's very kind of you to invite me** | è molto gentile da parte sua invitarmi | "e molto jayn**tee**lay da partay sooa eenvee**tar**mee" |
| **invoice** | la fattura | "fat**too**ra" |
| **Ireland** | l'Irlanda (f) | "eer**lan**da" |
| ▷ **Northern Ireland** | l'Irlanda del Nord | "eer**lan**da dayl nord" |
| ▷ **Republic of Ireland** | la Repubblica d'Irlanda | "ray**poob**leeka deer**lan**da" |
| **Irish** | irlandese | "eerlan**day**zay" |
| ▷ **I'm Irish** | sono irlandese | "sohnoh eerlan**day**zay" |
| **iron**[1] n (for clothes) (metal) | il ferro da stiro il ferro | "ferro da steero" "ferro" |
| ▷ **I need an iron** | ho bisogno di un ferro da stiro | "o bee**zohn**yo dee oon ferro da steero" |
| ▷ **I want to use my iron** | voglio usare il ferro da stiro | "volyo oo**zah**ray eel ferro da steero" |
| **to iron**[2] vb | stirare | "stee**rah**ray" |
| ▷ **where can I get this skirt ironed?** | dove posso far stirare questa gonna? | "dohvay posso fahr stee**rah**ray kwaysta gonna" |
| **ironmonger's** | il negozio di ferramenta | "nay**gots**yo dee ferra**mayn**ta" |
| **is** | è | "e" |
| **island** | l'isola (f) | "**ee**zola" |
| **it** | esso | "aysso" |
| **Italian** | italiano | "eetal**yah**no" |

| ABSOLUTE ESSENTIALS | | |
|---|---|---|
| **yes (please)** | sì (grazie) | "see (gratsyay)" |
| **no (thank you)** | no (grazie) | "no (gratsyay)" |
| **hello** | salve | "salvay" |
| **goodbye** | arrivederci | "arreevay**dayr**chee" |

|  | italiana | "eetal**yah**na" |
| ▷ **I don't speak Italian** | non parlo italiano | "nohn parlo ı eetal**yah**no" |
| **Italy** | l'Italia (f) | "eetalya" |
| ▷ **what part of Italy are you from?** | da che parte dell'Italia viene? | "da kay partaʏ delleetalya vyaynay" |
| **itch** | il prurito | "proo**ree**to" |
| **jack** (for car) | il cricco | "kreekko" |
| **jacket** | la giacca | "jakka" |
| **jam** (food) | la marmellata | "mahrmayl**lah**ta" |
| ▷ **strawberry jam** | marmellata di fragole | "mahrmayl**lah**ta dee **frah**golay" |
| ▷ **apricot jam** | marmellata di albicocche | "mahrmayl**lah**ta dee albee**kok**kay" |
| **jammed** | bloccato bloccata | "blok**kah**to" "blok**kah**ta" |
| ▷ **the drawer is jammed** | il cassetto è bloccato | "eel kas**sayt**to e blok**kah**to" |
| ▷ **the controls have jammed** | i comandi sono bloccati | "ee ko**man**dee sohno blok**kah**tee" |
| **January** | gennaio | "djayn**nay**o" |
| **jar** (container) | il vasetto | "va**zayt**to" |
| ▷ **a jar of coffee** | un vaso di caffè | "oon vazo di kaf**fe**" |
| **jazz** | il jazz | "jazz" |
| **jazz festival** | il festival del jazz | "feste**eval** del jazz" |
| **jeans** | i jeans | "jeans" |
| **jelly** (dessert) | la gelatina | "jayla**tee**na" |
| **jellyfish** | la medusa | "may**doo**za" |
| ▷ **I've been stung by a jellyfish** | mi ha pizzicato una medusa | "mee a peedsee**kah**to oona may**doo**za" |
| **jersey** | la maglia | "malya" |

ABSOLUTE ESSENTIALS

| I don't understand | non capisco | "nohn ka**pee**sko" |
| I don't speak Italian | non parlo l'italiano | "nohn parloh leetal**yah**no" |
| do you speak English? | parla inglese? | "parla eeng**lay**zay" |
| could you help me? | può aiutarmi? | "pwo ayoo**tar**mee" |

| | | |
|---|---|---|
| **jet lag** | i problemi dovuti allo sbalzo di fuso orario | "ee problemee dohvootee allo sbaltso dee foozo ohrahreeo" |
| ▷ **I'm suffering from jet lag** | non mi sento bene a causa dello sbalzo di fuso orario | "nohn mee saynto benay a cowza dayllo sbaltso dee foozo ohrahreeo" |
| **jet ski** | l'acquascooter (m) | "akwaskooter" |
| **jet skiing:** | | |
| ▷ **I'd like to go jet skiing** | vorrei andare a fare un giro con l'acquascooter | "vorreee andahray a fahray oon jeero kohn lakwaskooter" |
| **jeweller's** | la gioielleria | "joyayllayreea" |
| **jewellery** | i gioielli | "joyellee" |
| ▷ **I would like to put my jewellery in a safe** | vorrei mettere i gioielli in cassaforte | "vorreee mayttayray ee joyellee een kassafortay" |
| **Jewish** | ebreo | "aybreo" |
| | ebrea | "aybrea" |
| **job** | il lavoro | "lavohro" |
| ▷ **what's your job?** | che lavoro fa? | "kay lavohro fa" |
| **jog:** | | |
| ▷ **to go jogging** | fare footing | "fahray footing" |
| **joke** | lo scherzo | "skayrtso" |
| **journey** | il viaggio | "veeadjo" |
| ▷ **how was your journey?** | com'è andato il viaggio? | "kome andahto eel veeadjo" |
| **jug** | la brocca | "brokka" |
| ▷ **a jug of water** | una brocca d'acqua | "oona brokka dakwa" |
| **juice** | il succo | "sookko" |
| **July** | luglio | "loolyo" |

ABSOLUTE ESSENTIALS

| | | |
|---|---|---|
| **I would like ...** | vorrei... | "voreee" |
| **I need ...** | ho bisogno di... | "o beezohnyo dee" |
| **where is ...?** | dov'è...? | "doveh" |
| **I'm looking for ...** | sto cercando... | "sto chayrkando" |

| | | |
|---|---|---|
| **jump leads** | i cavi per far partire la macchina | "kahvee payr fahr par**tee**ray la **mak**keena" |
| **junction** (*road*) | l'incrocio (*m*) | "een**kroh**cho" |
| ▷ **go left at the next junction** | giri a sinistra al prossimo incrocio | "**jee**ree a see**nee**stra al **pross**eemo een**kroh**cho" |
| **June** | giugno | "**djoon**yo" |
| **just:** | | |
| ▷ **just two** | solamente due | "sola**mayn**tay **doo**ay" |
| ▷ **I've just arrived** | sono appena arrivato | "**soh**noh ap**pay**na arree**vah**to" |
| **to keep** (*retain*) | tenere | "tay**nay**ray" |
| ▷ **keep the door locked** | tenga la porta chiusa a chiave | "**tayn**ga la porta kee**oo**za a kee**ah**vay" |
| ▷ **may I keep it?** | lo posso tenere? | "loh posso tay**nay**ray" |
| ▷ **could you keep me a loaf of bread?** | può tenermi da parte un filone di pane? | "pwo tay**nayr**mee da partay oon fee**loh**nay dee **pah**nay" |
| ▷ **how long will it keep?** | per quanto si mantiene fresco? | "payr **kwan**to see man**tyay**nay fresko" |
| ▷ **keep to the path** | continui lungo il sentiero | "kohn**tee**nooee loongo eel sayn**tye**ro" |
| **kettle** | il bollitore | "bollee**toh**ray" |
| **key** | la chiave | "kee**ah**vay" |
| ▷ **which is the key for the front door?** | qual è la chiave della porta principale? | "kwal e la kee**ah**vay daylla porta preenchee**pah**lay" |
| ▷ **I've lost my key** | ho perso la mia chiave | "o payrso la **mee**a kee**ah**vay" |
| ▷ **can I have my key?** | posso avere la mia chiave? | "posso a**vay**ray la **mee**a kee**ah**vay" |
| **kidneys** (*Anat*) | i reni | "**ray**nee" |
| (*as food*) | i rognoni | "ron**yoh**nee" |
| **kilo** | il chilo | "**kee**lo" |

| | *ABSOLUTE ESSENTIALS* | |
|---|---|---|
| **do you have ...?** | avete...? | "a**vay**tay" |
| **is there ...?** | c'è...? | "che" |
| **are there ...?** | ci sono...? | "chee **soh**noh" |
| **how much is ...?** | quanto costa...? | "**kwan**to kosta" |

| **kilometre** | il chilometro | "kee**lo**maytro" |
|---|---|---|
| **kind**[1] *n (sort, type)* | il tipo | "**tee**po" |
| ▷ what kind of...? | che tipo di...? | "kay **tee**po dee" |
| **kind**[2] *adj (person)* | gentile | "jayn**tee**lay" |
| ▷ that's very kind of you | molto gentile da parte sua | "**moh**lto jayn**tee**lay da **par**tay **soo**a" |
| **kiss**[1] *n* | il bacio | "**ba**cho" |
| to **kiss**[2] *vb* | baciare | "ba**chah**ray" |
| **kitchen** | la cucina | "koo**chee**na" |
| **knife** | il coltello | "kol**tel**lo" |
| to **know** *(facts)* | sapere | "sa**pay**ray" |
| *(be acquainted with)* | conoscere | "ko**no**shayray" |
| ▷ I don't know | non lo so | "non loh so" |
| ▷ do you know a good place to go? | conosce qualche bel posto dove si potrebbe andare? | "ko**no**shay kwalkay bel posto dovay see po**trayb**bay an**dah**ray" |
| ▷ do you know where I can ...? | sa dove posso...? | "sa **do**vay **po**sso" |
| ▷ do you know Paul? | conosce Paul? | "ko**no**shay Paul" |
| ▷ do you know how to do this? | sa come si fa? | "sa **co**may see fah" |
| **kosher** | kasher | "**ka**sher" |
| **laces** *(for shoes)* | i lacci | "**lat**chee" |
| **ladder** | la scala | "**skah**la" |
| **ladies** | la toilette (per signore) | "twa**let** (payr seen**yoh**ray)" |
| ▷ where is the ladies? | dov'è la toilette per signore? | "doh**ve** la twa**let** payr seen**yoh**ray" |
| **lady** | la signora | "seen**yoh**ra" |
| **lager** | la birra chiara | "**beer**ra kee**a**ra" |

| lake | il lago | "lahgo" |
|------|---------|---------|
| lamb | l'agnello (m) | "anyello" |
| lamp | la lampada | "lampada" |
| ▷ the lamp is not working | la lampada non funziona | "la lampada non foontsyohna" |
| lane | la stradina | "stradeena" |
| (of motorway) | la corsia | "korseea" |
| ▷ you're in the wrong lane | è nella corsia sbagliata | "e nayla korseea sbalyahta" |
| language | la lingua | "leengwa" |
| ▷ what languages do you speak? | che lingue parla? | "kay leengway parla" |
| large | grande | "granday" |
| larger | più grande | "peeoo granday" |
| ▷ do you have a larger one? | ne ha uno più grande? | "nay a oono peeoo granday" |
| last¹ adj | scorso | "skorso" |
| | scorsa | "skorsa" |
| (final) | ultimo | "oolteemo" |
| | ultima | "oolteema" |
| ▷ last week | la settimana scorsa | "la saytteemahna skorsa" |
| to last² vb | durare | "doorahray" |
| ▷ how long will it last? | quanto dura? | "kwanto doora" |
| late | tardi | "tardee" |
| ▷ the train is late | il treno è in ritardo | "eel trayno e een reetardo" |
| ▷ sorry we are late | scusi il ritardo | "skoozee eel reetardo" |
| ▷ we went to bed late | siamo andati a dormire tardi | "seeyahmo andahtee a dormeeray tardee" |
| ▷ late last night | ieri sera tardi | "yeree sayra tardee" |
| ▷ it's too late | è troppo tardi | "e troppo tardee" |

ABSOLUTE ESSENTIALS

| I don't understand | non capisco | "nohn kapeesko" |
|--------------------|-------------|------------------|
| I don't speak Italian | non parlo l'italiano | "nohn parloh leetalyahno" |
| do you speak English? | parla inglese? | "parla eenglayzay" |
| could you help me? | può aiutarmi? | "pwo ayootarmee" |

| | | |
|---|---|---|
| ▷ we are 10 minutes late | siamo in ritardo di 10 minuti | "see**yah**mo een ree**tar**do dee dee**ee**chay mee**noo**tee" |
| **later** | più tardi | "pee**oo** tardee" |
| ▷ shall I come back later? | ritorno più tardi? | "ree**tor**no peeoo tardee" |
| ▷ see you later | a dopo | "a dopo" |
| **launderette** | la lavanderia automatica | "lavanday**ree**a owto**mat**eeka" |
| **laundry service:** | | |
| ▷ is there a laundry service? | c'è un servizio di lavanderia? | "che oon sayr**veets**yo dee lavanday**ree**a" |
| **lavatory** | il gabinetto | "gabee**nayt**to" |
| **lawyer** | l'avvocato (m) | "avvo**kah**to" |
| **laxative** | il lassativo | "lassa**tee**vo" |
| **lay-by** | la piazzola di sosta | "pee**ats**ola dee sosta" |
| **lead¹** n (electric) | il filo | "feelo" |
| **to lead²** vb: | | |
| ▷ you lead the way | ci faccia strada | "chee fatcha strada" |
| **leader** | il capo | "kapo" |
| (guide) | guida | "gweeda" |
| **leak** (of gas, liquid) | la perdita | "**payr**deeta" |
| (in roof) | il buco | "booko" |
| ▷ there is a leak in the petrol tank/radiator | il serbatoio/radiatore perde | "eel sayrba**to**yo/radya**toh**ray payrday" |
| **to learn** | imparare | "eempa**rah**ray" |
| **least:** | | |
| ▷ at least | almeno | "al**may**no" |
| **leather** | il cuoio | "kwoyo" |
| **to leave** (leave behind) | lasciare | "la**shah**ray" |

ABSOLUTE ESSENTIALS

| | | |
|---|---|---|
| I would like ... | vorrei... | "vor**eee**" |
| I need ... | ho bisogno di... | "o bee**zohn**yo dee" |
| where is ...? | dov'è...? | "do**veh**" |
| I'm looking for ... | sto cercando... | "sto chayr**kan**do" |

| | | |
|---|---|---|
| ▷ **when does the train leave?** | quando parte il treno? | "kwando partay eel treno" |
| ▷ **I shall be leaving at 8.00 tomorrow morning** | partirò domani mattina alle otto | "pahrteero domahnee matteena allay otto" |
| **leeks** | i porri | "porree" |
| **left¹** *n* | la sinistra | "seeneestra" |
| ▷ **(on/to the) left** | a sinistra | "a seeneestra" |
| ▷ **take the third street on the left** | prenda la terza strada a sinistra | "prenda la tertsa strada a seeneestra" |
| **left²** *vb*: | | |
| ▷ **I've been left behind** | mi hanno lasciato indietro | "mee anno lashahto eendeeeetro" |
| ▷ **I left my bags in the taxi** | ho lasciato le borse nel taxi | "o lashahto lay borsay nel taksee" |
| ▷ **I left the keys in the car** | ho lasciato le chiavi in macchina | "o lashahto lay keeahvee een makkeena" |
| **left-luggage (office)** | il deposito bagagli | "daypozeeto bagalyee" |
| **leg** | la gamba | "gamba" |
| **lemon** | il limone | "leemohnay" |
| **lemonade** | la limonata | "leemonahta" |
| **lemon tea** | il tè al limone | "te al leemohnay" |
| **to lend** | prestare | "praystahray" |
| ▷ **could you lend me some money?** | mi potrebbe prestare dei soldi? | "mee potraybbay prestahray dayee soldee" |
| ▷ **could you lend me a towel?** | mi potrebbe prestare un asciugamano? | "mee potraybbay prestahray oon ashoogamahno" |
| **lens** | l'obiettivo (*m*) | "obyaytteevo" |
| ▷ **I wear contact lenses** | porto le lenti a contatto | "porto lay lentee a contatto" |

*ABSOLUTE ESSENTIALS*

| | | |
|---|---|---|
| **do you have ...?** | avete...? | "avaytay" |
| **is there ...?** | c'è...? | "che" |
| **are there ...?** | ci sono...? | "chee sohnoh" |
| **how much is ...?** | quanto costa...? | "kwanto kosta" |

| **less** | meno | "mayno" |
| **lesson** | la lezione | "laytsyohnay" |
| ▷ **do you give lessons?** | dà lezioni? | "da laytsyohnee" |
| ▷ **can we take lessons?** | possiamo prendere delle lezioni? | "posyahmo prendayray dayllay laytsyohnee" |
| **to let** (allow) | permettere | "payrmayttayray" |
| (hire out) | affittare | "affeettahray" |
| **letter** | la lettera | "lettayra" |
| ▷ **how much is a letter to England?** | quanto costa un francobollo per l'Inghilterra? | "kwanto kosta oon frankobohllo payr leengeelterra" |
| ▷ **are there any letters for me?** | c'è posta per me? | "che posta payr may" |
| **lettuce** | la lattuga | "lattooga" |
| **level crossing** | il passaggio a livello | "eel passadjo a leevayllo" |
| **library** | la biblioteca | "beebleeoteka" |
| **licence** | il permesso | "payrmesso" |
| **lid** | il coperchio | "kopayrkyo" |
| **to lie down** | sdraiarsi | "zdrayahrsee" |
| **lifeboat** | la scialuppa di salvataggio | "shalooppa dee salvatadjo" |
| ▷ **call out the lifeboat!** | fate venire la scialuppa di salvataggio! | "fahtay vayneeray la shalooppa dee salvatadjo" |
| **lifeguard** | il bagnino | "banyeeno" |
| ▷ **get the lifeguard!** | chiamate il bagnino! | "keeamahtay eel banyeeno" |
| **lifejacket** | il giubbotto salvagente | "joobbotto salvajentay" |
| **lift** (in hotel etc) | l'ascensore (m) | "ashaynsohray" |
| (by car etc) | il passaggio | "passadjo" |

| | | |
|---|---|---|
| ▷ is there a lift in the building? | c'è un ascensore nell'edificio? | "che oon ashayn**soh**ray nelledee**fee**cho" |
| ▷ can you give me a lift to the garage? | mi può dare un passaggio fino all'officina? | "mee pwo dahray oon pas**sadj**o feeno alloffee**chee**na" |
| **lift pass** (*on ski slopes*) | la tessera per gli impianti di risalita | "**tes**sayra payr lyee eempee**ahn**tee dee reesa**lee**ta" |
| **light**[1] *n* | la luce | "**loo**chay" |
| ▷ have you got a light? | ha da accendere? | "a da at**chayn**dayray" |
| ▷ do you mind if I turn off the light? | le dispiace se spengo la luce? | "lay deespee**a**chay say spengo la **loo**chay" |
| **light**[2] *adj* (*not dark*) | chiaro chiara | "kee**a**ro" "kee**a**ra" |
| ▷ light blue/green | blu/verde chiaro | "bloo/verday kee**a**ro" |
| **light bulb** | la lampadina | "lampa**dee**na" |
| **lighter** | l'accendino (*m*) | "atchayn**dee**no" |
| **lighter fuel** | il gas per accendini | "gaz payr atchayn**dee**nee" |
| **like**[1] *prep* | come | "**koh**may" |
| ▷ like you | come lei | "**koh**may layee" |
| ▷ like this | così | "ko**zee**" |
| to **like**[2] *vb* | piacere | "peea**chay**ray" |
| ▷ I like coffee | mi piace il caffè | "mee pee**a**chay eel kaffe" |
| ▷ I would like a newspaper | vorrei un giornale | "vor**reee** oon jor**nah**lay" |
| **lime** (*fruit*) | la limetta | "lee**may**tta" |
| **line** (*row, queue*) (*telephone*) | la fila la linea | "**fee**la" "**lee**naya" |
| ▷ I'd like an outside line, please | mi dà la linea, per favore | "mee dah la **lee**naya payr fa**voh**ray" |
| ▷ the line's engaged | la linea è occupata | "la **lee**naya e okkoo**pah**ta" |

| | | |
|---|---|---|
| ▷ it's a bad line | si sente male | "see sayntay mahlay" |
| **lip salve** | il burro di cacao | "boorro dee kakao" |
| **lipstick** | il rossetto | "ross**sayt**to" |
| **liqueur** | il liquore | "lee**kwoh**ray" |
| ▷ what liqueurs do you have? | quali liquori avete? | "kwahlee lee**kwoh**ree a**vay**tay" |
| **Lisbon** | Lisbona (f) | "leez**bo**na" |
| to **listen** | ascoltare | "askol**tah**ray" |
| **litre** | il litro | "leetro" |
| **little:** | | |
| ▷ a little village | un paesino | "oon paay**zee**no" |
| ▷ I'm a little tired | sono un po' stanco | "sohno oon po stanco" |
| ▷ a little milk | un po' di latte | "oon po dee lattay" |
| to **live** | vivere | "**vee**vayray" |
| ▷ I live in Edinburgh | abito ad Edimburgo | "**ah**beeto ad aydeem**boor**go" |
| ▷ where do you live? | dove abita? | "dohvay **ah**beeta" |
| **liver** | il fegato | "**fay**gato" |
| **living room** | la sala | "sahla" |
| **loaf** | il pane | "panay" |
| **lobby** (in hotel) (in theatre) | l'atrio (m) il foyer | "**ah**treeo" "fway**ay**" |
| ▷ I'll meet you in the lobby | ci vediamo nell'atrio (or nel foyer) | "chee vayd**yah**mo nell**ah**treeo (or nel fway**ay**)" |
| **lobster** | l'aragosta (f) | "ara**gos**ta" |
| **local** (wine, speciality) | locale | "lo**kah**lay" |
| ▷ what's the local speciality? | qual è la specialità locale? | "kwal e la spaychahlee**ta** lo**kah**lay" |
| ▷ I'd like to order something local | vorrei ordinare un piatto locale | "vorr**eee** ordee**nah**ray oon pee**at**to lo**kah**lay" |

ABSOLUTE ESSENTIALS

| | | |
|---|---|---|
| I would like ... | vorrei... | "vor**eee**" |
| I need ... | ho bisogno di... | "o bee**zohn**yo dee" |
| where is ...? | dov'è...? | "do**veh**" |
| I'm looking for ... | sto cercando... | "sto chayr**kan**do" |

| | | |
|---|---|---|
| **lock**[1] n (*on door, box*) | la serratura | "sayrra**too**ra" |
| ▷ **the lock is broken** | la serratura è rotta | "la sayrra**too**ra e rohtta" |
| to **lock**[2] vb (*door*) | chiudere a chiave | "kee**oo**dayray a kee**ah**vay" |
| ▷ **I have locked myself out of my room** | sono rimasto chiuso fuori della mia stanza | "sohnoh ree**mas**to kee**oo**zo fworee daylla meea stantsa" |
| **locker** | l'armadietto (*m*) | "armahdee**et**to" |
| ▷ **are there any luggage lockers?** | ci sono armadietti per il deposito bagagli? | "chee sohnoh armahdee**et**tee payr eel day**po**zeeto ba**gal**yee" |
| ▷ **where are the clothes lockers?** | dove sono gli armadietti per i vestiti? | "dohvay sohnoh lyee armahdee**et**tee payr ee vay**stee**tee" |
| **lollipop** | il lecca lecca | "laykka laykka" |
| **London** | Londra (*f*) | "**lohn**dra" |
| **long** | lungo | "**loon**go" |
| | lunga | "**loon**ga" |
| ▷ **for a long time** | a lungo | "ah **loon**go" |
| ▷ **how long will it take to get there?** | quanto ci vorrà per arrivarci? | "kwanto chee vor**ra** payr arree**vahr**chee" |
| ▷ **will it be long?** | dura tanto? | "**doo**ra tanto" |
| ▷ **how long will it be?** | quanto dura? | "kwanto **doo**ra" |
| **long-sighted:** | | |
| ▷ **I'm long-sighted** | sono presbite | "sohnoh **pres**beetay" |
| to **look** | guardare | "gwar**dah**ray" |
| ▷ **I'm just looking** | guardo soltanto | "gwardo sol**tan**to" |
| to **look after** | badare a | "ba**dah**ray ah" |
| ▷ **could you look after my case for a minute please?** | può tenere d'occhio la mia valigia per un attimo, per favore? | "pwo tay**nay**ray dokyo la meea va**lee**ja payr oon **at**teemo payr fa**voh**ray" |

*ABSOLUTE ESSENTIALS*

| | | |
|---|---|---|
| **do you have ...?** | avete...? | "avaytay" |
| **is there ...?** | c'è...? | "che" |
| **are there ...?** | ci sono...? | "chee sohnoh" |
| **how much is ...?** | quanto costa...? | "kwanto kosta" |

## look for

| | | |
|---|---|---|
| ▷ **I need someone to look after the children tonight** | ho bisogno di qualcuno che mi tenga i bambini questa sera | "o bee**zon**yo dee kwal**koo**no kay mee taynga ee bam**bee**nee kwesta sayra" |
| to **look for** | cercare | "chayr**kah**ray" |
| ▷ **we're looking for a hotel/an apartment** | cerchiamo un albergo/ un appartamento | "chayr**kyah**mo oon al**bayr**go/oon apparta**may**nto" |
| **lorry** | il camion | "**kam**yon" |
| to **lose** | perdere | "**payr**dayray" |
| **lost** (*object*) | perso | "**payr**so" |
| | persa | "**payr**sa" |
| ▷ **I have lost my wallet** | ho perso il portafoglio | "o payrso eel porta**fol**yo" |
| ▷ **I am lost** | mi sono perso | "mee sohnoh payrso" |
| ▷ **my son is lost** | non trovo più mio figlio | "nohn trovo peeoo meeo feelyo" |
| **lost property office** | l'ufficio (*m*) oggetti smarriti | "oof**fee**cho od**jet**tee zmar**ree**tee" |
| **lot:** | | |
| ▷ **a lot** | molto | "**mohl**to" |
| **lotion** | la lozione | "lohts**yoh**nay" |
| **loud** | forte | "**for**tay" |
| ▷ **it's too loud** | è troppo forte | "e troppo fortay" |
| **lounge** (*in hotel*) | il salone | "sa**loh**nay" |
| ▷ **could we have coffee in the lounge?** | potremmo prendere il caffè nel salone? | "po**tray**mmo **prayn**dayray eel kaffe nel sa**loh**nay" |
| to **love** | (*person*) amare | "a**mah**ray" |
| ▷ **I love you** | ti amo | "tee amo" |
| ▷ **I love swimming** | mi piace molto nuotare | "mee pee**a**chay mohlto nwo**tah**ray" |
| ▷ **I love seafood** | adoro i frutti di mare | "a**doh**ro ee frootee dee mahray" |
| **lovely** | bellissimo | "bayl**lees**seemo" |

| | bellissima | "bay**lees**seema" |
|---|---|---|
| ▷ **it's a lovely day** | è una bella giornata | "e oona bella jor**nah**ta" |
| **low** | basso | "basso" |
| | bassa | "bassa" |
| *(standard, quality)* | scadente | "ska**den**tay" |
| **low tide** | la bassa marea | "bassa ma**ray**a" |
| **lucky** | fortunato | "fortoo**nah**to" |
| | fortunata | "fortoo**nah**ta" |
| **luggage** | i bagagli | "ba**gal**yee" |
| ▷ **can you help me with my luggage, please?** | mi può aiutare con i bagagli, per favore? | "mee pwo ayoo**tah**ray kohn ee ba**gal**yee payr fa**voh**ray" |
| ▷ **please take my luggage to a taxi** | porti i bagagli al taxi, per favore | "portee ee ba**gal**yee al taksee payr fa**voh**ray" |
| ▷ **I sent my luggage on in advance** | ho spedito i bagagli prima di partire | "o spay**dee**to ee ba**gal**yee preema dee par**tee**ray" |
| ▷ **our luggage has not arrived** | i nostri bagagli non sono arrivati | "ee nostree ba**gal**yee nohn sohnoh arree**vah**tee" |
| ▷ **where do I check in my luggage?** | dove posso consegnare i bagagli? | "dohvay posso konsayn**yah**ray ee ba**gal**yee" |
| ▷ **could you have my luggage taken up?** | potete far portare su i miei bagagli? | "potetay fahr por**tah**ray soo i mee**ay**ee ba**gal**yee" |
| ▷ **can you send someone to collect my luggage?** | potrebbe mandare qualcuno a prendere i miei bagagli? | "po**treb**bay man**dah**ray kwal**koo**no a **pren**dayray ee mee**ay**ee ba**gal**yee" |
| **luggage allowance:** | | |
| ▷ **what's the luggage allowance?** | qual è il peso massimo consentito per il bagaglio? | "kwa**le** eel payso **mas**seemo konsen**tee**to payr eel ba**gal**yo" |
| **luggage rack** *(on car, in train)* | il portabagagli | "portaba**gal**yee" |

| | | |
|---|---|---|
| **luggage tag** | l'etichetta (f) (del bagaglio) | "ayteekaytta (dayl bagalyo)" |
| **luggage trolley** | il carrello | "karrello" |
| ▷ **are there any luggage trolleys?** | ci sono dei carrelli per i bagagli? | "chee sohnoh dayee karrellee payr ee bagalyee" |
| **lunch** | il pranzo | "prantso" |
| ▷ **what's for lunch?** | cosa c'è per pranzo? | "koza che payr prantso" |
| **Luxembourg** | il Lussemburgo | "loossemboorgo" |
| **luxury** | di lusso | "dee loosso" |
| **macaroni** | i maccheroni | "makkayrohnee" |
| **machine** | la macchina | "makkeena" |
| **mackerel** | lo sgombro | "sgombro" |
| **madam** | signora | "seenyohra" |
| **Madrid** | Madrid (f) | "madreed" |
| **magazine** | la rivista | "reeveesta" |
| ▷ **do you have any English magazines?** | avete riviste in inglese? | "avaytay reeveestay een eenglayzay" |
| **maid** (in hotel) | la cameriera | "kamayryera" |
| ▷ **when does the maid come?** | quando viene la cameriera? | "kwando veeenay la kamayryera" |
| **main** | principale | "preencheepahlay" |
| ▷ **the main station** | la stazione principale | "la statsyohnay preencheepahlay" |
| **main course** | il piatto principale | "peeatto preencheepahlay" |
| **mains** (electric): | | |
| ▷ **turn it off at the mains** | spenga l'interruttore generale | "spaynga leenterroottoray jenerahlay" |

| to **make** (*generally*) | fare | "fahray" |
|---|---|---|
| (*meal*) | preparare | "prayparahray" |

| I make | faccio | "fahtcho" |
|---|---|---|
| you make (*informal singular*) | fai | "fay" |
| (*formal singular*) | fa | "fa" |
| he/she/it/makes | fa | "fa" |
| we make | facciamo | "fahtchahmo" |
| you make (*plural*) | fate | "fahtay" |
| they make | fanno | "fahnno" |

| **make-up** | il trucco | "trookko" |
|---|---|---|
| **make-up remover** | lo struccante | "strookkahntay" |
| **mallet** | la mazza | "matssa" |
| **man** | l'uomo (*m*) | "womo" |
| ▷ **men** | uomini | "**wo**meenee" |
| **manager** | il direttore | "deerayttohray" |
| ▷ **I'd like to speak to the manager** | vorrei parlare col direttore | "vor**reee** par**lah**ray kohl deret**toh**ray" |
| **Mantua** | Mantova (*f*) | "**man**tova" |
| **many** | molti | "mohltee" |
| **map** | la cartina | "kahr**tee**na" |
| ▷ **can you show me on the map?** | può mostrarmelo sulla cartina? | "pwo mo**strahr**maylo soolla kahr**tee**na" |
| ▷ **I want a street map of the city** | voglio una piantina della città | "volyo oona peean**tee**na daylla chee**ta**" |
| ▷ **I need a road map of ...** | ho bisogno di una carta stradale di... | "o bee**zohn**yo dee oona kahrta stra**dah**lay dee" |
| ▷ **where can I buy a local map?** | dove posso comprare una cartina? | "dohvay posso kom**prah**ray oona kahr**tee**na" |

| **March** | marzo | "**mart**so" |
|---|---|---|

ABSOLUTE ESSENTIALS

| do you have ...? | avete...? | "avaytay" |
|---|---|---|
| is there ...? | c'è...? | "che" |
| are there ...? | ci sono...? | "chee sohnoh" |
| how much is ...? | quanto costa...? | "kwanto kosta" |

| | | |
|---|---|---|
| **margarine** | la margarina | "mahrga**ree**na" |
| **mark** (*stain*) | la macchia | "**mak**ya" |
| **market** | il mercato | "mayr**kah**to" |
| **market day** | il giorno di mercato | "**jor**no dee mayr**kah**to" |
| ▷ **when is market day?** | quando c'è il mercato? | "**kwan**do che eel mayr**kah**to" |
| **marmalade** | la marmellata di arance | "marmay**llah**ta dee **aran**chay" |
| **married** | sposato | "spo**zah**to" |
| | sposata | "spo**zah**ta" |
| **marzipan** | il marzapane | "martsa**pa**nay" |
| **mascara** | il mascara | "ma**ska**ra" |
| **mass** (*in church*) | la messa | "**may**ssa" |
| ▷ **when is mass?** | quando viene celebrata la messa? | "**kwan**do vee**ee**nay chaylay**brah**ta la **may**ssa" |
| **matches** | i fiammiferi | "feeam**mee**fayree" |
| **material** (*cloth*) | il tessuto | "tays**soo**to" |
| ▷ **what is the material?** | che stoffa è? | "kay **stoff**a e" |
| **matter:** | | |
| ▷ **it doesn't matter** | non importa | "nohn eem**por**ta" |
| ▷ **what's the matter?** | cosa c'è? | "**ko**sa che" |
| **May** | maggio | "**mad**joh" |
| **mayonnaise** | la maionese | "mayo**nay**zay" |
| **meal** | il pasto | "**pas**to" |
| to **mean** (*signify*) | voler dire | "vo**layr dee**ray" |
| ▷ **what does this mean?** | cosa vuol dire questo? | "**ko**za vwol **dee**ray **kways**to" |
| **measles** | il morbillo | "mor**beel**lo" |

**to measure:**

▷ **can you measure me please?** — può prendermi le misure? — "pwo **pren**dermee lay mee**zoo**ray"

**meat** — la carne — "**kar**nay"

▷ **I don't eat meat** — non mangio carne — "nohn manjo **kar**nay"

**mechanic** — il meccanico — "may**kka**neeko"

▷ **can you send a mechanic?** — può mandare un meccanico? — "pwo man**dah**ray oon may**kka**neeko"

**medicine** — la medicina — "maydee**chee**na"

**medium** — medio — "**med**yo"
media — "**med**ya"

**medium rare** — poco cotto — "poko **kot**to"
poco cotta — "poko **kot**ta"

**to meet** — incontrare — "eenkon**trah**ray"

▷ **pleased to meet you** — piacere di conoscerla — "peea**chay**ray dee ko**no**shayrla"

▷ **shall we meet afterwards?** — ci incontriamo dopo? — "chee eenkon**tryah**mo dopo"

▷ **where can we meet?** — dove ci vediamo? — "dohvay chee ved**yah**mo"

**melon** — il melone — "may**loh**nay"

**to melt** — sciogliere — "**shol**yayray"

**member** (*of club etc*) — il socio — "**so**cho"

▷ **do we need to be members?** — bisogna essere soci? — "bee**zohn**ya **es**sayray **so**chee"

**men** — gli uomini — "**wo**meenee"

**to mention** — menzionare — "mentsyo**nah**ray"

▷ **don't mention it** — prego — "**pray**go"

**menu** — il menù — "may**noo**"

▷ **may we see the menu?** — possiamo vedere il menù? — "pos**syah**mo vay**day**ray eel may**noo**"

ABSOLUTE ESSENTIALS

| | | |
|---|---|---|
| I don't understand | non capisco | "nohn ka**pee**sko" |
| I don't speak Italian | non parlo l'italiano | "nohn parloh leetal**yah**no" |
| do you speak English? | parla inglese? | "parla eeng**lay**zay" |
| could you help me? | può aiutarmi? | "pwo ayoo**tar**mee" |

| | | |
|---|---|---|
| ▷ do you have a special menu for children? | avete un menù speciale per bambini? | "a**vay**tay oon may**noo** spay**chah**lay payr bam**bee**nee" |
| ▷ we'll have the menu at ... lire | prendiamo il menù a... lire | "prayn**dyah**mo eel may**noo** a ... **lee**ray" |
| **meringue** | la meringa | "may**reen**ga" |
| **message** | il messaggio | "mays**sad**jo" |
| ▷ can I leave a message with his secretary? | posso lasciare un messaggio alla sua segretaria? | "posso la**shah**ray oon mays**sad**jo alla **soo**a saygray**tar**ya" |
| ▷ could you take a message please? | posso lasciare un messaggio, per favore? | "posso la**shah**ray oon mays**sad**jo payr fa**voh**ray" |
| **metal** | il metallo | "may**tal**lo" |
| **meter** | il contatore | "konta**toh**ray" |
| ▷ the meter is broken | il contatore è rotto | "eel konta**toh**ray e **roh**tto" |
| ▷ do you have change for the meter? | ha moneta per il contatore? | "a mo**nay**ta payr eel konta**toh**ray" |
| **metre** | il metro | "**me**tro" |
| **migraine** | l'emicrania (f) | "aymee**kran**ya" |
| **Milan** | Milano (f) | "mee**lah**no" |
| **mile** (*metric equiv= 1.60km*) | il miglio | "**mee**lyo" |
| ▷ twenty miles | venti miglia | "**vayn**tee **mee**lya" |
| **milk** | il latte | "**laht**tay" |
| ▷ skimmed milk | il latte scremato | "eel **laht**tay skray**mah**to" |
| ▷ semi-skimmed milk | il latte parzialmente scremato | "eel **laht**tay partseeal**mayn**ytay skray**mah**to" |
| **milkshake** | il frappé | "frap**pay**" |
| **millimetre** | il millimetro | "meel**lee**maytro" |

| ABSOLUTE ESSENTIALS | | |
|---|---|---|
| I would like ... | vorrei... | "vo**reee**" |
| I need ... | ho bisogno di... | "o bee**zohn**yo dee" |
| where is ...? | dov'è...? | "do**veh**" |
| I'm looking for ... | sto cercando... | "sto chayr**kan**do" |

| | | |
|---|---|---|
| **million** | il milione | "meel**yoh**nay" |
| **mince** | la carne macinata | "kahrnay machee**nah**ta" |
| **to mind:** | | |
| ▷ **I don't mind** | non importa | "nohn eem**por**ta" |
| ▷ **do you mind if I ...?** | le dispiace se...? | "lay deespee**ea**chay say" |
| **mine** | (il) mio | "meeo" |
| | (la) mia | "meea" |
| | (i) miei | "meeayee" |
| | (le) mie | "meeay" |
| **mineral water** | l'acqua (f) minerale | "akwa meenay**rah**lay" |
| **minimum** | il minimo | "**mee**neemo" |
| **minister** (*church*) | il sacerdote | "sachayr**do**tay" |
| **minor road** | la strada secondaria | "strahda saykon**dar**ya" |
| **mint** (*herb*) | la menta | "**mayn**ta" |
| (*sweet*) | la mentina | "mayn**tee**na" |
| **minute** | il minuto | "mee**noo**to" |
| ▷ **wait a minute** | aspetti un momento | "as**payt**tee oon mo**mayn**to" |
| **mirror** | lo specchio | "**spek**yo" |
| **Miss** | Signorina | "seenyo**ree**na" |
| **to miss** (*train etc*) | perdere | "**payr**dayray" |
| ▷ **I've missed my train** | ho perso il treno | "o **payr**so eel **tray**no" |
| **missing** | | |
| ▷ **my son is missing** | manca mio figlio | "**man**ka meeo **feel**yo" |
| ▷ **my handbag is missing** | ho perso la mia borsa | "o **payr**so la meea **bor**sa" |
| **mistake** | l'errore (m) | "ayr**roh**ray" |
| ▷ **there must be a mistake** | ci deve essere un errore | "chee **day**vay **ays**sayray oon ayr**roh**ray" |
| ▷ **you've made a mistake in the change** | ha sbagliato nel darmi il resto | "a sbal**yah**to nel **dahr**mee eel **rays**to" |

| | | |
|---|---|---|
| **misty** | nebbioso | "nayb**yoh**zo" |
| | nebbiosa | "nayb**yoh**za" |
| **misunderstanding** | il malinteso | "maleen**tay**zo" |
| ▷ there's been a misunderstanding | c'è stato un malinteso | "che stahto oon maleen**tay**zo" |
| **modern** | moderno | "mo**dayr**no" |
| | moderna | "mo**dayr**na" |
| **moisturizer** | l'idratante (m) | "eedra**tan**tay" |
| **monastery** | il monastero | "mona**stay**ro" |
| **Monday** | il lunedì | "loonay**dee**" |
| **money** | i soldi | "sol**dee**" |
| ▷ I have run out of money | sono rimasto senza soldi | "sohnoh ree**ma**sto sentsa sol**dee**" |
| ▷ I have no money | non ho soldi | "nohn o sol**dee**" |
| ▷ can I borrow some money? | posso avere un prestito? | "posso a**vay**ray oon pray**stee**to" |
| ▷ can you arrange to have some money sent over urgently? | può farmi spedire dei soldi urgentemente? | "pwo fahrmee spay**dee**ray dayee sol**dee** oorgentay**may**ntay" |
| **money belt** | il marsupio | "mar**soo**pyo" |
| **money order** | il vaglia | "**val**ya" |
| **month** | il mese | "**may**zay" |
| **monument** | il monumento | "monoo**may**nto" |
| **mop** (for floor) | la scopa per lavare i pavimenti | "**skoh**pa payr lav**vah**ray ee pavee**may**ntee" |
| **more (than)** | più (di) | "**peeoo** (dee)" |
| ▷ more wine, please | ancora vino, per favore | "an**ko**ra veeno payr fa**voh**ray" |
| **morning** | la mattina | "mat**tee**na" |
| ▷ in the morning | la mattina | "lah mat**tee**na" |

| | | |
|---|---|---|
| **mosquito** | la zanzara | "dzan**dzah**ra" |
| **mosquito bite** | la puntura di zanzara | "poon**too**ra dee dzan**dzah**ra" |
| **most:** | | |
| ▷ **the most popular disco** | la discoteca più frequentata | "la deesko**te**ka peeoo fraykwayn**tah**ta" |
| **mother** | la madre | "**mah**dray" |
| **motor** | il motore | "mo**toh**ray" |
| **motor boat** | la barca a motore | "barka a mo**htoh**ray" |
| ▷ **can we rent a motor boat?** | possiamo affittare una barca a motore? | "pos**yah**mo affeet**tah**ray oona barka a mo**htoh**ray" |
| **motor cycle** | la moto | "moto" |
| **motorway** | l'autostrada (f) | "owto**strah**da" |
| ▷ **how do I get onto the motorway?** | come faccio per entrare in autostrada? | "**koh**may fatcho payr ayn**trah**ray een owto**strah**da" |
| ▷ **is there a toll on this motorway?** | c'è da pagare il pedaggio su questa autostrada? | "che da pa**gah**ray eel pay**dad**jo soo kwaysta owto**strah**da" |
| **mountain** | la montagna | "mon**tan**ya" |
| **mountain bike** | la mountain bike | "**mown**taeen baeek" |
| **mousse** | la mousse | "mousse" |
| **mouth** | la bocca | "**bokk**a" |
| **to move** | muovere | "**mw**ovayray" |
| | muoversi | "**mv**ovayrsee" |
| ▷ **it isn't moving** | non si muove | "nohn see mwovay" |
| ▷ **he can't move** | non può muoversi | "nohn pwo **mwo**vayrsee" |
| ▷ **I can't move my leg** | non posso muovere la gamba | "nohn posso **mwo**vayray la gamba" |
| ▷ **don't move him** | non muovetelo | "nohn mwo**vay**telo" |

*ABSOLUTE ESSENTIALS*

| | | |
|---|---|---|
| I don't understand | non capisco | "nohn ka**pee**sko" |
| I don't speak Italian | non parlo l'italiano | "nohn parloh leetal**yah**no" |
| do you speak English? | parla inglese? | "parla eeng**lay**zay" |
| could you help me? | può aiutarmi? | "pwo ayoo**tar**mee" |

| | | |
|---|---|---|
| ▷ **could you move your car please?** | può spostare la macchina, per favore? | "pwo spostahray la **mak**keena payr fa**voh**ray" |
| **Mr** | Signor | "seenyohr" |
| **Mrs** | Signora | "seen**yoh**ra" |
| **much** | molto | "mohlto" |
| ▷ **it costs too much** | costa troppo | "kosta troppo" |
| ▷ **that's too much** | è troppo | "e troppo" |
| ▷ **there's too much ... in it** | c'è troppo... | "che troppo" |
| **muesli** | il müsli | "**moos**lee" |
| **mumps** | gli orecchioni | "orayk**yoh**nee" |
| **museum** | il museo | "moo**zay**o" |
| ▷ **the museum is open in the afternoon** | il museo è aperto al pomeriggio | "eel moo**zay**o e a**payr**to al pomay**reed**jo" |
| **mushrooms** | i funghi | "**foon**gee" |
| **music** | la musica | "**moo**zeeka" |
| ▷ **the music is too loud** | la musica è troppo forte | "la **moo**seeka e troppo fortay" |
| **Muslim** | musulmano musulmana | "moozool**mah**no" "moozool**mah**na" |
| **mussels** | le cozze | "kotssay" |
| **must** | dovere | "do**vay**ray" |

| I must | devo | "dayvo" |
|---|---|---|
| you must | | |
| (*singular*) | deve | "dayvay" |
| (*plural*) | dovete | "do**vay**tay" |
| he/she/it must | deve | "dayvay" |
| we must | dobbiamo | "dobbee**yah**mo" |
| they must | devono | "**day**vohno" |

ABSOLUTE ESSENTIALS

| I would like ... | vorrei... | "voreee" |
|---|---|---|
| I need ... | ho bisogno di... | "o bee**zoh**nyo dee" |
| where is ...? | dov'è...? | "doveh" |
| I'm looking for ... | sto cercando... | "sto chayr**kan**do" |

| | | |
|---|---|---|
| ▷ **I must make a phone call** | devo fare una telefonata | "dayvo fahray oona taylayfonahta" |
| **mustard** | la senape | "senapay" |
| **mutton** | il montone | "montohnay" |
| **my:** | | |
| ▷ **my hat** | il mio cappello | "eel meeo kappello" |
| ▷ **my car** | la mia macchina | "la meea makkeena" |
| ▷ **my books** | i miei libri | "ee meeayee leebree" |
| ▷ **my shoes** | le mie scarpe | "lay meeay skarpay" |
| **nail** (*fingernail*) | l'unghia (*f*) | "oongya" |
| (*metal*) | il chiodo | "keeodo" |
| **nail file** | la limetta per le unghie | "leemaytta payr lay oongyay" |
| **nail polish** | lo smalto per le unghie | "zmalto payr lay oongyay" |
| **nail polish remover** | l'acetone (*m*) | "achaytohnay" |
| **naked** | nudo | "noodo" |
| | nuda | "nooda" |
| **name** | il nome | "nohmay" |
| ▷ **what's your name?** | come si chiama? | "komay see keeahma" |
| ▷ **my name is ...** | mi chiamo... | "mee keeahmo" |
| **napkin** | il tovagliolo | "tovalyolo" |
| **Naples** | Napoli (*f*) | "nahpolee" |
| **nappies** | i pannolini per bambini | "pannoleenee payr bambeenee" |
| **narrow** | stretto | "straytto" |
| | stretta | "straytta" |

| | | |
|---|---|---|
| **nationality** | la nazionalità | "natsyonalee**ta**" |
| **navy blue** | il blu scuro | "bloo skooro" |
| **near** | vicino | "vee**chee**no" |
| | vicina | "vee**chee**na" |
| ▷ **near the bank/hotel** | vicino alla banca/ all'albergo | "vee**chee**no alla banka/ allal**bayr**go" |
| **necessary** | necessario | "naychays**sar**yo" |
| | necessaria | "naychays**sar**ya" |
| **neck** | il collo | "kollo" |
| **necklace** | la collana | "kol**lah**na" |
| to **need** | | |
| ▷ **I need ...** | ho bisogno di... | "o bee**zohn**yo dee" |
| ▷ **do you need anything?** | ha bisogno di qualcosa? | "a bee**zohn**yo dee kwal**ko**za" |
| **needle** | l'ago (m) | "ahgo" |
| ▷ **a needle and thread** | un ago e del filo | "oon ahgo ay dayl feelo" |
| **negative** (photography) | il negativo | "nayga**tee**vo" |
| **neighbour** | il vicino | "vee**chee**no" |
| ▷ **our neighbours** | i nostri vicini | "ee nostree vee**chee**nee" |
| **never** | mai | "maee" |
| ▷ **I never drink wine** | non bevo mai il vino | "nohn bayvo maee eel veeno" |
| ▷ **I've never been to Italy** | non sono mai stato in Italia | "nohn sohnoh maee stahto een eet**al**ya" |
| **new** | nuovo | "nwovo" |
| | nuova | "nwova" |
| **news** | le notizie | "no**teets**yay" |
| **newsagent** | il giornalaio | "jorna**la**yo" |
| **newspaper** | il giornale | "jor**nah**lay" |

| | | |
|---|---|---|
| ▷ do you have any English newspapers? | avete giornali inglesi? | "a**vay**tay jor**nah**lee een**glay**zee" |

**New Year** — l'anno (*m*) nuovo — "**an**no **nwo**vo"

▷ **Happy New Year!** — buon Anno! — "bwon **an**no"

**New Zealand** — la Nuova Zelanda — "**nwo**va dzay**lan**da"

**next** — prossimo — "**pros**seemo"
prossima — "**pros**seema"

▷ **the next stop** — la prossima fermata — "la **pros**seema fayr**mah**ta"

▷ **next week** — la settimana prossima — "la saytee**mah**na **pros**seema"

▷ **when's the next bus to town?** — quando c'è il prossimo autobus per il centro? — "kwando che eel **pros**seemo **ow**toboos payr eel chentro"

▷ **take the next turning on the left** — prenda la prossima strada a sinistra — "**pray**nda la **pros**seema strahda a see**nee**stra"

**nice** — piacevole — "peea**chay**volay"
(*person*) — simpatico — "seem**pah**teeko"
simpatica — "seem**pah**teeka"

▷ **we are having a nice time** — ci stiamo divertendo — "chee stee**yah**mo deevayr**tayn**do"

▷ **it doesn't taste very nice** — non ha un buon sapore — "nohn a oon bwon sa**poh**ray"

▷ **yes, that's very nice** — sì, buonissimo — "see bwon**ees**seemo"

▷ **nice to have met you** — è stato un piacere conoscerla — "e stahto oon peea**chay**ray ko**no**shayrla"

**night** — la notte — "**not**tay"

▷ **at night** — di notte — "dee **not**tay"

▷ **on Saturday night** — sabato sera — "**sa**bato **say**ra"

▷ **last night** — ieri sera — "**ye**ree **say**ra"

▷ **tomorrow night** — domani sera — "do**mah**nee **say**ra"

**night club** — il night — "night"

**nightdress** — la camicia da notte — "ka**mee**cha da **not**tay"

*ABSOLUTE ESSENTIALS*

| | | |
|---|---|---|
| I don't understand | non capisco | "nohn ka**pee**sko" |
| I don't speak Italian | non parlo l'italiano | "nohn parloh leetaly**ah**no" |
| do you speak English? | parla inglese? | "parla een**glay**zay" |
| could you help me? | può aiutarmi? | "pwo ayoo**tar**mee" |

| **nine** | nove | "nohvay" |
| **nineteen** | diciannove | "deechannohvay" |
| **ninety** | novanta | "nohvanta" |
| **no** | no | "no" |
| ▷ **no thank you** | no grazie | "no gratsyay" |
| ▷ **there's no coffee** | non c'è caffè | "nohn che kaffe" |
| **nobody** | nessuno | "nayssoono" |
| **noisy** | rumoroso | "roomorohzo" |
| | rumorosa | "roomorohza" |
| ▷ **it's too noisy** | c'è troppo rumore | "che troppo roomohray" |
| **non-alcoholic** | analcolico | "analkoleeko" |
| | analcolica | "analkoleeka" |
| ▷ **what non-alcoholic drinks do you have?** | quali bibite analcoliche avete? | "kwalee beebeetay analkoleekay avaytay" |
| **none** | nessuno | "nessoono" |
| ▷ **there's none left** | non ce n'è più | "nohn chay nay peeoo" |
| **non-smoking** (*compartment*) | per non-fumatori | "payr nohnfoomatohree" |
| ▷ **is this a non-smoking area?** | questa è una zona per non-fumatori? | "kwaysta e oona zona payr nohnfoomatohree" |
| ▷ **I want to book a seat in a non-smoking compartment** | voglio prenotare un posto in uno scompartimento non fumatori | "volyo praynotahray oon posto een oono skomparteemaynto nohnfoomatohree" |
| **north** | il nord | "nord" |
| **Northern Ireland** | L'Irlanda (*f*) del Nord | "eerlanda dayl nord" |
| **not:** | | |
| ▷ **I am not coming** | non vengo | "nohn vayngo" |
| ▷ **I don't know** | non lo so | "nohn loh so" |
| **note** (*bank note*) | la banconota | "bankonota" |
| (*letter*) | il biglietto | "beelyaytto" |

| | | |
|---|---|---|
| ▷ **do you have change of this note?** | può cambiarmi questa banconota? | "pwo kamb**yah**rmee kwaysta banko**nota**" |
| **note pad** | il bloc-notes | "blok**not**" |
| **nothing** | niente | "nee**en**tay" |
| ▷ **nothing to declare** | niente da dichiarare | "nee**en**tay da deekya**rah**ray" |
| **notice** (*sign*) | il cartello | "kar**tayllo**" |
| **November** | novembre | "no**vaym**bray" |
| **now** | adesso | "a**desso**" |
| **number** | il numero | "**noo**mayro" |
| ▷ **car number** | la targa | "la **tahr**ga" |
| ▷ **what's your room number?** | qual è il numero della sua stanza? | "kwal e eel **noo**mayro dayla sooa stantsa" |
| ▷ **what's the telephone number?** | qual è il numero di telefono? | "kwal e eel **noo**mayro dee tay**le**fono" |
| ▷ **sorry, wrong number** | scusi, ho sbagliato numero | "skoozee o sbal**yah**to **noo**mayro" |
| **nurse** | l'infermiere (*m*) | "eenfayrm**ye**ray" |
| | l'infermiera (*f*) | "eenfayrm**ye**ra" |
| **nursery slope** | la pista per principianti | "peesta payr preencheep**yan**tee" |
| **nut** (*to eat*) | la noce | "**noh**chay" |
| (*for bolt*) | il dado | "**dah**do" |
| **occasionally** | ogni tanto | "**on**yee tanto" |
| **o'clock:** | | |
| ▷ **at 2 o'clock** | alle 2 | "**allay dooay**" |
| ▷ **it's 10 o'clock** | sono le 10 | "**sohno lay deeechee**" |
| **October** | ottobre | "ot**tob**ray" |
| **of** | di | "dee" |
| **of course** | naturalmente | "natooral**mayn**tay" |

| | | |
|---|---|---|
| **do you have ...?** | avete...? | "a**vay**tay" |
| **is there ...?** | c'è...? | "che" |
| **are there ...?** | ci sono...? | "chee sohnoh" |
| **how much is ...?** | quanto costa...? | "kwanto kosta" |

| | | |
|---|---|---|
| **off** (*machine etc*) | spento | "spento" |
| | spenta | "spenta" |
| ▷ **this meat is off** | questa carne è andata a male | "kwaysta karnay e andahta a mahlay" |
| ▷ **let me off here, please** | mi faccia scendere qui, per favore | "mee fatcha shayndayray kwee payr favohray" |
| ▷ **the lights are off** | le luci sono spente | "lay loochay sohno spentay" |
| to **offer** | offrire | "offreeray" |
| **office** | l'ufficio (*m*) | "ooffeecho" |
| ▷ **I work in an office** | lavoro in un ufficio | "lavohro een oon ooffeecho" |
| **often** | spesso | "spesso" |
| **oil** | l'olio (*m*) | "olyo" |
| **oil filter** | il filtro dell'olio | "feeltro dayllolyo" |
| **ointment** | l'unguento (*m*) | "oongwento" |
| **O.K.** | va bene | "va benay" |
| **old** | vecchio | "vaykyo" |
| | vecchia | "vaykya" |
| ▷ **how old are you?** | quanti anni ha? | "kwantee annee a" |
| **old-age pensioner** | il pensionato | "paynseeonahto" |
| | la pensionata | "paynseeonahta" |
| **olive oil** | l'olio (*m*) d'oliva | "olyo doleeva" |
| **olives** | le olive | "oleevay" |
| **omelette** | l'omelette (*f*) | "omaylet" |
| **on**[1] *adj* (*light, engine*) | acceso | "atchayzo" |
| | accesa | "atchayza" |
| (*tap*) | aperto | "apayrto" |
| | aperta | "apayrta" |
| **on**[2] *prep* | su | "soo" |
| ▷ **on the table** | sulla tavola | "soolla tahvola" |

| | | |
|---|---|---|
| **once** | una volta | "oona volta" |
| ▷ once a day/year | una volta al giorno/ all'anno | "oona volta al jorno/ all**ahn**no" |
| **one** | uno<br>una | "oono"<br>"oona" |
| **one-way** (*street*) | a senso unico | "a senso **oo**neeko" |
| **onions** | le cipolle | "cheepohllay" |
| **only** | solo | "sohlo" |
| ▷ we only want 3 | ne vogliamo solo 3 | "nay vol**yah**mo sohlo tre" |
| **open**[1] *adj* | aperto<br>aperta | "a**payr**to"<br>"a**payr**ta" |
| ▷ are you open? | è aperto? | "e a**payr**to" |
| ▷ is the castle open to the public? | il castello è aperto al pubblico? | "eel kas**te**llo e a**payr**to al **poob**bleeko" |
| to **open**[2] *vb* | aprire | "a**pree**ray" |
| ▷ what time does the museum open? | a che ora apre il museo? | "a kay ohra apray eel moo**zay**o" |
| ▷ I can't open the window | non riesco ad aprire la finestra | "nohn ree**es**ko ad a**pree**ray la fee**nes**tra" |
| **opera** | l'opera (*f*) | "**o**payra" |
| **operator** | il/la centralinista | "chayntralee**nee**sta" |
| **opposite:** | | |
| ▷ opposite the hotel | di fronte all'albergo | "dee frontay allal**bayr**go" |
| **or** | o | "oh" |
| **orange**[1] *n* | l'arancia (*f*) | "a**ran**cha" |
| **orange**[2] *adj* | arancione | "aran**choh**nay" |
| **orange juice** | il succo d'arancia | "sookko da**ran**cha" |
| to **order** | ordinare | "ordee**nah**ray" |
| ▷ can you order me a taxi, please | può chiamarmi un taxi, per favore? | "pwo keea**mahr**mee oon taxee payr fa**voh**ray" |

*ABSOLUTE ESSENTIALS*

| | | |
|---|---|---|
| I don't understand | non capisco | "nohn ka**pees**ko" |
| I don't speak Italian | non parlo l'italiano | "nohn parloh leetal**yah**no" |
| do you speak English? | parla inglese? | "parla eeng**lay**zay" |
| could you help me? | può aiutarmi? | "pwo ayoo**tar**mee" |

| | | |
|---|---|---|
| ▷ **can I order now please?** | posso ordinare ora, per piacere? | "posso ordee**nah**ray ora payr peea**chay**ray" |
| **oregano** | l'origano (*m*) | "or**ee**gano" |
| **original** | originale | "oreejee**nah**lay" |
| **other** | altro | "altro" |
| | altra | "altra" |
| ▷ **the other one** | l'altro | "laltro" |
| ▷ **do you have any others?** | ce ne sono altri? | "chay nay sohno altree" |
| ▷ **where are the others?** | dove sono gli altri? | "dohvay sohno lyee altree" |
| **ounce** (*metric equiv = 28.35g*) | l'oncia (*f*) | "oncha" |
| **our:** | | |
| ▷ **our apartment** | il nostro appartamento | "eel nostro apparta**mayn**to" |
| ▷ **our car** | la nostra macchina | "la nostra **mak**keena" |
| ▷ **our books** | il nostri libri | "ee nostree leebree" |
| ▷ **our shoes** | le nostre scarpe | "lay nostray skarpay" |
| **ours** | (il) nostro | "nostro" |
| | (la) nostra | "nostra" |
| | (i) nostri | "nostree" |
| | (le) nostre | "nostray" |
| **out** (*light*) | spento | "spento" |
| | spenta | "spenta" |
| (*outside*) | fuori | "fworee" |
| ▷ **she's out** | è fuori | "e fworee" |
| **outdoor** (*pool etc*) | all'aperto | "alla**payr**to" |
| ▷ **what are the outdoor activities?** | quali attività ricreative si possono fare all'aperto? | "kwalee atteevee**ta** reekraya**tee**vay see **pos**sono fahray alla**payr**to" |
| **outside** | fuori | "fworee" |
| ▷ **let's go outside** | andiamo fuori | "andy**ah**mo fworee" |

| | | |
|---|---|---|
| ▷ **an outside line please** | la linea esterna, per favore | "la **lee**naya es**ter**na payr fa**voh**ray" |
| **oven** | il forno | "forno" |
| **over** (*on top of*) | sopra | "sohpra" |
| **to overcharge** | far pagare troppo | "far pa**gah**ray troppo" |
| ▷ **I've been overcharged** | mi hanno fatto pagare troppo | "mee anno fatto pa**gah**ray troppo" |
| **overheating:** | | |
| ▷ **the engine is overheating** | il motore è surriscaldato | "eel moh**toh**ray e soorreeskal**dah**to" |
| **overnight** (*travel*) | di notte | "dee nottay" |
| **to owe** | dovere | "do**vay**ray" |
| ▷ **I owe you ...** | le devo... | "lay dayvo" |
| ▷ **what do I owe you?** | quanto le devo? | "kwanto lay dayvo" |
| **owner** | il proprietario | "propreeay**tar**yo" |
| ▷ **could I speak to the owner please?** | posso parlare al proprietario, per favore? | "posso par**lah**ray al propreeay**tar**yo payr fa**voh**ray" |
| **oyster** | l'ostrica (*f*) | "**os**treeka" |
| **to pack** (*luggage*) | fare le valigie | "**fah**ray lay va**lee**jay" |
| ▷ **I need to pack now** | devo fare le valigie adesso | "dayvo **fah**ray lay va**lee**jay a**des**so" |
| **package** | il pacco | "pakko" |
| **package tour** | il viaggio organizzato | "vee**ad**jo organeed**zzah**to" |
| **packed lunch** | il cestino con il pranzo | "chay**stee**no kohn eel prantso" |
| **packet** | il pacchetto | "pak**kay**to" |
| ▷ **a packet of cigarettes** | un pacchetto di sigarette | "oon pak**kay**to dee seega**rayt**tay" |

| | | |
|---|---|---|
| **paddling pool** | la piscina per bambini | "pee**shee**na payr bam**bee**nee" |
| ▷ is there a paddling pool for the children? | c'è una piscina per bambini? | "che oona pee**shee**na payr bam**bee**nee" |
| **Padua** | Padova (f) | "**pah**dova" |
| **paid** | pagato | "pa**gah**to" |
| | pagata | "pa**gah**ta" |
| **pain** | il dolore | "doh**loh**ray" |
| ▷ I have a pain here/in my chest | ho un dolore qui/al petto | "o oon doh**loh**ray kwee/al petto" |
| **painful** | doloroso | "dolo**roh**zo" |
| | dolorosa | "dolo**roh**za" |
| **painkiller** | l'antidolorifico (m) | "anteedolo**ree**feeko" |
| **painting** | il quadro | "**kwadro**" |
| **pair** | il paio | "**payo**" |
| ▷ a pair of sandals | un paio di sandali | "oon payo dee san**dah**lee" |
| **palace** | il palazzo | "pa**lats**so" |
| ▷ is the palace open to the public? | il palazzo è aperto al pubblico? | "eel pa**lats**so e a**payr**to al **poob**bleeko" |
| **pan** | la padella | "pa**dayl**la" |
| **pancake** | la crêpe | "krep" |
| **panties** | le mutandine | "mootan**dee**nay" |
| **pants** | le mutande | "moo**tan**day" |
| **paper** | la carta | "**karta**" |
| **paraffin** | il cherosene | "kayro**ze**nay" |
| **paragliding** | il volo col paracadute (a profilo alare) | "volo kohl paraka**doo**tay (a pro**fee**lo a**lah**ray)" |
| **parascending** | il volo trainato col paracadute | "volo try**nah**to kohl paraka**doo**tay" |

| | | |
|---|---|---|
| **parasol** | il parasole | "para**soh**lay" |
| **parcel** | il pacco | "pakko" |
| ▷ **I want to send this parcel** | voglio spedire questo pacco | "volyo spay**dee**ray kwaysto pakko" |
| **pardon** (*I didn't understand*) | scusi? | "skoozee" |
| ▷ **I beg your pardon** | mi scusi | "mee skoozee" |
| **parents** | i genitori | "jaynee**toh**ree" |
| **Paris** | Parigi (*f*) | "pa**reed**jee" |
| **park¹** *n* | il parco | "parko" |
| **to park²** *vb* | parcheggiare | "parkayd**jah**ray" |
| ▷ **can we park our caravan there?** | possiamo mettere là la nostra roulotte? | "pos**yah**mo mayt**tay**ray la la nostra roo**lot**" |
| ▷ **where can I park?** | dove posso parcheggiare? | "dohvay posso parkayd**jah**ray" |
| ▷ **can I park here?** | posso parcheggiare qui? | "posso parkayd**jah**ray kwee" |
| **parking disc** | il disco orario | "deesko o**rar**yo" |
| **parking meter** | il contatore | "konta**toh**ray" |
| **parsley** | il prezzemolo | "prayts**se**molo" |
| **part** | la parte | "partay" |
| **party** (*group*) | il gruppo | "grooppo" |
| **passenger** | il passeggero | "passayd**jay**ro" |
| **passport** | il passaporto | "passa**por**to" |
| ▷ **I have forgotten my passport** | ho dimenticato il passaporto | "o deemayntee**kah**to eel passa**por**to" |
| ▷ **please give me my passport back** | mi restituisca il passaporto, per favore | "mee raysteetoo**ees**ka eel passa**por**to payr fa**voh**ray" |

ABSOLUTE ESSENTIALS

| | | |
|---|---|---|
| **I don't understand** | non capisco | "nohn ka**pee**sko" |
| **I don't speak Italian** | non parlo l'italiano | "nohn parloh leetal**yah**no" |
| **do you speak English?** | parla inglese? | "parla eeng**lay**zay" |
| **could you help me?** | può aiutarmi? | "pwo ayoo**tar**mee" |

| | | |
|---|---|---|
| ▷ my wife/husband and I have a joint passport | io e mia moglie/mio marito siamo sullo stesso passaporto | "eeoh ay meea molyay/meeo mareeto seeyahmo soollo staysso passaporto" |
| ▷ the children are on this passport | i bambini sono su questo passaporto | "ee bambeenee sohnoh soo kwaysto passaporto" |
| ▷ my passport number is ... | il numero del mio passaporto è... | "eel noomayro dayl meeo passaporto e" |
| ▷ I've lost my passport | ho perso il passaporto | "o payrso eel passaporto" |
| ▷ my passport has been stolen | mi hanno rubato il passaporto | "mee anno roobahto eel passaporto" |
| ▷ I've got a visitor's passport | ho un passaporto valido per un anno | "o oon passaporto vahleedo payr oon anno" |
| passport control | il controllo passaporti | "kontrollo passaportee" |
| pasta | la pasta | "pasta" |
| pastry (cake) | la pasta il pasticcino | "pasta" "pasteetcheeno" |
| pâté | il pâté | "patay" |
| path | il sentiero | "sayntyero" |
| ▷ where does this path lead? | dove porta questo sentiero? | "dohvay porta kwaysta sayntyero" |
| to pay | pagare | "pagahray" |
| ▷ do I pay now or later? | pago adesso o dopo? | "pahgo adesso o dopo" |
| payment | il pagamento | "pagamaynto" |
| peaches | le pesche | "peskay" |
| peanuts | le arachidi | "arakeedee" |
| pears | le pere | "payray" |
| peas | i piselli | "peezellee" |
| to peel (fruit) | sbucciare | "sbootchahray" |
| peg (for clothes) | la molletta | "mollaytta" |

ABSOLUTE ESSENTIALS

| I would like ... | vorrei... | "voreee" |
| I need ... | ho bisogno di... | "o beezohnyo dee" |
| where is ...? | dov'è...? | "doveh" |
| I'm looking for ... | sto cercando... | "sto chayrkando" |

| | | |
|---|---|---|
| (for tent) | il picchetto | "peek**kayt**to" |
| **pen** | la penna | "**payn**na" |
| ▷ do you have a pen I could borrow? | mi può prestare una penna? | "mee pwo pres**tah**ray oona **payn**na" |
| **pencil** | la matita | "ma**tee**ta" |
| **penicillin** | la penicillina | "payneechee**llee**na" |
| ▷ I am allergic to penicillin | sono allergico alla penicillina | "sohno al**layr**jeeko alla payneechee**llee**na" |
| **penknife** | il temperino | "taympay**ree**no" |
| **pensioner** | il pensionato | "paynseeo**nah**to" |
| | la pensionata | "paynseeo**nah**ta" |
| ▷ are there reductions for pensioners? | ci sono sconti per pensionati? | "chee sohno skontee payr paynseeo**nah**tee" |
| **pepper** (spice) | il pepe | "**pay**pay" |
| (vegetable) | il peperone | "paypay**roh**nay" |
| **per:** | | |
| ▷ per hour | all'ora | "al**loh**ra" |
| ▷ per week | alla settimana | "alla sayttee**mah**na" |
| ▷ 60 miles per hour | 60 miglia all'ora | "ses**san**ta meelya al**loh**ra" |
| **perfect** | perfetto | "payr**fayt**to" |
| | perfetta | "payr**fayt**ta" |
| **performance** | lo spettacolo | "spayt**tah**kolo" |
| ▷ what time does the performance begin? | a che ora comincia lo spettacolo? | "a kay ora ko**meen**cha loh spayt**tah**kolo" |
| ▷ how long does the performance last? | quanto dura lo spettacolo? | "kwanto doora loh spayt**tah**kolo" |
| **perfume** | il profumo | "pro**foo**mo" |
| **perhaps** | forse | "**for**say" |
| **period** (of time) | il periodo | "pe**ree**eodo" |
| (menstruation) | le mestruazioni | "maystrooats**yoh**nee" |
| **perm** | la permanente | "payrma**nen**tay" |
| ▷ my hair is permed | ho la permanente | "o la payrma**nen**tay" |

| | | |
|---|---|---|
| **permit** | il permesso | "payr**mes**so" |
| ▷ do I need a fishing permit? | devo avere una licenza di pesca? | "dayvo a**vay**ray oona lee**chay**ntsa dee paysca" |
| **person** | la persona | "payr**soh**na" |
| **petrol** | la benzina | "baynd**zee**na" |
| ▷ 20 litres of unleaded petrol | 20 litri di benzina senza piombo | "vayntee leetree dee baynd**zee**na sentsa pee**om**bo" |
| ▷ I have run out of petrol | sono rimasto senza benzina | "sohnoh ree**mas**to sentsa bend**zee**na" |
| **petrol station** | il distributore di benzina | "deestreeboo**toh**ray dee baynd**zee**na" |
| **pheasant** | il fagiano | "fad**jah**no" |
| **phone**[1] *n* | il telefono | "tay**le**fono" |
| to **phone**[2] *vb* | telefonare | "taylefo**nah**ray" |
| ▷ can I phone from here? | posso telefonare da qui? | "posso taylefo**nah**ray da kwee" |
| **phone box** | la cabina telefonica | "ka**bee**na taylefo**nee**ka" |
| **phone card** | la scheda telefonica | "skayda taylefo**nee**ka" |
| ▷ do you sell phone cards? | vendete schede telefoniche? | "vayn**day**tay skayday taylefo**nee**kay" |
| **photocopy**[1] *n* | la fotocopia | "foto**kop**ya" |
| ▷ I'd like a photocopy of this please | mi fa una fotocopia, per cortesia? | "mee fah oona foto**kop**ya payr cortay**zee**a" |
| to **photocopy**[2] *vb* | fotocopiare | "fotokop**yah**ray" |
| ▷ where can I get some photocopying done? | dove posso far fare delle fotocopie? | "dohvay posso fahr fahray dayllay foto**kop**yay" |
| **photo(graph)** | la fotografia | "fotogra**fee**a" |
| ▷ when will the photos be ready? | quando saranno pronte le foto? | "kwando sa**ran**no **proh**ntay lay foto" |

| | | |
|---|---|---|
| ▷ **can I take photos in here?** | posso fare delle foto qui dentro? | "posso fahray dayllay foto kwee dayntro" |
| ▷ **would you take a photo of us, please?** | può farci una foto, per favore? | "pwo fahrchee oona foto payr favohray" |
| **picnic** | il picnic | "peekneek" |
| ▷ **a picnic lunch** | un pranzo al sacco | "oon prantso al sacco" |
| **picture** (*painting*) | il quadro | "kwadro" |
| (*photo*) | la foto | "foto" |
| **pie** | la torta | "torta" |
| **piece** | il pezzo | "petsso" |
| ▷ **a piece of cake** | una fetta di dolce | "oona faytta dee dohlchay" |
| **pill** | la pillola | "**peel**lola" |
| ▷ **I'm on the pill** | prendo la pillola | "prendo la **peel**lola" |
| ▷ **I'm not on the pill** | non prendo la pillola | "nohn prendo la **peel**lola" |
| **pillow** | il cuscino | "eel coo**shee**no" |
| ▷ **I would like an extra pillow** | vorrei ancora un cuscino | "vor**reee** an**koh**ra oon coo**shee**no" |
| **pillowcase** | la federa | "**fe**dayra" |
| **pin** | lo spillo | "speello" |
| **pineapple** | l'ananas (*m*) | "**a**nanas" |
| **pink** | rosa | "roza" |
| **pint** (*metric equiv = 0.56l*) | la pinta | "peenta" |
| ▷ **a pint of beer** | una birra grande | "oona beerra granday" |
| **pipe** | la pipa | "peepa" |
| **pipe tobacco** | il tabacco da pipa | "tabakko da peepa" |
| **pistachio** | il pistacchio | "pees**tahk**yo" |
| **plane** | l'aereo (*m*) | "**ae**rayo" |
| ▷ **my plane leaves at ...** | il mio aereo parte alle... | "eel mee **ae**rayo partay allay" |

*ABSOLUTE ESSENTIALS*

| | | |
|---|---|---|
| **I don't understand** | non capisco | "nohn ka**pees**ko" |
| **I don't speak Italian** | non parlo l'italiano | "nohn parloh leetal**yah**no" |
| **do you speak English?** | parla inglese? | "parla eeng**lay**zay" |
| **could you help me?** | può aiutarmi? | "pwo ayoo**tar**mee" |

| | | |
|---|---|---|
| ▷ **I've missed my plane** | ho perso l'aereo | "o payrso l'**ae**rayo" |
| **plaster** (*sticking plaster*) | il cerotto | "chay**rott**o" |
| **plastic** | la plastica | "**plast**eeka" |
| ▷ **a plastic bag** | una borsa di plastica | "oon borsa dee **plast**eeka" |
| **plate** | il piatto | "pee**att**o" |
| **platform** | il binario | "bee**nar**yo" |
| ▷ **which platform for the train to ...?** | da che binario parte il treno per...? | "da kay bee**nar**yo pahrtay eel treno payr" |
| to **play** (*games*) | giocare | "jo**kah**ray" |
| ▷ **we'd like to play tennis** | vorremmo giocare a tennis | "vor**raym**mo jo**kah**ray a **ten**nees" |
| **playroom** | la stanza dei giochi | "stantsa dayee jokee" |
| **please** | per piacere | "payr peea**chay**ray" |
| | per favore | "payr fa**voh**ray" |
| ▷ **yes, please** | sì grazie | "see **grat**syay" |
| **pleased** | contento | "kon**tent**o" |
| | contenta | "kon**tent**a" |
| ▷ **pleased to meet you** | piacere | "peea**chay**ray" |
| **pliers** | le pinze | "**peent**say" |
| **plug** (*electrical*) | la spina | "**speen**a" |
| (*for sink*) | il tappo | "**tapp**o" |
| **plum** | la susina | "soo**seen**a" |
| **plumber** | l'idraulico (*m*) | "ee**drow**leeko" |
| **points** (*in car*) | le puntine | "poon**teen**ay" |
| **police** | la polizia | "poleet**see**a" |
| ▷ **we will have to report it to the police** | dovremo comunicarlo alla polizia | "do**vray**mo komoonee**kahr**lo alla poleet**see**a" |
| ▷ **get the police!** | chiamate la polizia! | "keea**mah**tay la poleet**see**a" |

---

ABSOLUTE ESSENTIALS

| | | |
|---|---|---|
| **I would like ...** | vorrei... | "vo**ree**" |
| **I need ...** | ho bisogno di... | "o bee**zohn**yo dee" |
| **where is ...?** | dov'è...? | "do**veh**" |
| **I'm looking for ...** | sto cercando... | "sto chayr**kan**do" |

| | | |
|---|---|---|
| policeman | il poliziotto | "poleets**yot**to" |
| police station | il commissariato | "kommeessar**yah**to" |
| ▷ where is the police station? | dov'è il commissariato? | "doh**ve** eel kommeessar**yah**to" |
| polish *(for shoes)* | il lucido | "**loo**cheedo" |
| polluted | inquinato | "eenkwee**nah**to" |
| | inquinata | "eenkwee**nah**ta" |
| pony trekking: | | |
| ▷ we'd like to go pony trekking | vorremmo andare a fare il trekking a cavallo | "vor**ray**mmo an**dah**ray a **fah**ray eel trekkeeng a ca**vah**llo" |
| pool *(swimming)* | la piscina | "pee**shee**na" |
| ▷ is there a children's pool? | c'è una piscina per bambini? | "che oona pee**shee**na payr bam**bee**nee" |
| ▷ is the pool heated? | è riscaldata la piscina? | "e reeskal**dah**ta la pee**shee**na" |
| ▷ is it an outdoor pool? | è una piscina all'aperto? | "e oona pee**shee**na alla**payr**to" |
| Pope | il papa | "papa" |
| popular | popolare | "popo**lah**ray" |
| pork | il maiale | "ma**yah**lay" |
| port *(seaport, wine)* | il porto | "porto" |
| porter *(in hotel)* | il portiere | "port**ye**ray" |
| *(in station)* | il facchino | "fak**kee**no" |
| Portugal | il Portogallo | "porto**gah**llo" |
| Portuguese | portoghese | "porto**gay**zay" |
| possible | possibile | "pos**see**beelay" |
| ▷ as soon as possible | prima possibile | "preema pos**see**beelay" |
| to post | spedire | "spay**dee**ray" |
| *(letter)* | imbucare | "eemboo**kah**ray" |

ABSOLUTE ESSENTIALS

| | | |
|---|---|---|
| do you have ...? | avete...? | "a**vay**tay" |
| is there ...? | c'è...? | "che" |
| are there ...? | ci sono...? | "chee **soh**noh" |
| how much is ...? | quanto costa...? | "**kwan**to **kos**ta" |

| | | |
|---|---|---|
| ▷ **where can I post these cards?** | dove posso imbucare queste cartoline? | "dohvay posso eembookahray kwaystay kartoleenay" |
| **postbox** | la cassetta delle lettere | "kassaytta dayllay lettayray" |
| **postcard** | la cartolina | "kartoleena" |
| ▷ **do you have any postcards?** | avete cartoline? | "avaytay kartoleenay" |
| ▷ **where can I buy some postcards?** | dove posso comprare delle cartoline? | "dohvay posso komprahray dayllay kartoleenay" |
| **postcode** | il codice postale | "kodeechay postahlay" |
| **post office** | l'ufficio (m) postale | "ooffeecho postahlay" |
| **pot** (for cooking) | la pentola | "payntola" |
| **potatoes** | le patate | "patahtay" |
| **pottery** | la terracotta | "tayrrakotta" |
| **pound** (weight: metric equiv = 1.60kg) (money) | la libbra la sterlina | "leebbra" "stayrleena" |
| **powdered milk** | il latte in polvere | "lattay een polvayray" |
| **pram** | la carrozzina | "karrotsseena" |
| **prawn** | il gambero | "gambayro" |
| **to prefer** | preferire | "prayfayreeray" |
| ▷ **I'd prefer to go ...** | preferirei andare... | "prayfayreerayee andahray" |
| ▷ **I prefer ... to ...** | preferisco... | "prayfayreesko" |
| **pregnant** | incinta | "eencheenta" |
| **to prepare** | preparare | "prayparahray" |
| **prescription** | la ricetta | "reechaytta" |

ABSOLUTE ESSENTIALS

| | | |
|---|---|---|
| **yes (please)** | sì (grazie) | "see (gratsyay)" |
| **no (thank you)** | no (grazie) | "no (gratsyay)" |
| **hello** | salve | "salvay" |
| **goodbye** | arrivederci | "arreevaydayrchee" |

|  |  |  |
|---|---|---|
| ▷ where can I get this prescription made up? | dove posso farmi fare questa ricetta? | "dohvay posso fahrmee fahray kwaysta reechaytta" |
| **present** (*gift*) | il regalo | "raygahlo" |
| ▷ I want to buy a present for my husband/my wife | voglio comprare un regalo per mio marito/mia moglie | "volyo komprahray oon raygahlo payr meeoo mareeto/meea molyay" |
| **pretty** | carino | "kareeno" |
| | carina | "kareena" |
| **price** | il prezzo | "pretsso" |
| **price list** | il listino prezzi | "leesteeno pretssee" |
| **priest** | il prete | "pretay" |
| ▷ I want to see a priest | voglio vedere un prete | "volyo vaydayray oon pretay" |
| **private** | privato | "preevahto" |
| | privata | "preevahta" |
| ▷ can I speak to you in private? | le posso parlare in privato? | "lay posso parlahray een preevahto" |
| ▷ this is private | è una questione privata | "e oona kwaystyohnay preevahta" |
| ▷ I have private health insurance | ho un'assicurazione sanitaria privata | "o oonasseekooratsyoh nay saneetahreea preevahta" |
| **probably** | probabilmente | "probabeelmayntay" |
| **problem** | il problema | "problema" |
| **programme** | il programma | "programma" |
| to **pronounce** | pronunciare | "pronoonchahray" |
| ▷ how do you pronounce it? | come si pronuncia? | "kohmay see pronooncha" |
| **Protestant** | protestante | "protaystantay" |
| **prunes** | le prugne | "proonyay" |

ABSOLUTE ESSENTIALS

|  |  |  |
|---|---|---|
| I don't understand | non capisco | "nohn kapeesko" |
| I don't speak Italian | non parlo l'italiano | "nohn parloh leetalyahno" |
| do you speak English? | parla inglese? | "parla eenglayzay" |
| could you help me? | può aiutarmi? | "pwo ayootarmee" |

| | | |
|---|---|---|
| **public** | pubblico | "**poob**bleeko" |
| | pubblica | "**poob**bleeka" |
| ▷ **is the castle open to the public?** | il castello è aperto al pubblico? | "eel kas**tello** e a**payr**to al **poob**bleeko" |
| **public holiday** | la festa nazionale | "festa natsyo**nah**lay" |
| **pudding** | il dolce | "dohlchay" |
| **to pull** | tirare | "tee**rah**ray" |
| **pullover** | il pullover | "pull**over**" |
| **puncture** | la foratura | "fora**too**ra" |
| ▷ **I have a puncture** | ho una ruota a terra | "o oona rwota a terra" |
| **purple** | viola | "vee**o**la" |
| **purse** | il borsellino | "borsayl**lee**no" |
| ▷ **my purse has been stolen** | mi hanno rubato il borsellino | "mee anno roo**bah**to eel borsayl**lee**no" |
| ▷ **I've lost my purse** | ho perso il borsellino | "o payrso eel borsayl**lee**no" |
| **push**[1] *n* | la spinta | "**speen**ta" |
| ▷ **my car's broken down, can you give me a push?** | la mia macchina è in panne, mi può dare una spinta? | "la meea **makk**eena e een **pahn**nay mee pwo dahray oona **speen**ta" |
| **to push**[2] *vb* | spingere | "**speen**jayray" |
| **to put** (*insert*) | mettere | "**mayt**tayray" |
| **to put down** | posare | "po**zah**ray" |
| ▷ **put it down over there, please** | lo posi lì, per favore | "loh pohzee lee payr fa**voh**ray" |
| **pyjamas** | il pigiama | "pee**ja**ma" |
| **quarter** | il quarto | "kwarto" |
| ▷ **quarter to 10** | 10 meno un quarto | "dee**ee**chee mayno oon kwarto" |
| ▷ **quarter past 3** | le 3 e un quarto | "lay tre ay oon kwarto" |

*ABSOLUTE ESSENTIALS*

| | | |
|---|---|---|
| **I would like ...** | vorrei... | "vor**eee**" |
| **I need ...** | ho bisogno di... | "o bee**zohn**yo dee" |
| **where is ...?** | dov'è...? | "do**veh**" |
| **I'm looking for ...** | sto cercando... | "sto chayr**kan**do" |

*rare*

| | | |
|---|---|---|
| **queue** | la fila | "feela" |
| ▷ is this the end of the queue? | comincia qui la fila? | "komeencha kwee la feela" |
| **quick** | veloce | "vaylohchay" |
| **quickly** | velocemente | "vaylochaymayntay" |
| **quiet** (*place*) | tranquillo | "trankweello" |
| | tranquilla | "trankweella" |
| **quilt** | il piumino | "peeoomeeno" |
| **quite:** | | |
| ▷ it's quite good | è abbastanza buono | "abbastantsa bwono" |
| ▷ it's quite expensive | è piuttosto caro | "e peeoottosto kahro" |
| **rabbit** | il coniglio | "koneelyo" |
| **racket** | la racchetta | "rakkaytta" |
| ▷ can we hire rackets? | possiamo noleggiare delle racchette? | "posyahmo nolaydjahray dayllay rakkayttay" |
| **radiator** | il radiatore | "radeeyahtohray" |
| **radio** | la radio | "rahdyo" |
| ▷ is there a radio/radio cassette in the car? | c'è una radio/radio con mangiacassette nella macchina? | "che oona rahdyo/rahdyo kohn manjakassaytay naylla makkeena" |
| **radishes** | i ravanelli | "ravanayllee" |
| **railway station** | la stazione | "statsyohnay" |
| **rain**[1] *n* | la pioggia | "peeodja" |
| to **rain**[2] *vb:* | | |
| ▷ is it going to rain? | pioverà? | "peeovayra" |
| ▷ it's raining | piove | "peeovay" |
| **raincoat** | l'impermeabile (*m*) | "eempayrmayahbeelay" |
| **raisin** | l'uvetta (*f*) | "oovaytta" |
| **rare** (*unique*) | raro | "rahro" |

*ABSOLUTE ESSENTIALS*

| | | |
|---|---|---|
| do you have ...? | avete...? | "avaytay" |
| is there ...? | c'è...? | "che" |
| are there ...? | ci sono...? | "chee sohnoh" |
| how much is ...? | quanto costa...? | "kwanto kosta" |

| | rara | "rahra" |
|---|---|---|
| (steak) | al sangue | "al sangway" |

**rash:**

| | | |
|---|---|---|
| ▷ I have a rash | ho un'irritazione alla pelle | "o ooneerreetat**syoh**nay alla payllay" |

| **raspberries** | i lamponi | "lam**poh**nee" |
|---|---|---|

| **rate** | la tariffa | "ta**reeff**a" |
|---|---|---|
| ▷ what is the daily/ weekly rate? | quanto costa al giorno/ alla settimana? | "kwanto kosta al jorno/alla sayttee**mah**na" |
| ▷ do you have a special rate for children? | avete delle riduzioni per bambini? | "a**vay**tay dayllay reeduts**yoh**nee payr bam**bee**nee" |
| ▷ what is the rate for sterling? | qual è il cambio per la sterlina? | "kwal e eel kambyo payr la stayr**lee**na" |
| ▷ rate of exchange | il cambio | "kambyo" |

| **raw** | crudo | "kroodo" |
|---|---|---|
| | cruda | "krooda" |

| **razor** | il rasoio | "ra**zo**yo" |
|---|---|---|

| **razor blades** | le lamette | "la**mayt**tay" |
|---|---|---|

| **ready** | pronto | "prohnto" |
|---|---|---|
| | pronta | "prohnta" |
| ▷ are you ready? | è pronto? | "e prohnto" |
| ▷ I'm ready | sono pronto | "sohnoh prohnto" |
| ▷ when will lunch be ready? | quando è pronto il pranzo? | "kwando e prohnto eel prantso" |
| ▷ when will dinner be ready? | quando è pronta la cena? | "kwando e prohnta la chayna" |

| **real** | vero | "vayro" |
|---|---|---|
| | vera | "vayra" |

| **receipt** | la ricevuta | "reechay**voo**ta" |
|---|---|---|
| ▷ I'd like a receipt, please | vorrei una ricevuta, per favore | "vor**reee** oona reechay**voo**ta payr fa**voh**ray" |

| **recently** | recentemente | "raychayntay**mayn**tay" |
|---|---|---|
| **reception** (desk) | la reception | "reception" |
| **recipe** | la ricetta | "ree**chett**a" |
| to **recommend** | consigliare | "konseel**yah**ray" |
| ▷ **what do you recommend?** | che cosa ci consiglia? | "kay koza chee kon**seel**ya" |
| ▷ **can you recommend a cheap hotel/a good restaurant?** | mi può consigliare un albergo poco costoso/un buon ristorante? | "mee pwo konseel**yah**ray oon al**bayr**go pohko ko**sto**zo/oon bwon reestor**ant**ay" |
| **record** (*music etc*) | il disco | "**dees**ko" |
| **red** | rosso | "**ross**o" |
| | rossa | "**ross**a" |
| **reduction** | la riduzione | "reedoots**yoh**nay" |
| ▷ **is there a reduction for children/for senior citizens/for a group?** | ci sono riduzioni per bambini/per anziani/per comitive? | "chee sohnoh reedoots**yoh**nay payr bam**bee**nee/payr ant**syah**nee/payr komee**tee**vay" |
| **refill** (*for pen*) | il ricambio | "ree**kamb**yo" |
| (*for lighter*) | la bomboletta di gas | "bombo**laytt**a dee gas" |
| **refund** | il rimborso | "reem**bors**o" |
| ▷ **I'd like a refund** | vorrei un rimborso | "vor**eee** oon reem**bors**o" |
| to **register:** | | |
| ▷ **where do I register?** | dove firmo il registro? | "dohvay feermo eel ray**jee**stro" |
| **registered** | raccomandato | "rakkoman**dah**to" |
| | raccomandata | "rakkoman**dah**ta" |
| **registered delivery** | la raccomandata | "rakkoman**dah**ta" |
| **regulations** | il regolamento | "raygola**mayn**to" |

*ABSOLUTE ESSENTIALS*

| I don't understand | non capisco | "nohn ka**pee**sko" |
|---|---|---|
| I don't speak Italian | non parlo l'italiano | "nohn parloh leetaly**ah**no" |
| do you speak English? | parla inglese? | "parla eeng**lay**zay" |
| could you help me? | può aiutarmi? | "pwo ayoo**tar**mee" |

| | | |
|---|---|---|
| ▷ **I'm very sorry, I didn't know the regulations** | mi scusi tanto, non conoscevo il regolamento | "mee skoozee tanto nohn kono**shay**vo eel raygola**mayn**to" |
| to **reimburse** | rimborsare | "reembor**sah**ray" |
| **relation** (family) | il/la parente | "pa**ren**tay" |
| to **relax** | rilassarsi | "reelas**sahr**see" |
| **reliable** (company, service) | sicuro sicura | "see**koo**ro" "see**koo**ra" |
| to **remain** | restare | "ray**stah**ray" |
| to **remember** | ricordare | "reekor**dah**ray" |
| to **rent** (house) (car) ▷ **I'd like to rent a room/villa** | affittare noleggiare vorrei affittare una stanza/villa | "affeet**tah**ray" "nolayd**jah**ray" "vor**ree**e affee**tah**ray oona stantsa/veella" |
| **rental** (house) (car) | l'affitto (m) il noleggio | "af**feet**to" "no**lay**djo" |
| to **repair** ▷ **can you repair this?** | riparare lo può riparare? | "reepa**rah**ray" "lo pwo reepa**rah**ray" |
| to **repeat** ▷ **please repeat that** | ripetere ripeta per favore | "reepe**tay**ray" "ree**pe**ta payr fa**voh**ray" |
| **reservation** ▷ **I'd like to make a reservation for 2 people** | la prenotazione vorrei fare una prenotazione per 2 persone | "praynotats**yoh**nay" "vor**ree**e fahray oona praynotats**yoh**nay payr dooay payr**soh**nay" |
| to **reserve** ▷ **we'd like to reserve two seats for tonight** | prenotare vorremmo prenotare due posti per stasera | "prayno**tah**ray" "vor**raym**mo prayno**tah**ray dooay pohstee payr sta**say**ra" |
| ▷ **I have reserved a room in the name of ...** | ho prenotato una stanza a nome di... | "o prayno**tah**to oona stantsa a nohmay dee" |

| | | |
|---|---|---|
| ▷ **I want to reserve a single room/a double room/a hotelroom/a family room** | voglio prenotare una stanza singola/una stanza doppia/una stanza in albergo/una stanza per la famiglia | "volyo praynotahray oona stantsa seengohla/oona stantsa doppya/oona stantsa een albayrgo/ oona stantsa payr la fameelya" |
| **reserved** | prenotato<br>prenotata | "praynotahto"<br>"praynotahta" |
| **rest¹** n (repose) | il riposo | "reepozo" |
| ▷ **the rest of the wine** | il resto del vino | "eel resto dayl veeno" |
| to **rest²** vb | riposarsi | "reepozahrsee" |
| **restaurant** | il ristorante | "reestorantay" |
| **restaurant car** | il vagone ristorante | "vagohnay reestorantay" |
| to **return** (go back)<br>(give back) | ritornare<br>restituire | "reetornahray"<br>"raysteetooeeray" |
| **return ticket** | il biglietto di andata e ritorno | "beelyaytto dee andahta ay reetorno" |
| ▷ **a return ticket to ...,<br>first class** | un biglietto di andata e ritorno per..., prima classe | "oon beelyaytto dee andahta ay reetorno payr ... preema classay" |
| **reverse charge call** | la chiamata a carico del destinatario | "keeamahta a kareeko dayl daysteenataryo" |
| ▷ **I'd like to make a<br>reverse charge call** | vorrei fare una chiamata a carico del destinatario | "vorreee fahray oona keeamahta a kareeko dayl daysteenataryo" |
| **rheumatism** | il reumatismo | "rayoomateezmo" |
| **rhubarb** | il rabarbaro | "rabarbaro" |
| **rice** | il riso | "reezo" |
| **ride:** | | |
| ▷ **to go for a ride** (in car) | andare a fare un giro in macchina | "andahray a fahray oon jeeroh een makkeena" |

| ABSOLUTE ESSENTIALS | | |
|---|---|---|
| do you have ...? | avete...? | "avaytay" |
| is there ...? | c'è...? | "che" |
| are there ...? | ci sono...? | "chee sohnoh" |
| how much is ...? | quanto costa...? | "kwanto kosta" |

| | | |
|---|---|---|
| (on horse) | andare a fare una cavalcata | "an**dah**ray a fahray oona kaval**kah**ta" |
| **riding** | l'equitazione (f) | "aykweetatsy**oh**nay" |
| ▷ **to go riding** | andare a cavallo | "an**dah**ray a ka**val**lo" |
| ▷ **can we go riding?** | possiamo andare a cavallo? | "posy**ah**mo an**dah**ray a ka**val**lo" |
| **right¹** n | la destra | "**destra**" |
| ▷ **(on/to the) right** | a destra | "a **destra**" |
| ▷ **right of way** | la precedenza | "praychay**dayn**tsa" |
| **right²** adj (correct) | giusto | "**joosto**" |
| | giusta | "**joosta**" |
| **ring** | l'anello (m) | "a**nel**lo" |
| **ripe** | maturo | "ma**too**ro" |
| | matura | "ma**too**ra" |
| **river** | il fiume | "fee**oo**may" |
| ▷ **can one swim in the river?** | si può nuotare nel fiume? | "see pwo nwo**tah**ray nayl fee**oo**may" |
| ▷ **am I allowed to fish in the river?** | posso pescare nel fiume? | "posso pes**kah**ray nel fee**oo**may" |
| **road** | la strada | "**strahda**" |
| ▷ **is the road to ... snowed up?** | la strada per... è chiusa per neve? | "la **strahda** payr... e kee**oo**za payr nayvay" |
| ▷ **which road do I take for ...?** | quale strada devo prendere per...? | "**kwah**lay **strahda** dayvo **pren**dayray payr" |
| ▷ **when will the road be clear?** | quando sarà libera la strada? | "kwando sa**ra lee**bayra la **strahda**" |
| **road map** | la carta stradale | "karta stra**dah**lay" |
| **roast** | arrosto | "ar**ros**to" |
| **to rob** | derubare | "dayroo**bah**ray" |
| ▷ **I've been robbed** | sono stato derubato | "**sohnoh** stahto dayroo**bah**to" |
| **rock climbing:** | | |
| ▷ **to go rock climbing** | andare a fare roccia | "an**dah**ray a fahray rotcha" |

| ABSOLUTE ESSENTIALS | | |
|---|---|---|
| yes (please) | sì (grazie) | "see (gratsyay)" |
| no (thank you) | no (grazie) | "no (gratsyay)" |
| hello | salve | "salvay" |
| goodbye | arrivederci | "arreevay**dayr**chee" |

| | | |
|---|---|---|
| **roll** (*bread*) | il panino | "pan**ee**no" |
| **roller skates** | i pattini a rotelle | "**pat**teenee a ro**tayl**lay" |
| **roller skating:** | | |
| ▷ **where can we go roller skating?** | dove possiamo andare a pattinare? | "dovay pos**yah**mo an**dah**ray a pattee**nah**ray" |
| **Rome** | Roma (f) | "**roh**ma" |
| **roof** | il tetto | "**tay**tto" |
| ▷ **the roof leaks** | entra acqua dal tetto | "**ayn**tra akwa dal **tay**tto" |
| **roof rack** | il portabagagli | "portaba**gal**yee" |
| **room** (*in house, hotel*) | la stanza | "**stan**tsa" |
| (*space*) | lo spazio | "**spat**syo" |
| **room service** | il servizio in camera | "sayr**veets**yo een **ka**mayra" |
| **rope** | il cavo | "**kah**vo" |
| **rosé** (*wine*) | il (vino) rosé | "veeno ro**zay**" |
| **rough** (*sea*) | mosso | "mosso" |
| | mossa | "mossa" |
| ▷ **is the sea rough today?** | c'è mare mosso oggi? | "che mahray mosso odjee" |
| ▷ **the crossing was rough** | c'era mare mosso durante la traversata | "chayra mahray mosso doo**ran**tay la travayr**sah**ta" |
| **round** (*object*) | rotondo | "ro**tohn**do" |
| | rotonda | "ro**tohn**da" |
| ▷ **round the corner** | dietro l'angolo | "dee**e**tro **lan**golo" |
| ▷ **whose round is it?** | a chi tocca? | "a kee **tohk**ka" |
| ▷ **a round of golf** | una partita a golf | "oona par**tee**ta a golf" |
| **route** | l'itinerario (*m*) | "eeteenay**rar**yo" |
| ▷ **is there a route that avoids the traffic?** | c'è un'altra strada per evitare il traffico? | "che oon**al**tra strahda payr ayvee**tah**ray eel **traf**feeko" |

| | | |
|---|---|---|
| **rowing boat** | la barca a remi | "barka a raymee" |
| ▷ **can we rent a rowing boat?** | possiamo affittare una barca a remi? | "pos**yah**mo affeet**tah**ray oona barka a raymee" |
| **rubber** | la gomma | "**goh**mma" |
| **rubber band** | l'elastico (m) | "ay**las**teeko" |
| **rubbish** | la spazzatura | "spatssa**too**ra" |
| **rucksack** | lo zaino | "dza**ee**no" |
| **rug** | il tappeto | "tap**pay**to" |
| **rugby** | il rugby | "regbee" |
| **ruins** | le rovine | "ro**vee**nay" |
| **rum** | il rum | "room" |
| **run¹** n (skiing) | la pista | "peesta" |
| ▷ **which are the easiest runs?** | quali sono le piste più facili? | "kwalee sohnoh lay peestay peeoo **fa**cheelee" |
| to **run²** vb | correre | "ko**rray**ray" |
| ▷ **the bus runs every twenty minutes** | c'è un autobus ogni venti minuti | "che oon **ow**toboos onyee vayntee mee**noo**tee" |
| ▷ **he runs the hotel** | è il direttore dell'albergo | "ay eel deerayt**to**ray dayllal**bayr**go" |
| ▷ **I run my own business** | ho una ditta | "oh oona deetta" |
| ▷ **I run courses in Marketing** | tengo corsi di marketing | "tayngo korsee dee **mar**kayteeng" |
| **running:** | | |
| ▷ **to go running** | andare a correre | "an**dah**ray a ko**rray**ray" |
| **rush hour** | l'ora (f) di punta | "ohra dee poonta" |
| **saccharine** | la saccarina | "sakka**ree**na" |
| **safe¹** n | la cassaforte | "kassa**for**tay" |

| | | |
|---|---|---|
| ▷ **please put this in the hotel safe** | per cortesia, lo metta nella cassaforte dell'albergo | "payr kortay**zee**a lo may**tta** naylla kassa**for**tay dayllal**bayr**go" |
| **safe**[2] *adj* (*beach, medicine*) | non pericoloso<br>non pericolosa | "nohn payreeko**loh**zo"<br>"nohn payreeko**loh**za" |
| ▷ **is it safe to swim here?** | si può nuotare senza pericolo qui? | "see pwo nwo**tah**ray sentsa pay**ree**kolo kwee" |
| ▷ **is it safe for children?** (*medicine*) | può essere presa da bambini? | "pwo **ays**sayray prayza da bam**bee**nee" |
| **safe sex** | il sesso sicuro | "saysso see**koo**ro" |
| **safety pin** | la spilla di sicurezza | "speella dee seekoo**rayts**sa" |
| ▷ **I need a safety pin** | ho bisogno di una spilla di sicurezza | "o bee**zohn**yo dee oona speella dee seekoo**rayts**sa" |
| **sail**[1] *n* | la vela | "vayla" |
| **to sail**[2] *vb* | navigare | "navee**gah**ray" |
| ▷ **when do we sail?** | quando partiamo? | "kwando par**tyah**mo" |
| **sailboard** | la tavola a vela<br>il windsurf | "**tah**vola a vayla"<br>"windsurf" |
| **sailboarding:** | | |
| ▷ **I'd like to go sailboarding** | vorrei fare windsurf | "vor**reee** fahray windsurf" |
| **sailing** (*sport*) | la vela | "vayla" |
| ▷ **I'd like to go sailing** | vorrei uscire in barca a vela | "voreee oo**shee**ray een barka a vayla" |
| ▷ **what time is the next sailing?** | quando parte la prossima nave? | "kwando partay la **pross**eema nahvay" |
| **salad** | l'insalata (*f*) mista | "eensa**lah**ta meesta" |
| ▷ **a mixed salad** | un'insalata mista | "ooneensa**lah**ta meesta" |
| **salad dressing** | il condimento per l'insalata | "kondee**mayn**to payr leensa**lah**ta" |

ABSOLUTE ESSENTIALS

| | | |
|---|---|---|
| **do you have ...?** | avete...? | "avaytay" |
| **is there ...?** | c'è...? | "che" |
| **are there ...?** | ci sono...? | "chee sohnoh" |
| **how much is ...?** | quanto costa...? | "kwanto kosta" |

| | | |
|---|---|---|
| **saline solution** *(for contact lenses)* | la soluzione salina | "soloot**syoh**nay sa**lee**na" |
| **salmon** | il salmone | "sal**moh**nay" |
| **salt** | il sale | "**sah**lay" |
| ▷ **pass the salt, please** | mi passa il sale, per favore? | "mee passa eel sahlay payr fa**voh**ray" |
| **same** | stesso / stessa | "**stay**sso" / "**stay**ssa" |
| ▷ **I'll have the same** | lo stesso per me | "lo **stay**sso payr may" |
| **sand** | la sabbia | "**sab**ya" |
| **sandals** | i sandali | "**san**dalee" |
| **sandwich** | il panino | "pa**nee**no" |
| ▷ **what kind of sandwiches do you have?** | che panini avete? | "kay pa**nee**nee a**vay**tay" |
| **sandy:** | | |
| ▷ **a sandy beach** | una spiaggia di sabbia | "oona spee**ad**ja dee sabya" |
| **sanitary towels** | gli assorbenti | "assor**bayn**tee" |
| **sardine** | la sardina | "sar**dee**na" |
| **Sardinia** | la Sardegna | "sar**dayn**ya" |
| **Saturday** | il sabato | "**sa**bato" |
| **sauce** | la salsa | "**sal**sa" |
| **saucepan** | la pentola | "**payn**tola" |
| **saucer** | il piattino | "peeat**tee**no" |
| **sauna** | la sauna | "**saoo**na" |
| **sausage** | la salsiccia | "sal**seet**cha" |
| **savoury** *(not sweet)* | salato / salata | "sa**lah**to" / "sa**lah**ta" |

| | | |
|---|---|---|
| to **say** | dire | "deeray" |
| **scallop** | la capasanta | "kapa**san**ta" |
| **scampi** | gli scampi | "skampee" |
| **scarf** | la sciarpa | "sharpa" |
| **school** | la scuola | "skwola" |
| **scissors** | le forbici | "**for**beechee" |
| **scotch** | lo scotch | "skotch" |
| **Scotland** | la Scozia | "skotsya" |
| **Scottish** | scozzese | "skots**say**zay" |
| ▷ **I'm Scottish** | sono scozzese | "sohnoh skots**say**zay" |
| **screw** | la vite | "veetay" |
| ▷ **the screw has come loose** | la vite si è allentata | "la veetay see e allayn**tah**ta" |
| **screwdriver** | il cacciavite | "katcha**vee**tay" |
| **scuba diving:** | | |
| ▷ **where can we go scuba diving?** | dove possiamo andare a fare immersione subacquea? | "dovay pos**yah**mo an**dah**ray a fahray eemayr**syoh**nay soo**bak**kwaya" |
| **sculpture** | la scultura | "skool**too**ra" |
| **sea** | il mare | "mahray" |
| **seafood** | i frutti di mare | "froottee dee mahray" |
| ▷ **do you like seafood?** | le piacciono i frutti di mare? | "lay pee**ach**ohno ee froottee dee mahray" |
| **seasickness** | il mal di mare | "mahl dee mahray" |
| **seaside:** | | |
| ▷ **at the seaside** | al mare | "al mahray" |
| **season ticket** | l'abbonamento (m) | "abbona**mayn**to" |

| **seat** (*chair*) | la sedia | "sedya" |
| (*in train, theatre*) | il posto | "posto" |
| ▷ **is this seat free?** | è libero questo posto? | "e **lee**bayro kwaysto posto" |
| ▷ **is this seat taken?** | è occupato questo posto? | "e okkoo**pah**to kwaysto posto" |
| ▷ **we'd like to reserve two seats for tonight** | vorremmo prenotare due posti per stasera | "vor**raym**mo prayno**tah**ray dooay postee payr sta**say**ra" |
| ▷ **I have a seat reservation** | ho un posto prenotato | "o oon posto prayno**tah**to" |
| **second** | secondo | "say**kohn**do" |
| | seconda | "say**kohn**da" |
| **second class** | la seconda classe | "say**kohn**da klassay" |
| **to see** | vedere | "vay**day**ray" |
| ▷ **see you soon** | a presto | "a presto" |
| ▷ **what is there to see here?** | che cosa c'è da vedere qui? | "kay koza che da vay**day**ray kwee" |
| **self-service** | il self-service | "self service" |
| **to sell** | vendere | "**ven**dayray" |
| ▷ **do you sell stamps?** | vendete francobolli? | "ven**day**tay franko**boh**lee" |
| **Sellotape®** | lo scotch | "scotch" |
| **semi-skimmed milk** | il latte parzialmente scremato | "**lah**tay partseeal**mayn**tay scray**mah**to" |
| **to send** | mandare | "man**dah**ray" |
| | spedire | "spay**dee**ray" |
| ▷ **please send my mail/ luggage on to this address** | mandi la posta/il bagaglio a questo indirizzo per favore | "mandee la posta/eel ba**ga**lyo a kwaysto eendee**reet**so payr fa**voh**ray" |
| **senior citizen** | l'anziano (*m*) | "antsyah**no**" |
| | l'anziana (*f*) | "antsyah**na**" |

| **ABSOLUTE ESSENTIALS** | | |
| I would like ... | vorrei... | "vor**eee**" |
| I need ... | ho bisogno di... | "o bee**zohn**yo dee" |
| where is ...? | dov'è...? | "do**veh**" |
| I'm looking for ... | sto cercando... | "sto chayr**kando**" |

| | | |
|---|---|---|
| ▷ **is there a reduction for senior citizens?** | ci sono sconti per anziani? | "chee sohnoh skohntee payr antsyahnee" |
| **separate** | separato | "sayparahto" |
| | separata | "sayparahta" |
| **September** | settembre | "sayttaymbray" |
| **serious** | grave | "grahvay" |
| **seriously:** | | |
| ▷ **he is seriously injured** | è ferito gravemente | "e fayreeto grahvaymayntay" |
| to **serve** | servire | "sayrveeray" |
| ▷ **we are still waiting to be served** | stiamo ancora aspettando di essere serviti | "steeyahmo ankohra aspayttando dee essayray sayrveetee" |
| **service** (in restaurant) | il servizio | "sayrveetsyo" |
| ▷ **is service included?** | il servizio è compreso nel prezzo? | "eel sayrveetsyo e komprayzo nayl pretsso" |
| ▷ **what time is the service?** (church) | a che ora è la messa? | "a kay ohra e la mayssa" |
| **service charge** | il servizio | "sayrveetsyo" |
| **service station** | la stazione di servizio | "statsyohnay dee sayrveetsyo" |
| **set menu** | il menù fisso | "maynoo feesso" |
| ▷ **we'll take the set menu** | prendiamo il menù fisso | "prayndyahmo eel maynoo feesso" |
| ▷ **do you have a set menu?** | avete un menù fisso? | "avaytay oon maynoo feesso" |
| ▷ **how much is the set menu?** | quant'è il menù fisso? | "kwante eel maynoo feesso" |
| **seven** | sette | "settay" |
| **seventeen** | diciassette | "deechassettay" |
| **seventy** | settanta | "settanta" |

| | | |
|---|---|---|
| **shade** | l'ombra (f) | "**ohm**bra" |
| ▷ **in the shade** | all'ombra | "all**ohm**bra" |
| **shallow** | poco profondo | "poko pro**fohn**do" |
| | poco profonda | "poko pro**fohn**da" |
| **shampoo** | lo shampoo | "shampo" |
| **shampoo and set** | shampoo e messa in piega | "shampo ay **may**sa een pee**ee**ga" |
| **shandy** | la birra con gassosa | "**beer**ra kohn gas**soh**za" |
| to **share** | dividere | "dee**vee**dayray" |
| ▷ **we could share a taxi** | potremmo prendere un taxi insieme | "po**tray**mo **prayn**dayray oon taksee eensee**ee**may" |
| to **shave** | farsi la barba | "far**see** la barba" |
| **shaving brush** | il pennello per barba | "payn**nayl**lo payr barba" |
| **shaving cream** | la crema da barba | "**krema** da barba" |
| **she** | lei | "layee" |
| **sheet** | il lenzuolo | "laynt**swo**lo" |
| **shellfish** | i frutti di mare | "**froo**tee dee mahray" |
| **sherry** | lo sherry | "sherry" |
| **ship** | la nave | "**nah**vay" |
| **shirt** | la camicia | "ka**mee**cha" |
| **shock absorber** | l'ammortizzatore (m) | "ammorteedzza**toh**ray" |
| **shoe** | la scarpa | "**skarpa**" |
| ▷ **there is a hole in my shoe** | ho un buco nella scarpa | "o oon bookoh naylla skarpa" |
| ▷ **can you reheel these shoes?** | può rifare i tacchi a queste scarpe? | "pwo ree**fah**ray ee takkee a kwaystay skarpay" |
| **shoe laces** | i lacci per le scarpe | "**lah**chee payr lay skarpay" |

| | | |
|---|---|---|
| **shoe polish** | il lucido per scarpe | "**loo**cheedo payr skarpay" |
| **shop** | il negozio | "nay**gots**yo" |
| ▷ **what time do the shops close?** | a che ora chiudono i negozi? | "a kay ohra kee**oo**dohnoh ee nay**gots**ee" |
| **shopping** | lo shopping | "**shop**peeng" |
| ▷ **to go shopping** | fare compere | "fahray **kom**payray" |
| ▷ **where is the main shopping area?** | dove sono i negozi principali? | "dohvay sohnoh ee nay**gots**ee preenchee**pah**lee" |
| **shopping centre** | il centro commerciale | "chayntro komayr**chah**lay" |
| **short** | corto corta | "korto" "korta" |
| **short cut** | la scorciatoia | "skorcha**toy**a" |
| **shorts** | i calzoncini corti | "kaltson**chee**nee kortee" |
| **short-sighted:** | | |
| ▷ **I'm short-sighted** | sono miope | "sohnoh **mee**ohpe" |
| **shoulder** | la spalla | "spalla" |
| ▷ **I've hurt my shoulder** | mi sono fatto male alla spalla | "mee sohnoh fahto mahlay alla spalla" |
| **show**[1] *n* | lo spettacolo | "spay**ttah**kolo" |
| to **show**[2] *vb* | mostrare | "mo**strah**ray" |
| ▷ **could you show me please?** | mi può far vedere per favore? | "mee pwo fahr vay**day**ray payr fa**voh**ray" |
| ▷ **could you show us around?** | ci può fare da guida? | "chee pwo fahray da gweeda" |
| **shower** | la doccia | "dotcha" |
| ▷ **how does the shower work?** | come funziona la doccia? | "kohmay foonts**yoh**na la dotcha" |
| ▷ **I'd like a room with a shower** | una camera con doccia, per favore | "oona **ka**mayra kohn dotcha payr fa**voh**ray" |
| **shrimps** | i gamberetti | "gambay**rayt**tee" |

*ABSOLUTE ESSENTIALS*

| | | |
|---|---|---|
| I don't understand | non capisco | "nohn ka**pees**ko" |
| I don't speak Italian | non parlo l'italiano | "nohn parloh leetal**yah**no" |
| do you speak English? | parla inglese? | "parla eeng**lay**zay" |
| could you help me? | può aiutarmi? | "pwo ayoo**tar**mee" |

| **Sicily** | la Sicilia | "see**chee**lya" |
| **sick** (*ill*) | malato | "ma**lah**to" |
| | malata | "ma**lah**ta" |
| ▷ **she has been sick** | ha vomitato | "a vomee**tah**to" |
| ▷ **I feel sick** | mi sento male | "mee saynto mahlay" |
| **sightseeing** | il turismo | "too**reez**mo" |
| ▷ **are there any sightseeing tours?** | ci sono delle gite turistiche? | "chee sohnoh dayllay jeetay too**ree**steekay" |
| **sign**[1] *n* | il segnale | "sayn**yah**lay" |
| to **sign**[2] *vb* | firmare | "feer**mah**ray" |
| ▷ **where do I sign?** | dove firmo? | "dohvay feermo" |
| **signature** | la firma | "feerma" |
| **silk** | la seta | "seta" |
| **silver** | l'argento(*m*) | "ar**jayn**to" |
| **similar** | simile | "**see**meelay" |
| **simple** | semplice | "**saym**pleechay" |
| **single** (*unmarried*) | non sposato | "nohn spo**zah**to" |
| | non sposata | "nohn spo**zah**ta" |
| (*not double*) | singolo | "**seen**golo" |
| | singola | "**seen**gola" |
| (*ticket*) | di (sola) andata | "dee (sohla) an**dah**ta" |
| ▷ **a single to ..., second class** | un biglietto di andata per ..., seconda classe | "oon beel**yayt**to dee an**dah**ta payr ... say**kohn**da klassay" |
| **single bed** | il letto a una piazza | "letto a oona pee**ats**sa" |
| **single room** | la camera singola | "**ka**mayra **seen**gola" |
| ▷ **I want to reserve a single room** | vorrei prenotare una camera singola | "vor**reee** prayno**tah**ray oona **ka**mayra **seen**gola" |
| **sir** | signore | "seen**yoh**ray" |

| | | |
|---|---|---|
| **sister** | la sorella | "so**rell**a" |
| to **sit** | sedere | "say**day**ray" |
| | sedersi | "say**dayr**see" |
| ▷ **please, sit down** | prego, si accomodi | "**praygo** see ak**kom**ohdee" |
| **six** | sei | "sayee" |
| **sixteen** | sedici | "**se**deechee" |
| **sixty** | sessanta | "ses**san**ta" |
| **size** | la misura | "mee**zoo**ra" |
| ▷ **I take a continental size 40** | porto la taglia 40 | "porto la **tal**ya kwa**ran**ta" |
| ▷ **do you have this in a bigger/smaller size?** | ce l'avete in una taglia più grande/una taglia più piccola? | "che la**vay**tay een oona **tal**ya peeoo gran**day**/una **tal**ya peeoo **peek**kola" |
| **skate** | il pattino | "**pat**teeno" |
| ▷ **where can we hire skates?** | dove possiamo noleggiare dei pattini? | "**dohvay** pos**yah**mo nole**djah**ray dayee **pat**teenee" |
| **skateboard** | lo skate-board | "skate-board" |
| **skating** | il pattinaggio | "patteen**ad**jo" |
| ▷ **where can we go skating?** | dove possiamo andare a pattinare? | "**dohvay** pos**yah**mo an**dah**ray a patteen**ah**ray" |
| **ski**[1] *n* | lo sci | "shee" |
| ▷ **can we hire skis here?** | possiamo noleggiare degli sci qui? | "pos**yah**mo nolay**djah**ray daylyee shee kwee" |
| **ski**[2] *vb* | sciare | "shee**ah**ray" |
| **ski boots** | gli scarponi da sci | "skar**poh**nee da shee" |
| **skid:** | | |
| ▷ **the car skidded** | la macchina è scivolata | "la **mak**keena e sheevo**lah**ta" |
| **skiing** (*downhill*) | lo sci | "shee" |

| | | |
|---|---|---|
| (cross-country) | lo sci di fondo | "shee deefondo" |
| ▷ to go skiing | andare a sciare | "andahray a sheeahray" |
| ▷ to go cross-country skiing | andare a fare lo sci di fondo | "andahray a fahray lo shee dee fondo" |
| **skiing lessons** | le lezioni di sci | "laytsyohnay dee shee" |
| ▷ do you organize skiing lessons? | organizzate lezioni di sci? | "organeedzahtay laytsyohnay dee shee" |
| **ski instructor** | il maestro di sci | "mystroh dee shee" |
| **ski jacket** | la giacca a vento | "djakka a vaynto" |
| **ski lift** | l'impianto (m) di risalita | "eempyanto dee reesaleeta" |
| **skimmed milk** | il latte scremato | "lahttay skraymahto" |
| **skin** | la pelle | "pellay" |
| **skin diving** | il nuoto subacqueo | "nwoto soobakwayo" |
| **ski pants** | i pantaloni da sci | "pantalohnee da shee" |
| **ski pass** | la tessera per gli impianti di risalita | "tessayra payr lyee eempeeahntee dee reesaleeta" |
| **ski pole** | la racchetta da sci | "rakkaytta da shee" |
| **ski resort** | la località sciistica | "lokahleeta sheeeesteeka" |
| **skirt** | la gonna | "gonna" |
| **ski run** | la pista | "peesta" |
| **ski suit** | il completo da sci | "kompleto da shee" |
| **sledge** | la slitta | "zleetta" |
| **sledging:** | | |
| ▷ where can we go sledging? | dove possiamo andare con la slitta? | "dohvay posyahmo andahray kohn la zleeta" |
| to **sleep** | dormire | "dormeeray" |

| | | |
|---|---|---|
| ▷ **I can't sleep for the noise/heat** | non riesco a dormire a causa del rumore/ caldo | "nohn reeesko a dormeeray a kowza dayl roomohray/kaldo" |
| **sleeper:** | | |
| ▷ **can I reserve a sleeper?** | posso prenotare un posto in vagone letto? | "posso praynotahray oon posto een vagohnay letto" |
| **sleeping bag** | il sacco a pelo | "sakko a paylo" |
| **sleeping car** | il vagone letto | "vagohnay letto" |
| **sleeping pill** | il sonnifero | "sonneefayro" |
| **slice** | la fetta | "faytta" |
| **slide** (*photograph*) | la diapositiva | "deeapozeeteeva" |
| **slippers** | le pantofole | "pantofolay" |
| **slow** | lento | "laynto" |
| | lenta | "laynta" |
| ▷ **slow down!** | piano! | "peeano" |
| **slowly** | lentamente | "layntamayntay" |
| ▷ **please speak slowly** | parli lentamente, per favore | "parlee layntamayntay payr favohray" |
| **small** | piccolo | "**peek**kolo" |
| | piccola | "**peek**kola" |
| **smaller (than)** | più piccolo (di) | "peeoo **peek**kolo (dee)" |
| | più piccola (di) | "peeoo **peek**kola (dee)" |
| **smell** (*pleasant*) | il profumo | "profoomo" |
| (*unpleasant*) | la puzza | "pootssa" |
| **smoke**[1] *n* | il fumo | "foomo" |
| to **smoke**[2] *vb* | fumare | "foomahray" |
| ▷ **do you mind if I smoke?** | le dispiace se fumo? | "lay deespeeachay say foomo" |
| ▷ **do you smoke?** | fuma? | "fooma" |
| **smoked** | affumicato | "affoomeekahto" |

*ABSOLUTE ESSENTIALS*

| | | |
|---|---|---|
| **I don't understand** | non capisco | "nohn ka**pee**sko" |
| **I don't speak Italian** | non parlo l'italiano | "nohn parloh leetalyahno" |
| **do you speak English?** | parla inglese? | "parla eenglayzay" |
| **could you help me?** | può aiutarmi? | "pwo ayootarmee" |

| | affumicata | "affoomee**kah**ta" |

### smoking:

▷ **I'd like a non-smoking room/seat** — una stanza/un posto per non-fumatori, per favore — "oona stantsa/oon posto payr nohnfooma**toh**ree payr fa**voh**ray"

▷ **I'd like a seat in the smoking area** — un posto nella zona fumatori, per favore — "oon posto naylla dzohna fooma**toh**ree payr fa**voh**ray"

### smoky:

▷ **it's too smoky here** — c'è troppo fumo qui — "che troppo foomo kwee"

**snack bar** — la tavola calda — "**tah**vola kalda"

**snorkel** — il boccaglio — "bok**kall**yo"

### snorkelling:

▷ **I'd like to go snorkelling** — vorrei andare a nuotare col tubo e la maschera — "vor**reee** an**dah**ray a **nwotah**ray kol tooboh ay la mas**kay**ra"

**snow¹** *n* — la neve — "**nay**vay"

▷ **what are the snow conditions?** — com'è la neve? — "koh**me** la nayvay"

**to snow²** *vb* — nevicare — "nayvee**kah**ray"

▷ **is it going to snow?** — nevicherà? — "nayveekah**ra**"

**snowboard** — lo snowboard — "snowboard"

### snowboarding:

▷ **where can we go snowboarding?** — dove si può andare con lo snowboard? — "**dohvay** see pwo an**dah**ray kohn lo snowboard"

**snowed up** — isolato a causa della neve — "eezo**lah**to a **kow**za daylla nayvay"
— isolata a causa della neve — "eezo**lah**ta a **kow**za daylla nayvay"

### snowing:

▷ **it's snowing** — nevica — "**nay**veeka"

| | | |
|---|---|---|
| **snowplough** | lo spazzaneve | "spatsa**nay**vay" |
| **so** | così | "koh**zee**" |
| ▷ **so much** | tanto | "**tanto**" |
| **soaking solution** (*for contact lenses*) | il liquido per lenti | "**leek**weedo payr layntee" |
| **soap** | la saponetta | "sapo**nay**tta" |
| ▷ **there is no soap** | non c'è sapone | "nohn che sa**po**nay" |
| **soap powder** | il detersivo | "daytayr**see**vo" |
| **sober** | sobrio | "**so**breeo" |
| | sobria | "**so**breea" |
| **socket** | la presa | "**pray**za" |
| ▷ **where is the socket for my electric razor?** | dov'è la presa per il rasoio elettrico? | "doh**ve** la prayza payr eel ra**zoy**o ray**lettreeko**" |
| **socks** | i calzini | "kalt**see**nee" |
| **soda** | la soda | "**soda**" |
| **soft** | soffice | "**sof**feechay" |
| **soft drink** | l'analcolico (*m*) | "anal**ko**leekoh" |
| **sole** (*fish*) | la sogliola | "**sohl**yohla" |
| **soluble aspirin** | l'aspirina (*f*) effervescente | "aspee**ree**na ayffayrvay**shay**ntay" |
| **solution** | la soluzione | "soloot**syoh**nay" |
| ▷ **saline solution** | la soluzione salina | "soloot**syoh**nay sa**lee**na" |
| ▷ **cleansing solution for contact lenses** | liquido per la pulizia delle lenti a contatto | "**leek**weedo payr la poolee**tsee**a dayllay layntee a kohn**tat**to" |
| **some** | del | "dayl" |
| | della | "**day**lla" |
| (*plural*) | alcuni | "al**koo**nee" |
| | alcune | "al**koo**nay" |
| ▷ **some bread** | del pane | "dayl pahnay" |

*ABSOLUTE ESSENTIALS*

| | | |
|---|---|---|
| **do you have ...?** | avete...? | "a**vay**tay" |
| **is there ...?** | c'è...? | "che" |
| **are there ...?** | ci sono...? | "chee **soh**noh" |
| **how much is ...?** | quanto costa...? | "**kwanto kosta**" |

| | | |
|---|---|---|
| ▷ **some people** | della gente | "daylla djayntay" |
| ▷ **some of you** | alcuni di voi | "alkoonee dee voy" |
| **someone** | qualcuno | "kwalkoono" |
| **something** | qualcosa | "kwalkoza" |
| **sometimes** | qualche volta | "kwalkay volta" |
| **son** | il figlio | "feelyo" |
| **song** | la canzone | "kantsohnay" |
| **soon** | presto | "presto" |
| **sore** | | |
| ▷ **my back is sore** | mi fa male la schiena | "mee fa mahlay la skeeena" |
| ▷ **I have a sore throat** | ho mal di gola | "o mahl dee gohla" |
| ▷ **my feet/eyes are sore** | mi fanno male i piedi/gli occhi | "mee fahnno mahlay ee peeedee/lyee okee" |
| **sorry** | | |
| ▷ **I'm sorry!** | mi scusi! | "mee skoozee" |
| **sort** | | |
| ▷ **what sort of cheese?** | che tipo di formaggio? | "kay teepo dee formadjo" |
| **soup** | la minestra | "meenestra" |
| ▷ **what is the soup of the day?** | qual è la minestra del giorno? | "kwal e la meenestra dayl johrno" |
| **south** | il sud | "sood" |
| **souvenir** | il souvenir | "soovneer" |
| **space** | lo spazio | "spatsyo" |
| ▷ **parking space** | il posto | "posto" |
| **spade** | la paletta | "palaytta" |
| **spanner** | la chiave | "keeahvay" |
| **spare wheel** | la ruota di scorta | "rwota dee skorta" |

| | | |
|---|---|---|
| **sparkling wine** | lo spumante | "spoo**man**tay" |
| **spark plug** | la candela | "kan**day**la" |
| **to speak** | parlare | "par**lah**ray" |
| ▷ **can I speak to ...?** | posso parlare con...? | "posso par**lah**ray kohn" |
| ▷ **please speak louder/ (more) slowly** | per favore parli più forte/più lentamente | "payr fa**voh**ray parlee peeoo fortay/peeoo laynta**mayn**tay" |
| **special** | speciale | "spay**chah**lay" |
| ▷ **do you have a special menu for children?** | avete un menù speciale per bambini? | "a**vay**tay oon may**noo** spay**chah**lay payr bam**bee**nee" |
| **speciality** | la specialità | "spaychalee**ta**" |
| ▷ **is there a local speciality?** | c'è una specialità locale? | "che oona spaychalee**ta** lo**kah**lay" |
| ▷ **what is the house speciality?** | qual è la specialità della casa? | "kwal e la spaychalee**ta** **day**lla kasa" |
| **speed** | la velocità | "vaylochee**ta**" |
| **speed limit** | il limite di velocità | "**lee**meetay dee vaylochee**ta**" |
| ▷ **what is the speed limit on this road?** | qual è il limite di velocità su questa strada? | "kwal e eel **lee**meetay dee vaylochee**ta** soo kwaysta strahda" |
| **speedometer** | il tachimetro | "ta**kee**maytro" |
| **to spell:** | | |
| ▷ **how do you spell it?** | come si scrive? | "**koh**may see skreevay" |
| **spicy** | piccante | "peek**kan**tay" |
| **spinach** | gli spinaci | "spee**na**chee" |
| **spirits** | i liquori | "lee**kwoh**ree" |
| **sponge** | la spugna | "**spoo**nya" |
| **spoon** | il cucchiaio | "kook**ya**yo" |

*ABSOLUTE ESSENTIALS*

| | | |
|---|---|---|
| I don't understand | non capisco | "nohn ka**pee**sko" |
| I don't speak Italian | non parlo l'italiano | "nohn parloh leetal**yah**no" |
| do you speak English? | parla inglese? | "parla eeng**lay**zay" |
| could you help me? | può aiutarmi? | "pwo ayoo**tar**mee" |

| | | |
|---|---|---|
| **sport** | lo sport | "sport" |
| ▷ **which sports activities are available here?** | quali sport si possono fare qui? | "kwalee sport see **pos**sono fahray kwee" |
| **spring** (*season*) | la primavera | "preema**ve**ra" |
| **square** (*in town*) | la piazza | "pee**ats**sa" |
| **squash** (*game*) | lo squash | "squash" |
| (*drink*) | la spremuta | "spray**moo**ta" |
| **stain** | la macchia | "makya" |
| ▷ **this stain is coffee** | è una macchia di caffè | "e oona makya dee kaffe" |
| ▷ **can you remove this stain?** | può togliere questa macchia? | "pwo **tol**yayray kwaysta makya" |
| **stairs** | le scale | "skahlay" |
| **stalls** (*theatre*) | la platea | "plataya" |
| **stamp** | il francobollo | "franko**bohl**lo" |
| ▷ **do you sell stamps?** | vende francobolli? | "vaynday franko**bohl**lee" |
| ▷ **I'd like six stamps for postcards to America, please** | vorrei sei francobolli per cartolina per l'America, per favore | "vor**reee** say franko**bohl**lee payr karto**lee**na payr la**may**reeka payr fa**voh**ray" |
| ▷ **twelve 600-lira stamps, please** | dodici francobolli da 600 lire, per favore | "**doh**deechee franko**bohl**lee da say**chayn**to leeray payr fa**voh**ray" |
| ▷ **where can I buy stamps?** | dove posso comprare francobolli? | "dohvay posso kom**prah**ray franko**bohl**lee" |
| **to start** | cominciare | "komeen**chah**ray" |
| ▷ **when does the film/ show start?** | quando comincia il film/lo spettacolo? | "kwando ko**meen**cha eel feelm/lo spayt**tah**kolo" |
| **starter** (*in meal*) | l'antipasto (*m*) | "antee**pas**to" |
| (*in car*) | il motorino d'avviamento | "moto**ree**no davveea**mayn**to" |

| ABSOLUTE ESSENTIALS | | |
|---|---|---|
| I would like ... | vorrei... | "vor**eee**" |
| I need ... | ho bisogno di... | "o bee**zohn**yo dee" |
| where is ...? | dov'è...? | "do**veh**" |
| I'm looking for ... | sto cercando... | "sto chayr**kando**" |

# stomach

| | | |
|---|---|---|
| **station** | la stazione | "stats**yoh**nay" |
| ▷ **to the main station** | alla stazione centrale | "alla stats**yoh**nay chayn**trah**lay" |
| **stationer's** | la cartoleria | "kartolay**ree**a" |
| **to stay** | (*remain*) restare | "ray**stah**ray" |
| ▷ **I'm staying at a hotel** | sto in un albergo | "sto een oon al**bayr**go" |
| ▷ **I want to stay an extra night** | voglio stare ancora una notte | "volyo staray an**koh**ra oona nottay" |
| ▷ **where are you staying?** | dove alloggia? | "dohvay allodja" |
| **steak** | la bistecca | "bee**stayk**ka" |
| **steep** | ripido | "**ree**peedo" |
| | ripida | "**ree**peeda" |
| **sterling** | la sterlina | "stayr**lee**na" |
| ▷ **what is the rate for sterling?** | qual è il cambio per la sterlina? | "kwal e eel kambyo payr la stayr**lee**na" |
| **stew** | lo stufato | "stoo**fah**to" |
| **steward** | lo steward | "steward" |
| **stewardess** | la hostess | "hostess" |
| **sticking plaster** | il cerotto | "chay**rott**o" |
| **still** (*motionless*) | fermo | "**fayr**mo" |
| | ferma | "**fayr**ma" |
| ▷ **is it/he still there?** | è ancora lì? | "e an**koh**ra lee" |
| **sting** | la puntura | "poon**too**ra" |
| **stockings** | le calze | "**kalt**say" |
| **stolen** | rubato | "roo**bah**to" |
| | rubata | "roo**bah**ta" |
| ▷ **my passport/my watch has been stolen** | mi hanno rubato il passaporto/l'orologio | "mee anno roo**bah**to eel passa**por**to/loro**lod**joh" |
| **stomach** | la pancia | "**pan**cha" |

| | | |
|---|---|---|
| **do you have ...?** | avete...? | "a**vay**tay" |
| **is there ...?** | c'è...? | "che" |
| **are there ...?** | ci sono...? | "chee **soh**noh" |
| **how much is ...?** | quanto costa...? | "**kwan**to **kos**ta" |

| | | |
|---|---|---|
| **stomach ache** | il mal di pancia | "mal dee pancha" |
| **stomach upset** | il mal di stomaco | "mal dee **sto**mako" |
| ▷ **I have a stomach upset** | ho dei disturbi allo stomaco | "o dayee dee**stoor**bee allo **sto**mako" |
| to **stop** | fermarsi | "fayr**mahr**see" |
| ▷ **please stop here/at the corner** | si fermi qui/all'angolo per favore | "see fayrmee kwee/ allangolo payr fa**voh**ray" |
| ▷ **do we stop at ...?** | ci fermiamo a...? | "chee fayrm**yah**mo a" |
| ▷ **where do we stop for lunch?** | dove ci fermiamo per pranzo? | "dohvay chee fayrm**yah**mo payr prahntso" |
| ▷ **please stop the bus** | fermi l'autobus, per favore | "fayrmee **low**toboos payr fa**voh**ray" |
| **stopover** | la sosta | "sosta" |
| **storm** | la tempesta | "taym**pes**ta" |
| **stormy:** | | |
| ▷ **it's (very) stormy** | c'è burrasca | "che boo**rah**ska" |
| **straight on** | diritto | "dee**reet**to" |
| | diritta | "dee**reet**ta" |
| **strap** | la cinghietta | "cheeng**yay**ta" |
| ▷ **I need a new strap** | ho bisogno di una cinghietta nuova | "o bee**zohn**yo dee oona cheeng**yay**ta nwova" |
| **straw** (for drinking) | la cannuccia | "kan**noot**cha" |
| **strawberries** | le fragole | "**frah**golay" |
| **street** | la strada | "strahda" |
| **street map** | la piantina | "peean**tee**na" |
| **string** | lo spago | "spahgo" |
| **striped** | a strisce | "a streeshay" |
| **strong** | forte | "fortay" |
| **stuck** | | |
| ▷ **it's stuck** | è inceppato | "e eenchayp**pah**to" |

| | | |
|---|---|---|
| **student** (*male*) | lo studente | "stoo**dayn**tay" |
| (*female*) | la studentessa | "stoodayn**tess**a" |
| **stung:** | | |
| ▷ **he has been stung** | è stato punto | "e **stah**to **poon**to" |
| **stupid** | stupido | "**stoo**peedo" |
| | stupida | "**stoo**peeda" |
| **suddenly** | improvvisamente | "eemprooveeza**mayn**tay" |
| **suede** | il camoscio | "ka**mo**sho" |
| **sugar** | lo zucchero | "**tsook**kayro" |
| **suit** (*man's*) | l'abito (*m*) | "**a**beeto" |
| (*woman's*) | il tailleur | "ta**yer**" |
| **suitcase** | la valigia | "va**lee**ja" |
| ▷ **my suitcase was damaged in transit** | la mia valigia è stata danneggiata durante il viaggio | "la **mee**a va**lee**ja e **stah**ta dannayd**jah**ta doo**ran**tay eel vee**ad**jo" |
| ▷ **my suitcase is missing** | manca la mia valigia | "**man**ka la **mee**a va**lee**ja" |
| **summer** | l'estate (*f*) | "ay**stah**tay" |
| **sun** | il sole | "**soh**lay" |
| to **sunbathe** | prendere il sole | "**prayn**dayray eel **soh**lay" |
| **sunbed** | il lettino solare | "layt**tee**no so**lah**ray" |
| **sunburn** | la scottatura solare | "skotta**too**ra so**lah**ray" |
| ▷ **can you give me anything for sunburn?** | ha qualcosa contro le scottature solari? | "a kwal**ko**za **kohn**tro lay skotta**too**ray so**lah**ree" |
| **sunburnt:** | | |
| ▷ **I am sunburnt** | mi sono scottato al sole | "mee **soh**noh skot**tah**to al **soh**lay" |
| **Sunday** | la domenica | "do**may**neeka" |
| **sunglasses** | gli occhiali da sole | "ok**yah**lee da **soh**lay" |
| **sun lounger** | il lettino | "layt**tee**no" |

| | | |
|---|---|---|
| **I don't understand** | non capisco | "nohn ka**pees**ko" |
| **I don't speak Italian** | non parlo l'italiano | "nohn **par**lo leetal**yah**no" |
| **do you speak English?** | parla inglese? | "**par**la eeng**lay**zay" |
| **could you help me?** | può aiutarmi? | "pwo ayoo**tar**mee" |

| | | |
|---|---|---|
| **sunny** | assolato | "asso**lah**to" |
| | assolata | "asso**lah**ta" |
| ▷ **it's sunny** | c'è il sole | "che eel sohlay" |
| **sunshade** | l'ombrellone (*m*) | "ombrayl**loh**nay" |
| **sunstroke** | l'insolazione (*f*) | "eensolats**yoh**nay" |
| **suntan lotion** | la lozione solare | "lohts**yoh**nay so**lah**ray" |
| **supermarket** | il supermercato | "soopayrmayr**kah**to" |
| **supper** (*dinner*) | la cena | "chayna" |
| **supplement** | il supplemento | "soopplay**mayn**to" |
| ▷ **is there a supplement to pay?** | bisogna pagare un supplemento? | "bee**zoh**nya pa**gah**ray oon soopplay**mayn**to" |
| **sure** | sicuro | "see**koo**ro" |
| | sicura | "see**koo**ra" |
| **surface mail** | la posta ordinaria | "posta ordee**nar**ya" |
| **surfboard** | la tavola per il surf | "**tah**vola payr eel surf" |
| ▷ **can I rent a surfboard?** | posso noleggiare una tavola per il surf? | "posso nolayd**jah**ray oona **tah**vola payr eel surf" |
| **surfer** | il/la surfista | "surf**ees**ta" |
| **surfing** | il surf | "surf" |
| ▷ **I'd like to go surfing** | vorrei andare a fare surf | "vor**reee** an**dah**ray a fahray surf" |
| **surname** | il cognome | "kon**yoh**may" |
| **suspension** | la sospensione | "sospaynsy**oh**nay" |
| **sweater** | il maglione | "maly**oh**nay" |
| **sweet** | dolce | "dohlchay" |
| **sweetener** | il dolcificante | "dohlcheefee**kan**tay" |
| **sweets** | le caramelle | "kara**mel**lay" |
| to **swim** | nuotare | "nwo**tah**ray" |

| | | |
|---|---|---|
| ▷ **can one swim in the river?** | si può nuotare nel fiume? | "see pwo nwo**tah**ray nayl fee**oo**may" |
| ▷ **is it safe to swim here?** | si può nuotare senza pericolo qui? | "see pwo nwo**tah**ray sentsa payr**eek**olo kwee" |
| ▷ **can you swim?** | sa nuotare | "sah nwo**tah**ray" |
| **swimming:** | | |
| ▷ **let's go swimming** | andiamo a fare una nuotata | "and**yah**mo a fahray oona nwo**tah**ta" |
| **swimming pool** | la piscina | "pee**shee**na" |
| ▷ **is there a swimming pool?** | c'è una piscina? | "che oona pee**shee**na" |
| ▷ **where is the municipal swimming pool?** | dov'è la piscina comunale? | "doh**ve** la pee**shee**na comoo**nah**lay" |
| **swimsuit** | il costume da bagno | "ko**stoo**may da banyo" |
| **Swiss** | svizzero svizzera | "**zveet**sayro" "**zveet**sayra" |
| **switch** | l'interruttore (*m*) | "eentayrroot**toh**ray" |
| **to switch off** | spegnere | "**spen**yayray" |
| ▷ **can I switch the light/ radio off?** | posso spegnere la luce/ la radio | "posso **spen**yayray la loochay/la radyo" |
| **to switch on** | accendere | "at**chen**dayray" |
| ▷ **can I switch the light/ radio on?** | posso accendere la luce/la radio | "posso at**chen**dayray la loochay/la radyo" |
| **Switzerland** | la Svizzera | "**zveet**sayra" |
| **synagogue** | la sinagoga | "seena**go**ga" |
| **table** | la tavola | "**tah**vola" |
| ▷ **a table for four, please** | un tavolo per quattro, per favore | "oon **tah**volo payr kwattro payr fa**voh**ray" |
| ▷ **the table is booked for ... o'clock this evening** | il tavolo è riservato per le... di questa sera | "eel **tah**volo e reezayr**vah**to payr lay ... dee kwaysta sayra" |
| **tablecloth** | la tovaglia | "tova**lya**" |

ABSOLUTE ESSENTIALS

| | | |
|---|---|---|
| **do you have ...?** | avete...? | "a**vay**tay" |
| **is there ...?** | c'è...? | "che" |
| **are there ...?** | ci sono...? | "chee sohnoh" |
| **how much is ...?** | quanto costa...? | "kwanto kosta" |

| | | |
|---|---|---|
| **tablespoon** | il cucchiaio | "kook**ya**yo" |
| **tablet** | la pastiglia | "past**eel**ya" |
| **table tennis** | il ping-pong | "peeng pong" |
| **to take** (*carry*) | portare | "por**tah**ray" |
| (*grab, seize*) | prendere | "**pren**dayray" |
| ▷ **I take a continental size 40** | porto la taglia 40 | "portoh la talya kwa**ran**ta" |
| ▷ **how long does it take?** | quanto tempo ci vuole? | "kwanto tempo chee vwolay" |
| ▷ **I'd like to take a shower** | vorrei fare una doccia | "vor**ree**e fahray oona dotcha" |
| ▷ **could you take a photograph of us?** | ci fa una foto, per favore? | "chee fa oona fohtoh payr fa**voh**ray" |
| **talc** | il borotalco | "boro**tal**ko" |
| **to talk** | parlare | "par**lah**ray" |
| **tall** | alto | "alto" |
| | alta | "alta" |
| ▷ **how tall are you?** | quanto sei alto? | "kwanto say alto" |
| ▷ **I am 1m 80 tall** | sono alto 1m e 80 | "sohnoh alto oon metro ay ot**tan**ta" |
| ▷ **how tall is it?** | quanto è alto? | "kwanto e alto" |
| ▷ **it's 10m tall** | è alto 10m | "e alto dee**ee**chee metree" |
| **tampons** | i tamponi | "tam**poh**nee" |
| **tap** | il rubinetto | "roobee**nayt**to" |
| **tape** (*cassette*) | la cassetta | "kas**say**tta" |
| (*video*) | la videocassetta | "veedayokas**say**tta" |
| (*ribbon*) | il nastro | "nastro" |
| **tape recorder** | il registratore | "rayjeestra**toh**ray" |
| **tart** (*cake*) | la crostata | "kro**stah**ta" |
| **tartar sauce** | la salsa tartara | "salsa **tar**tara" |
| **taste**[1] n | il sapore | "sa**poh**ray" |

| | | |
|---|---|---|
| to **taste**[2] *vb*: | | |
| ▷ **can I taste some?** | ne posso assaggiare un po'? | "nay posso assad**ja**ray oon po" |
| ▷ **can I taste it?** | posso assaggiarlo? | "posso assad**jar**lo" |
| **tax** | la tassa | "tassa" |
| **taxi** | il taxi | "tak**see**" |
| ▷ **can you order me a taxi, please?** | può chiamarmi un taxi, per favore? | "pwo kee**amah**rmee oon taksee payr fa**voh**ray" |
| **taxi rank** | il posteggio dei taxi | "po**stayd**jo dayee taksee" |
| **tea** | il tè | "te" |
| **tea bag** | la bustina di tè | "boo**stee**na dee te" |
| to **teach** | insegnare | "eensayn**yah**ray" |
| **teacher** | l'insegnante (*m/f*) | "eensayn**yan**tay" |
| **team** | la squadra | "skwadra" |
| **team games** | i giochi di squadra | "johkee dee skwadra" |
| **teapot** | la teiera | "tay**ye**ra" |
| **teaspoon** | il cucchiaino | "kookya**ee**no" |
| **teat** | la tettarella | "taytta**rel**la" |
| **tee shirt** | la maglietta | "mal**yayt**ta" |
| **teeth** | i denti | "dentee" |
| **telegram** | il telegramma | "taylay**gram**ma" |
| ▷ **where can I send a telegram from?** | da dove posso mandare un telegramma? | "da dohvay posso man**dah**ray oon taylay**gram**ma" |
| ▷ **I want to send a telegram** | voglio mandare un telegramma | "volyo man**dah**ray oon taylay**gram**ma" |
| **telephone** | il telefono | "tay**le**fono" |

_ABSOLUTE ESSENTIALS_

| | | |
|---|---|---|
| I don't understand | non capisco | "nohn ka**pee**sko" |
| I don't speak Italian | non parlo l'italiano | "nohn parloh leetal**yah**no" |
| do you speak English? | parla inglese? | "parla eeng**lay**zay" |
| could you help me? | può aiutarmi? | "pwo ayoo**tar**mee" |

| | | |
|---|---|---|
| ▷ **how much is it to telephone England?** | quanto costa telefonare in Inghilterra? | "kwanto kosta taylayfonahray een eengeelterra" |
| ▷ **can I telephone from here?** | posso telefonare da qui? | "posso taylayfonahray da kwee" |
| **telephone book** | l'elenco (m) telefonico | "aylenko taylayfoneeko" |
| **telephone box** | la cabina telefonica | "kabeena taylayfoneeka" |
| **telephone call** | la telefonata | "taylayfonahta" |
| ▷ **I'd like to make a telephone call** | vorrei fare una telefonata | "vorreee fahray oona taylayfonata" |
| **telephone directory** | l'elenco (m) telefonico | "aylenko taylayfoneeko" |
| **television** | la televisione | "taylayveezyohnay" |
| **television lounge** | la sala TV | "sahla teevoo" |
| ▷ **is there a television lounge?** | c'è una sala TV? | "che oona sahla teevoo" |
| **television set** | il televisore | "taylayveezohray" |
| **telex** | il telex | "telex" |
| **to tell** | dire | "deeray" |
| **temperature** | la temperatura | "taympayratoora" |
| ▷ **to have a temperature** | avere la febbre | "avayray la febbray" |
| ▷ **what is the temperature?** | quanti gradi ci sono? | "kwantee gradee chee sohnoh" |
| **temporary** | temporaneo temporanea | "taymporahnayo" "taymporahnaya" |
| **ten** | dieci | "deeechee" |
| **tennis** | il tennis | "tennees" |
| ▷ **where can we play tennis?** | dove possiamo giocare a tennis? | "dohvay posyahmo jokahray a tennees" |
| **tennis ball** | la pallina da tennis | "palleena da tennees" |

| | | |
|---|---|---|
| **tennis court** | il campo da tennis | "kampo da tennees" |
| ▷ **how much is it to hire a tennis court?** | quanto costa affittare un campo da tennis? | "kwanto kosta affeettahray oon kampo da tennees" |
| **tennis racket** | la racchetta da tennis | "rakkaytta da tennees" |
| **tent** | la tenda | "tenda" |
| ▷ **can we pitch our tent here?** | possiamo piantare la tenda qui? | "posyahmo peeantahray la tenda kwee" |
| **tent peg** | il picchetto | "peekaytto" |
| **terminus** (*for buses*) (*station*) | il capolinea la stazione di testa | "kapoleenaya" "statsyohnay dee testa" |
| **terrace** | la terrazza | "tayrratssa" |
| ▷ **can I eat on the terrace?** | posso mangiare sulla terazza? | "posso manjahray soolla tayrratssa" |
| **than** | di | "dee" |
| ▷ **better than this** | meglio di così | "maylyo dee kozee" |
| **thank you** | grazie | "gratsyay" |
| ▷ **thank you very much** | tante grazie | "tantay gratsyay" |
| ▷ **no thank you** | no grazie | "no gratsyay" |
| **that** | quel quello quella | "kwayl" "kwayllo" "kwaylla" |
| ▷ **that one** | quello là | "kwayllo la" |
| **to thaw:** | | |
| ▷ **it's thawing** | sta sgelando | "sta zjaylando" |
| **theatre** | il teatro | "tayatro" |
| **their:** | | |
| ▷ **their apartment** | il loro appartamento | "eel loro appartamaynto" |
| ▷ **their car** | la loro macchina | "la loro makkeena" |
| ▷ **their books** | i loro libri | "ee loro leebree" |
| ▷ **their shoes** | le loro scarpe | "lay loro skarpay" |

| **theirs** | (il) loro | "loro" |
| | (la) loro | "loro" |
| | (i) loro | "loro" |
| | (le) loro | "loro" |

**then:**

| ▷ **they will be away then** | a quell'epoca saranno via | "a kwayll**e**poka sar**ah**no veea" |

| **there** | lì | "lee" |
| ▷ **there is** | c'è | "che" |
| ▷ **there are** | ci sono | "chee sohno" |

| **thermometer** | il termometro | "tayr**mo**maytro" |

| **these** | questi | "kwaystee" |
| | queste | "kwaystay" |

| **they** | loro | "lohroh" |

| **thief** | il ladro | "lahdro" |

| **thing** | la cosa | "koza" |
| ▷ **my things** | la mia roba | "la meea roba" |

| **to think** | pensare | "payn**sah**ray" |

| **third** | terzo | "tayrtso" |
| | terza | "tayrtsa" |

**thirsty:**

| ▷ **I'm thirsty** | ho sete | "o saytay" |

| **thirteen** | tredici | "**tray**deechee" |

| **thirty** | trenta | "traynta" |

| **this** | questo | "kwaysto" |
| | questa | "kwaysta" |

| ▷ **this one** | questo qui | "kwaysto kwee" |

| **those** | quelli | "kwayllee" |

|  | quelle | "kwayllay" |
|---|---|---|
| **thousand** | mille | "meellay" |
| **thread** | il filo | "feelo" |
| **three** | tre | "tre" |
| **throat** | la gola | "gohla" |
| ▷ **I want something for a sore throat** | voglio qualcosa per il mal di gola | "volyo kwal**ko**za payr eel mal dee gohla" |
| **throat lozenges** | le pastiglie per la gola | "pa**steel**yay payr la gohla" |
| **through:** |  |  |
| ▷ **I can't get through** | non riesco a prendere la linea | "nohn ree**es**ko a **pren**dayray la **lee**naya" |
| ▷ **is it/this a through train?** | è un treno diretto? | "e oon trayno dee**rayt**to" |
| **to thunder:** |  |  |
| ▷ **I think it's going to thunder** | credo che ci saranno i tuoni | "kraydo kay chee sa**ran**no ee twonee" |
| **thunderstorm** | il temporale | "taympo**rah**lay" |
| ▷ **will there be a thunderstorm?** | ci sarà un temporale? | "chee sa**ra** oon taympo**rah**lay" |
| **Thursday** | il giovedì | "djovay**dee**" |
| **ticket** | il biglietto | "beel**yayt**to" |
| ▷ **can you book the tickets for us?** | può prenotarci i biglietti? | "pwo prayno**tahr**chee ee beel**yayt**tee" |
| ▷ **where do I buy a ticket?** | dove posso comprare il biglietto? | "dohvay posso kom**prah**ray eel beel**yayt**to" |
| ▷ **can I buy the tickets here?** | posso comprare qui i biglietti? | "posso kom**prah**ray kwee ee beel**yayt**tee" |
| ▷ **a single ticket** | un biglietto di sola andata | "oona beel**yayt**to dee sohla an**dah**ta" |
| ▷ **a return ticket** | un biglietto di andata e ritorno | "oon beel**yayt**to dee an**dah**ta ay ree**tor**no" |

| | | |
|---|---|---|
| ▷ **2 tickets for the opera** | 2 biglietti per l'opera | "dooay beel**yayt**tee payr **loh**payra" |
| ▷ **a book of tickets** | un blocchetto di biglietti | "oon blok**kayt**to dee beel**yayt**tee" |
| **ticket collector** | il controllore | "kontro**loh**ray" |
| **ticket office** | la biglietteria | "beelyayttay**ree**a" |
| **tide** | la marea | "mar**ay**a" |
| **tie** | la cravatta | "kra**vat**ta" |
| **tights** | i collant | "kol**lant**" |
| **till**[1] *n* | la cassa | "**kass**a" |
| **till**[2] *prep* | fino a | "**feen**o a" |
| ▷ **I want to stay three nights** | voglio restare per tre notti | "**voly**o ray**stah**ray payr tray **not**tee" |
| **time** | il tempo | "**tempo**" |
| ▷ **this time** | questa volta | "**kwaysta volta**" |
| ▷ **what time is it?** | che ora è? | "kay **ohra** eh" |
| ▷ **do we have time to visit the town?** | abbiamo tempo per visitare la città? | "ab**yah**mo **tempo** payr veezee**tah**ray la **cheet**ta" |
| ▷ **what time do we get to ...?** | a che ora arriviamo a...? | "a kay **ohra** arreev**yah**mo a" |
| ▷ **is it time to go?** | è ora di andare? | "e **ohra** dee an**dah**ray" |
| **timetable** | l'orario *(m)* | "oh**rah**reeo" |
| ▷ **can I have a timetable?** | potrei avere un orario? | "po**tray** a**vay**ray oon oh**rah**reeo" |
| **timetable board** | il tabellone degli orari | "tabayl**loh**nay **dayl**lyee o**rah**ree" |
| **tin** | la scatola | "**skah**tola" |
| **tinfoil** | la carta stagnola | "**karta** stan**yo**la" |
| **tin-opener** | l'apriscatole *(m)* | "apree**skah**tolay" |

**tinted:**

| | | |
|---|---|---|
| ▷ my hair is tinted | i miei capelli sono tinti | "ee myay ka**pay**llee sohnoh **teen**tee" |
| **tip** (to waiter etc) | la mancia | "**man**cha" |
| ▷ is it usual to tip? | si deve dare la mancia? | "see **day**vay **dah**ray la **man**cha" |
| ▷ how much should I tip? | quanto devo lasciare di mancia? | "**kwan**to **day**vo la**shah**ray dee **man**cha" |
| ▷ is the tip included? | è compresa la mancia? | "e kom**pray**za la **man**cha" |
| **tired** | stanco | "**stan**ko" |
| | stanca | "**stan**ka" |
| **tiring** | stancante | "stan**kan**tay" |
| **tissues** | i fazzoletti di carta | "fatsso**layt**tee dee **kar**ta" |
| **to** | a | "ah" |
| ▷ to London | a Londra | "ah **lohn**dra" |
| ▷ to Spain | in Spagna | "een **span**ya" |
| **toast** | il pane tostato | "**pah**nay to**stah**to" |
| ▷ two slices of toast | due fette di pane tostato | "**dooay** **fayt**tay dee **pah**nay to**stah**to" |
| **tobacco** | il tabacco | "ta**bak**ko" |
| **tobacconist** | il tabaccaio | "tabak**ka**yo" |
| **today** | oggi | "**od**jee" |
| ▷ is it open today? | è aperto oggi? | "e a**payr**to **od**jee" |
| **together** | insieme | "eensee**ee**may" |
| **toilet** | la toilette | "twa**let**" |
| ▷ is there a toilet for the disabled? | c'è una toilette per portatori di handicap? | "che **oo**na twa**let** payr portah**toh**ree dee **an**deekap" |
| ▷ where are the toilets, please? | dov'è la toilette, per favore? | "doh**ve** la twa**let** payr fa**voh**ray" |

*ABSOLUTE ESSENTIALS*

| | | |
|---|---|---|
| do you have ...? | avete...? | "a**vay**tay" |
| is there ...? | c'è...? | "che" |
| are there ...? | ci sono...? | "chee **soh**noh" |
| how much is ...? | quanto costa...? | "**kwan**to **kos**ta" |

| | | |
|---|---|---|
| ▷ is there a toilet on board? | c'è una toilette a bordo? | "che oona twalet a bordo" |
| ▷ the toilet won't flush | non funziona lo sciacquone | "nohn foontsyohna loh shahkwohnay" |
| **toilet paper** | la carta igienica | "karta eejeneeka" |
| ▷ there is no toilet paper | non c'è carta igienica | "nohn che karta eejeneeka" |
| **toll** | il pedaggio | "paydadjo" |
| ▷ is there a toll on this motorway? | c'è da pagare il pedaggio su questa autostrada? | "che da pagahray eel paydadjo soo kwaysta owtostrahda" |
| **tomato** | il pomodoro | "pomodoro" |
| **tomato juice** | il succo di pomodoro | "sookko dee pomodoro" |
| **tomato soup** | la zuppa di pomodoro | "tsoopa dee pomodoro" |
| **tomorrow** | domani | "domahnee" |
| ▷ tomorrow morning | domani mattina | "domahnee matteena" |
| ▷ tomorrow afternoon | domani pomeriggio | "domahnee pomayreedjo" |
| ▷ tomorrow night | domani sera | "domahnee sayra" |
| ▷ is it open tomorrow? | è aperto domani? | "e apayrto domahnee" |
| **tongue** | la lingua | "leengwa" |
| **tonic water** | l'acqua (f) tonica | "akwa toneeka" |
| **tonight** | stasera | "stasayra" |
| **too** (also) | anche | "ankay" |
| (excessively) | troppo | "troppo" |
| ▷ me too | anch'io | "ankeeo" |
| ▷ it's too big | è troppo grande | "e troppo granday" |
| **tooth** | il dente | "dentay" |
| ▷ I've broken a tooth | mi sono spezzato un dente | "mee sohnoh spaytssahto oon dentay" |
| **toothache** | il mal di denti | "mal dee dentee" |
| ▷ I have toothache | ho mal di denti | "o mal dee dentee" |

|  |  |  |
|---|---|---|
| ▷ **I want something for toothache** | voglio qualcosa per il mal di denti | "volyo kwal**ko**za payr eel mal dee **den**tee" |
| **toothbrush** | lo spazzolino da denti | "spatsso**lee**no da **den**tee" |
| **toothpaste** | il dentifricio | "daynteefree**cho**" |
| **toothpick** | lo stuzzicadenti | "stootseeka**den**tee" |
| **top¹** *n (of mountain)* | la cima | "**chee**ma" |
| ▷ **on top of ...** | sopra... | "**so**pra" |
| **top²** *adj:* | | |
| ▷ **the top floor** | l'ultimo piano | "**lool**teemo pee**ah**no" |
| **torch** | la pila | "**pee**la" |
| **torn** | strappato | "strap**pah**to" |
| | strappata | "strap**pah**ta" |
| **total** | il totale | "to**tah**lay" |
| **tough** *(meat)* | duro | "**doo**ro" |
| | dura | "**doo**ra" |
| **tour** | il giro | "**jee**ro" |
| ▷ **when is the bus tour of the town?** | quando inizia il giro della città in autobus? | "kwando ee**neets**ya eel **jee**ro daylla chee**tta** een **ow**toboos" |
| ▷ **the tour starts at about ...** | il giro comincia alle... circa | "eel **jee**ro ko**meen**cha allay... **cheer**ka" |
| ▷ **how long does the tour take?** | quanto dura la gita? | "kwanto **doo**ra la **jee**ta" |
| **tourist** | il turista | "too**ree**sta" |
| **tourist office** | l'ufficio (*m*) informazioni turistiche | "oo**ffee**cho eenformats**yoh**nee too**ree**steekay" |
| ▷ **I'm looking for the tourist office** | sto cercando l'ufficio informazioni turistiche | "sto chayr**kan**do loo**ffee**cho eenformats**yoh**nee too**ree**steekay" |

*ABSOLUTE ESSENTIALS*

| | | |
|---|---|---|
| I don't understand | non capisco | "nohn ka**pee**sko" |
| I don't speak Italian | non parlo l'italiano | "nohn parloh leetaly**ah**no" |
| do you speak English? | parla inglese? | "parla eeng**lay**zay" |
| could you help me? | può aiutarmi? | "pwo ayoo**tar**mee" |

# tourist ticket

| | | |
|---|---|---|
| **tourist ticket** | il biglietto turistico | "beel**yayt**to tooree**stee**ko" |
| to **tow**: | | |
| ▷ **can you tow me to a garage?** | può trainarmi da un meccanico? | "pwo traee**nahr**mee da oon mayk**ka**neeko" |
| **towel** | l'asciugamano (m) | "ashooga**mah**no" |
| ▷ **the towels have run out** | sono finiti gli asciugamani | "sohnoh fee**nee**tee lyee ashooga**mah**nee" |
| **town** | la città | "cheet**ta**" |
| **town centre** | il centro | "**chen**tro" |
| **town plan** | la pianta della città | "pee**an**ta daylla cheet**ta**" |
| **tow rope** | il cavo da rimorchio | "**kah**vo da ree**mork**yo" |
| **toy** | il giocattolo | "jo**kat**tolo" |
| **toy shop** | il negozio di giocattoli | "nay**gots**yo dee jo**kat**tolee" |
| **traditional** | tradizionale | "tradeetsyo**nah**lay" |
| **traffic** | il traffico | "**traf**feeko" |
| ▷ **is the traffic heavy on the motorway?** | c'è molto traffico sull'autostrada? | "che moltoh **traf**feeko soollowto**strah**da" |
| ▷ **is there a route that avoids the traffic?** | c'è un'altra strada per evitare il traffico? | "che oon**al**tra strahda payr ayvee**tah**ray eel **traf**feeko" |
| **traffic jam** | l'ingorgo (m) | "een**gor**go" |
| **trailer** | il rimorchio | "ree**mork**yo" |
| **train** | il treno | "**tre**no" |
| ▷ **is this the train for ...?** | è questo il treno per...? | "e kwaysto eel **tre**no payr" |
| ▷ **what times are the trains?** | a che ora ci soni i treni? | "a kay ohra chee sohnoh ee **tre**nee" |
| ▷ **are there any cheap train fares?** | ci sono biglietti ferroviari a tariffa ridotta? | "chee sohnoh beel**yayt**tee fayrrovee**ea**ree a tah**ree**ffa ree**doht**ta" |

ABSOLUTE ESSENTIALS

| | | |
|---|---|---|
| **I would like ...** | vorrei... | "vo**ree**ee" |
| **I need ...** | ho bisogno di... | "o bee**zohn**yo dee" |
| **where is ...?** | dov'è...? | "do**veh**" |
| **I'm looking for ...** | sto cercando... | "sto chayr**kan**do" |

| | | |
|---|---|---|
| ▷ **does this train go to ...?** | questo treno va a...? | "kwaysto treno va a" |
| ▷ **how frequent are the trains to town?** | ogni quanto ci sono i treni per la città? | "onyee kwanto chee sohnoh ee trenee payr la cheetta" |
| ▷ **does this train stop at ...?** | questo treno ferma a...? | "kwesto treno fayrma a" |
| ▷ **when is the first train to ...?** | quando c'è il primo treno per ...? | "kwando che eel preemo treno payr" |
| **training shoes** | le scarpe da ginnastica | "skarpay da jeennasteeka" |
| **tram** | il tram | "tram" |
| **trampoline** | la pedana elastica per ginnasti | "paydahna aylahsteeka payr jeennastee" |
| **to transfer:** | | |
| ▷ **I should like to transfer some money from my account** | vorrei trasferire dei soldi dal mio conto | "vorreee trasfayreeray day soldee dal meeo kohnto" |
| **to translate** | tradurre | "tradoorray" |
| ▷ **could you translate this for me?** | me lo può tradurre? | "may lo pwo tradoorray" |
| **translation** | la traduzione | "tradootsyohnay" |
| **to travel** | viaggiare | "veeadjahray" |
| ▷ **I am travelling alone** | viaggio da solo | "veeadjo da sohlo" |
| **travel agent** | l'agente (*m*) di viaggio | "ajentay dee veeadjo" |
| **traveller's cheques** | i traveller's cheque | "**tra**vellers cheque" |
| ▷ **do you accept traveller's cheques?** | accettate i traveller's cheque? | "atchayttahtay ee **tra**vellers cheque" |
| ▷ **can I change my traveller's cheques here?** | si possono cambiare traveller's cheque qui? | "see possono kambyahray **tra**vellers cheque kwee" |
| **travel-sick:** | | |
| ▷ **I get travel-sick** | viaggiare mi fa star male | "veeadjahray mee fa stahr mahlay" |

| **tray** | il vassoio | "vas**soy**o" |
| **tree** | l'albero (m) | "**al**bayro" |
| **trim** (haircut) | la spuntata | "spoon**tah**ta" |
| ▷ can I have a trim? | mi dà una spuntata, per favore? | "mee da oona spoon**tah**ta payr fa**voh**ray" |
| **trip** | la gita | "**jee**ta" |
| ▷ this is my first trip to ... | questo è il mio primo viaggio a... | "**kwaysto** e eel meeo **pree**mo vee**adj**o a" |
| ▷ a business trip | un viaggio d'affari | "oon vee**adj**o daf**fah**ree" |
| ▷ do you run day trips to ...? | organizzate gite in giornata a...? | "organeed**zah**tay jeetay een jor**nah**ta a" |
| **trolley** | il carrello | "kar**rayl**lo" |
| **trouble** | la difficoltà | "deeffeekol**ta**" |
| ▷ I am in trouble | ho bisogno di aiuto | "o bee**zohn**yo dee a**yoo**to" |
| ▷ I'm sorry to trouble you | mi scusi se la disturbo | "mee skoozee say la dees**toor**bo" |
| ▷ I'm having trouble with the phone | ho problemi col telefono | "o prob**lay**mee kohl tay**le**fono" |
| **trousers** | i pantaloni | "pantal**oh**nee" |
| **trout** | la trota | "**troh**ta" |
| **true** | vero | "**vay**ro" |
| | vera | "**vay**ra" |
| **trunk** (luggage) | il baule | "ba**oo**lay" |
| ▷ I'd like to send my trunk on ahead | vorrei spedire il mio baule | "vor**reee** spay**dee**ray eel meeo ba**oo**lay" |
| **trunks** | i calzoncini da bagno | "kaltson**chee**nee da banyo" |
| to **try** | provare | "pro**vah**ray" |
| to **try on** | provare | "pro**vah**ray" |

| ABSOLUTE ESSENTIALS | | |
| --- | --- | --- |
| yes (please) | sì (grazie) | "see (**grat**syay)" |
| no (thank you) | no (grazie) | "no (**grat**syay)" |
| hello | salve | "**sal**vay" |
| goodbye | arrivederci | "arreevay**dayr**chee" |

| | | |
|---|---|---|
| ▷ **may I try on this dress?** | posso provare questo vestito? | "posso pro**vah**ray kwaysto vay**stee**to" |
| **T-shirt** | la maglietta | "mal**yayt**ta" |
| **Tuesday** | il martedì | "martay**dee**" |
| **tuna** | il tonno | "tonno" |
| **tunnel** | la galleria | "gallay**ree**a" |
| ▷ **the Channel tunnel** | il tunnel sotto la Manica | "toonel sohtto la **man**eeka" |
| **Turin** | Torino (f) | "to**ree**no" |
| **turkey** | il tacchino | "tak**kee**no" |
| **to turn** (handle, wheel) | girare | "jee**rah**ray |
| ▷ **it's my turn** | tocca a me | "tokka a me" |
| **to turn down** (sound, heating etc) | abbassare | "abbas**sah**ray" |
| **turning:** | | |
| ▷ **is this the turning for ...?** | devo girare qui per...? | "dayvo jee**rah**ray kwee payr" |
| ▷ **take the second/third turning on your left** | giri la seconda/terza a sinistra | "**jee**ree la say**kon**da/ tayrtsa a see**nee**stra" |
| **turnip** | la rapa | "**rah**pa" |
| **to turn off** (light etc) | spegnere | "spayn**yay**ray" |
| (tap) | chiudere | "kee**oo**dayray" |
| ▷ **I can't turn the heating off** | non riesco a spegnere il riscaldamento | "nohn ree**es**ko a **spayn**yayray eel reeskaldah**mayn**to" |
| **to turn on** (light etc) | accendere | "at**chen**dayray" |
| (tap) | aprire | "a**pree**ray" |
| ▷ **I can't turn the heating on** | non riesco ad accendere il riscaldamento | "nohn ree**es**ko ad at**chen**dayray eel reeskalda**mayn**to" |
| **to turn up** (sound, heating etc) | alzare | "alt**sah**ray" |

| tweezers | la pinzette | "peent**sayt**tay" |
| twelve | dodici | "**doh**deechee" |
| twenty | venti | "**vayn**tee" |
| twenty-one | ventuno | "vayn**too**no" |
| twenty-two | ventidue | "vayntee**doo**ay |
| twice | due volte | "dooay voltay" |
| twin-bedded room | la camera con letti gemelli | "**ka**mayra kohn lettee jay**mel**lee" |
| two | due | "dooay" |
| typical | tipico<br>tipica | "**tee**peeko"<br>"**tee**peeka" |
| ▷ have you anything typical of this region? | avete qualcosa di tipico di questa regione? | "a**vay**tay kwalkoza dee **tee**peeko dee kwaysta re**joh**nay" |
| tyre | la gomma | "**goh**mma" |
| tyre pressure | la pressione delle gomme | "prays**yoh**nay dayllay gohmmay" |
| ▷ what should the tyre pressure be? | che pressione dovrebbero avere le gomme? | "kay prays**yoh**nay dov**rayb**bayro a**vay**ray lay gohmmay" |
| UK | il Regno Unito | "**rayn**yo oo**nee**to" |
| umbrella (for rain)<br>(on beach) | l'ombrello (m)<br>l'ombrellone (m) | "om**brel**lo"<br>"ombrel**loh**nay" |
| uncomfortable | scomodo<br>scomoda | "**sko**modo"<br>"**sko**moda" |
| ▷ the bed is uncomfortable | il letto è scomodo | "eel letto e **sko**modo" |
| unconscious | svenuto<br>svenuta | "zvay**noo**to"<br>"zvay**noo**ta" |
| under | sotto | "**soh**tto" |

| | | |
|---|---|---|
| **underground** | la metropolitana | "maytropolee**tah**na" |
| **underground station** | la stazione della metropolitana | "stats**yoh**nay daylla maytropolee**tah**na" |
| **underpass** | il sottopassaggio | "sottopas**sad**jo" |
| **to understand** | capire | "ka**pee**ray" |
| ▷ **I don't understand** | non capisco | "nohn ka**pee**sko" |
| **underwear** | la biancheria intima | "beeankay**ree**a **een**teema" |
| **United States** | gli Stati Uniti | "stahtee oo**nee**tee" |
| **university** | l'università (f) | "ooneevayr**see**ta" |
| **unleaded petrol** | la benzina senza piombo | "baynd**zee**na sentsa pee**om**bo" |
| **to unpack** | disfare le valigie | "dees**fah**ray lay va**lee**jay" |
| ▷ **I have to unpack** | devo disfare le valigie | "**day**vo dees**fah**ray lay va**lee**jay" |
| **up** | su | "soo" |
| ▷ **up there** | lassù | "las**soo**" |
| **upstairs** | di sopra | "dee **soh**pra" |
| **urgent** | urgente | "oor**jen**tay" |
| **USA** | gli USA | "**oo**sa" |
| **to use** | usare | "oo**zah**ray" |
| ▷ **can I use the toilet?** | posso usare il bagno? | "posso oo**zah**ray eel **ban**yo" |
| ▷ **may I use your phone?** | posso fare una telefonata? | "posso **fah**ray oona taylayfo**nah**ta" |
| **useful** | utile | "**oo**teelay" |
| **usual** | solito | "**so**leeto" |
| | solita | "**so**leeta" |
| **usually** | di solito | "dee**so**leeto" |

*ABSOLUTE ESSENTIALS*

| | | |
|---|---|---|
| **do you have ...?** | avete...? | "a**vay**tay" |
| **is there ...?** | c'è...? | "che" |
| **are there ...?** | ci sono...? | "chee **soh**noh" |
| **how much is ...?** | quanto costa...? | "**kwan**to **kos**ta" |

**vacancies:**

▷ **do you have any vacancies?** (*in hotel*)    avete stanze libere?    "**avay**tay stantsay **lee**bayray"

    (*at campsite*)    avete dei posti liberi?    "**avay**tay dayee postee **lee**bayree"

**to vacate:**

▷ **when do I have to vacate the room?**    quando devo lasciare la stanza?    "kwando dayvo la**shah**ray la stantsa"

**vacuum cleaner**    l'aspirapolvere (*m*)    "aspeera**pohl**vayray"

**valid**    valido    "**val**eedo"
     valida    "**val**eeda"

**valley**    la valle    "val**lay**"

**valuable**    di valore    "dee va**loh**ray"

**valuables**    i valori    "va**loh**ree"

**van**    il furgone    "foor**goh**nay"

**vase**    il vaso    "**vah**zo"

**VAT**    l'IVA (*f*)    "**ee**va"

▷ **does the price include VAT?**    l'IVA è compresa nel prezzo?    "**ee**va e kom**pray**zo nayl prettso"

**veal**    il vitello    "vee**tayl**lo"

**vegan**    vegetaliano    "vayjaytal**yah**no"
     vegetaliana    "vayjaytal**yah**na"

▷ **is this suitable for vegans?**    va bene per vegetaliani?    "va benay payr vayjaytal**yah**nee"

▷ **do you have any vegan dishes?**    avete piatti vegetaliani?    "a**vay**tay peeatee vayjaytal**yah**nee"

**vegetables**    le verdure    "vayr**doo**ray"
  (*in restaurant*)    i contorni    "kon**tor**nee"

**vegetarian**    il vegetariano    "vayjaytar**yah**no"
     la vegetariana    "vayjaytar**yah**na"

---

**ABSOLUTE ESSENTIALS**

| | | |
|---|---|---|
| yes (please) | sì (grazie) | "see (gratsyay)" |
| no (thank you) | no (grazie) | "no (gratsyay)" |
| hello | salve | "salvay" |
| goodbye | arrivederci | "arreevay**dayr**chee" |

| ▷ is this suitable for vegetarians? | va bene per vegetariani? | "va benay payr vayjaytaryahnee" |
| ▷ do you have any vegetarian dishes? | avete piatti vegetariani? | "avaytay peeatee vayjaytaryahnee" |
| **Venice** | Venezia (f) | "vaynaytsya" |
| **venison** | la carne di cervo | "karnay dee chayrvo" |
| **ventilator** | il ventilatore | "vaynteelatohray" |
| **vermouth** | il vermut | "vayrmoot" |
| **vertigo:** | | |
| ▷ I suffer from vertigo | soffro di vertigini | "sohffro dee vayrteejeenee" |
| **very** | molto | "mohlto" |
| **vest** | la canottiera | "kanottyera" |
| **via** | via | "veea" |
| **video** | il video | "veedayo" |
| **view** | la vista | "veesta" |
| ▷ I'd like a room with a view of the sea/the mountains | vorrei una camera con vista sul mare/sulle montagne | "vorreee oona kamayra kohn veesta sool mahray/soollay montanyay" |
| **villa** | la villa | "veella" |
| **village** | il paese | "paayzay" |
| **vinegar** | l'aceto (m) | "achayto" |
| **vineyard** | la vigna | "veenya" |
| **visa** | il visto | "veesto" |
| ▷ I have an entry visa | ho un visto d'ingresso | "o oon veesto deengraysso" |
| **to visit** | visitare | "veezeetahray" |

ABSOLUTE ESSENTIALS

| I don't understand | non capisco | "nohn kapeesko" |
| I don't speak Italian | non parlo l'italiano | "nohn parloh leetalyahno" |
| do you speak English? | parla inglese? | "parla eenglayzay" |
| could you help me? | può aiutarmi? | "pwo ayootarmee" |

| | | |
|---|---|---|
| ▷ **can we visit the vineyard?** | possiamo visitare il vigneto? | "posyahmo veezeetahray eel veenyayto" |
| **vitamin** | la vitamina | "veetameena" |
| **vodka** | la vodka | "vodka" |
| **volleyball** | la pallavolo | "pallavohloh" |
| **voltage** | il voltaggio | "voltadjo" |
| ▷ **what's the voltage?** | che voltaggio è? | "kay voltadjo e" |
| **waist** | la cintura | "cheentoora" |
| **waistcoat** | il panciotto | "panchohtto" |
| **to wait (for)** | aspettare | "aspayttahray" |
| ▷ **can you wait here for a few minutes?** | può aspettare qui per alcuni minuti? | "pwo aspayttahray kwee payr alkoonee meenootee" |
| ▷ **please wait for me** | mi aspetti, per favore | "mee aspayttee payr favohray" |
| **waiter** | il cameriere | "kamayryeray" |
| **waiting room** | la sala d'aspetto | "sahla daspetto" |
| **waitress** | la cameriera | "kamayryera" |
| **to wake** | svegliare | "svaylyahray" |
| ▷ **please wake me at 8.00** | mi svegli alle 8.00, per favore | "mee svaylyee ahllay ohtto payr favohray" |
| **to wake up** | svegliarsi | "svaylyarsee" |
| **Wales** | il Galles | "gallays" |
| **walk¹** *n:* | | |
| ▷ **to go for a walk** | fare una passeggiata | "fahray oona passaydjahta" |
| ▷ **are there any interesting walks nearby?** | ci sono delle belle passeggiate da fare qui vicino? | "chee sohnoh dayllay bellay passaydjahtay da fahray kwee veecheeno" |
| **to walk²** *vb* | andare a piedi | "andahray a peeedee" |

| **wallet** | il portafoglio | "porta**fol**yo" |
|---|---|---|
| **walnut** | la noce | "**no**chay" |
| **to want** | volere | "vo**lay**ray" |
| ▷ **I want ...** | voglio... | "**vol**yo" |
| **warm** | caldo | "**kal**do" |
|  | calda | "**kal**da" |
| **warning triangle** | il triangolo | "tree**an**golo" |
| **to wash** | lavare | "la**vah**ray" |
| ▷ **to wash oneself** | lavarsi | "la**vahr**see" |
| ▷ **where can I wash my clothes?** | dove posso lavare i vestiti? | "**do**vay posso la**vah**ray ee vay**stee**tee" |
| ▷ **where can I wash my hands?** | dove mi posso lavare le mani? | "**do**vay mee posso la**vah**ray lay **mah**nee" |
| **washable:** |  |  |
| ▷ **is it washable?** | si può lavare? | "see pwo la**vah**ray" |
| **washbasin** | il lavandino | "lavan**dee**no" |
| ▷ **the washbasin is dirty** | il lavandino è sporco | "eel lavan**dee**no e **spor**ko" |
| **washing** | il bucato | "boo**kah**to" |
| ▷ **where can I do some washing?** | dove posso fare il bucato? | "**do**vay posso **fah**ray eel boo**kah**to" |
| **washing machine** | la lavatrice | "lava**tree**chay" |
| ▷ **how do you work the washing machine?** | come funziona la lavatrice? | "**ko**may foonts**yoh**na la lava**tree**chay" |
| **washing powder** | il detersivo | "daytayr**see**vo" |
| **washing-up liquid** | il detersivo per i piatti | "daytayr**see**vo payr ee pee**at**tee" |
| **wasp** | la vespa | "**vespa**" |
| **waste bin** | il bidone della spazzatura | "bee**doh**nay daylla spatssa**too**ra" |
| **watch**[1] *n* | l'orologio *(m)* | "oro**lo**djo" |

*ABSOLUTE ESSENTIALS*

| **do you have ...?** | avete...? | "a**vay**tay" |
|---|---|---|
| **is there ...?** | c'è...? | "che" |
| **are there ...?** | ci sono...? | "chee **soh**noh" |
| **how much is ...?** | quanto costa...? | "**kwan**to **kos**ta" |

| | | |
|---|---|---|
| ▷ **I think my watch is slow/fast** | credo che il mio orologio sia indietro/avanti | "kraydo kay eel meeo orolodjo seea eendeeeetro/avantee" |
| ▷ **my watch has stopped** | il mio orologio si è fermato | "eel meeo orolodjo see e fayrmahto" |
| to **watch**[2] *vb (look at)* | guardare | "gwardahray" |
| ▷ **could you watch my bag for a minute, please?** | può tenere d'occhio la mia borsa un attimo, per favore? | "pwo taynayray dokkyo la meea bohrsa oon atteemo payr favohray" |
| **water** | l'acqua *(f)* | "akwa" |
| ▷ **there is no hot water** | non c'è acqua calda | "nohn che akwa kalda" |
| ▷ **a glass of water** | un bicchiere d'acqua | "oon beekyayray dakwa" |
| **waterfall** | la cascata | "kaskahta" |
| **water heater** | lo scaldabagno | "skaldabanyo" |
| **watermelon** | l'anguria *(f)* | "angooreea" |
| **waterproof** | impermeabile | "eempayrmayahbeelay" |
| **water-skiing** | lo sci d'acqua | "shee dakwa" |
| ▷ **is it possible to go water-skiing?** | si può fare lo sci d'acqua? | "see pwo fahray loh shee dakwa" |
| **wave** *(on sea)* | l'onda | "onda" |
| **wax** | la cera | "chayra" |
| **way** *(manner)* | il modo | "modo" |
| *(route)* | la strada | "strahda" |
| ▷ **what's the best way to get to ...?** | qual è il modo migliore per andare a...? | "kwal e eel modo meelyohray payr andahray a" |
| ▷ **this way** | di qua | "dee kwa" |
| ▷ **which is the way to ...?** | come si va a...? | "komay see vah a" |
| ▷ **this way** | da questa parte | "da kwaysta partay" |
| ▷ **that way** | per di là | "payr dee la" |
| **we** | noi | "nohee" |

| | | |
|---|---|---|
| **weak** (*person*) | debole | "**day**bolay" |
| (*coffee*) | leggero | "led**jer**o" |
| | leggera | "led**jer**a" |
| to **wear** | portare | "por**tah**ray" |
| ▷ **what should I wear?** | come mi devo vestire? | "kohmay mee dayvo ve**stee**ray" |
| **weather** | il tempo | "**tempo**" |
| ▷ **is the weather going to change?** | il tempo cambierà? | "eel tempo kambye**ra**" |
| ▷ **what dreadful weather!** | che tempaccio! | "kay tem**pa**tcho" |
| **weather forecast:** | | |
| ▷ **what's the weather forecast for tomorrow?** | come sono le previsioni del tempo per domani? | "kohmay sohnoh lay prayveez**yoh**nee dayl tempo payr do**mah**nee" |
| **wedding** | il matrimonio | "matree**mon**yo" |
| ▷ **we are here for a wedding** | siamo qui per un matrimonio | "see**yah**mo kwee payr oon matree**mon**yo" |
| **Wednesday** | il mercoledì | "mayrkolay**dee**" |
| **week** | la settimana | "saytteemahna" |
| ▷ **this week** | questa settimana | "kwaysta saytteemahna" |
| ▷ **last week** | la settimana scorsa | "la saytteemahna skorsa" |
| ▷ **next week** | la settimana prossima | "la saytteemahna prosseema" |
| ▷ **for two weeks** | per due settimane | "payr dooay saytteemahnay" |
| **weekday** | il giorno feriale | "jorno fayryahlay" |
| **weekend** | il week-end | "weekend" |
| **weekly rate** | la tariffa settimanale | "tareeffa saytteemanahlay" |
| **weight** | il peso | "payzo" |
| **welcome** | benvenuto | "baynvaynooto" |

*ABSOLUTE ESSENTIALS*

| | | |
|---|---|---|
| **I don't understand** | non capisco | "nohn ka**pees**ko" |
| **I don't speak Italian** | non parlo l'italiano | "nohn parloh leetalyahno" |
| **do you speak English?** | parla inglese? | "parla eeng**lay**zay" |
| **could you help me?** | può aiutarmi? | "pwo ayoo**tar**mee" |

| | | |
|---|---|---|
| ▷ **thank you! – you're welcome** | grazie! – prego | "grahtseeay – praygo" |
| **well** | bene | "benay" |
| ▷ **he's not well** | non sta bene | "nohn sta benay" |
| **well done** (*steak*) | ben cotto<br>ben cotta | "ben kotto"<br>"ben kotta" |
| **Welsh** | gallese | "gallayzay" |
| ▷ **I'm Welsh** | sono gallese | "sohnoh gallayzay" |
| **west** | l'ovest (*m*) | "ovest" |
| **wet** | bagnato<br>bagnata | "banyahto"<br>"banyahta" |
| **wetsuit** | la muta | "moota" |
| **what** | che | "kay" |
| ▷ **what is it?** | cos'è? | "koze" |
| **wheel** | la ruota | "rwota" |
| **wheelchair** | la sedia a rotelle | "sedya a rotellay" |
| **when** | quando | "kwando" |
| **where** | dove | "dovay" |
| ▷ **where are you from?** | di dov'è? | "dee dove" |
| **which** | quale | "kwalay" |
| ▷ **which is it?** | qual è? | "kwal e" |
| ▷ **which man?** | che uomo? | "kay womo" |
| ▷ **which woman?** | che donna? | "kay donna" |
| ▷ **which book?** | che libro? | "kay leebro" |
| **while**[1] *n*:<br>▷ **in a while** | fra poco | "fra poko" |
| **while**[2] *conj*:<br>▷ **while I was there ...** | mentre ero lì... | "mayntray ayro lee" |

*ABSOLUTE ESSENTIALS*

| | | |
|---|---|---|
| I would like ... | vorrei... | "voreee" |
| I need ... | ho bisogno di... | "o beezohnyo dee" |
| where is ...? | dov'è...? | "doveh" |
| I'm looking for ... | sto cercando... | "sto chayrkando" |

| ▷ can you do it while I wait? | lo fa subito? | "loh fa **soo**beeto" |
| **whipped cream** | la panna montata | "panna mon**tah**ta" |
| **whisky** | il whisky | "**whee**skee" |
| ▷ I'll have a whisky | prendo un whisky | "prendo oon **whee**skee" |
| ▷ whisky and soda | whisky e soda | "**whee**skee ay sohda" |
| **white** | bianco | "bee**an**ko" |
| | bianca | "bee**an**ka" |
| **who** | chi | "kee" |
| ▷ who is it? | chi è? | "kee e" |
| **whole** | tutto | "**toot**to" |
| | tutta | "**toot**ta" |
| **wholemeal** | integrale | "eentay**grah**lay" |
| **wholemeal bread** | il pane integrale | "panay eentay**grah**lay" |
| **whose:** | | |
| ▷ whose is it? | di chi è? | "dee kee e" |
| **why** | perché | "pay**rkay**" |
| **wide** | largo | "largo" |
| | larga | "larga" |
| **wife** | la moglie | "**mol**yay" |
| **window** | la finestra | "fee**nes**tra" |
| (in car, plane) | il finestrino | "feenes**tree**no" |
| ▷ I'd like a window seat | vorrei un posto vicino al finestrino | "vor**reee** oon posto vee**chee**no al feenes**tree**no" |
| ▷ I can't open the window | non riesco ad aprire la finestra | "nohn ree**es**ko ad a**pree**ray la fee**nes**tra" |
| ▷ I have broken the window | ho rotto un vetro | "o **roht**toh oon vaytro" |
| ▷ may I open the window? | posso aprire il finestrino? | "posso a**pree**ray eel feenay**stree**no" |

ABSOLUTE ESSENTIALS

| do you have ...? | avete...? | "a**vay**tay" |
| is there ...? | c'è...? | "che" |
| are there ...? | ci sono...? | "chee sohnoh" |
| how much is ...? | quanto costa...? | "kwanto kosta" |

| window | la vetrina | "vay**tree**na" |
|---|---|---|
| ▷ **in the window** | in vetrina | "een vay**tree**na" |

**windscreen** · il parabrezza · "para**braydz**za"

▷ **could you clean the windscreen?** · potrebbe pulire il vetro? · "po**treb**bay poo**lee**ray eel vaytro"

▷ **the windscreen has shattered** · il parabrezza si è rotto · "eel para**braydz**za see e rohtto"

**windscreen washers:**

▷ **can you top up the windscreen washers?** · aggiunge del liquido ai lavacristalli? · "a**joon**jay dayl **lee**kweedo ayee lavakree**stahl**lee"

**windscreen wiper** · il tergicristallo · "tayrjeekree**stahl**lo"

**windsurfer** (*person*) · chi fa windsurf · "kee fah windsurf"
(*board*) · il windsurf · "windsurf"
▷ **can I hire a windsurfer?** · posso noleggiare un windsurf? · "posso nolay**djah**ray oon windsurf"

**windsurfing** · il windsurf · "windsurf"
▷ **can I go windsurfing?** · posso andare a fare windsurf? · "posso an**dah**ray a fahray windsurf"

**windy:**
▷ **it's windy** · c'è vento · "che vaynto"
▷ **it's too windy** · c'è troppo vento · "che troppo vaynto"

**wine** · il vino · "veeno"

▷ **this wine is not chilled** · questo vino non è stato messo in fresco · "kwaysto veeno nohn e stahto maysso een fraysko"

▷ **can you recommend a good red wine?** · ci può consigliare un buon vino rosso? · "chee pwo konseel**yah**ray oon bwon veeno rosso"

▷ **a bottle of house wine** · una bottiglia di vino della casa · "oona bot**teel**ya dee veeno **dayl**la kasa"

▷ **red/white wine** · vino rosso/bianco · "veeno rosso/bee**an**ko"
▷ **rosé wine** · vino rosé · "veeno ro**ze**"
▷ **sparkling wine** · lo spumante · "spoo**man**tay"

*ABSOLUTE ESSENTIALS*

| yes (please) | sì (grazie) | "see (gratsyay)" |
|---|---|---|
| no (thank you) | no (grazie) | "no (gratsyay)" |
| hello | salve | "salvay" |
| goodbye | arrivederci | "arreevay**dayr**chee" |

| | | |
|---|---|---|
| ▷ sweet/medium-sweet wine | vino dolce/amabile | "veeno dolchay/ amahbeelay |
| ▷ dry/medium-dry wine | vino secco/demi-sec | "veeno sayko/**de**meesek" |
| wine list | la lista dei vini | "leesta dayee veenee" |
| ▷ may we see the wine list? | possiamo vedere la lista dei vini? | "pos**yah**mo vay**day**ray la leesta dayee veenee" |
| winter | l'inverno (m) | "een**vayr**no" |
| with | con | "kohn" |
| without | senza | "sentsa" |
| woman | la donna | "donna" |
| wood (material) (forest) | il legno il bosco | "laynyo" "bosko" |
| wool | la lana | "lana" |
| word | la parola | "par**o**la" |
| ▷ what is the word for ...? | come si dice...? | "kohmay see deechay" |
| to work (person) (machine, car) | lavorare funzionare | "lavo**rah**ray" "foontsyoh**nah**ray" |
| ▷ where do you work? | dove lavora? | "dovay la**voh**ra" |
| ▷ this does not work | questo non funziona | "kwaysto nohn foonts**yoh**na" |
| ▷ how does this work? | come funziona? | "kohmay foonts**yoh**na" |
| worried | preoccupato preoccupata | "prayokkoo**pah**to" "prayokkoo**pah**ta" |
| worse | peggio | "pedjo" |
| worth: | | |
| ▷ it's worth £100 | vale 100 sterline | "vahlay chento stayr**lee**nay" |
| ▷ how much is it worth? | quanto vale? | "kwanto vahlay" |
| would: | | |
| ▷ I would like to ... | mi piacerebbe ... | "mee peeachay**ray**bay " |

*ABSOLUTE ESSENTIALS*

| | | |
|---|---|---|
| I don't understand | non capisco | "nohn ka**pee**sko" |
| I don't speak Italian | non parlo l'italiano | "nohn parloh leetaly**ah**no" |
| do you speak English? | parla inglese? | "parla eeng**lay**zay" |
| could you help me? | può aiutarmi? | "pwo ayoo**tar**mee" |

| | | |
|---|---|---|
| ▷ we would like to ... | ci piacerebbe ... | "chee peeachay**ray**bay" |
| to **wrap (up)** | incartare | "eenkar**tah**ray" |
| ▷ could you wrap it up for me, please? | può incartarlo per favore? | "pwo eenkahr**tahr**lo payr fa**voh**ray" |
| **wrapping paper** | la carta da pacchi | "karta da **pakk**ee" |
| to **write** | scrivere | "**skree**vayray" |
| ▷ could you write that down, please? | me lo può scrivere, per favore? | "may loh pwo **skree**vayray payr fa**voh**ray" |
| **writing paper** | la carta da lettera | "karta da **lett**ayra" |
| **wrong** | sbagliato | "sbal**yah**to" |
| | sbagliata | "sbal**yah**ta" |
| ▷ sorry, wrong number | scusi, ho sbagliato numero | "skoozee o sbal**yah**to **noo**mayro" |
| ▷ I think you've given me the wrong change | credo che si sia sbagliato nel darmi il resto | "kraydo kay see seea sbal**yah**to nayl darmee eel raysto" |
| ▷ there is something wrong with the brakes/the electrics | c'è qualcosa che non va nei freni/nell'impianto elettrico | "che kwal**ko**za kay nohn va nayee fraynee/ nelleemp**yan**to ay**let**treeko" |
| ▷ what's wrong? | cosa c'è? | "koza che" |
| **yacht** | lo yacht | "yacht" |
| **year** | l'anno (m) | "anno" |
| ▷ this year | quest'anno | "kwest**ann**o" |
| ▷ last year | l'anno scorso | "lanno skorso" |
| ▷ next year | l'anno prossimo | "lanno **pross**eemo" |
| ▷ every year | ogni anno | "onyee anno" |
| **yellow** | giallo | "jallo" |
| | gialla | "jala" |
| **yes** | sì | "see" |
| ▷ yes please | sì, grazie | "see gratsyay" |
| **yesterday** | ieri | "yeree" |

| **yet** | ancora | "an**ko**ra" |
| *(however)* | tuttavia | "toota**vee**a" |
| ▷ **not yet** | non ancora | "non an**ko**ra" |
| **yoghurt** | lo yogurt | "yogurt" |
| **you** | tu | "too" |
| *(plural)* | voi | "**vo**yee" |
| *(polite form)* | lei | "**la**yee" |
| **young** | giovane | "**joh**vanay" |
| **your** | il tuo | "**too**o" |
| | la tua | "**too**a" |
| | i tuoi | "**two**yee" |
| | le tue | "**too**ay" |
| ▷ **where is your mother?** | dov'è la tua mamma? | "**doh**ve la **too**a mamma" |
| *(plural)* | il vostro | "**vo**stro" |
| | la vostra | "**vo**stra" |
| | i vostri | "**vo**stree" |
| | le vostre | "**vo**stray" |
| *(polite form)* | il suo | "**soo**o" |
| | la sua | "**soo**a" |
| | i suoi | "**swo**yee" |
| | le sue | "**soo**ay" |
| ▷ **your keys, madam** | le sue chiavi, signora | "lay **soo**ay kee**ah**vay seen**yo**ra" |
| **yours** | (il) tuo | "**too**o" |
| | (la) tua | "**too**a" |
| | (i) tuoi | "**two**yee" |
| | (le) tue | "**too**ay" |
| *(plural)* | (il) vostro | "**vo**stro" |
| | (la) vostra | "**vo**stra" |
| | (i) vostri | "**vo**stree" |
| | (le) vostre | "**vo**stray" |
| *(polite form)* | (il) suo | "**soo**o" |
| | (la) sua | "**soo**a" |
| | (i) suoi | "**syo**yee" |
| | (le) sue | "**soo**ay" |

ABSOLUTE ESSENTIALS

| **do you have ...?** | avete...? | "a**vay**tay" |
| **is there ...?** | c'è...? | "che" |
| **are there ...?** | ci sono...? | "chee **soh**noh" |
| **how much is ...?** | quanto costa...? | "**kwan**to **kos**ta" |

| **youth hostel** | l'ostello (*m*) della gioventù | "ostello daylla jovayntoo" |
| :-- | :-- | :-- |
| ▷ **is there a youth hostel?** | c'è un ostello della gioventù? | "che oon ostello daylla jovayntoo" |
| **zebra crossing** | il passaggio pedonale | "passadjo paydonahlay" |
| **zero** | lo zero | "dzero" |
| **zip** | la cerniera | "chayrnyera" |
| **zoo** | lo zoo | "dzooh" |

In the pronunciation system used in this book, Italian sounds are represented by spellings of the nearest possible sounds in English. Hence, when you read out the pronunciation – shown in the third column, after the translation – sound the letters as if you were reading an English word. Whenever we think it is not sufficiently clear where to stress a word or phrase, we have used **bold** to highlight the syllable to be stressed. The following notes should help you:

|    | REMARKS | EXAMPLE | PRONUNCIATION |
|----|---------|---------|---------------|
| *ay* | As in *day* | **dei** | *dayee* |
| *ah* | As *a* in *father* | **prendiamo** | *prend**yah**mo* |
| *e* | As in *bed* | **letto** | *letto* |
| *oh* | As in *go, low* | **sono** | *sohnoh* |
| *y* | As in *yet* | **aiuto** | *ayooto* |

Spelling in Italian is very regular and, with a little practice, you will soon be able to pronounce Italian words from their spelling alone. The only letters which may cause problems are:

| | | | |
|---|---|---|---|
| **i** | As *ee* in *meet* | **vino** | *veeno* |
| | Or as *y* in *yet* | **aiuto** | *ayooto* |
| **u** | As *oo* in *boot* | **luna** | *loona* |
| | Or as *w* in *will* | **buon** | *bwon* |
| **c** | Before *e, i* as *ch* in *chat* | **centro** | *chentro* |
| | Before *a, o, u* as *c* in *cat* | **cosa** | *koza* |
| **ch** | As *c* in *cat* | **chi** | *kee* |
| **g** | Before *e, i* as in *gin* | **giorno** | *jorno* |
| | Before *a, h, o, u* as in *get* | **regalo** | *raygahlo* |
| **gl** | As *lli* in *million* | **figlio** | *feelyo* |
| **gn** | As *ni* in *onion* | **bisogno** | *beezohnyo* |
| **h** | Silent | **ho** | *o* |
| **sc** | Before *e, i*, as *sh* in *shop* | **uscita** | *oosheeta* |
| | Before *a, o, u* as in *scar* | **capisco** | *ka**pee**sko* |
| **z** | As *ts* in *cats* or *ds* in *rods* | **senza** | *sentsa* |
| | | **mezzo** | *medzzo* |

1

In the weight and length charts the middle figure can be either metric or imperial. Thus 3.3 feet = 1 metre, 1 foot = 0.3 metres, and so on.

| feet | | metres | inches | | cm | lbs | | kg |
|---|---|---|---|---|---|---|---|---|
| 3.3 | 1 | 0.3 | 0.39 | 1 | 2.54 | 2.2 | 1 | 0.45 |
| 6.6 | 2 | 0.61 | 0.79 | 2 | 5.08 | 4.4 | 2 | 0.91 |
| 9.9 | 3 | 0.91 | 1.18 | 3 | 7.62 | 6.6 | 3 | 1.4 |
| 13.1 | 4 | 1.22 | 1.57 | 4 | 10.6 | 8.8 | 4 | 1.8 |
| 16.4 | 5 | 1.52 | 1.97 | 5 | 12.7 | 11.0 | 5 | 2.2 |
| 19.7 | 6 | 1.83 | 2.36 | 6 | 15.2 | 13.2 | 6 | 2.7 |
| 23.0 | 7 | 2.13 | 2.76 | 7 | 17.8 | 15.4 | 7 | 3.2 |
| 26.2 | 8 | 2.44 | 3.15 | 8 | 20.3 | 17.6 | 8 | 3.6 |
| 29.5 | 9 | 2.74 | 3.54 | 9 | 22.9 | 19.8 | 9 | 4.1 |
| 32.9 | 10 | 3.05 | 3.9 | 10 | 25.4 | 22.0 | 10 | 4.5 |
| | | | 4.3 | 11 | 27.9 | | | |
| | | | 4.7 | 12 | 30.1 | | | |

| °C | 0 | 5 | 10 | 15 | 17 | 20 | 22 | 24 | 26 | 28 | 30 | 35 | 37 | 38 | 40 | 50 | 100 |
|---|---|---|---|---|---|---|---|---|---|---|---|---|---|---|---|---|---|
| °F | 32 | 41 | 50 | 59 | 63 | 68 | 72 | 75 | 79 | 82 | 86 | 95 | 98.4 | 100 | 104 | 122 | 212 |

| Km | 10 | 20 | 30 | 40 | 50 | 60 | 70 | 80 | 90 | 100 | 110 | 120 |
|---|---|---|---|---|---|---|---|---|---|---|---|---|
| Miles | 6.2 | 12.4 | 18.6 | 24.9 | 31.0 | 37.3 | 43.5 | 49.7 | 56.0 | 62.0 | 68.3 | 74.6 |

## Tyre pressures

| lb/sq in | 15 | 18 | 20 | 22 | 24 | 26 | 28 | 30 | 33 | 35 |
|---|---|---|---|---|---|---|---|---|---|---|
| kg/sq cm | 1.1 | 1.3 | 1.4 | 1.5 | 1.7 | 1.8 | 2.0 | 2.1 | 2.3 | 2.5 |

## Liquids

| gallons | 1.1 | 2.2 | 3.3 | 4.4 | 5.5 | pints | 0.44 | 0.88 | 1.76 |
|---|---|---|---|---|---|---|---|---|---|
| litres | 5 | 10 | 15 | 20 | 25 | litres | 0.25 | 0.5 | 1 |

## CAR PARTS

| accelerator | l'acceleratore (m) | "achaylayratohray" |
|---|---|---|
| air conditioning | l'aria (f) condizionata | "ahreea kohndeetsyohnahta" |
| antifreeze | l'antigelo (m) | "anteejaylo" |
| automatic | automatico | "owtomateeko" |
| | automatica | "owtomateeka" |
| battery | la batteria | "battayreea" |
| boot | il portabagagli | "portahbagalyee" |
| brake fluid | l'olio (m) per i freni | "olyo payr ee fraynee" |
| brakes | i freni | "fraynee" |
| car | la macchina | "makkeena" |
| carburettor | il carburatore | "kahrbooratohray" |
| car number | il numero di targa | "noomayro dee tahrga" |
| chain | la catena | "katayna" |
| de-ice | liberare dal ghiaccio | "leebayrahray dal geeatcho" |
| diesel | il gasolio | "gazolyo" |
| engine | il motore | "motohray" |
| exhaust pipe | il tubo di scappamento | "toobo dee skappamaynto" |
| fan belt | la cinghia del ventilatore | "cheengya dayl vaynteelatohray" |
| fuel pump | la pompa di benzina | "pompa dee bayndzeena" |
| garage | l'officina (f) | "offeecheena" |
| gear | la marcia | "mahrcha" |
| headlights | i fari | "fahree" |
| indicator | la freccia | "fraycha" |
| jack | il cricco | "kreekko" |
| jump leads | i cavi per far partire la macchina | "kahvee payr fahr parteeray la makkeena" |
| leak | la perdita | "payrdeeta" |
| luggage rack | il portabagagli | "portahbagalyee" |
| oil filter | il filtro dell'olio | "feeltro dayllolyo" |
| petrol | la benzina | "bayndzeena" |
| points | le puntine | "poonteenay" |
| radiator | il radiatore | "radeeyahtohray" |
| roof rack | il portabagagli | "portahbagalyee" |
| shock absorber | l'ammortizzatore (m) | "ammorteedzzatohray" |
| spare wheel | la ruota di scorta | "rwota dee skorta" |
| spark plug | la candela | "kandayla" |
| speedometer | il tachimetro | "takeemaytro" |
| suspension | la sospensione | "sospaynsyohnay" |
| tyre | la gomma | "gohmma" |
| tyre pressure | la pressione delle gomme | "praysyohnay dayllay gohmmay" |
| warning triangle | il triangolo | "treeangolo" |
| windscreen | il parabrezza | "parabraydzza" |
| windscreen washers | i lavacristalli | "lavakreestahllee" |
| windscreen wiper | il tergicristallo | "tayrjeekreestahllo" |

## COLOURS

| black | nero | "nayro" |
| | nera | "nayra" |
| blue | blu | "bloo" |
| brown | marrone | "marrohnay" |
| colour | il colore | "kolohray" |
| dark | scuro | "skooro" |
| | scura | "skoora" |
| green | verde | "vayrday" |
| grey | grigio | "greejo" |
| | grigia | "greeja" |
| light | chiaro | "keearo" |
| | chiara | "keeara" |
| navy blue | il blu scooro | "bloo skooro" |
| orange | arancione | "aranchohnay" |
| pink | rosa | "roza" |
| purple | viola | "veeola" |
| red | rosso | "rosso" |
| | rossa | "rossa" |
| white | bianco | "beeanko" |
| | bianca | "beeanka" |
| yellow | giallo | "jallo" |
| | gialla | "jalla" |

## COUNTRIES

| America | l'America *(f)* | "**amay**reeka" |
|---|---|---|
| Australia | l'Australia *(f)* | "ow**strahl**ya" |
| Austria | l'Austria *(f)* | "**ows**treeya" |
| Belgium | il Belgio | "**bel**jo" |
| Britain | la Gran Bretagna | "gran bray**tan**ya" |
| Canada | il Canada | "**ka**nada" |
| England | l'Inghilterra *(f)* | "eengeel**terra**" |
| Europe | l'Europa *(f)* | "ayoo**ro**pa" |
| France | la Francia | "**fran**cha" |
| Germany | la Germania | "jayr**mahn**ya" |
| Greece | la Grecia | "**gray**cha" |
| Ireland | l'Irlanda *(f)* | "eer**lan**da" |
| Italy | l'Italia *(f)* | "ee**tal**ya" |
| Luxembourg | il Lussemburgo | "loossem**boor**go" |
| New Zealand | la Nuova Zelanda | "nwova dzay**lan**da" |
| Northern Ireland | l'Irlanda *(f)* del Nord | "eer**lan**da dayl nord" |
| Portugal | il Portogallo | "porto**gah**llo" |
| Scotland | la Scozia | "**skots**ya" |
| Spain | la Spagna | "**span**ya" |
| Switzerland | la Svizzera | "**zveet**sayra" |
| United States | gli Stati Uniti | "**stah**tee oo**nee**tee" |
| USA | gli USA | "**oo**sa" |
| Wales | il Galles | "**gal**les" |

7

## DRINKS

| | | |
|---|---|---|
| alcohol | l'alcool *(m)* | "alko**ol**" |
| alcoholic | alcolico | "al**ko**leeko" |
| | alcolica | "al**ko**leeka" |
| apéritif | l'aperitivo *(m)* | "apayree**tee**vo" |
| beer | la birra | "**beer**ra" |
| brandy | brandy | "brandy" |
| champagne | lo champagne | "shang**panye**" |
| cider | il sidro | "**seedro**" |
| cocktail | il cocktail | "cocktail" |
| cocoa | il cacao | "ka**ka**o" |
| coffee | il caffè | "**kaffe**" |
| coke® | la coca | "**ko**ka" |
| draught beer | la birra alla spina | "**beer**ra alla **speena**" |
| drinking chocolate | la cioccolata calda | "chokko**lah**ta kalda" |
| drinking water | l'acqua *(f)* potabile | "**akwa** po**tah**beelay" |
| fruit juice | il succo di frutta | "**sookko** dee **frootta**" |
| gin | il gin | "jeen" |
| gin and tonic | il gin tonic | "jeen **toneek**" |
| grapefruit juice | il succo di pompelmo | "**sookkho** dee pom**pelmo**" |
| juice | il succo | "**sookko**" |
| lager | la birra chiara | "**beer**ra kee**ara**" |
| lemonade | la limonata | "leemo**nah**ta" |
| lemon tea | il tè al limone | "te al lee**moh**nay" |
| liqueur | il liquore | "leek**woh**ray" |
| milk | il latte | "**lahttay**" |
| milkshake | il frappé | "frap**pay**" |
| mineral water | l'acqua *(f)* minerale | "**akwa** meenay**rah**lay" |
| non-alcoholic | analcolico | "anal**ko**leeko" |
| | analcolica | "anal**ko**leeka" |
| orange juice | il succo d'arancia | "**sookko** da**ran**cha" |
| rosé (wine) | il (vino) rosé | "(**veeno**) ro**zay**" |
| shandy | la birra con gassosa | "**beer**ra kohn gas**sohza**" |
| sherry | lo sherry | "sherry" |
| skimmed milk | il latte scremato | "**lattay** skray**mahto**" |
| soda | la soda | "**soda**" |
| soft drink | l'analcolico *(m)* | "anal**ko**leekoh" |
| spirits | i liquori | "leek**woh**ree" |
| squash | la spremuta | "spray**moo**ta" |
| tea | il tè | "te" |
| tomato juice | il succo di pomodoro | "**sookko** dee pomo**do**ro" |
| tonic water | l'acqua *(f)* tonica | "**akwa** **toneeka**" |
| vermouth | il vermut | "vayr**moot**" |
| vodka | la vodka | "vodka" |
| whisky | il whisky | "**wheeskee**" |
| wine | il vino | "**veeno**" |

# FISH AND SEAFOOD

|  |  |  |
|---|---|---|
| anchovy | l'acciuga *(f)* | "ah**choo**ga" |
| caviar | il caviale | "ka**vya**lay" |
| cod | il merluzzo | "mayr**loo**tso" |
| crab | il granchio | "**gran**kyo" |
| fish | il pesce | "**pay**shay" |
| haddock | l'eglefino *(m)* | "ayglay**fee**no" |
| hake | il nasello | "na**zay**llo" |
| herring | l'aringa *(f)* | "a**reen**ga" |
| lobster | l'aragosta *(f)* | "ara**gos**ta" |
| mackerel | lo sgombro | "**sgom**bro" |
| mussels | le cozze | "**kot**ssay" |
| oyster | l'ostrica *(f)* | "**os**treeka" |
| prawn | il gambero | "**gam**bayro" |
| salmon | il salmone | "sal**moh**nay" |
| sardine | la sardina | "sar**dee**na" |
| scallop | la cappa santa | "**kap**pa **san**ta" |
| scampi | gli scampi | "**skam**pee" |
| seafood | i frutti di mare | "**froot**tee dee **mah**ray" |
| shellfish | i frutti di mare | "**froot**tee dee **mah**ray" |
| shrimps | i gamberetti | "gambay**rayt**tee" |
| sole | la sogliola | "**sohl**yohla" |
| trout | la trota | "**troh**ta" |
| tuna | il tonno | "**ton**no" |

## FRUIT AND NUTS

| | | |
|---|---|---|
| almond | la mandorla | "**man**dorla" |
| apple | la mela | "**may**la" |
| apricot | l'albicocca (f) | "albee**kok**ka" |
| banana | la banana | "ba**nan**a" |
| blackcurrant | il ribes nero | "**ree**bes **nay**ro" |
| cherries | le ciliegie | "cheel**yay**jay" |
| chestnut | la castagna | "kas**tan**ya" |
| coconut | la noce di cocco | "**noh**chay dee **kok**ko" |
| currant | l'uva sultanina (f) | "**oo**vah soolta**nee**na" |
| date | il dattero | "**dat**tayro" |
| fig | il fico | "**fee**ko" |
| fruit | la frutta | "**froot**ta" |
| grapefruit | il pompelmo | "pom**pel**mo" |
| grapes | l'uva (f) | "**oo**va" |
| hazelnut | la nocciola | "not**cho**la" |
| lemon | il limone | "lee**moh**nay" |
| lime | la limetta | "lee**mayt**ta" |
| melon | il melone | "may**loh**nay" |
| nut | la noce | "**noh**chay" |
| olives | le olive | "o**lee**vay" |
| orange | l'arancia (f) | "a**ran**cha" |
| peaches | le pesche | "**pes**kay" |
| peanuts | le arachidi | "a**ra**keedee" |
| pears | le pere | "**pay**ray" |
| pineapple | l'ananas (m) | "**a**nanas" |
| pistachio | il pistacchio | "pees**tahk**yo" |
| plum | la susina | "soo**see**na" |
| prunes | le prugne | "**proon**yay" |
| raisin | l'uvetta (f) | "oo**vayt**ta" |
| raspberries | i lamponi | "lam**poh**nee" |
| strawberries | le fragole | "**frah**golay" |
| walnut | la noce | "**noh**chay" |
| watermelon | l'anguria (f) | "an**goo**reea" |

## MEATS

| bacon | la pancetta | "pan**chaytt**a" |
|---|---|---|
| beef | il manzo | "**mandzo**" |
| beefburger | l'hamburger *(m)* | "am**boor**gayr" |
| breast | il petto | "**paytto**" |
| cheeseburger | il cheeseburger | "**cheez**boorgayr" |
| chicken | il pollo | "**pohllo**" |
| chop | la costoletta | "kostoh**laytt**a" |
| cold meat | gli affettati | "affayt**tah**tee" |
| duck | l'anatra *(f)* | "**anatra**" |
| goose | l'oca *(f)* | "**oka**" |
| ham | il prosciutto | "pro**shoott**o" |
| hamburger | l'hamburger *(m)* | "am**boor**gayr" |
| kidneys | i rognoni | "ron**yoh**nee" |
| liver | il fegato | "**fay**gato" |
| meat | la carne | "**karnay**" |
| mince | la carne macinata | "**karnay** machee**nah**ta" |
| mutton | il montone | "mon**toh**nay" |
| pâté | il pâté | "pa**tay**" |
| pheasant | il fagiano | "fadj**ah**no" |
| pork | il maiale | "ma**yah**lay" |
| rabbit | il coniglio | "ko**neel**yo" |
| salami | il salami | "sa**lah**mee" |
| sausage | la salsiccia | "sal**seet**cha" |
| steak | la bistecca | "bee**stayk**kha" |
| stew | lo stufato | "stoo**fah**to" |
| turkey | il tacchino | "tak**kee**no" |
| veal | il vitello | "vee**tayl**lo" |

## SHOPS

| | | |
|---|---|---|
| baker's | la panetteria | "panayttay**ree**a" |
| barber | il barbiere | "barb**yer**ay" |
| bookshop | la libreria | "leebray**ree**a" |
| butcher | il macellaio | "machay**lla**yo" |
| café | il caffè | "ka**ffe**" |
| chemist's | la farmacia | "farma**chee**a" |
| dry-cleaner's | la tintoria | "teento**ree**a" |
| duty-free shop | il duty free | "duty free" |
| grocer's | il negozio di alimentari | "nay**gots**yo dee aleemayn**tah**ree" |
| hairdresser | il parrucchiere | "parrook**yer**ay" |
| | la parrucchiera | "parrook**yer**a" |
| health food shop | il negozio di prodotti dietetici | "nay**gots**yo dee pro**doht**tee deeay**tay**teechee" |
| ironmonger's | il negozio di ferramenta | "nay**gots**yo dee ferra**mayn**ta" |
| jeweller's (shop) | la gioielleria | "joyayllay**ree**a" |
| launderette | la lavanderia automatica | "lavanday**ree**a owto**ma**teeka" |
| market | il mercato | "mayr**kah**to" |
| newsagent | il giornalaio | "jorna**la**yo" |
| post office | l'ufficio (m) postale | "oo**ffee**cho po**stah**lay" |
| shop | il negozio | "nay**gots**yo" |
| stationer's | la cartoleria | "kartolay**ree**a" |
| supermarket | il supermercato | "soopayrmayr**kah**to" |
| tobacconist | il tabaccaio | "tabak**ka**yo" |
| toy shop | il negozio di giocattoli | "nay**gots**yo dee jo**kat**tolee" |

# VEGETABLES

| | | |
|---|---|---|
| **artichoke** | il carciofo | "kar**choh**fo" |
| **asparagus** | gli asparagi | "a**spa**rajee" |
| **aubergine** | la melanzana | "maylant**sah**na" |
| **avocado** | l'avocado *(m)* | "avo**kah**do" |
| **beans** | i fagioli | "fa**jo**lee" |
| **beetroot** | la barbabietola | "bahrbab**ye**tola" |
| **broccoli** | i broccoli | "**broh**kohlee" |
| **Brussels sprouts** | i cavoletti di Bruxelles | "kahvo**layt**tee dee brooksel" |
| **cabbage** | il cavolo | "**kah**volo" |
| **carrots** | le carote | "ka**ro**tay" |
| **cauliflower** | il cavolfiore | "kahvolf**yoh**ray" |
| **celery** | il sedano | "**se**dano" |
| **chives** | l'erba *(f)* cipollina | "ayrba cheepoh**lee**na" |
| **courgettes** | gli zucchini | "tsook**kee**nee" |
| **cucumber** | il cetriolo | "chaytree**o**lo" |
| **French beans** | i fagiolini | "fajo**lee**nee" |
| **garlic** | l'aglio *(m)* | "**a**lyo" |
| **green pepper** | il peperone verde | "paypay**roh**nay vayrday" |
| **onions** | le cipolle | "chee**poh**llay" |
| **parsley** | il prezzemolo | "prayts**se**molo" |
| **peas** | i piselli | "pee**zel**lee" |
| **pepper** | il peperone | "paypay**roh**nay" |
| **potatoes** | le patate | "pa**tah**tay" |
| **radishes** | i ravanelli | "rava**nayl**lee" |
| **spinach** | gli spinaci | "spee**na**chee" |
| **spring onion** | la cipollina | "cheepoh**llee**na" |
| **tomato** | il pomodoro | "pomo**do**ro" |
| **turnip** | la rapa | "**rah**pa" |
| **vegan** | vegetaliano | "vayjaytal**yah**no" |
| | vegetaliana | "vayjaytal**yah**na" |
| **vegetables** | le verdure | "vayr**doo**ray" |
| **vegetarian** | vegetariano | "vayjaytar**jah**no" |
| | vegetariana | "vayjaytar**jah**na" |

# ITALIAN-ENGLISH

## A

**a** at; in; to; **a 30 chilometri** 30 kilometres away; **due volte al giorno** twice a day; **uno a uno** one by one

**AAST** (abbreviation of **azienda autonoma di soggiorno e turismo**) Italian tourist board

**abbacchio** m baby lamb

**abbaglianti** mpl: **accendere gli abbaglianti** to put one's headlights on full beam

**abbagliare** to dazzle

**abbassare** to lower; to turn down; to dip (headlights)

**abbastanza** enough; quite

**abbattere** to knock down

**abbazia** f abbey

**abbigliamento** m clothes; **abbigliamento intimo** underwear; **abbigliamento sportivo** casual wear; **abbigliamento uomo/donna/bambino** men's/ladies/children's wear

**abboccato(a)** semi-sweet (wine)

**abbonamento** m subscription; season ticket; **spedizione in abbonamento** postal subscription

**abbonato(a)** m/f subscriber; season ticket holder

**abbozzo** m sketch; draft

**abbracciare** to embrace; to hug

**abbronzante** m suntan oil/cream

**abbronzarsi** to tan

**abbronzatura** f suntan

**abete** m fir (tree)

**abitante** m/f inhabitant

**abitare** to live (reside); to live in

**abito** m dress; suit; **abito da sera** evening dress (woman's)

**abituale** usual

**abituarsi a** to get used to

**abitudine** f habit

**abside** f apse

**abuso** m: **ogni abuso sarà punito** penalty for improper use

**accadere** to happen

**accamparsi** to camp

**accanto** nearby; **accanto a** beside

**accappatoio** m bathrobe

**accelerare** to accelerate; to speed up

**acceleratore** m accelerator

**accendere** to turn on; to light; **vietato accendere fuochi** do not light a fire

**accendino** m cigarette lighter

**accensione** f ignition; **l'accensione della luce rossa segnala il fuori servizio** machine not in use when red light shows

**accento** m accent; stress

**acceso(a)** on

**accesso** m access; fit; **divieto di accesso** no entry; **divieto di accesso ai non addetti ai lavori** authorized personnel only

**accessori** mpl accessories

**accettare** to accept; **non si accettano assegni** we

do not accept cheques

**accettazione** f acceptance; reception; check-in; **accettazione bagagli** check-in

**acchiappare** to catch

**acciaio** m steel

**acciuga** f anchovy

**accoglienza** f welcome

**accogliere** to receive (guest); to welcome

**accomodarsi** to make oneself comfortable

**accompagnare** to escort; to accompany

**accompagnatore** m escort; **accompagnatore turistico** courier

**acconciatura** f hairstyle

**acconto** m down payment

**accorciare** to shorten

**accordare** to tune; to grant

**accordo** m agreement; **essere d'accordo** to agree

**accostare: accostare (a)** to bring near (to); to draw up (at); **accostare la banconota a destra** place the banknote on the right

**accreditare** to credit

**accusa** f charge; accusation

**acerbo(a)** unripe; sour

**aceto** m vinegar; **aceto di vino** wine vinegar; **aceto balsamico** balsamic vinegar

**ACI** ≈ A.A.

**acido(a)** acid; sour

**acqua** f water; **acqua corrente** running water; **acqua distillata** distilled water; **acqua minerale** mineral water; **acqua potabile** drinking water;

**acqua tonica** tonic water; **fare acqua** to leak (boat)
**acquaio** m sink
**acquazzone** m shower (rain)
**acquedotto** m aqueduct
**acquirente** m/f purchaser
**acquistare** to acquire
**acquisti** mpl shopping
**acquisto** m purchase
**acuto(a)** sharp; acute
**adattare** to adapt
**adatto(a)** suitable
**addebitare** to debit
**addetto(a): personale addetto** relevant staff
**addobbi** mpl decorations
**addome** m abdomen
**addormentato(a)** asleep
**adesione** f adhesion; agreement
**adolescente** m/f teenager
**Adriatico** m Adriatic (Sea)
**adulto(a)** m/f adult
**aereo** m plane; aircraft; **in aereo** by plane; on the plane
**aereo(a)** air; **per via aerea** by air
**aeromobile** m aircraft
**aeroplano** m aeroplane
**aeroporto** m airport
**aeroportuale: formalità aeroportuali** fpl airport formalities
**afa** f closeness
**affamato(a)** starving
**affare** m affair (matter); deal; **affari** business; **per affari** on business
**affascinante** fascinating; glamorous
**affatto** at all
**afferrare** to seize; to grab
**affettato** m (sliced) cold meat
**affetto** m affection
**affettuoso(a)** affectionate
**affidabilità** f reliability
**affilato(a)** sharp
**affissione f: divieto di affissione** post no bills
**affittanze** fpl: **vendite e affittanze** property for sale or rent

**affittare** to rent; to let
**affittasi** to let
**affitto** m lease; rent; hire; **affitto ombrelloni** beach umbrellas for hire
**affogato(a)** drowned; poached (egg)
**affollato(a)** crowded
**affondare** to sink
**affrancare** to stamp (letter)
**affresco** m fresco
**affrettarsi** to hurry
**affrontare** to tackle
**affumicato(a)** smoked
**afoso(a)** close (stuffy)
**agenda** f diary
**agente** m agent; broker; **agente immobiliare** estate agent; **agente marittimo** shipping agent; **agente di polizia** police officer; **agente verificatore** ticket inspector; **agente di viaggi** travel agent; **agenti portuali** port inspectors
**agenzia** f agency; **agenzia immobiliare** estate agent's (office); **agenzia di navigazione** shipping agency; **agenzia di viaggi** travel agency; **agenzia viaggiatori Ferrovie dello Stato** rail travel agency
**aggiornato(a)** up-to-date; adjourned
**aggiungere** to add
**aggiustare** to repair; to adjust
**agire** to act
**agitare** to shake
**agitato(a)** rough; restless; upset
**agli = a + gli**
**aglio** m garlic
**agnello** m lamb; **agnello arrosto** roast lamb
**agnolotti** mpl squares or circles of pasta with meat filling
**ago** m needle
**agosto** m August
**agricolo(a)** agricultural
**agricoltore** m farmer
**agrodolce: in agrodolce** in a sweet and sour sauce

**ai = a + i**
**aia** f farmyard
**aiuola** f flowerbed; **è vietato calpestare le aiuole** keep off the grass
**aiutare** to help
**aiuto** m help
**ala** f wing
**alba** f dawn
**albergatore** m hotelier
**alberghiero(a): catena alberghiera** hotel chain
**albergo** m hotel
**albero** m tree; mast; **albero di Natale** Christmas tree; **alberi in banchina** overhanging trees
**albicocca** f apricot
**alcolici** mpl liquor
**alcolico(a)** alcoholic (drink)
**alcolizzato(a)** m/f alcoholic
**alcool** m alcohol; **alcool denaturato** methylated spirits
**alcuni(e)** some
**alcuno(a)** any
**alghe** fpl seaweed
**aliante** m glider
**alici: filetti di alici** mpl anchovy fillets
**alimentari** mpl: **negozio di alimentari** grocer's (shop)
**aliscafo** m hydrofoil
**allacciare** to fasten; **allacciare la cintura di sicurezza** to fasten one's seat belt
**allappante** slightly tart (wine)
**allarme** m alarm; **allarme antincendio** fire alarm
**alleanza** f alliance
**allegare** to enclose
**allegro(a)** cheerful
**allenamento** m training
**allenatore** m coach (instructor)
**allergia** f allergy
**allestimento m: mostra/vetrina in allestimento** exhibition/window display in preparation
**allevamento** m rearing; stock farm

**alleviare** to ease
**alloggiare** to put up (*accommodate*); to live (*reside*)
**alloggio** *m* lodgings; accommodation
**allora** then; **d'allora in poi** from then on
**allungare** to lengthen
**almeno** at least
**Alpi** *fpl* Alps
**alpinismo** *m* mountaineering
**alt: alt dogana/polizia** stop; customs/police
**altalena** *f* swing; seesaw
**altare** *m* altar
**altezza** *f* height
**altitudine** *f* altitude
**alto** high; aloud; **in alto** high; up, upward(s)
**alto(a)** high; tall; **alta stagione** high season
**altoparlante** *m* loudspeaker
**altopiano** *m* plateau
**altrimenti** otherwise
**altro(a)** other
**altrove** somewhere else
**alunno(a)** *m/f* pupil
**alzare** to raise; to turn up
**alzarsi** to get up; stand up; to rise
**amabile** sweet (*wine*)
**amaca** *f* hammock
**amante** *m/f* lover; mistress
**amare** to love
**amaro(a)** bitter
**amarognolo(a)** slightly bitter
**ambasciata** *f* embassy
**ambasciatore** *m* ambassador
**ambedue** both
**ambiente** *m* environment
**ambulanza** *f* ambulance
**ambulatorio** *m* consulting room; **ambulatorio comunale** health centre
**America** *f* America; **America del Sud** South America; **America del Nord** North America; **America Latina** Latin America

**amianto** *m* asbestos
**amichevole** friendly
**amico(a)** *m/f* friend
**amido** *m* starch
**ammaccatura** *f* dent; bruise
**ammaestrare** to train (*animal*)
**ammandorlato(a): vino ammandorlato** wine with a flavour of almonds
**amministrazione** *f* administration; **amministrazione statale** civil service
**ammiraglia** *f*: **(nave) ammiraglia** flagship
**ammirare** to admire
**ammobiliare** to furnish
**ammontare a** to amount to
**ammorbidente** *m* softener
**ammortizzatore** *m* shock absorber
**amo** *m* (fish) hook
**amore** *m* love
**ampère** *m* amp
**ampio(a)** loose; wide; full-bodied (*wine*)
**amplificatore** *m* amplifier
**analcolico(a)** nonalcoholic; soft (*drink*)
**analisi** *f* analysis; test; **analisi cliniche** medical tests
**analizzare** to analyse
**ananas** *m* pineapple
**anatra** *f* duck; **anatra arrosto** roast duck; **anatra in agrodolce** duck in sweet and sour sauce
**anca** *f* hip
**anche** too; also; even
**ancora**[1] still; yet; again; **ancora del formaggio** more cheese
**ancora**[2] *f* anchor
**andare** to go; **andiamo** let's go; **andare in macchina** to drive; **andare in bicicletta** to cycle; **andarsene** to go away
**anello** *m* ring; **anello di fidanzamento** engagement

ring; **anello di fondo** cross-country skiing circuit
**anfiteatro** *m* amphitheatre
**angolo** *m* corner; angle
**angoscia** *f* distress
**anguilla** *f* eel; **anguilla in umido** eel stew
**anguria** *f* watermelon
**anima** *f* soul
**animale** *m* animal; **animale domestico** pet
**animato(a)** *adj* busy (*place*)
**animatore** *m* organizer; compère
**animazione** *f*: **programma di animazione** organized entertainment; **animazione sportiva e ricreativa** organized sports and recreational activities
**animelle** *fpl* sweetbreads
**annaffiare** to water; to wash down (*meal*)
**annata** *f* vintage; year; **vino d'annata** vintage wine
**annegare** to drown
**anno** *m* year; **quanti anni ha?** how old are you?
**annodare** to tie; to knot
**annoiare** to bore
**annotare** to write down
**annotazioni** *fpl* notes
**annullamento** *m* cancellation; **spese per l'annullamento del servizio** cancellation fee
**annullare** to cancel
**annuncio** *m* announcement; advertisement
**ansia** *f* anxiety
**antenato(a)** *m/f* ancestor
**antenna** *f* aerial; antenna; **antenna trasmittente** radio mast
**anteprima** *f* preview
**anteriore** front
**antiappannante** *m* demister
**antibiotico** *m* antibiotic
**antichità** *f* antique; antiquity
**anticipare** to advance (*money*)
**anticipo** *m* advance (*loan*); **in anticipo** in advance;

early
**antico(a)** antique; ancient
**anticoncezionale** *m* contraceptive
**anticongelante** *m* antifreeze
**antifurto** *n* anti-theft device
**antigelo** *m* antifreeze; de-icer
**antincendio: bombola antincendio** *f* fire extinguisher
**antipasto** *m* hors d'œuvre; **antipasto misto** mixed hors d'œuvre, usually containing cured hams and pickles; **antipasto di pesce** fish hors d'œuvre; **antipasto di frutti di mare** seafood starter
**antiquario** *m* antique dealer
**antiquato(a)** out of date; old-fashioned
**antisettico** *m* antiseptic
**antistaminico** *m* antihistamine
**ape** *f* bee
**aperitivo** *m* apéritif
**aperto(a)** open; on; **all'aperto** in the open (air); open-air
**apertura: apertura a spinta** push to open
**apparecchiare** to lay (table)
**apparecchiatura** *f* equipment; device; **apparecchiatura fotografica** photographic equipment
**apparecchio** *m* appliance; **apparecchio acustico** hearing aid; **apparecchi pubblici** public telephones
**apparentemente** apparently
**apparire** to appear
**appartamento** *m* flat, apartment
**appartenere a** to belong to
**appassionato(a)** keen
**appena** scarcely; just

**appendere** to hang
**appendicite** *f* appendicitis
**appetito** *m* appetite; **buon appetito!** enjoy your meal!
**appezzamento** *m* plot (of land)
**appiccicoso(a)** sticky
**applaudire** to clap; to cheer
**appoggiarsi: appoggiarsi a** to lean against; **è pericoloso appoggiarsi** do not lean against the door(s)
**apposta** on purpose; specially
**apprendista** *m/f* apprentice; trainee
**apprezzare** to appreciate
**appropriato(a)** suitable
**approssimativamente** roughly
**approvare** to approve of
**approvazione** *f* approval
**appuntamento** *m* appointment; date
**apribottiglie** *m* bottle opener
**aprile** *m* April
**aprire** to open; to turn on; **non aprire prima che il treno sia fermo** do not open while the train is in motion
**apriscatole** *m* can-opener
**APT** abbreviation of **azienda di promozione turistica**
**aquila** *f* eagle
**aquilone** *m* kite
**arachide** *f* peanut
**aragosta** *f* lobster
**arancia** *f* orange
**aranciata** *f* orangeade
**arancino** *m* rice croquette stuffed with meat
**arancione** orange
**arbitro** *m* umpire; referee
**arbusto** *m* shrub
**archeologico(a): museo archeologico** archaeological museum
**architettura** *f* architecture
**archivio** *m* file; filing cabinet
**arco** *m* arch; bow (for arrow, violin)

*arrow, violin)*
**ardere** to burn
**area** *f* area; **area di parcheggio** parking area; **area di servizio** service area
**argenteria** *f* silverware
**argento** *m* silver
**argilla** *f* clay
**argomento** *m* topic
**aria** *f* air; tune; **con aria condizionata** air-conditioned; **all'aria aperta** in the open (air); outdoor
**arieggiare** to air
**aringa** *f* herring
**arista** *f* chine of pork
**arma** *f* weapon; **arma da fuoco** firearm
**armadietto** *m* locker
**armadio** *m* cupboard; wardrobe
**armeria** *f* armoury; collection of arms
**armi** *fpl* arms (*weapons*)
**arnese** *m* tool
**aromi** *mpl* seasoning; herbs
**arpa** *f* harp
**arrabbiato(a)** angry
**arrampicarsi su** to climb (*tree, wall*)
**arrangiarsi** to manage
**arredare** to furnish
**arredato(a): appartamento arredato** furnished flat
**arredo** *m*: **arredo bagno** bathroom furnishings
**arretrati** *mpl* arrears
**arrivare** to arrive; **arrivare a** to reach
**arrivederci** goodbye
**arrivo** *m* arrival; **arrivi/partenze nazionali** domestic arrivals/departures; **arrivi/partenze internazionali** international arrivals/departures
**arrostire** to roast
**arrosto** *m* roast meat; **arrosto di manzo/tacchino/vitello** roast beef/turkey/veal

**arrugginirsi** to rust
**arte** f art; craft
**articolo** m article; **articoli da pesca** fishing equipment; **articoli da spiaggia** beachwear and accessories; **articoli sportivi** sports goods; **articoli da toeletta** toiletries; **articoli di vetro** glassware
**artificiale** artificial; man-made
**artigiano** m craftsman
**artista** m/f artist
**artrite** f arthritis
**ascensore** m lift
**asciugacapelli** m hair-drier
**asciugamano** m towel
**asciugare** to dry; to wipe
**asciugatoio** m hair-drier (at swimming pool)
**asciutto(a)** dry
**ascoltare** to listen
**asilo d'infanzia** m nursery school
**asino** m donkey
**asma** f asthma
**asparagi** mpl asparagus
**aspettare** to wait; to wait for; to expect
**aspetto** m appearance
**aspirapolvere** m vacuum cleaner
**aspirina** f aspirin
**aspro(a)** sharp; sour
**assaggiare** to taste
**assalire** to attack
**assassino** m killer
**asse¹** m axle
**asse²** f board; **asse da stiro** ironing board
**assegnare** to allocate
**assegno** m cheque; allowance (state payment)
**assente** absent
**assetato(a)** thirsty
**assicurare** to assure; to insure
**assicurarsi** to make sure; to insure oneself
**assicurazione** f insurance; **assicurazione contro terzi** third party insurance; **assicurazione casco**

comprehensive insurance
**assistente** m/f assistant; **assistente sanitario** doctor; **assistente sociale** social worker
**assistenza** f assistance; **assistenza qualificata** expert service; **assistenza sanitaria** health service
**assistere** to assist; **assistere a** to attend (meeting etc)
**asso** m ace
**associazione** f society; association; **associazione turistica giovanile** tourist association for young people
**assoluto(a)** absolute
**assomigliare a** to resemble
**assorbente** absorbent; **assorbente igienico** m sanitary towel
**assorbire** to absorb
**assortito(a)** assorted
**assumere** to recruit (personnel)
**assurdo(a)** absurd
**asta** f auction; **asta dell'olio** dipstick
**astenersi** to abstain
**astice** m lobster
**astuccio** m case
**atlante** m atlas
**Atlantico** m Atlantic Ocean
**attaccapanni** m coat peg; hat stand; coat hanger
**attaccare** to attach; to attack; to fasten
**attacco** m attack; **attacco cardiaco** heart attack
**atteggiamento** m attitude
**attendere** to wait for
**attento(a)** careful; **attenti al cane** beware of the dog
**attenzione** f attention; **attenzione allo scalino** mind the step; **attenzione alla corrente elettrica** danger: electricity
**atterraggio** m landing (of plane); **atterraggio di emergenza** emergency

landing; **atterraggio di fortuna** crash-landing
**atterrare** to land (plane)
**attestare: si attesta che ...** it is hereby declared that ...
**attestazione** f: **attestazione di versamento** proof of payment
**attico** m attic; penthouse
**attività** f activity; **attività di bordo** fpl activities on board; **attività sportive** fpl sporting activities
**attivo(a)** active
**atto** m act; action; deed
**attore** m actor
**attracco** m berthing; berth; **divieto di attracco a imbarcazioni non autorizzate** berths for authorized craft only
**attraversamento pedonale** m pedestrian crossing
**attraversare** to cross; **vietato attraversare i binari** do not cross the track
**attraverso** through
**attrazione** f attraction
**attrezzatura** f equipment
**attrice** f actress
**attuale** present
**audace** bold
**audiovisivo(a)** audio-visual
**auguri** mpl: **tanti auguri** all the best; **auguri di buon compleanno** best wishes on your birthday
**aula** f classroom; lecture room; **aula del tribunale** courtroom; **aula magna** main hall
**aumentare** to increase; to turn up
**aumento** m increase; rise; raise; growth
**austriaco(a)** Austrian
**autentico(a)** genuine
**autista** m driver; chauffeur
**autobus** m bus
**autocorriera** f bus
**autocorsa** f bus

**autoforniture** fpl car parts and accessories
**autogrù** f breakdown van
**automatico(a)** automatic
**automobile** f car; **automobile decappottabile** convertible
**automobilista** m/f motorist
**automotrice** f railcar
**autonoleggio** m car hire; **autonoleggio con autista** chauffeur-drive service
**autopompa** f fire engine
**autopullman** m bus; coach
**autore** m author
**autorimessa** f garage (for parking)
**autoritratto** m self-portrait
**autorizzare** to authorize
**autorizzazione** f authorization; **autorizzazione scritta** written authorization
**autoscuola** f driving school
**autostop** m hitchhiking
**autostoppista** m/f hitchhiker
**autostrada** f motorway; **autostrada a pedaggio** toll road
**autovettura** f motor car
**autunno** m autumn
**avanti** in front; forward(s)
**avanzare** to remain (be left over); to advance
**avaria** f breakdown (of car); failure
**avena** f oats
**avere** to have
**aviazione** f air force; aviation
**aviogetto** m jet
**avorio** m ivory
**avvenimento** m event
**avvenuto(a): l'avvenuta accettazione è indicata da un segnale acustico** an acoustic signal indicates that your money has been accepted
**avverso(a): avverse condizioni atmosferiche** fpl adverse weather conditions

**avvertire** to warn
**avviarsi** to set off
**avvicinarsi** to approach
**avvisare** to inform; to warn
**avviso** m warning; announcement; advertisement; notice; **avviso alla clientela** notice to customers
**avvocato** m barrister; lawyer
**avvolgere** to wind; to wrap
**azienda** f business, firm; **azienda turismo** or **di soggiorno** local tourist board
**azione** f action
**azzurro(a)** blue

## B

**baccalà** m dried salted cod; **baccalà alla vicentina** salt cod cooked in milk with white wine, spices, anchovies, onion and garlic
**bacheca** f display case; notice board
**baciare** to kiss
**bacino** m pelvis; basin
**bacio** m kiss
**badare a** to look after; to pay attention to
**baffi** mpl moustache
**bagagliaio** m boot (of car); luggage van
**bagaglio** m luggage; **bagaglio a mano** hand luggage; **bagaglio personale** personal luggage
**bagliore** m flash; glare (of light)
**bagnare** to wet
**bagnarsi** to get wet; to bathe
**bagnino** m lifeguard
**bagno** m bathroom; bath; **bagni** mpl bathing establishment
**bagnomaria: cuocere a bagnomaria** to cook in a

double saucepan
**baia** f bay
**balcone** m balcony
**balena** f whale
**ballare** to dance
**balletto** m ballet
**ballo** m ball; dance
**balneazione** f: **è proibita la balneazione** bathing strictly prohibited
**balsamo** m hair conditioner
**bambinaia** f nurse(maid)
**bambino(a)** m/f child; baby
**bambola** f doll
**banca** f bank
**bancarella** f stall; stand
**bancarotta** f bankruptcy
**banchetto** m banquet
**banchina** f platform; quay; quayside
**banco** m counter; bench; **banco di registrazione** check-in (desk); **banco di sabbia** sandbank
**bancogiro** m bank giro (system)
**Bancomat®** m autobank
**banconota** f bank note
**banda** f gang; band
**bandiera** f banner; flag
**bandito** m gunman
**bar** m bar; pub
**barattolo** m tin; jar
**barba** f beard
**barbabietola** f beetroot
**Barbera** f dry, full-bodied, deep-red wine from Piedmont
**barbiere** m barber
**barbo** m barbel
**barca** f boat
**barcone** m: **barconi per escursioni** boat excursions
**Bardolino** m light, dry red wine from the sea around Verona
**barella** f stretcher
**barile** m barrel
**barista** m/f barman; barmaid
**Barolo** m dry, full-bodied red wine with a taste of violets, from Piedmont
**basare** to base

**base** f base; basis; **pranzo a base di pesce/carne** lunch with fish/meat as the main course

**basso(a)** low; short

**bastare** to be enough

**bastoncini** mpl chopsticks; **bastoncini di merluzzo** cod fish fingers; **bastoncini di pesce** fish fingers

**bastone** m stick; walking stick

**battaglia** f battle

**battello** m boat; **battello da diporto** pleasure boat; **battello di salvataggio** lifeboat

**battere** to hit; to beat; **battere bandiera inglese** etc to fly the British etc flag

**batteria** f battery (in car); heat (sports)

**battersi** to fight

**battesimo** m baptism

**battistero** m baptistry

**baule** m trunk

**beccaccia** f woodcock

**beccaccino** m snipe

**bellezza** f beauty

**bello(a)** beautiful; handsome; lovely; fine; **fa bello** the weather's fine

**Bel Paese®** m soft, mild creamy cheese

**benché** although

**benda** f blindfold; bandage

**bene** well; all right; **stare bene** to be well; **va bene** okay; it's okay

**beneficiario** m payee

**beni** mpl goods; property

**benvenuto(a)** welcome

**benzina** f petrol

**bere** to drink

**berlina** f saloon (car)

**bernoccolo** m bump

**berretto** m cap

**bersaglio** m target

**bestemmiare** to swear

**bestiame** m cattle

**betulla** f birch

**bevanda** f drink

**biancheria** f linen (for beds, table); **biancheria per la casa** household linens;

**biancheria da letto** bedding; **biancheria intima** underwear

**bianco(a)** white; blank; **assegno in bianco** blank cheque; **lasciate in bianco per favore** please leave blank; **pesce/carne in bianco** boiled fish/meat

**Bibbia** f Bible

**biberon** m baby's bottle

**bibita** f soft drink

**biblioteca** f library; bookcase

**bicchiere** m glass; **bicchiere da vino** wineglass

**bicicletta** f bicycle

**bidone** m dustbin

**bigiotteria** f costume jewellery

**bigliettaio** m bus conductor

**biglietteria** f ticket office; **biglietteria aerea** air travel ticket office

**biglietto** m note; ticket; card; **biglietto di andata e ritorno** return ticket; **biglietto di solo andata** single ticket; **biglietto orario** ticket valid for one hour from time of issue; **il biglietto deve essere convalidato all'inizio del viaggio e conservato per il controllo** tickets must be punched at start of journey and kept ready for inspection

**bignè** m cream puff

**bigodino** m curler

**bilancia** f scales

**bilanciare** to balance

**bilancio** m balance sheet; **bilancio preventivo** budget

**bilia** f marble

**biliardo** m billiards

**bin.** abbreviation of **binario**

**binario** m track; line; platform

**binocolo** m binoculars

**biondo(a)** blond(e); fair

**birra** f beer; **birra alla**

spina draught beer; **birra chiara** lager; **birra piccola/grande** half-pint/ pint of beer; **birre estere** foreign beers; **birre nazionali** Italian beers

**birreria** f brewery; bierkeller

**bis** m encore

**biscotto** m biscuit

**bisognare** to have to

**bisogno** m need; **avere bisogno di** to need

**bistecca** f steak; **bistecca ai ferri** grilled steak; **bistecca di filetto** fillet steak; **bistecca alla fiorentina** T-bone steak

**bivio** m fork

**bloccare** to block; **bloccare un assegno** to stop a cheque

**bloccarsi** to jam

**blocchetto** m notebook; **blocchetto di biglietti** book of tickets

**blocco** m block; notepad; **per evitare il blocco dell'ascensore ...** to prevent the lift from jamming ...

**blu** blue

**blusa** f smock

**boa** f buoy

**bocca** f mouth

**bocce** fpl bowls (game)

**boccone** m bite (of food)

**bolla** f bubble; blister

**bollettino** m bulletin

**bollire** to boil

**bollito** m boiled meat; **bollito misto** assorted boiled meats

**bollitore** m kettle

**bombetta** f bowler hat

**bombola** f cylinder (for gas); **bombola spray** spray

**bombolone** m doughnut

**bordo** m border; edge; **a bordo** on board; **salire a bordo** to go aboard; **a bordo della nave** aboard ship

**borghese** middle-class; **in borghese** in plain clothes

**borgo** m district
**borsa** f handbag; holdall; bag; briefcase; **la Borsa** the stock market; the stock exchange; **borsa dell'acqua calda** hot water bottle; **borsa nera** black market; **borsa per la spesa** shopping bag; **borsa di studio** grant; **borsa da toletta** sponge-bag
**borsellino** m purse
**borsetta** f handbag
**bosco** m wood (*forest*)
**botte** f barrel, cask
**bottega** f shop; **bottega artigiana** crafts shop
**botteghino** m box office
**bottiglia** f bottle
**bottone** m button
**bovino(a): carni bovine** fpl beef
**box** m playpen; garage
**braccialetto** m bracelet
**braccio** m arm
**braciola** f chop; **braciola di maiale** pork chop
**brandina** f camp-bed
**brano** m passage (*from book*)
**branzino** m bass
**brasato** m braised beef
**breve** brief
**brezza** f breeze
**briciola** f crumb
**bricolage** m do-it-yourself
**briglia** f rein; bridle
**brillare** to shine
**brindare a** to toast (*drink to*)
**brindisi** m toast (*drink, speech*)
**britannico(a)** British
**brocca** f jug
**broccoletti** mpl broccoli
**brodetto** m: **brodetto di pesce** spicy fish soup
**brodo** m stock; **riso/pasta in brodo** rice/noodle soup
**bruciare** to burn
**bruciore di stomaco** m heartburn
**bruno(a)** brown; dark
**brusco(a)** abrupt; sharp
**brutto(a)** ugly

**buca** f hole; **buca per le lettere** letter box
**bucato** m washing; laundry; **per bucato in lavatrice** for machine washing; **per bucato a mano** for hand washing
**buccia** f peel, skin
**buco** m hole; **buco della serratura** keyhole
**budino** m pudding
**bufera** f storm; **bufera di neve** blizzard
**buffé** m buffet
**bugia** f lie
**buio(a)** dark
**buongustaio** m gourmet
**buono** m voucher; coupon; token
**buono(a)** good; **buon giorno!** good morning/afternoon!; **buona notte!** good night!; **a buon mercato** cheap
**burrasca** f storm
**burrascoso(a)** gusty; rough
**burro** m butter
**bussare** to knock
**bussola** f compass
**busta** f envelope
**bustina** f sachet; **bustina di tè** tea bag
**busto** m bust
**buttare via** to throw away

# C

**cabina** f cabin; beach hut; cubicle; **cabina interna/esterna** cabin below/above deck; **cabina telefonica** telephone booth; **cabina doppia/tripla/quadrupla** two-/three-/four-berth cabin
**cabinato** m cabin cruiser
**cabinovia** f two-seater cablecar
**cacao** m cocoa; **cacao amaro** cocoa with no added sugar
**caccia** f hunting; shooting

**cacciagione** f game (*hunting*)
**cacciare** vt to hunt; to chase away
**cacciatora: alla cacciatora** with tomatoes, mushrooms, shallots, ham and wine
**cacciavite** m screwdriver
**cacciucco** m: **cacciucco alla livornese** spiced fish soup with garlic and sage
**caciocavallo** m firm cheese made from cow's or sheep's milk
**cadavere** m body (*corpse*)
**cadere** to fall; to fall over; to fall down; to drop
**caduta** f fall; **caduta massi/sassi** danger, falling rocks/stones
**caffè** m café; coffee; **caffè corretto** coffee containing a liqueur; **caffè decaffeinato** decaffeinated coffee; **caffè in grani** coffee beans; **caffè lungo** weak black coffee; **caffè macchiato** coffee with a dash of milk; **caffè nero** black coffee; **caffè ristretto** strong black coffee; **caffè tostato** roasted coffee
**caffellatte** m white coffee
**caffettiera** f coffeepot
**calamaretti ripieni** mpl stuffed baby squid
**calamari** mpl: **calamari fritti/alla griglia** fried/grilled squid
**calamita** f magnet
**calare** to fall
**calcestruzzo** m concrete
**calcio** m kick; football (*game*); calcium
**calcolare** to calculate; to allow
**calcolo** m calculation
**caldarroste** fpl roast chestnuts
**caldo(a)** warm; hot; **ho caldo** I'm warm/hot
**calendario** m calendar; **calendario partenze**

departure dates
**callo** m corn
**calma** f calm
**calmante** m painkiller
**calmarsi** to calm down
**calmo(a)** calm
**calore** m warmth; heat
**calpestare** to tread on
**calza** f stocking; sock
**calzatura** f footwear
**calzino** m sock
**calzoleria** f shoeshop
**calzoncini** mpl shorts
**calzone** m savoury turnover made with pizza dough, usually filled with cheese and ham
**calzoni** mpl trousers
**cambiale** f draft (*financial*)
**cambiamento** m change
**cambiare** to change; to exchange; **cambiare casa** to move house
**cambiarsi** to change one's clothes
**cambio** m change; exchange; rate of exchange; gears; **cambio di asciugamani/delle lenzuola** change of towels/sheets; **cambio filtri** oil filter change; **cambio olio rapido** quick oil change; **cambio medio applicato** average rate of exchange applied; **cambio valute** exchange office
**camera** f room; **camera (da letto)** bedroom; **camera dei bambini** nursery; **camera blindata** strongroom; **camera di commercio** Chamber of Commerce; **camera libera** vacancy; **camera matrimoniale** double room; **camera degli ospiti** guest-room; **camera singola** single room
**cameriera** f waitress; chambermaid; **cameriera al banco** barmaid
**cameriere** m waiter
**camerini prova** mpl fitting rooms

**camiceria** f shirt shop
**camicetta** f blouse
**camicia** f shirt; **camicia da notte** nightdress; nightshirt
**caminetto** m mantelpiece
**camino** m chimney; fireplace
**camion** m lorry
**camionabile** for heavy vehicles
**camionista** m lorry driver
**camminare** to walk
**campagna** f country; countryside; campaign
**campana** f bell
**campanello** m bell; doorbell
**campeggio** m camping; camp(ing) site; **campeggio libero** free camp site
**campionato** m championship
**campione** m sample; specimen; champion
**campo** m field; **campo da gioco** playing field; **campo di golf** golf course; **campo sportivo** sports ground; **campo da tennis** tennis court
**camposanto** m cemetery
**canale** m canal; channel
**cancellare** to rub out; to cancel
**cancellata** f railings
**cancellazione** f cancellation
**cancelleria** f stationery
**cancello** m gate; **cancello motorizzato controllato a distanza** gate operated by remote control
**cancro** m cancer
**candeggina** f bleach
**candela** f spark(ing) plug; candle
**cane** m dog
**canna da pesca** f fishing rod
**cannella** f cinnamon
**cannelloni** mpl tubes of pasta stuffed with sauce and baked
**cannolo** m cream horn
**cannone** m gun; cannon

**canoa** f canoe
**canocchia** f squill
**canottaggio** m rowing
**canottiera** f vest
**canovaccio** m teacloth
**cantare** to sing
**cantiere** m building site; **cantiere navale** shipyard
**cantina** f cellar; wine cellar
**cantiniere** m cellarman
**canto** m song; singing
**canzone** f song
**capace** capable
**capacità** f ability
**capanna** f hut
**capelli** mpl hair; **capelli grassi/secchi** greasy/dry hair
**capello** m hair (*single strand*)
**capienza** f capacity
**capire** to understand
**capitale**[1] f capital (*city*)
**capitale**[2] m capital (*finance*)
**capitaneria** f: **capitaneria (di porto)** port authorities
**capitano** m captain; **capitano del porto** harbour master
**capitello** m capital
**capitolo** m chapter
**capo** m head; leader; boss; **capo di vestiario** item of clothing; **detersivo per capi delicati** soap powder for delicates
**capocuoco** m chef
**Capodanno** m New Year's Day
**capogruppo** m group leader
**capolavoro** m masterpiece
**capolinea** m terminus
**capoluogo** m ≈ county town
**capotreno** m guard (*on train*)
**cappella** f chapel
**cappello** m hat
**cappotto** m overcoat
**cappuccino** m frothy white coffee
**cappuccio** m hood
**capra** f goat
**capretto** m kid
**capriolo** m roe deer

**carabiniere** *m* (military) policeman

**caraffa** *f* decanter; carafe

**caramella** *f* sweet

**caramello** *m* caramel

**caratteristica** *f* characteristic; feature

**caratteristico(a)** characteristic; typical

**carbone** *m* coal

**carburante** *m* fuel; **pompa del carburante** fuel pump

**carburatore** *m* carburettor

**carcere** *m* prison

**carciofino** *m*: **carciofini sott'olio** artichoke hearts in oil

**carciofo** *m* artichoke

**cardiologia** *f* cardiology

**carenza** *f* shortage

**caricare** to load; to wind up; to charge (*battery*)

**carico** *m* shipment; cargo; load; **accesso consentito per operazioni di carico e scarico** access for loading and unloading only

**carino(a)** lovely; pretty; nice

**carnagione** *f* complexion

**carne** *f* meat; flesh; **carne di cervo** venison; **carne di maiale** pork; **carne di manzo** beef; **carne di montone** mutton; **carne tritata** mince; **carni bianche** white meats; **carni nere** game meats; **carni rosse** red meats

**carnevale** *m* carnival

**caro(a)** dear

**carota** *f* carrot

**carpa** *f* carp

**carpaccio** *m* thin slices of rare beef with oil, salt and pepper and sometimes grated cheese

**carpione**: **pesce in carpione** soused fish

**careggiata doppia** *f* dual carriageway

**carrello** *m* trolley; **carrello per bagagli** luggage trolley

**carriera** *f* career

**carro** *m* cart; **carro attrezzi** breakdown van

**carrozza** *f*: **carrozza ferroviaria** railway carriage; **carrozza a salone** open-plan carriage; **carrozze cuccette** carriages with couchettes; **carrozze letto** sleepers

**carrozzeria** *f* bodywork; body repairer's

**carrozzina** *f* pram

**carta** *f* paper; card; **alla carta** à la carte; **Carta d'Argento** Senior Citizen's rail card; **carta carbone** carbon paper; **carta di credito** credit card; **Carta Famiglia** Family rail card; **carta geografica** map (*of country*); **carta da gioco** playing card; **carta d'identità** identity card; **carta igienica** toilet paper; **carta d'imbarco** boarding pass; **carta da lettere** notepaper; **carta nautica** chart (*map*); **carta da pacchi** wrapping paper; **carta da parati** wallpaper; **carta da regalo** (gift) wrapping paper; **carta da scrivere** writing paper; **carta stradale** road map; **carta verde** green card

**cartella** *f* folder; briefcase; schoolbag

**cartello** *m* sign; signpost; cartel

**cartoccio** *m* paper bag; **pesce/pollo al cartoccio** fish/chicken baked in tinfoil

**cartoleria** *f* stationer's (shop)

**cartolina** *f* postcard; greetings card; **cartolina di Natale** Christmas card

**cartoncino** *m* card

**cartone** *m* cardboard; cardboard box; **cartone animato** cartoon (*animated*)

**cartuccia** *f* cartridge

**casa** *f* house; home; **offerto(a) dalla casa** on the house; **casa di cura** nursing home; **casa colonica** farmhouse; **casa dello studente** student hostel

**casalinga** *f* housewife

**casalinghi** *mpl* household articles

**casamento** *m* block of flats

**cascata** *f* waterfall

**casco** *m* helmet; crash helmet

**casella postale** *f* post-office box

**casello** *m*: **casello autostradale** motorway tollgate

**caserma** *f* barracks; **caserma dei pompieri** fire station

**caso** *m* case (*instance*); **nel caso che** in case; **a caso** at random; **per caso** by accident; by chance; **in caso di necessità rompere il vetro** in an emergency break the glass

**cassa** *f* cash desk; cash register; **cassa chiusa** checkout closed; position closed; **cassa continua** night safe; **cassa da imballaggio** packing case; **cassa di risparmio** savings bank; **cassa da morto** coffin

**cassaforte** *f* strongbox; safe

**cassata** *f* tutti-frutti ice cream

**casseruola** *f* saucepan; casserole (*dish*)

**cassetta** *f* box; cartridge (*of tape*); cassette; **cassetta di pronto soccorso** first-aid kit; **cassetta per le lettere** letterbox; **cassetta di sicurezza** safe-deposit box

**cassetto** *m* drawer

**cassiere(a)** *m/f* cashier; teller

**castagna** *f* chestnut

**castagnaccio** *m* chestnut cake with pine nuts and

sultanas
**castano(a)** brown *(hair)*
**castello** m castle
**casuale** chance
**catarifrangente** m reflector *(on cycle, car)*
**catena** f chain; range *(of mountains)*; **catene (da neve)** snow chains; **obbligo di catene** snow chains compulsory
**catrame** m tar
**cattedrale** f cathedral
**cattivo(a)** bad; nasty; evil; naughty
**cattolico(a)** Roman Catholic
**catturare** to capture
**causa** f cause; case *(lawsuit)*; **a causa di** because of
**causare** to cause
**cauzionale: deposito cauzionale** deposit
**cauzione** f security *(for loan)*; bail *(for prisoner)*; deposit *(for key etc)*; **su cauzione** on bail
**cavalcare** to ride
**cavalcavia** m flyover *(road)*
**cavallo** m horse; **cavallo da corsa** racehorse
**cavare** to take out; **cavarsela** to manage
**cavatappi** m corkscrew
**caviale** m caviar(e)
**caviglia** f ankle
**cavo** m cable
**cavolfiore** m cauliflower
**cavolini di Bruxelles** mpl Brussels sprouts
**cavolo** m cabbage; **cavolo cappuccio** spring cabbage; **cavolo rapa** kohlrabi
**c'è** there is
**ce** before lo, la, li, le, ne = ci
**cedere** to give in *(yield)*
**cedro** m cedar; lime *(fruit)*
**C.E.E.** f E.E.C.
**cefalo** m grey mullet
**celibe** single *(not married: man)*
**cena** f dinner; supper;

dinner party
**cenere** f ash *(cinders)*
**cenno** m sign; nod; wave
**cenone** m: **cenone di Capodanno** New Year's Eve dinner
**centesimo(a)** hundredth; cent *(US)*
**centinaio** m a hundred; about a hundred
**cento** hundred
**centrale** central; **centrale telefonica** f telephone exchange
**centralinista** m/f switchboard operator
**centralino** m switchboard
**centro** m centre; **centro arredamenti** furniture centre; **centro assistenza tecnica** after-sales department; **centro città** city centre; town centre; **centro commerciale** shopping centre
**ceppo** m log *(of wood)*
**cera** f wax; polish *(for floor)*
**ceramica** f pottery
**cerasella** f cherry liqueur
**cercare** to look for; to look up *(word)*; **cercare di fare** to try to do
**cerchio** m ring; hoop; circle
**cernia** f: **cernia (gigante)** grouper; **cernia (di fondo)** stone bass
**cerniera lampo** f zip(-fastener)
**cerotto** m sticking-plaster
**certamente** definitely; certainly
**certificato** m certificate
**certo(a)** certain; sure; definite
**cervella** fpl brains *(food)*
**cervello** m brain; brains *(as food)*
**cervo** m deer; **carne di cervo** venison
**cespuglio** m bush
**cesta** f hamper
**cestino** m waste paper basket
**cetriolino** m gherkin

**cetriolo** m cucumber
**che** that; than; who; whom; which; what; what's wrong?; **che c'è?** what's wrong?; **non era che un errore** it was just a mistake
**chi** who; whom; **di chi è questo libro?** whose book is this?
**chiacchierare** to chat; to gossip
**chiamare** to call; to page
**chiamarsi** to be called
**chiamata** f call; **chiamata d'emergenza** emergency call; **chiamata urbana/interurbana** local/long-distance call
**Chianti** m dry red/white wine from Tuscany
**chiaretto** m claret
**chiaro(a)** clear; light *(bright, pale)*
**chiatta** f barge
**chiave** f key; spanner; **chiave dell'accensione** ignition key
**chiavistello** m bolt
**chiedere** to ask; to ask for
**chiesa** f church
**chile** m chili
**chilo** m kilo
**chilogrammo** m kilogram(me)
**chilometraggio** m ≈ mileage; **chilometraggio illimitato** unlimited mileage
**chilometrico(a): biglietto chilometrico** special ticket which can be used to travel a certain number of kilometres
**chilometro** m kilometre
**chimico(a)** chemical
**chinarsi** to bend *(person)*
**chinotto** m bitter orange drink
**chiocciola** f snail
**chiodo** m nail *(metal)*; stud; **chiodo di garofano** clove
**chiosco** m kiosk
**chirurgia** f surgery *(operation)*

**chirurgo** m surgeon
**chitarra** f guitar
**chiudere** to shut; to close; to turn off; **chiudere a chiave** to lock
**chiudersi** to shut; to close; **si chiude da sé** door closes automatically
**chiunque** whoever; anybody
**chiusa** f lock (in canal)
**chiuso(a)** shut; off (tap, light etc)
**chiusura** f end; closure; closing down; lock; **(orario di) chiusura** closing time
**ci** us; to us; ourselves; one another; there; **ci sono** there are
**cialda** f waffle
**ciao** hello; goodbye
**ciascuno(a)** each
**cibo** m food
**cicatrice** f scar
**ciclismo** m cycling
**ciclista** m/f cyclist
**ciclomotore** m moped
**cicoria** f endive; chicory
**cieco(a)** blind
**cielo** m sky
**cifra** f figure (number); **cifra tonda** round figure/number
**ciglia** fpl eyelashes
**ciglio** m: **sul ciglio della strada** on the roadside
**cigno** m swan
**ciliegia** f cherry
**cilindro** m cylinder
**cima** f peak; top; **cima alla genovese** cold veal stuffed with sausage, eggs and mushrooms
**cimice** f (bed)bug
**cimitero** m cemetery
**cincin** cheers!
**cinepresa** f cine-camera
**cinese** Chinese
**cinghia** f strap; **cinghia della ventola** fanbelt
**cinghiale** m wild boar
**cinquanta** fifty
**cinque** five
**cintura** f belt (for waist); **cintura di sicurezza** seat belt; **cintura di**

**salvataggio** lifebelt
**cinturato(a)** radial(-ply)
**ciò** this; that; **ciò che** what
**cioccolata** f chocolate; **cioccolata calda** hot chocolate
**cioccolatino** m chocolate; **cioccolatini assortiti** assorted chocolates
**cioccolato** m chocolate; **cioccolato scuro** plain chocolate
**cioè** that is (to say) ...
**ciottolo** m pebble
**cipolla** f onion
**cipollina** f spring onion
**cipria** f face powder
**circa** about
**circo** m circus
**circolare** to move (traffic)
**circolazione** f circulation; movement; **circolazione stradale** (road) traffic; **valido per la circolazione all'estero** valid for driving abroad; **tassa di circolazione** road tax
**circolo** m circle
**circondare** to surround
**circonvallazione** f ring road; bypass
**circostanze** fpl circumstances
**citazione** f quotation (passage); summons
**citofono** m intercom
**città** f town; city
**clacson** m horn (of car)
**classe** f class; **classe economica** economy class; **classe turistica** tourist class
**cliente** m/f customer; guest (at hotel); client; **cliente successivo** next customer
**clientela** f customers; clients
**clima** m climate
**climatizzato(a)** air-conditioned
**cocco** m coconut
**coccodrillo** m crocodile
**cocktail** m: **cocktail di scampi** prawn cocktail
**cocomero** m watermelon

**coda** f tail; queue; train (of dress); **fare la coda** to queue; **coda di rospo** monkfish
**codice** m code; **codice fiscale** tax code; **codice postale** postcode; **codice stradale** Highway Code
**cofano** m bonnet (of car)
**cognata** f sister-in-law
**cognato** m brother-in-law
**cognome** m surname; **cognome da nubile** maiden name
**coincidenza** f connection (train etc); coincidence; **questo treno fa coincidenza con quello delle 16.45** this train connects with the 16.45; **coincidenze nazionali/internazionali** domestic/international connections
**coincidere** to coincide
**colapasta** m colander
**colare** to strain (tea etc)
**colazione** f breakfast; **colazione all'inglese** English breakfast; **colazione in stanza** breakfast in one's room
**colino** m strainer; **colino da tè** tea strainer
**colla** f glue; paste
**collana** f necklace
**collant** m tights
**collaudare** to test
**collega** m/f colleague
**collegamento** m: **collegamenti internazionali** international connections
**collera** f anger
**colletto** m collar
**collezione** f collection
**collina** f hill
**collinoso(a)** hilly
**collo**[1] m neck; **collo alto** polo neck; **collo a V** V-neck
**collo**[2] m parcel; piece of luggage; **colli a mano** hand luggage
**collocare** to place
**colloquio** m interview

**colomba** f dove
**Colonia** f: **(acqua di) Colonia** (eau de) cologne
**colonia** f colony; holiday camp
**colonna** f column; **colonna sonora** sound track; **colonna dello sterzo** steering column
**colonnato** m colonnade
**colorante** m: **senza coloranti** no artificial colouring
**colore** m colour; **di colore** coloured (person)
**colpa** f fault (blame)
**colpevole** guilty
**colpire** to hit; to beat; to strike; to knock
**colpo** m knock; blow; hit; shot (from gun); stroke; bang (of gun etc); thump (noise)
**coltello** m knife
**coltivare** to grow (plants); to cultivate
**comandante** m captain (of ship, plane)
**comandi** mpl controls
**combattimento** m fight
**combustibile** m fuel
**come** like; as; how; **come?** pardon?; **com'è?** what's it like?; **come va?** how are you?
**comico** m comedian
**comignolo** m chimney
**cominciare** to start, begin
**comitiva** f group; **sconti per comitive** discounts for group bookings
**commedia** f comedy; play
**commensali** mpl table companions
**commerciante** m/f dealer; trader
**commercio** m commerce; trade
**commesso(a)** m/f assistant; clerk
**commettere** to commit (crime)
**commissariato** m police station
**commozione** f emotion;

**commozione cerebrale** concussion
**comodità** fpl amenities
**comodo(a)** comfortable
**compagnia** f company; **compagnia aerea** airline; **compagnia di navigazione** shipping company
**compensato** m plywood
**compito** m job; duty; task
**compleanno** m birthday; **buon compleanno!** happy birthday!
**complesso(a)** complex; **complesso pop** m pop group
**completamente** completely
**completare** to complete
**completo(a)** complete; full up (bus etc); **un completo** a suit; an outfit; a two-piece; **al completo** full; no vacancies
**complicato(a)** complex; elaborate; complicated
**complimento** m compliment; **complimenti!** congratulations!
**comporre** to dial (number)
**comportamento** m behaviour
**comportarsi** to behave; to act
**compositore** m composer
**comprare** to buy
**comprensione** f understanding
**compreso(a)** including; **servizio compreso** inclusive of service; **... non compreso(a)** exclusive of ...
**comune¹** common
**comune²** m town council; town hall; municipality
**comunicazione** f communication; **comunicazione telefonica** telephone call; **ottenere la comunicazione** to get through (on phone)
**comunque** in any case; nevertheless; however
**con** with

**concessionario** m agent; dealer
**conchiglia** f shell
**conciliare: conciliare una contravvenzione** to settle a fine on the spot
**concorrenza** f competition
**concorso** m contest
**condimento** m dressing; seasoning
**condizionamento dell'aria** m air-conditioning
**condizione** f condition; proviso; **a condizione che ...** on condition that ...
**condizioni** fpl terms (of contract); **condizioni del tempo permettendo** weather permitting
**condominio** m block of flats; condominium
**condomino** m: **riservato ai condomini** residents only
**conducente** m driver (of taxi, bus)
**conduttori elettrici** mpl jump leads
**conferenza** f lecture; conference
**confermare** to confirm
**confezionato(a)** ready-made (clothes)
**confezione** f packaging; **confezione gigante** giant economy size; **confezione regalo** gift pack; **confezioni per signora** ladies' wear; **confezioni da uomo** menswear
**confine** m boundary; border
**confondere** to mix up; to confuse
**confrontare** to compare
**congedo** m leave (holiday); **in congedo** on leave
**congelato(a)** frozen (food)
**congelatore** m deep-freeze
**congratularsi con** to congratulate
**coniglio** m rabbit; **coniglio stufato** rabbit stew
**connazionale** m/f fellow

countryman/woman

**cono** *m* cone; **cono gelato** ice-cream cone

**conoscenza** *f* acquaintance; knowledge

**conoscere** to know

**conoscersi** to know one another; to meet

**conoscitore** *m* connoisseur

**consegna** *f* delivery; consignment

**consegnare** to deliver (*goods*)

**conseguenza** *f* consequence

**conservante** *m*: **senza conservanti** no preservatives

**conservare** to keep; to preserve; **conservare in luogo fresco e asciutto** store in a cool, dry place

**conservarsi** to keep; **da conservarsi in frigo** keep refrigerated

**conservatorio** *m* academy of music

**consigliare** to advise

**consiglio** *m* advice; **consigli per l'uso** instructions for use

**consistere in** to consist of

**consolato** *m* consulate

**console** *m* consul

**consultare** to consult; to refer to

**consumare** to consume

**consumarsi: da consumarsi entro il ...** best before ...

**consumatore** *m* consumer

**consumazione** *f* drink; **buono per una consumazione** voucher for one drink; **la consumazione è obbligatoria** customers only, please

**contachilometri** *m* ≈ milometer

**contante** *m* cash; **pagare in contanti** to pay cash

**contare** to count; **contare su** to rely on

**contatore** *m* meter

**contattare** to reach (*contact*)

**contatto** *m* contact; **mettersi in contatto con** to contact

**contenere** to hold; to contain

**contento(a)** happy; pleased; content(ed)

**contenuto** *m* contents

**contestare** to dispute

**continuare** to continue

**continuo(a)** continuous; continual

**conto** *m* bill; account; **conto corrente** current account; **conto in banca** bank account; **per conto di** on behalf of

**contorno** *m* vegetables

**contrario** *m* opposite; **al contrario** on the contrary

**contratto** *m* contract; **contratto di viaggio** travel agreement terms

**contravvenzione** *f* fine

**contribuire** to contribute

**contro** against; versus

**controllare** to check; to control; to inspect (*ticket*)

**controllo** *m* check; control; **controllo acque** radiator check; **controllo gomme** tyre check; **controllo passaporti** passport control

**controllore** *m* ticket inspector; **controllore di volo** air traffic controller

**contusione** *f* bruise

**convalidare** to punch; to stamp; **convalida** punch (*or* stamp) this side; **il biglietto va convalidato nella obliteratrice all'inizio del viaggio** insert your ticket in the machine at the start of your journey

**convegno** *m* conference

**convento** *m* monastery; convent

**conversazione** *f* talk; conversation

**convocazione** *f*: **area convocazione gruppi** group rendezvous point

**coperchio** *m* cover; lid

**coperta** *f* cover; blanket

**coperte** *fpl* bedclothes

**coperto** *m* place setting; cover charge; **al coperto** indoor (*games*)

**copertura** *f* cover (*insurance*)

**copia** *f* copy; print (*photographic*)

**copiare** to copy

**copisteria** copy bureau

**coppa**[1] *f* cup (*trophy*); dish; **coppa dell'olio** sump (*in car*); **coppa gelato** dish of ice cream; tub of ice cream

**coppa**[2] *f* large pork sausage

**coppia** *f* pair (*of people*); couple

**coprire** to cover

**coraggio** *m* courage

**coraggioso(a)** brave

**corda** *f* cord (*twine*); rope; string

**cordialmente** yours sincerely

**cornamusa** *f* (bag)pipes

**cornetto** *m* small croissant

**cornice** *f* frame (*of picture*)

**corno** *m* horn

**coro** *m* choir

**corona** *f* crown

**corpo** *m* body

**corposo(a)** full-bodied

**corredo** *m* kit; trousseau; **corredi neonato** baby clothes

**correggere** to correct

**corrente** *f* power (*electricity*); current; **corrente d'aria** draught

**correntemente** fluently

**correre** to run

**correttamente** properly

**corretto(a)** right; correct; proper

**corridoio** *m* corridor

**corrimano** *m* handrail

**corrispondere** to correspond

**corrompere** to corrupt;

to bribe
**corrotto(a)** corrupt
**corsa** f race; journey; **corsa semplice** single fare; **ultimate corsa** last bus; **corse ippiche** horse-racing
**corsetteria** f corsetry
**corsetto** m corset
**corsia** f lane; ward (in hospital); **corsia di emergenza** hard shoulder; **corsia di sorpasso** outside lane
**corso** m course; main street; **corso dei cambi** exchange rates; **corso per corrispondenza** correspondence course; **corso intensivo** crash course; **corso di lingua** language course
**corteo** m parade
**cortile** m courtyard; yard; playground
**corto(a)** short; **essere a corto di qualcosa** to be short of something
**cosa** f thing; **cosa vuole?** what do you want?
**coscia** f thigh; **coscia di pollo** chicken leg
**cosciotto** m leg; **cosciotto d'agnello** leg of lamb
**così** so; thus (in this way)
**cosmetici** mpl cosmetics
**cospargere di** to sprinkle with
**costa** f coast
**Costa Azzurra** f French Riviera
**costare** to cost; **quanto costa?** how much is it?
**costata** f: **costata di manzo** beef entrecôte
**costo** m cost
**costola** f rib
**costoletta** f cutlet; **costoletta di vitello alla milanese** veal cutlet coated in breadcrumbs and fried
**costoso(a)** expensive
**costringere** to force
**costruire** to build; to construct

**costruzione** f construction
**costume** m custom; fancy dress; costume; **costume da bagno** swimsuit; swimming trunks; **costume nazionale** national dress
**cotechino** m spiced pork sausage
**cotoletta** f cutlet; **cotoletta alla milanese** chop/cutlet coated in breadcrumbs and fried
**cotone** m cotton; **cotone idrofilo** cotton wool
**cotto(a)** done (cooked); **poco cotto(a)** underdone
**cottura** f cooking; baking
**cozza** f mussel; **cozze alla marinara** breaded mussels cooked in wine with herbs, carrot and onion
**crauti** mpl sauerkraut
**cravatta** f tie; **cravatta a farfalla** bow tie
**creare** to create
**credenza** f sideboard; belief
**credere** to believe
**credito** m credit; **non si fa credito** no credit given; **credito residuo** credit remaining
**crema** f cream; custard; **crema per barba** shaving cream; **crema per calzature** shoe cream; **crema fredda ai cetrioli** cucumber with yoghurt, milk, cream and parsely; **crema per le mani** hand cream; **crema con pomodori** cream of tomato soup; **crema solare** sun cream; **crema per il viso** face cream
**crepuscolo** m dusk
**crescere** to grow; to grow up
**crescione** m cress
**crescita** f growth
**crespella** f fried pastry twist
**cric** m jack (for car)
**crimine** m crime
**cristallo** m crystal

**criticare** to criticize
**croccante** crisp
**crocchetta** f croquette; **crocchette di patate** potato croquettes
**croce** f cross
**crocevia** m crossroads
**crociera** f cruise; **crociera d'altura** sea cruise
**croco** m crocus
**crollare** to collapse; to slump
**crollo** m collapse; slump; **pericolo di crollo** danger: building unsafe
**cromo** m chrome
**cronaca** f news
**cronista** m/f reporter
**cronometro** m stopwatch
**crosta** f crust; scab
**crostacei** mpl shellfish
**crostino** m crouton
**crudele** cruel
**crudo(a)** raw (uncooked)
**cruscotto** m dash(board)
**cubetto di ghiaccio** m ice cube
**cuccetta** f couchette; berth
**cucchiaiata** f tablespoon (measure); spoonful
**cucchiaino** m teaspoon
**cucchiaio** m spoon; dessertspoon
**cucina** f kitchen; cooker; cooking; **cucina a gas** gas cooker
**cucinare** to cook
**cucinino** m kitchenette; **cucinino accessoriato** fully-equipped kitchenette; **cucinino con frigorifero e blocco cottura** kitchenette with fridge and cooker
**cucire** to sew
**cuffia** f headphones; **cuffia da bagno** bathing cap
**cugino(a)** m/f cousin
**cui** that, which; whose
**culla** f cradle
**cullare** to rock
**cultura** f culture
**cumulo** m pile; **cumulo di neve** snowdrift
**cunetta** f gutter (in street)
**cuocere** to cook; **cuocere**

**al forno** to bake; **cuocere ai ferri** to grill
**cuoco(a)** m/f cook
**cuoio** m leather; **cuoio verniciato** patent leather
**cuore** m heart
**cura** f care; treatment (medical)
**curare** to treat; to cure; to look after
**curioso(a)** curious; funny; quaint
**curva** f bend; corner; curve; **curva a gomito** hairpin bend; **curva senza visibilità** blind corner
**curvare** to bend
**cuscinetti** mpl bearings (in car)
**cuscino** m cushion
**custode** m caretaker
**custodia valori** f valuables accepted for safekeeping
**custodire** to keep; to guard
**C.V.** horse power, h.p.

# D

**da** from; by; since; with; **dal giornalaio** at/to the newsagent's
**dadi** mpl dice
**dado** m stock cube
**dagli = da + gli, dai = da + i**
**dama** f draughts; partner (dancing)
**danneggiare** to spoil; to damage
**danni** mpl damages
**danno** m damage; harm
**dappertutto** everywhere
**dapprima** at first
**dare** to give; **dare su** to overlook; to give onto
**data** f date (day)
**dati** mpl data
**datore di lavoro** m employer
**dattero** m date (fruit)
**dattilografo(a)** m/f typist
**davanti** in front; opposite

**dazio** m customs duty
**debito** m debt; debit
**debole** weak; faint
**decaffeinato(a)** decaffeinated
**decennio** m decade
**decente** decent
**decidere** to decide
**decidersi** to decide
**decimo(a)** tenth
**decollare** to take off (plane)
**decollo** m takeoff
**decorare** to decorate
**deficienza** f shortage
**degli = di + gli**
**degustare** to sample (wine)
**degustazione** f: **degustazione caffè** specialist coffee shop and coffee bar; **degustazione vini** specialist wine bar
**dei = di + i, del = di + il**
**delegazione** f delegation
**delicato(a)** delicate; dainty
**delitto** m crime
**delizioso(a)** delightful; delicious
**deludere** to disappoint
**deluso(a)** disappointed
**demi-sec: spumante demi-sec** m medium-dry sparkling wine
**denaro** m money; **denaro liquido** cash
**denominazione** f: **denominazione di origine controllata** mark guaranteeing the quality and origin of a wine; **denominazione di origine controllata e garantita** as above, but of a higher standard: awarded to only a few top-quality wines
**denso(a)** thick; dense
**dente** m tooth
**dentiera** f dentures
**dentifricio** m toothpaste
**dentista** m/f dentist
**dentro** in; inside
**depositare** to settle (wine); to deposit
**deposito** m deposit;

**deposito bagagli** left luggage office; **deposito valori** place where valuables may be left
**deriva: andare alla deriva** to drift
**derubare** to rob
**descrivere** to describe
**descrizione** f description
**desiderare** to wish for; to desire
**desiderio** m wish; desire
**destinazione** f destination; **con destinazione Messina** bound for Messina
**destra** f right; **a destra** on/to the right
**destro(a)** right
**detersivo** m detergent; **detersivo (in polvere)** soap powder
**detrarre** to deduct
**detrazione** f deduction
**dettagliatamente** in detail
**dettaglio** m detail; **al dettaglio** retail
**dettatura** f: **dettatura telegrammi** telemessage service
**deviare** to reroute; to divert; to swerve
**deviazione** f diversion; detour
**di** of; some; **di giorno/notte** by day/night; **meglio di lui** better than him
**diagnosi** f diagnosis
**dialetto** m dialect
**diamante** m diamond
**diapositiva** f slide (photo)
**diarrea** f diarrhoea
**dibattito** m debate
**dicembre** m December
**dichiarare** to declare; **niente da dichiarare** nothing to declare
**dichiarazione** f declaration; statement; **dichiarazione doganale** customs declaration
**diciannove** nineteen
**diciassette** seventeen
**diciotto** eighteen
**dieci** ten
**dieta** f diet

**dietro** behind; after
**difendere** to defend
**difesa** f defence
**difetto** m defect; fault
**differenza** f difference
**difficile** difficult
**difficoltà** f difficulty
**diffondere** to spread (*news*)
**diga** f dam; dyke
**digestivo** m after-dinner liqueur
**dilettante** m amateur
**diluire** to dilute
**dimagrire** to lose weight
**dimensioni** *fpl* size; dimensions
**dimenticare** to forget
**diminuire** to reduce; to diminish
**diminuzione** f reduction; fall
**dimostrazione** f demonstration
**dindio** m: **dindio ripieno** stuffed turkey
**dintorni** *mpl* surroundings
**dio** m god; **Dio** God
**dipendere da** to depend on; **dipende** it depends
**dipingere** to paint
**dipinto** m painting
**diramazione** f fork
**dire** to tell; to say; **si dice che ...** they say that ...
**direttamente** straight; directly
**diretto(a)** direct; **treno diretto** through train
**direttore** m conductor (*of orchestra*); governor (*of institution*); manager; president (*of company*); director (*of firm*); **direttore di banca** bank manager
**direttrice** f manageress
**direzione** f management; direction; **direzione amministrativa** administration; **direzione regionale del turismo** regional tourist board headquarters
**dirigere** to manage
**dirigersi: dirigersi a** or

**verso** to make one's way towards
**dirimpetto** opposite
**diritto** m right; right side (*of cloth etc*); **diritto per esazioni in treno** fine payable if not in possession of a train ticket; **diritti portuali/aeroportuali** harbour/airport taxes
**diritto(a)** straight; **sempre diritto** straight on
**dirottare** to hijack
**disagio** m discomfort; difficulty
**disapprovare** to disapprove of
**disarmato(a)** unarmed
**disastro** m disaster
**disbrigo** m: **disbrigo (di)** dealing (with)
**discesa** f descent; **in discesa** downhill
**disco** m disc; record; **disco orario** parking disc
**discorso** m speech
**discoteca** f disco(theque)
**discreto(a)** discreet; fair
**discussione** f discussion; **fuori discussione** out of the question
**discutere** to discuss
**disdire** to cancel
**disegno** m plan; design; pattern; drawing
**disfare** to unpack; to undo; to unwrap
**disinfettante** m disinfectant
**disoccupazione** f unemployment
**disordinato(a)** untidy
**disordine** m mess
**dispari** odd (*number*)
**dispensa** f larder
**dispensario** m dispensary
**disperso(a)** missing
**dispiacere a** to displease; **mi dispiace (l'm)** sorry
**disponibile** available
**disporre** to arrange
**dispositivo** m gadget
**disposizione** f arrangement; order; measure; **per disposizione**

**di legge** by law; **tempo a disposizione per fare spese** free time for shopping; **siamo a vostra completa disposizione** we are entirely at your disposal
**disposto(a)** willing
**dissenso** m disagreement
**dissestato(a): strada dissestata** road up
**distanza** f distance; **a poca distanza dal mare** within easy reach of the sea
**distinguere** to distinguish
**distintivo** m badge
**distorsione** f sprain
**distrarre** to distract
**distributore** m distributor; **distributore automatico** vending machine; **distributore automatico di benzina** self-service petrol pump; **distributore di benzina** petrol pump
**distribuzione** f distribution; delivery
**distruggere** to destroy
**disturbare** to disturb; **pregasi non disturbare** do not disturb; **non disturbare il conducente** do not distract the driver
**disturbarsi** to put oneself out
**disturbo** m trouble; **disturbi di stomaco** stomach trouble
**disubbidire** to disobey
**dito** m finger; **dito del piede** toe
**ditta** f business; firm; company
**diurno(a)** day(time); **programma diurno** daytime programme; **albergo diurno** public toilets with washing and shaving facilities *etc*
**divano** m sofa; divan; **divano letto** bed settee
**diventare** to become
**diversi(e)** several
**diverso(a)** different
**divertente** funny

**divertire** to amuse
**divertirsi** to enjoy oneself
**dividere** to divide; to share
**divieto: è fatto severo divieto ...** it is strictly forbidden to ...; **divieto di parcheggio** no parking
**divisa** f uniform; **divisa estera** foreign currency
**divo(a)** m/f star
**divorzio** m divorce
**dizionario** m dictionary
**DOC** abbreviation of **denominazione di origine controllata**
**doccia** f shower (bath)
**DOCG** abbreviation of **denominazione di origine controllata e garantita**
**documenti** mpl papers (passport etc)
**dodicesimo(a)** twelfth
**dodici** twelve
**dogana** f customs
**doganiere** m customs officer
**dolce¹** sweet; mild
**dolce²** m sweet; dessert; cake; **dolci assortiti** assorted cakes/desserts; **dolci della casa** our own cakes/desserts
**dolcelatte** m mild, creamy blue cheese
**Dolcetto** m dry red wine with slighty bitter taste
**dolciumi** mpl sweets
**dolore** m grief; pain
**doloroso(a)** painful
**domanda** f question; demand; application (for job); **fare domanda per** to apply for
**domandare** to ask; to ask for; to demand
**domandarsi** to wonder
**domani** tomorrow
**domattina** tomorrow morning
**domenica** f Sunday
**domestico(a)** m/f servant
**donare** to donate
**donatore** m: **donatore di sangue** blood donor
**dondolarsi** to swing

**donna** f woman; **donna delle pulizie** cleaning lady
**dono** m gift; donation
**dopo** after; afterward(s); **4 anni dopo** 4 years later; **dopo di che** after which
**dopobarba** m aftershave (lotion)
**dopodomani** the day after tomorrow
**doppio(a)** double
**dorato(a)** golden
**dormire** to sleep
**dormitorio** m dormitory
**dosaggio** m dosage
**dottore** m doctor
**dottoressa** f (female) doctor
**dove** where; **di dove è?** where are you from?
**dovere¹** m duty
**dovere²** to have to; must; to owe (money)
**dovunque** wherever; everywhere
**dozzina** f dozen
**dragoncello** m tarragon
**dramma** m drama; play
**droga** f drug
**drogheria** f grocery shop
**droghiere** m grocer
**dubbio** m doubt
**dubitare** to doubt
**duca** m duke
**due** two; **tutti(e) e due** both
**dunque** so
**duomo** m cathedral
**durante** during
**durare** to last
**duro(a)** hard; tough; harsh

# E

**E** abbreviation of **est**; road symbol for international route
**e** and
**è: Lei è** you are; **lui è** he is
**ebreo(a)** Jewish; Jew
**ecc** etc
**eccedenza** f excess; surplus

**eccellente** excellent
**eccesso** m excess; **eccesso di velocità** speeding
**eccezionale** exceptional
**eccezione** f exception; **fatta eccezione per ...** except for ...
**eccitazione** f excitement
**ecco** here is/are; **eccolo** here he/it is
**economico(a)** economic; economical
**edicola** f newsstand
**edificio** m building
**Edimburgo** f Edinburgh
**editore** m publisher
**editrice: casa editrice** f publishing house
**educato(a)** well-mannered
**effetto** m effect; **effetti personali** belongings
**efficace** effective
**egli** he
**egoistico(a)** selfish
**egregio(a)** distinguished; **Egregio Signor Smith** Dear Mr Smith
**elastico(a)** elastic
**eleggere** to elect
**elementare** elementary; primary (school)
**elemento** m unit (of machinery, furniture); element
**elencare** to list
**elenco** m list; **elenco telefonico** telephone directory
**elettrauto** m workshop for car electrical repairs; car electrician
**elettricista** m electrician
**elettricità** f electricity
**elettrico(a)** electric(al)
**elettrodomestico** m domestic (electrical) appliance
**elettronico(a)** electronic
**elettroricambi** mpl electrical spares
**elevatore** m ramp (in garage)
**elezione** f election
**elicottero** m helicopter
**ella** she
**emergenza** f emergency

emicrania *f* migraine
emissione *f* issue
emorragia nasale *f* nosebleed
emorroidi *fpl* haemorrhoids
emozionante exciting
emozione *f* emotion
energico(a) energetic
enfasi *f* stress; emphasis
enorme enormous
enoteca *f* wine bar
ente *m* body, corporation; ente nazionale/ provinciale turismo national/provincial tourist board
entrambi(e) both
entrare to come in; to enter; to go in
entrata *f* entrance; entrata abbonati porta anteriore season ticket holders' entrance at front of vehicle
entrate *fpl* takings; income
entusiasta enthusiastic
epidemia *f* epidemic
epilessia *f* epilepsy
epoca *f* age (*era*)
eppure and yet
equilibrio *m* balance; perdere l'equilibrio to lose one's balance
equino(a): carni equine *fpl* horsemeat
equipaggiamento *m* equipment; gear
equipaggio *m* crew
equitazione *f* horse-riding
erba *f* grass
erbaccia *f* weed
erbaceo(a): vino erbaceo wine with a flavour of herbs
erbe *fpl* herbs; erbe aromatiche herbs
erbette *fpl* beet tops
erboristeria *f* herbalist's (shop)
ereditare to inherit
ermetico(a) airtight
ernia *f* hernia
errare to wander
errore *m* error; mistake; errore di stampa misprint

eruzione *f* rash
esagerare to exaggerate
esame *m* examination
esaminare to examine; to test
esatto(a) exact; accurate
esaurimento *m* exhaustion; esaurimento nervoso nervous breakdown
esaurito(a) exhausted; out of print; sold out; tutto esaurito sold out; house full
esausto(a) exhausted
esca *f* bait
esclamare to exclaim
escludere to exclude
esclusivo(a) exclusive
escluso(a): escluso taxi etc except for taxis etc; escluse le bevande excluding drinks
escursione *f* excursion; escursione a piedi hike
eseguire to carry out (*order*)
esempio *m* example
esente exempt; esente da dogana/tasse duty-/tax-free
esercitarsi to practise
esercito *m* army
esercizio *m* exercise; business; questo esercizio resta chiuso nel giorno di ... this shop (*or* restaurant *etc*) is closed on ...
esigenza *f* requirement
esigere to demand
esistere to exist
esitare to hesitate
esito *m* result
espatrio *m*: valido per l'espatrio valid for travel abroad
esperienza *f* experience
esperto(a) expert; experienced
esplorazione *f* exploration
esplosione *f* explosion
esporre to expose; to explain; to display
esportare to export
esportazione *f* export

esposto(a) exposed; esposto(a) a nord facing north
espresso *m* express letter; express train; espresso (coffee)
esprimere to express
essere to be
essi(e) they; them
esso(a) it
est *m* east
estate *f* summer
esterno(a) outside; external
estero(a) foreign; all'estero abroad
estetista *m/f* beautician
estintore *m* fire extinguisher
estratto *m*: estratto di carne meat extract
estremi *mpl* details, particulars
estremo(a) extreme
età *f* age
etichetta *f* etiquette; tag; label
Europa *f* Europe
europeo(a) European
eventuale possible
evitare to avoid
extrasec: spumante extrasec *m* extra-dry sparkling wine

# F

fa[1] ago
fa[2]: lui lo fa he does it; cosa fa qui? what is he (*or* she) doing here?; what are you doing here?
fabbrica *f* factory
fabbricante *m* manufacturer
fabbricare to manufacture; fabbricato in serie mass-produced
facchino *m* porter (*for luggage*)
faccia *f* face
facciata *f* façade
facile easy

**facilmente** easily
**facoltativo(a)** optional
**faggio** m beech
**fagiano** m pheasant
**fagioli** mpl beans; **fagioli borlotti** kidney beans; **fagioli con le cotiche** beans in a ham and tomato sauce with onion, garlic, basil and parsley
**fagiolini** mpl runner beans
**fai da te** m do-it-yourself
**falegname** m carpenter; joiner
**fallimento** m failure; bankruptcy
**fallo** m error; **senza fallo** without fail
**falò** m bonfire
**falsificazione** f forgery
**falso** false; fake
**fama** f fame; reputation
**fame** f hunger; **avere fame** to be hungry
**famiglia** m family
**familiare** family; familiar; m relative
**fanale** m light (on car); **fanali di posizione** sidelights; **fanali dei freni** stoplights
**fango** m mud
**fanghi** mpl mud baths
**fantascienza** f science fiction
**fantasma** m ghost
**fantino** m jockey
**faraona** f guinea fowl
**farcito(a)** stuffed (chicken etc)
**fare** to do; to make; **ti fa bene** it's good for you; **fa caldo** it is warm/hot
**farfalla** f butterfly
**farina** f flour; **farina di granturco** cornflour; **farina integrale** wholemeal flour
**farmacia** f chemist's shop; **farmacie di turno** duty chemists
**faro** m headlight; lighthouse
**farsa** f farce
**fascia** f band; bandage; **fascia oraria** time band

**fascino** m charm
**fascio** m bundle
**fastidio** m bother; **dare fastidio a** to annoy
**fatto** m fact
**fattore** m factor
**fattoria** f farm
**fattorino d'albergo** m bellboy
**fattura** f invoice; **la fattura si richiede all'atto del pagamento** an invoice should be requested when making payment
**fave** fpl broad beans
**favore** m favour; **per favore** please; **per favore silenzio** quiet please
**fazzolettino di carta** m tissue (handkerchief)
**fazzoletto** m handkerchief; (head)scarf
**febbraio** m February
**febbre** f fever; **avere la febbre** to have a temperature; **febbre da fieno** hay fever
**fede** f faith; belief; wedding ring
**fedeltà** f faithfulness; **ad alta fedeltà** hi-fi
**federa** f pillowcase, pillowslip
**fegatelli** mpl: **fegatelli alla fiorentina** pig's liver kebabs with fried croutons, bay leaves, fennel and garlic
**fegatini** mpl: **fegatini d'anatra** duck livers; **fegatini di pollo** chicken livers
**fegato** m liver; **fegato di maiale/vitello** pig's/calf's liver; **fegato alla veneziana** calf's liver fried with onions
**felice** glad
**felicissimo(a)** delighted
**felicità** f happiness
**felicitazioni** fpl congratulations
**feltro** m felt (cloth)
**femmina** f female
**femminile** feminine

**fendinebbia:** (proiettori) **fendinebbia** mpl fog lamps
**feriale: giorno feriale** working day, weekday
**ferie** fpl holiday(s)
**ferita** f wound; injury; cut
**ferito(a)** injured
**fermaglio** m: **fermaglio per capelli** hair slide
**fermare** to stop
**fermarsi** to stop; **si ferma automaticamente** (it) stops automatically
**fermata** f stop; **fermata dell'autobus** bus stop; **fermata a richiesta** request stop; **divieto di fermata** no waiting
**fermo(a)** firm; steady; stationary; off (machine); **ferme restando le condizioni di cui sopra** in accordance with the terms as set out above
**feroce** fierce; **animali feroci** wild animals
**ferragosto** national holiday on August 15th
**ferramenta** fpl hardware; (negozio di) **ferramenta** ironmonger's (shop)
**ferri: ai ferri** grilled
**ferro** m iron; **ferro da calza** knitting needle; **ferro da stiro** iron (for clothes)
**ferrovia** railway; **ferrovia pacchi dogana** border customs office for rail parcels
**ferroviario(a)** rail(way); **carta ferroviaria** rail map
**fesa** f: **fesa di vitello** rump of veal
**fessura** f slot; crack
**festa** f party; holiday (day); **festa danzante** dance
**festeggiare** to celebrate
**fetta** f slice; **fette biscottate** rusks
**fettuccine** fpl ribbon-shaped pasta
**FF SS** Italian State Railways
**fiamma** f flame
**fiammifero** m match
**fiasco** m straw-covered

flask
**fiato** m breath
**fibbia** f clasp; buckle
**fibra** f fibre
**fico** m fig
**fidanzato(a)** engaged; fiancé(e)
**fidarsi di** to trust
**fidato(a)** reliable
**fiducia** f confidence (*trust*)
**fieno** m hay
**fiera** f fair
**fieristico(a): sede fieristica** trade fair centre
**figlia** f daughter
**figliastra** f stepdaughter
**figliastro** m stepson
**figlio** m son
**figura** f figure
**fila** f row; queue; **fare la fila** to queue
**filetto** m fillet; **filetto alla Carpaccio** raw strips of fillet steak with mayonnaise, cream, Worcester cause, red peppers, capers and brandy; **filetto di manzo alla griglia** grilled fillet steak; **filetto al pepe verde** fillet steak with green peppercorns; **filetti di merluzzo/sogliola** cod/sole fillets
**filiale** f branch; subsidiary
**film** m film; **film per soli adulti** film for adults only; **film giallo/di fantascienza** detective/science fiction film; **film dell'orrore** horror film
**filo** m thread; flex; wire; edge (*of blade*)
**filo di ferro** m wire; **filo di ferro spinato** barbed wire
**filone** m: **filone di vitello** veal marrow bone
**filtro** m filter; **con filtro** tipped (*cigarettes*); **filtro dell'olio** oil filter; **filtro dell'aria** air filter
**finalmente** finally
**finanza** f finance
**finanziario(a)** financial
**finanziera** f sauce made

with truffles, mushrooms, offal and Marsala
**finché** as long as; until
**fine**[1] f end; **alla fine** at last; eventually; **fine settimana** weekend
**fine**[2] m purpose
**fine**[3] fine; thin
**finestra** f window
**finestrino** m window (*in car, train*)
**fingere** to pretend
**finire** to finish
**fino** even; **fino a** until; as far as; **fino a 6** up to 6
**fino(a)** fine
**finocchio** m fennel; **semi di finocchio** fennel seeds
**finora** up till now
**fiocco** m flake; bow (*in ribbon*)
**fioraio(a)** m/f florist
**fior di latte** m cream
**fiore** m flower; **fiori di zucca fritti** fried courgette flowers
**fiorista** m/f florist
**Firenze** f Florence
**firma** f signature
**firmare** to sign
**fiscale** fiscal
**fischio** m whistle
**fisco** m Inland Revenue
**fissare** to stare at; to fix; to arrange
**fitta** f stitch (*pain*)
**fitto(a)** dense
**fiume** m river
**flauto** m flute
**flipper** m pinball
**flotta** f fleet
**flusso** m flow
**focaccia** f kind of pizza; bun
**focolare** m fireplace
**fodera** f lining
**foglia** f leaf
**foglio** m sheet (*of paper*)
**fogna** f drain
**folaga** f coot
**folclore** m folklore
**folla** f crowd
**folle** mad; **in folle** in neutral (*car*)
**fondale** m bottom;

**attenzione fondale basso** warning: shallow water
**fondamentalmente** basically
**fondare** to establish
**fondere** to melt
**fondersi** to melt; to merge
**fondi** mpl funds
**fondo** m back (*of room*); bottom; **fondi di caffè** coffee grounds
**fonduta** f melted cheese with milk, egg yolk and truffles
**fontana** f fountain
**fonte** f source; **fonte battesimale** baptismal font
**fontina** f soft, creamy cheese from Piedmont
**footing** m jogging
**forare** to pierce; to punch (*ticket etc*)
**foratura** f puncture
**forbici** fpl scissors
**forchetta** f fork
**forcina** f hairpin
**forfora** f dandruff
**forma** f form; **in forma** in good shape
**formaggio** m cheese; **formaggi piccanti/teneri** strong/mild cheeses
**formica** f ant
**fornaio** m baker
**fornello** m stove; hotplate; ring; **fornello a gas** gas ring; camping stove
**fornire** to provide; to supply
**fornitore** m supplier
**forno** m oven
**foro** m hole; forum; law court; **foro competente** court of jurisdiction
**forse** perhaps
**forte** strong; loud; **forte nel golf** good at golf
**fortuna** f fortune (*wealth*); luck
**forza** f strength; force; **per causa di forza maggiore** by reason of an act of God; due to circumstances beyond one's control
**foschia** f mist

**fossa** f pit
**fossato** m ditch
**foto** f photo; **foto ritratto** portrait photo
**fotocopia** f photocopy
**fotografare** to photograph
**fotografia** f photography; photograph
**foto-ottica** f photographic and optical instruments dealer
**fototessera** f passport(-type) photo
**fra** between; among(st); **fra 2 giorni** in 2 days
**fracasso** m crash (noise)
**fragola** f strawberry; **fragole al limone** strawberries with lemon juice and sugar; **fragole con la panna** strawberries and cream
**fragore** m roar; rumble
**frana** f landslide
**francese** French
**franchigia** f: **in franchigia** duty free; **franchigia bagaglio** luggage allowance
**Francia** f France
**francobollo** m (postage) stamp
**frangia** f fringe
**frappé** m milk shake
**Frascati** m dry or medium-dry white wine from the Frascati area near Rome
**frase** f phrase; sentence
**fratello** m brother
**frattaglie** fpl offal; giblets
**frattura** f fracture
**frazione** f village
**freccette** fpl darts
**freccia** f arrow; indicator (of car); **mettere la freccia** to use one's indicator
**freddo(a)** cold; **ho freddo** I'm cold
**fregare** to rub; to cheat
**frenare** to brake
**freno** m brake; **freno a mano** handbrake; **freno a pedale** footbrake; **freni a disco** disc brakes
**fresco(a)** cool; fresh; wet

(paint)
**fretta** f rush; haste; **avere fretta** to be in a hurry
**fricassea** f: **coniglio/pollo** etc **in fricassea** rabbit/chicken etc fricassee
**friggere** to fry
**frigo** m fridge
**frigorifero** m refrigerator
**frittata** f omelette; **frittata con le erbe/le verdure** omelette with herbs/vegetables
**frittella** f fritter
**frizzante** fizzy; sparkling
**fritto** m: **fritto misto** mixed fry
**fritto(a)** fried
**frizione** f clutch (of car)
**frontale** head-on
**fronte** f forehead; **di fronte** facing; **la casa di fronte** the house opposite
**frontiera** f frontier; border
**frullato** m milkshake
**frullatore** m blender
**frullino** m whisk
**frumento** m wheat
**frusta** f whip
**frutta** f fruit; **frutta secca** dried fruit
**fruttato(a)** fruity (wine)
**frutteto** m orchard
**fruttivendolo** m greengrocer
**frutto** m fruit; **frutti di mare** seafood; **frutti di bosco** fruits of the forest (blackberries etc)
**FS** Italian State Railways
**fu** was; late (deceased)
**fucile** m rifle; gun
**fuga** f escape; leak (gas)
**fuggire** to run away; to escape
**fumare** to smoke
**fumatore** m smoker
**fumo** m smoke
**fungere da** to act as
**fungo** m mushroom; **funghi ovoli** royal agaric mushrooms; **funghi porcini** boletus mushrooms; **funghi secchi** dried mushrooms

**funzionare** to work (mechanism); **funziona a nafta** it runs on diesel; **fare funzionare** to operate (machine)
**funzionario(a) statale** m/f civil servant
**fuoco** m fire; focus; **fuochi d'artificio** fireworks; **mettere a fuoco** to focus
**fuori** outside; out (not at home)
**fuoribordo** m outboard
**furgone** m van
**furto** m robbery
**fusibile** m fuse
**fuso orario** m time zone
**futuro** m future

# G

**gabbia** f cage; crate
**gabinetto** m toilet; **gabinetto medico** doctor's surgery
**galleggiante** m float
**galleria** f tunnel; gallery; circle (in theatre); arcade; **prima galleria** dress circle; **galleria interi/ridotti** full-price/concessionary circle tickets; **galleria d'arte** art gallery
**Galles** m Wales
**gallese** Welsh
**gallina** f hen
**gallo** m cock
**gamba** f leg
**gamberetto** m shrimp; prawn
**gambero** m crayfish
**gamma** f range
**gancio** m hook; **gancio per rimorchio** tow-bar (on car)
**garanzia** f guarantee; warranty; **garanzia assicurativa** insurance cover; **garanzie infortuni al conducente** cover in the event of an accident to the driver
**garofano** m carnation
**garza** f gauze; lint

**gas** *m* gas; **gas di scappamento** exhaust (fumes)

**gasolio** *m* diesel oil

**gassato(a): bevanda gassata** fizzy drink

**gassoso(a)** fizzy

**gatto** *m* cat; **gatto delle nevi** snow plough

**gelare** to freeze

**gelateria** *f* ice-cream shop

**gelatina** *f* jelly

**gelato** *m* ice-cream

**gelo** *m* frost

**geloso(a)** jealous

**gemelli** *mpl* twins; cuff links

**genere** *m* kind (*type*); gender

**generi alimentari** *mpl* foodstuffs

**genero** *m* son-in-law

**gengiva** *f* gum

**genitori** *mpl* parents

**gennaio** *m* January

**Genova** *f* Genoa

**gente** *f* people

**gentile** kind; polite

**geometra** *m* surveyor

**gergo** *m* slang

**Germania** *f* Germany

**gesso** *m* chalk; plaster (*for limb*); plaster of Paris

**gesto** *m* gesture

**gettacarte** *m* wastepaper basket

**gettare** to throw; **non gettare alcun oggetto dal finestrino** do not throw anything out of the window

**gettone** *m* token (*for machine*); chip (*in gambling*); counter; **gettone telefonico** telephone token; **gettoni esauriti** telephone tokens sold out

**gettoniera** *f* telephone-token dispenser

**ghiacciaia** *f* icebox

**ghiaccio** *m* ice

**ghiacciolo** *m* ice lolly

**ghiaia** *f* gravel

**ghiandola** *f* gland

**ghisa** *f* cast iron

**già** already

**giacca** *f* jacket; **giacca a vento** anorak; **giacca di salvataggio** life jacket; **giacca sportiva** sports jacket; **in giacca e cravatta** a jacket and tie must be worn

**giallo** *m* detective story/ thriller

**giallo(a)** yellow

**giardinetta** *f* estate (*car*)

**giardiniere** *m* gardener

**giardino** *m* garden; **giardino botanico** botanical gardens

**giarrettiere** *fpl* suspenders

**giglio** *m* lily

**ginepro** *m* juniper; **bacche di ginepro** juniper berries

**Ginevra** *f* Geneva

**gingerino** *m* drink similar to ginger ale

**ginnastica** *f* gymnastics; **ginnastica presciistica** pre-ski exercises

**ginocchio** *m* knee; **mettersi in ginocchio** to kneel down

**giocare** to play; to gamble

**giocatore(trice)** *m/f* player

**giocattolo** *m* toy

**gioco** *m* game; **essere in gioco** to be at stake; **gioco d'azzardo** gambling; **giochi di società** parlour games

**gioia** *f* joy

**gioielli** *mpl* jewellery

**gioielliere** *m* jeweller

**gioiello** *m* jewel

**giornalaio** *m* newsagent

**giornale** *m* newspaper; **giornale a fumetti** comic; **giornale radio** radio news; **giornale della sera** evening paper

**giornalista** *m/f* journalist

**giornata** *f* day

**giorno** *m* day; **di giorno in giorno** day by day; **giorno festivo** holiday; **giorno feriale** weekday; **giorno di mercato** market-day

**giostra** *f* merry-go-round

**giovane** young; young person

**giovedì** *m* Thursday

**gioventù** *f* youth

**giradischi** *m* record-player

**girare** to turn; to spin

**giro** *m* tour; turn; rev (*in engine*); lap (*of track*); **fare un giro in macchina** to go for a drive

**gita** *f* trip; excursion; **gita di gruppo** group excursion

**giù** down; downstairs

**giudicare** to judge

**giudice** *m* judge

**giugno** *m* June

**giuntura** *f* joint

**giurare** to swear

**giustizia** *f* justice

**giusto(a)** right; fair

**glassa** *f* icing

**gli** the; to him/it; **glielo dia** give it to him/her

**gliela = gli + la**

**gliele = gli + le**

**glieli = gli + li**

**glielo = gli + lo**

**gliene = gli + ne**

**globale** inclusive (*costs*); global

**gnocchi** *mpl* small dumplings made of potato or semolina; **gnocchi di semolino alla romana** semolina dumplings made with butter, egg yolks, milk and nutmeg

**goccia** *f* drop (*of liquid*); drip

**gocciolare** to drip

**gola** *f* throat

**golf** *m* golf; cardigan

**golfo** *m* gulf

**goloso(a)** greedy

**gomito** *m* elbow

**gomitolo** *m* ball (*of string, wool*)

**gomma** *f* rubber; tyre; **gomma per cancellare** rubber (*eraser*); **gomma da masticare** chewing gum

**gommone** *m* dinghy

(inflatable)
**gonfiare** to inflate
**gonfiarsi** to swell (up)
**gonfio(a)** swollen
**gonfiore** m swelling
**gonna** f skirt
**gorgonzola** m rich, soft blue-veined cheese with a pungent smell
**governante** f housekeeper
**GR** abbreviation of **giornale radio**
**gradazione** f: a bassa **gradazione alcolica** low in alcohol
**gradevole** pleasant
**gradinata** f flight of steps; terracing
**gradino** m step; stair
**gradire** to accept; to like; **gradisce qualcosa da bere?** would you like something to drink?
**grado** m grade; standard; degree; **a 2 gradi sotto zero** at minus 2 degrees; **un whisky di 40 gradi** a 70° proof whisky
**graffetta** f paper clip; staple
**graffiare** to scratch
**grafico** m graph; chart
**grammatica** f grammar
**grammo** m gram(me)
**grana** m hard cheese similar to Parmesan
**granaio** m barn
**Gran Bretagna** f Great Britain
**grancevola** f spiny spider crab
**granchio** m crab; **polpa di granchio** crab meat
**grande** great; large; big; **di gran lunga** by far
**grandine** f hail
**granita** f water ice
**grano** m grain
**granturco** m maize
**grasso(a)** fat; greasy; grease
**grata** f grating
**gratinato(a)** sprinkled with grated cheese and breadcrumbs and browned

in the oven
**grato(a)** grateful
**grattacielo** m skyscraper
**grattugia** f grater
**gratuito(a)** free; **il servizio è gratuito** the service is free of charge
**grazie** thank you
**grazioso(a)** charming; graceful
**Grecia** f Greece
**greco(a)** Greek
**grezzo(a)** raw (unprocessed); crude (oil etc)
**gridare** to shout
**grigio(a)** grey
**griglia** f grill (gridiron): **alla griglia** grilled
**grigliata** f grill; **grigliata mista** mixed grill
**Grignolino** m dry red wine from Piedmont, with the scent of roses
**grissino** m bread-stick
**grondaia** f gutter
**grongo** m conger eel
**grossista** m/f wholesaler
**grosso(a)** big; thick
**grossolano(a)** rude
**groviera** f mild cheese with holes; Italian version of the Swiss cheese, gruyère
**gru** f crane
**gruccia** f crutch; coat hanger
**grumo** m lump (in sauce)
**gruppo** m group; **gruppo sanguigno** blood group
**gruviera** f = **groviera**
**guadagnare** to earn; to win
**guado** m ford
**guai** mpl trouble (problems)
**guancia** f cheek
**guanciale** m pillow
**guanto** m glove
**guardacoste** m coastguard
**guardare** to watch; to look at; to look
**guardaroba** m wardrobe; cloakroom
**guardia** f guard; **guardia del corpo** bodyguard; **Guardia di Finanza**

Customs and Excise
**guardiano** m warder; caretaker
**guardrail** m crash barrier
**guarire** to cure; to heal; to recover
**guarnizione** f gasket
**guastarsi** to go bad (food); to fail (brakes); to break down (car etc)
**guasto** m failure (mechanical); **guasto al motore** engine trouble; **guasto tecnico** technical failure
**guasto(a)** out of order
**guerra** f war
**guida** f directory; guide; guidebook; **guida a sinistra** left-hand drive; **guida telefonica** telephone directory
**guidare** to drive; to steer
**guidato(a): visita guidata** guided tour
**guidatore** m driver
**guinzaglio** m lead, leash; **cani al guinzaglio** dogs must be on a lead
**guscio** m shell
**gustare** to taste; to enjoy
**gusto** m taste; flavour

# H

**ha: Lei ha** you have; **lui ha** he has
**ho: io ho** I have

# I

**i** the
**idraulico** m plumber
**ieri** yesterday; **ieri l'altro** the day before yesterday
**igienico(a)** hygienic
**ignorare** to ignore (person); to be unaware of
**il** the
**illimitato(a)** unlimited
**illuminato(a)** floodlit

**illuminazione** f lighting; illumination; **illuminazione elettrica** electric lighting; **illuminazione al neon** strip-lighting

**imballaggio** m packing

**imballare** to pack (goods); to wrap up (parcel); to rev

**imbarazzato(a)** embarrassed

**imbarcarsi** to embark

**imbarcazione** f boat

**imbarco** m boarding; **carta d'imbarco** boarding card

**imbattibile** unbeatable

**imbottigliato(a)** bottled

**imbottito(a)** stuffed (cushion etc)

**imbrogliare** to mix up; to cheat

**imbucare** to post

**immagazzinare** to store

**immaginare** to imagine

**immangiabile** inedible

**immediato(a)** immediate; instant

**immergere** to dip (into liquid)

**immersione** f: **immersione in apnea** diving without breathing apparatus

**immobile** still

**immondizie** fpl rubbish

**imparare** to learn

**impasto** m mixture

**impaziente** impatient

**impedire** to hinder; to prevent

**impegnarsi a** to undertake

**impegno** m undertaking; commitment

**imperatore** m emperor

**impermeabile** waterproof; m raincoat

**impero** m empire

**impiegare** to employ; to spend; to take

**impiegato(a)** m/f employee

**impiego** m use; employment; job

**imporre** to impose

**importanza** f importance

**importare** to import; to

matter; **non importa** it doesn't matter

**importazione** f import

**importo** m (total) amount

**imposta** f tax (on income); shutter (on window);
**imposta sul valore aggiunto** value-added tax

**impresa** f venture; enterprise; undertaking

**impressionare** to impress; to upset

**improbabile** unlikely

**improvviso(a)** sudden

**in** in; to; into; **in treno/macchina** by train/car; **in marmo** made of marble; **siamo in quattro** there are four of us

**inadatto(a)** unsuitable

**inadempienza** f: **eventuali inadempienze dei nostri agenti di viaggio ...** any negligence on the part of our travel agents ...

**incantevole** charming

**incaricarsi di** to take charge of

**incendio** m fire

**incerto(a)** uncertain; doubtful

**inchino** m bow

**inchiodare** to nail

**inchiostro** m ink

**inciampare** to trip

**incidente** m accident; **incidente stradale/aereo** road accident/plane crash

**incinta** pregnant

**inclinare** to tip

**incluso(a)** included; enclosed; inclusive

**incollare** to glue

**incolpare** to blame

**incontrare** to crack

**incrocio** m crossroads; **incrocio a T** T-junction

**incubo** m nightmare

**indicare** to show; to point to

**indicatore** m gauge; indicator

**indicazioni** fpl directions

**indice** m index; contents

**indietro** backwards; back;

behind; **il mio orologio è indietro** my watch is slow; **fare marcia indietro** to reverse

**indigesto(a)** indigestible

**indirizzare** to send; to address

**indirizzo** m address

**indivia** f endive

**indomani** m: **l'indomani** the next day

**indossare** to put on (clothes)

**indossatrice** f to put on (clothes)

**indossatrice** f (fashion) model

**indovinare** to guess

**indumento** m garment

**industria** f industry

**infatti** in fact; actually

**infelice** miserable; unhappy

**inferiore** inferior; lower

**infermiera** f nurse

**infettivo(a)** infectious

**infezione** f infection

**infiammabile** inflammable

**infiammazione** f inflammation

**influenza** f influence; flu

**influire su** to influence

**informare** to inform; **informarsi (di)** to inquire (about)

**informazioni** fpl information; **per informazioni e prenotazioni di gruppi ...** for information and group bookings ...

**infortunio** m accident

**infrangibile** unbreakable

**ingannare** to trick; to deceive

**inganno** m trick; deceit

**ingegnere** m engineer

**Inghilterra** f England

**inghiottire** to swallow

**inginocchiarsi** to kneel

**ingiusto(a)** unfair

**inglese** English

**ingombrante: bagaglio ingombrante** luggage exceeding the dimensions allowed

**ingombrare: non ingombrare l'uscita** do not obstruct the exit

**ingorgo** m blockage; **ingorgo stradale** traffic jam

**ingrandire** to enlarge

**ingresso** m entry; entrance; **prezzo d'ingresso** admission fee; **ingresso libero** admission free; no obligation to buy; **ingresso a pagamento** admission charge; **ingresso pedonale** pedestrian entrance; **ingresso riservato al personale** staff only; **ingresso vietato ai non addetti ai lavori** no entry to unauthorised personnel; **vietato l'ingresso alle persone sprovviste di biglietto di viaggio** ticket-holders only beyond this point

**ingrosso: all'ingrosso** wholesale

**iniezione** f injection

**inizio** m start

**innamorarsi** to fall in love

**innestato(a)** in gear

**inno** m hymn; **inno nazionale** national anthem

**innocuo(a)** harmless

**inoltre** besides

**inondazione** f flood

**inossidabile** rustproof; stainless (steel)

**inquilino(a)** m/f tenant; lodger

**inquinamento** m pollution

**insaccati** mpl sausages

**insalata** f salad; **insalata verde** green salad; **insalata mista/di pomodori/di riso/di cetrioli** mixed/tomato/rice/cucumber salad; **insalata di pesce** seafood salad; **insalata russa** mixed boiled vegetables in mayonnaise

**insegna** f sign

**insegnante** m/f teacher

**insegnare** to teach

**inseguire** to chase

**inserire** to insert; **inserire le banconote una per volta** insert the banknotes one at a time

**inserzione** f advertisement

**insettifugo** m insect repellent

**insetto** m insect

**insieme** together; m outfit

**insistere** to insist

**insolazione** f sunstroke

**insolito(a)** unusual

**insopportabile** unbearable

**installarsi** to settle in

**insuccesso** m failure

**insulina** f insulin

**intanto** meanwhile

**intelligenza** f intelligence

**intenzionale** deliberate

**intenzione** f intention

**interessante** interesting

**interessarsi a** to be interested in

**interesse** m interest

**internazionale** international

**interno** m inside; telephone extension; flat number

**interno(a)** internal

**intero(a)** whole

**interpretazione** f interpretation; performance (of actor)

**interprete** m/f interpreter

**interregionale: (treno) interregionale** m (slow) long-distance train

**interrompere** to interrupt

**interruttore** m switch

**interurbano(a)** long-distance

**intervallo** m half-time; interval (in performance)

**intervento** m intervention; operation (medical)

**intervenuto** m: **gli intervenuti** those present

**intervista** f interview

**intestato(a)** a registered in the name of; made out in the name of

**intimi donna** mpl lingerie

**intingolo** m sauce; tasty dish

**intirizzito(a)** numb (with cold)

**intonaco** m plaster

**intonarsi** to match

**intorno** round

**intossicazione alimentare** f food poisoning

**intraprendere** to undertake

**intrattenere** to entertain

**introdurre** to introduce

**inutile** unnecessary; useless

**invalido(a)** disabled; invalid

**invano** in vain

**invecchiamento** m ageing; maturing

**invece** instead; but; **invece di** instead of

**inventario** m inventory; stocktaking

**inverno** m winter

**inversione** f U-turn

**investigatore** m detective

**investire** to run down; to invest

**invidiare** to envy

**invitare** to invite

**invito** m invitation

**involtino** m stuffed meat roll

**io** I

**iodio** m iodine

**ipermercato** m hypermarket

**ipoteca** f mortgage

**ippodromo** m racecourse

**Irlanda** f Ireland

**irlandese** Irish

**irruzione** f raid (by police)

**iscritto** m member; **per iscritto** in writing

**iscrizione** f inscription; enrolment; registration

**isola** f island; **isola pedonale** pedestrian precinct

**isolato** m block

**isolato(a)** isolated

**ispettore di polizia** m police inspector

**ispezione** f inspection

**istituto** m institute; **istituto di bellezza** beauty salon

**istruttore(trice)** m/f instructor/instructress

**istruzione** f education
**istruzioni** fpl instructions; directions
**Italia** f Italy
**Italia Nostra** f ≈ National Trust
**itinerario** m route; **itinerario di massima** general itinerary; **itinerari d'arte** routes of artistic interest; **itinerario turistico** scenic route
**I.V.A.** f V.A.T.

# J

**jolly** m joker (cards)

# L

**l'** the; him; her; it; you
**la** the; her; it; you
**là** there; **per di là** that way
**labbra** f lips
**labbro** m lip
**laboratorio** m laboratory; workshop; **laboratorio orafo** goldsmith's
**lacca** f lacquer; hair spray
**laccio** m lace (of shoe)
**lacrima** f tear
**ladro** m thief
**laggiù** down there; over there
**lagnarsi** to complain
**lago** m lake
**lama** f blade
**Lambrusco** m sparkling red wine from Emilia-Romagna
**lamentarsi (di)** to complain (about)
**lametta** f razor blade
**lamiera** f sheet (of metal)
**lampada** f lamp; **lampada a raggi ultravioletti** sunlamp; **lampada a stelo** standard lamp
**lampadina** f light bulb; **lampadina tascabile** torch
**lampione** m streetlamp;

lamppost
**lampo** m flash of lightning
**lampone** m raspberry
**lana** f wool; **di lana** woollen; **pura lana vergine** pure new wool; **lana di vetro** fibre-glass
**lancetta** f needle (on dial); hand (of clock)
**lanciare** to throw; to launch
**larghezza** f width; breadth
**largo(a)** wide; broad; **al largo** offshore
**lasagne** fpl thin layers of pasta with meat sauce, white sauce and grated cheese, baked in the oven; **lasagne verdi** thin layers of spinach pasta, served as above
**lasciare** to leave; to let go of; to let (allow); **lasciare libero il passaggio** keep clear
**lassativo** m laxative
**lassù** up there
**lastra** f slab; plate
**lastricato** m paving
**lastricato(a): stradine lastricate** fpl narrow, paved streets
**laterale: via laterale** f side street
**lato** m side
**latta** f can
**lattaio** m milkman
**latte** m milk; **latte condensato** condensed milk; **latte detergente** cleansing milk; **latte evaporato** evaporated milk; **latte intero** full-cream milk; **latte macchiato** hot milk with a dash of coffee; **latte in polvere** dried milk; **latte scremato** skimmed milk; **latte solare** suncream
**latteria** f dairy
**lattuga** f lettuce; **lattuga romana** cos lettuce
**laurea** f degree (university)
**laureato(a)** m/f graduate
**lavabile** washable

**lavabo** m washbasin
**lavacristallo** m windscreen washer
**lavaggio** m washing; **qui lavaggio rapido** rapid car wash; **per lavaggi frequenti** for frequent shampooing
**lavanderia** f laundry (place); **servizio lavanderia e stireria** laundry and ironing service
**lavandino** m sink
**lavare** to wash; **lavare a secco** to dry-clean
**lavarsi** to wash (oneself)
**lavasecco** m dry-cleaner's (shop)
**lavastoviglie** m dishwasher
**lavatrice** f washing machine
**lavorare** to work
**lavoratore(trice)** m/f worker
**lavoro** m work; **lavori domestici** housework; **lavori stradali** road works; **lavori in corso** work in progress; road works ahead
**le** the; them; to her/it; to you
**lecca-lecca** m lollipop
**leccare** to lick
**legare** to tie
**legenda** f key
**legge** f law
**leggere** to read; **leggere attentamente le avvertenze** read the instructions carefully
**leggero(a)** light (not heavy); weak; mild; slight; minor
**legno** m wood (material); **di legno** wooden
**legumi** mpl: **legumi secchi** dried pulses
**lei** she; her; you; **Lei** you
**lente** f lens (of glasses); **lenti a contatto** contact lenses
**lenticchie** fpl lentils
**lento(a)** slow; slack
**lenzuolo** m sheet
**leone** m lion

**lepre** f hare; **lepre in salmì** jugged hare
**lesso** m boiled meat
**lettera** f letter; **lettera di accompagnamento** covering letter; **lettera raccomandata** registered letter
**letteratura** f literature
**lettino** m cot
**letto** m bed; **letto a una piazza** single bed; **letto matrimoniale** double bed; **letti a castello** bunk beds; **letti gemelli** twin beds
**lettura** f reading
**leva** f lever
**levare** to remove; to take away; to take off
**levata** f collection (of mail); **orario della levata** collection times
**lezione** f lesson; lecture
**li** them
**lì** there
**libbra** f pound (weight)
**liberare** to release
**libero(a)** free; clear (not blocked); vacant (seat, toilet); **giorno libero** day off; **ingresso libero** admission free
**libreria** f bookshop; **libreria antiquaria** shop selling old and rare books
**libretto** m booklet; **libretto di circolazione** logbook (of car); **libretto degli assegni** cheque-book; **libretto di banca** bankbook
**libro** m book; **libro di grammatica** grammar (book); **libro tascabile** paperback; **libro paga** payroll
**licenziare** to dismiss; to lay off
**liceo** m secondary school (for 14- to 19-year-olds)
**lieto(a)** glad; **molto lieto** pleased to meet you
**lievito** m yeast
**lima** f file (tool)
**limetta** f nailfile

**limitare** to restrict
**limite** m limit; boundary; **limite di velocità** speed limit
**limonata** f lemonade
**limone** m lemon
**linea** f line; **linea urbana** urban bus service; **linee marittime** sea routes; shipping lines; **Linee FS** Italian State railway network
**lingeria** f lingerie
**lingua** f language; tongue; **lingua salmistrata** pickled ox tongue
**linguaggio** m language
**lino** m linen
**liofilizzato(a)** freeze-dried
**liquidazione** f liquidation
**liquido(a)** liquid; **denaro liquido** cash
**liquirizia** f licorice
**liquore** m liqueur
**liquori** mpl spirits
**liquoroso(a): vino liquoroso** dessert wine
**liscio(a)** smooth; straight
**lista** f list; **lista dei vini** wine list; **lista d'attesa** waiting list; **lista delle pietanze** menu
**listino prezzi** m price list
**lite** f argument; quarrel
**litigare** to argue; to quarrel
**litro** m litre
**livello** m level; **livello del mare** sea level
**lo** the; him; it
**locale** m room; place; **locale notturno** nightclub
**località** f: **località balneare/di villeggiatura** seaside/holiday resort
**locanda** f inn
**locomotiva** f engine (of train)
**loggione** m: **il loggione** the gods (in theatre)
**logorare** to wear out
**logoro(a)** worn; worn-out
**Londra** f London
**lontananza** f distance
**lontano(a)** far

**lordo(a)** gross; pretax
**loro** they; them; to them; you; to you; **Loro** you; to you; **il loro padre** their/ your father
**lotta** f struggle; wrestling
**lotto** m lottery; lot (at auction)
**lozione** f lotion
**lucchetto** m padlock
**luccio** m pike
**luce** f light
**lucidare** to polish
**lucido** m polish (for shoes)
**luglio** m July
**lui** he; him
**lumache** fpl snails
**luna** f moon; **luna di miele** honeymoon
**luna-park** m amusement park
**lunedì** m Monday
**lunghezza** f length
**lungo(a)** long; **lungo la strada** along the street; **a lungo** for a long time
**lungomare** m promenade; seafront
**lungometraggio** m feature film
**luogo** m place; **in nessun luogo** nowhere; **sul luogo** on the spot
**lupo** m wolf
**lusso** m luxury; **di lusso** de luxe; luxury

# M

**ma** but
**maccheroni** mpl macaroni; **maccheroni alla siciliana** macaroni in a sauce containing tomato, capers, garlic, green and black olives, chilli pepper; **maccheroni alla chitarra** macaroni in a sauce containing bacon, tomato, cheese, onion, basil
**macchia** f spot; stain; blot
**macchiare** to stain; to mark

**macchina** f car; machine; **macchina da scrivere** typewriter; **macchina per cucire** sewing maching; **macchina fotografica** camera; **macchina della polizia** police car; **macchina sportiva** sports car

**macchinetta per il caffè** f percolator

**macedonia** f fruit salad

**macellaio** m butcher

**macelleria** f butcher's (shop)

**macinare** to mill; to grind

**macinato(a)** ground (coffee)

**macinino** m mill (for coffee, pepper)

**madera** m Madeira (wine)

**madre** f mother

**madrelingua** f mother tongue

**madrina** f godmother

**maestra** f teacher (primary school)

**maestro** m master; teacher (primary school)

**magazzino** m store room; warehouse; **grande magazzino** department store

**maggio** m May

**maggioranza** f majority

**maggiorazione** f increase

**maggiore** larger; greater; largest; greatest; elder; eldest

**magia** f magic

**maglia** f jersey (sweater); **lavorare a maglia** to knit

**maglieria** f knitwear

**maglietta** f T-shirt

**maglione** m sweater

**magnetofono** m tape recorder

**magnifico(a)** great (excellent); magnificent; grand

**magro(a)** thin (person); lean (meat)

**mai** never; ever

**maiale** m pig; pork; **maiale al latte** pork cooked in

milk with bacon, garlic, cinnamon and rosemary; **maiale arrosto** roast pork

**maialino** m: **maialini da latte** suckling pigs

**maionese** f mayonnaise

**mais** m maize

**maiuscola** f capital letter

**mal** m see **male²**

**malato(a)** ill; sick; sick person; patient

**malattia** f illness; disease

**male¹** badly (not well)

**male²** m pain; ache; **fare male** to hurt; **mal d'auto** car-sickness; **mal di mare** seasickness; **mal di cuore/ di fegato** heart/liver complaint; **mal di denti/di gola/d'orecchi/di stomaco/di testa** toothache/sore throat/ earache/stomach ache/ headache

**malgrado** in spite of

**maltempo** m bad weather

**malva** mauve

**malvagio(a)** wicked

**Malvasia** f sweet, aromatic dessert wine

**mamma** f mum(my)

**mancanza** f lack; shortage

**mancare** to miss

**mancato(a): mancate coincidenze** fpl missed (rail/air etc) connections

**mancia** f tipp (money given)

**mancino(a)** left-handed

**mandare** to send

**mandarino** m mandarin (orange)

**mandorla** f almond

**maneggio** m riding school

**manette** fpl handcuffs

**mangia-e-bevi** m ice cream with nuts, fruit and liqueur

**mangiare** to eat; **vietato dare da mangiare agli animali** do not feed the animals

**Manica** f Channel

**manica** f sleeve

**manico** m handle

**maniere** fpl manners

**manifestazione** f demonstration (political); rally

**manifesto** m poster

**maniglia** f handle; strap (on bus)

**mano** f hand; trick (in cards); **fatto(a) a mano** handmade

**manopola** f knob (on radio etc); mitt(en); **manopola di spugna** facecloth

**manovale** m labourer

**manovella** f handle (for winding)

**mantello** m cloak; coat

**mantenere** to support (financially); to keep

**Mantova** f Mantua

**manubrio** m handlebar(s)

**manutenzione** f upkeep; maintenance

**manzo** m beef

**marca** f brand; brand name

**marchio** m hallmark; **marchio di fabbrica** trademark; **marchio depositato** registered trademark

**marcia** f march; gear (of car); **quarta/prima marcia** top/bottom gear

**marciapiede** m pavement

**marcio(a)** rotten (wood etc)

**marcire** to rot; to go bad

**mare** m sea; seaside; **avere mal di mare** to be seasick

**marea** f tide; **c'è alta/ bassa marea** the tide is in/out

**margine** m margin

**marina** f navy

**marinaio** m sailor

**marito** m husband

**maritozzo** m sort of currant bun

**marmellata** f jam; **marmellata d'arance** marmalade

**marmitta** f silencer (on car); **marmitta catalitica** catalytic converter

**marmo** m marble (material)

**marrone** brown; m chestnut

**Marsala** *m* red dessert wine from Sicily

**martedì** *m* Tuesday; **martedì grasso** Shrove Tuesday

**martello** *m* hammer

**marzo** *m* March

**mascarpone** *m* soft, creamy cheese often served as a dessert

**mascella** *f* jaw

**maschera** *f* mask; usherette

**maschile** masculine

**maschio** male

**massaggiare** to massage

**massiccio(a)** massive

**massimale** *m* maximum sum insurable

**massimo(a)** maximum

**masticare** to chew

**mastro** *m* ledger

**materassino** *m* air bed

**materasso** *m* mattress

**materia** *f* subject (in *school*); **materie prime** raw materials

**maternità** *f* maternity hospital

**matita** *f* pencil

**matrice** *f* stub (*counterfoil*)

**matrimonio** *m* wedding; marriage

**matterello** *m* rolling pin

**mattina** *f* morning

**mattino** *m* morning

**mattone** *m* brick

**maturarsi** to ripen; to accrue

**maturo(a)** ripe; mature

**mazza** *f* club; bat

**mazzo** *m* pack (of cards); bunch

**me** me; to me; myself

**meccanismo** *m* mechanism; works

**medaglioni** *mpl*: **medaglioni di filetto/di pollo** round fillets of beef/chicken

**media** *f* average

**medicina** *f* medicine; **medicina d'urgenza** emergency treatment

**medicinale** *m* drug (*medicine*)

**medico** *m* doctor; **medico generico** general practitioner, G.P.

**medusa** *f* jellyfish

**meglio** better; best

**mela** *f* apple; **mela cotogna** quince

**melagrana** *f* pomegranate

**melanzana** *f* aubergine; **melanzane alla parmigiana** aubergines baked with tomatoes, Parmesan cheese and spices; **melanzane ripiene** stuffed aubergines

**melassa** *f* treacle

**melo** *m* apple tree

**melone** *m* melon; **melone ghiacciato** iced melon

**membro** *m* member

**memoria** *f* memory; **a memoria** by heart

**mendicante** *m/f* beggar

**meno** less; minus; **a meno che** unless; **il meno caro** the least expensive; **meno errori** fewer errors

**mensa** *f* canteen

**mensile** monthly

**menta** *f* mint (*herb*)

**mente** *f* mind

**mentire** to lie (*tell a lie*)

**mento** *m* chin

**mentre** while; whereas

**menù** *m*: **menù del giorno** menu of the day; **menù turistico** tourist or low-price menu; **menù vegetariano** vegetarian menu

**menzione** *f* mention

**meraviglioso(a)** wonderful, marvellous

**mercante** *m* merchant

**mercatino** *m*: **mercatino dell'usato** flea market

**mercato** *m* market; **Mercato Comune** Common Market; **mercato ittico** fish market

**merce** *f* goods; **la merce si paga alle casse del piano dove è stata scelta** goods must be paid for on the floor from which they have been selected

**merceria** *f* haberdashery

**merci** *fpl* freight; goods

**mercoledì** *m* Wednesday; **mercoledì delle Ceneri** Ash Wednesday

**merenda** *f* snack

**meridionale** southern

**meritare** to deserve

**merlango** *m* whiting

**merlo** *m* blackbird

**Merlot** *m* dry red table wine

**merluzzo** *m* cod

**meschino(a)** mean

**mescolanza** *f* mixture

**mescolare** to blend; to mix

**mescolarsi** to mix

**mese** *m* month

**messa** *f* mass (*church*); **messa in piega** set (of *hair*)

**messaggio** *m* message

**mestiere** *m* job; trade

**mestruazioni** *fpl* menstruation

**metà** *f* half

**metro** *m* metre; **metro a nastro** tape measure

**metropolitana** *f* underground

**mettere** to put; to put on (*clothes*); **mettere in comunicazione** to put through (on *phone*); **mettersi in posa** to pose

**mezzanotte** *f* midnight

**mezzi** *mpl* means

**mezzo** *m* means; means of transport; middle; **per mezzo di** by means of; **mezzo di trasporto** means of transport

**mezzo(a)** half; **di mezza età** middle-aged

**mezzogiorno** *m* midday, noon; **il Mezzogiorno** the south of Italy

**mezz'ora** *f* half-hour; half-an-hour

**mi** me; to me; myself

**mia** my; mine

**microfono** *m* microphone

**mie** my; mine
**miei** my; mine
**miele** *m* honey
**mietere** to harvest (*grain*)
**miglio** *m* mile
**migliorare** to improve
**migliore** better; best
**miliardo** *m* thousand million
**milione** *m* million
**militare** *m* serviceman
**mille** thousand
**mina** *f* lead (*in pencil*)
**minacciare** to threaten
**minatore** *m* miner
**minestra** *f* soup; **minestra in brodo** clear soup with rice or noodles; **minestra di verdura** vegetable soup
**miniera** *f* mine (*for coal etc*)
**minigonna** *f* miniskirt
**minimo(a)** minimum
**ministero** *m* ministry (*political*)
**ministro** *m* minister (*political*)
**minoranza** *f* minority
**minore** less; smaller; lower; younger; **vietato ai minori di anni 18** no admission to anyone under 18 years of age
**minorenne** under age
**mio** my; mine
**miope** shortsighted
**mira** *f* aim
**mirtillo** *m* cranberry
**miscela** *f* blend
**misto** *m*: **misto mare** mixed fish salad
**misto(a)** mixed
**misura** *f* measure; measurement; **fatto(a) su misura** made-to-measure
**mite** mild; gentle
**mitili** *mpl* mussels
**mittente** *m/f* sender
**MM** *abbreviation of* metropolitana
**mobile** *m* piece of furniture
**mobili** *mpl* furniture
**moda** *f* fashion; **l'ultima moda** the latest fashions; **di moda** fashionable

**modalità** *f*: **secondo le modalità previste** according to what has already been agreed; **modalità di pagamento** method of payment; **seguire le modalità d'uso** follow the instructions
**modificare** to modify
**modisteria** *f* milliner's shop
**modo** *m* way; manner; **ad ogni modo** in any case; **in tutti i modi** at all costs; **in qualche modo** somehow
**modulo** *m* form (*document*)
**mogano** *m* mahogany
**moglie** *f* wife
**molla** *f* spring (*coil*)
**molletta** *f* clothes-peg; **molletta per capelli** hairgrip
**mollica** *f*: **mollica (di pane)** crumb
**molluschi** *mpl* molluscs
**molo** *m* pier; **molo per attracco** docking pier
**molti(e)** many
**moltiplicare** to multiply
**molto** a lot; much; very
**molto(a)** much; **molta gente** lots of people
**momento** *m* moment; **per il momento** for the time being
**monaca** *f* nun
**monaco** *m* monk
**monastero** *m* monastery
**mondo** *m* world
**moneta** *f* coin
**monorotaia** *f* monorail
**montagna** *f* mountain
**montare** to go up; to put up; to assemble (*parts of machine*); to whip (*cream, eggs*)
**montatura** *f* frames (*of glasses*)
**montone** *m*: **carne di montone** mutton; **giacca di montone** sheepskin jacket
**montuoso(a)** mountainous
**moquette** *f* wall-to-wall carpet(ing)

**mora** *f* blackberry
**morbido(a)** soft
**morbillo** *m* measles
**mordere** to bite
**morire** to die
**morso** *m* bite (*by animal*)
**mortadella** *f* type of salted pork meat
**morte** *f* death
**morto(a)** dead
**mosca** *f* fly
**moscato** *m* muscatel: red or white dessert wine; **moscato spumatizzato** sparkling muscatel; **Moscato d'Asti** sweet, sparkling white wine
**moscerino** *m* gnat
**moscone** *m* pedalo (with oars)
**mosella** *m* Moselle (*wine*)
**mostarda** *f* mustard
**mostra** *f* show; exhibition; **mostra permanente** permanent exhibition; **mostra convegno** conference and exhibition
**mostrare** to show
**motocicletta** *f* motorbike
**motociclista** *m/f* motorcyclist
**motociclo** *m* motorbike
**motolancia** *f* launch
**motonautica** *f* speedboat racing
**motore** *m* engine; motor; **vietato tenere motori e luci non elettriche accesi** switch off engine and extinguish any cigarettes
**motorino d'avviamento** *m* starter (*in car*)
**motoscafo** *m* motorboat
**movimento** *m* motion; movement
**mozzarella** *f* mozzarella (moist Neapolitan curd cheese); **mozzarella in carrozza** mozzarella with either anchovies or ham between 2 slices of bread, fried in batter
**mucchio** *m* pile; heap
**mulino** *m* mill; **mulino a vento** windmill

**multa** f fine; **multa per sosta vietata** parking ticket

**municipio** m town hall

**muovere** to move

**muratura** f: **villette in muratura** stonebuilt or brickbuilt villas

**muro** m wall

**muscolo** m muscle

**museo** m museum; **museo civico di storia naturale** municipal museum of natural history; **museo storico** museum of history

**musica** f music; **musica leggera/da camera/di sottofondo** light/chamber/ background music

**musicista** m/f musician

**mutande** fpl underpants

**mutandine** fpl panties

**muto(a)** dumb

# N

**nafta** f diesel oil

**nailon** m nylon

**Napoli** f Naples

**narrativa** f fiction

**nascere** to be born

**nascita** f birth

**nascondere** to hide

**nasello** m hake

**naso** m nose

**nastro** m ribbon; tape; **nastro adesivo** sellotape

**Natale** m Christmas

**nato(a)** born

**naufragio** m shipwreck

**navata** f nave

**nave** f ship; **nave cisterna** tanker (ship)

**nave-traghetto** f ferry

**navigare** to sail

**nazione** f nation

**ne** of him/her/it/them

**né... né** neither...nor; **né l'uno né l'altro** neither

**neanche** not even; neither

**nebbia** f fog

**Nebbiolo** m light, dry red wine from Piedmont

**negare** to deny

**negli** = in + gli

**negoziante** m shopkeeper

**negozio** m shop

**nei** = in + i, **nel** = in + il

**nemico** m enemy

**nemmeno, neppure** not even; neither

**nero(a)** black

**nervetti** mpl: **nervetti in insalata** thin strips of sinewy beef or veal served cold with beans, shallots and pickles

**nessuno(a)** no; any; nobody; none; anybody

**netto(a)** net; **al netto di IVA** net of VAT

**neve** f snow

**nevicare** to snow

**nevischio** m sleet

**nido** m nest; **nido d'infanzia** day nursery, crèche

**niente** nothing; anything

**nipote** m/f grandson/ granddaughter; nephew/ niece

**Nizza** f Nice

**no** no (as answer)

**nocciolo** m stone (in fruit)

**noce** f walnut

**nocivo(a)** harmful

**nodo** m knot; bow (ribbon); **nodo ferroviario** junction (railway)

**noi** we; us

**noioso(a)** dull; boring; annoying

**noleggiare** to hire; to rent; to charter (plane, bus); **si noleggiano biciclette** bicycles for hire

**noleggio** m: **noleggio biciclette** bicycles for hire; **noleggio furgoni** vans for hire

**nolo** m = **noleggio**

**nome** m name; first name; **nome di battesimo** Christian name

**nominare** to appoint; to mention

**non** not

**nondimeno** all the same

**non-fumatore** m nonsmoker

**nonna** f grandmother

**nonno** m grandfather

**nono(a)** ninth

**nord** m north

**norma** f norm; par (golf)

**nostalgia** f homesickness; nostalgia

**nostro(a)** our; ours

**nota** f note; memo(randum)

**notaio** m notary (public)

**notare** to notice

**notevole** remarkable

**notiziario** m news (on TV etc)

**notizie** fpl news

**notte** f night

**novanta** ninety

**nove** nine

**novembre** m November

**novità** f novelty; news

**nubile** single (woman)

**nudo(a)** naked; nude; bare

**nulla** nothing; anything

**nullo(a)** void (contract)

**numero** m number (figure); act (at circus etc); issue (of magazine); size (of shoes)

**nuora** f daughter-in-law

**nuotare** to swim

**nuovo(a)** new; **di nuovo** again

**nutrire** to feed

**nuvola** f cloud

**nuvoloso(a)** cloudy

# O

**o** or; **o... o** either...or

**obbligo** m obligation

**obiettare a** to object to

**obiettivo** m lens (of camera); target; objective; **obiettivo grandangolare** wide angle lens

**obliterare** to stamp (ticket); **lato da obliterare** side to be stamped

**obliteratrice** f stamping machine

**oblò** *m* porthole
**oca** *f* goose
**occasione** *f* opportunity; occasion; bargain
**occhiali** *mpl* glasses; goggles; **occhiali da sole** sunglasses
**occhio** *m* eye
**Occidente** *m*: **l'Occidente** the West
**occorrere** to be necessary
**occuparsi: me ne occupo io** I'll take care of it
**occupato(a)** busy; engaged
**odiare** to hate
**odierno(a): in data odierna** today
**odio** *m* hatred
**odore** *m* smell; scent
**offerta** *f* bid; offer; **in offerta (speciale)** on (special) offer
**officina** *f* workshop; **officina autorizzata** authorized garage; **officina per autovetture nazionali ed estere** repairs carried out on all makes of car
**offrire** to offer; to bid (*amount*)
**oggettistica** *f* fancy goods; **oggettistica regalo** giftware
**oggetto** *m* object; **oggetto d'antiquariato** antique
**oggi** today
**oggigiorno** nowadays
**ogni** every; each
**ognuno** everyone
**Olanda** *f* Holland
**oleodotto** *m* pipeline
**olio** *m* oil; **olio solare** suntan oil; **olio di ricino** castor oil; **olio d'oliva** olive oil
**oltre** beyond; besides
**oltremare** overseas
**ombra** *f* shadow; shade
**ombrello** *m* umbrella
**ombrellone** *m* sunshade (*over table*); beach umbrella
**ombretto** *m* eyeshadow
**omettere** to omit
**omicidio** *m* murder; **omicidio colposo** manslaughter
**omissione di soccorso** *f* failure to stop and give assistance
**omogeneizzati** *mpl* baby foods
**oncia** *f* ounce
**onda** *f* wave; **onde medie** medium wave; **onde corte** short wave; **onde lunghe** long wave
**onesto(a)** decent (*respectable*); honest
**onorario** *m* fee
**opera** *f* work (*art, literature*); opera
**operaio** *m* workman
**operaio(a)** working-class
**opuscolo** *m* brochure
**ora[1]** now
**ora[2]** *f* hour; **ora di pranzo** lunchtime; **ora di punta** rush hour; **che ora è?** what's the time?
**orario** *m* timetable; schedule; **in orario** punctual; on schedule; **orario di apertura/chiusura** opening/closing times; **orario di cassa** banking hours; **orario definitivo/indicativo** final/approximate schedule; **orario delle partenze** timetable for departures; **orario degli uffici per il pubblico** hours of opening to the public; **orario di vendita** opening hours; **orario di visite** visiting times
**orata** *f* sea bream
**ordinare** to order (*goods, meal*)
**ordinato(a)** neat, tidy
**ordinazione** *f* order (*for goods, meal*)
**ordine** *m* command; order; **di prim'ordine** high class
**orecchino** *m* earring
**orecchio** *m* ear
**orecchioni** *mpl* mumps
**oreficeria** *f* jeweller's (shop)
**organizzare** to organize
**orgoglio** *m* pride
**orientarsi** to take one's bearings
**Oriente** *m*: **l'Oriente** the East
**origano** *m* oregano
**orizzontale** level; horizontal
**orizzonte** *m* horizon
**orlo** *m* hem; verge
**ormeggiare** to moor
**ornare** to decorate
**oro** *m* gold; **oro massiccio** solid gold; **placcato oro** gold-plated
**orologeria** *f* watchmaker's (shop)
**orologio** *m* watch; clock
**orso** *m* bear
**ortaggi** *mpl* vegetables
**ortofrutticolo(a): mercato ortofrutticolo** fruit and vegetable market
**Orvieto** *m* light, straw-coloured wine from Umbria: dry, sweet or semi-sweet
**orzo** *m* barley; **orzo tostato solubile** instant barley coffee
**osare** to dare
**oscuro(a)** dim; obscure
**ospedale** *m* hospital; **ospedale infantile/psichiatrico** children's/mental hospital
**ospite** *m/f* guest; host; hostess
**osservazione** *f* remark; observation
**ossigeno** *m* oxygen
**osso** *m* bone
**ossobuco** *m* marrowbone; stew made with knuckle of veal in tomato and wine sauce
**ostacolare** to obstruct; to hinder
**ostacolo** *m* obstacle
**ostaggio** *m* hostage
**ostello** *m* hostel; **ostello della gioventù** youth hostel
**osteria** *f* inn
**ostrica** *f* oyster

**ostruzione** f blockage
**ottanta** eighty
**ottavo(e)** eighth
**ottenere** to obtain; to get; **ottenere la linea** to get through (on phone)
**ottico** m optician
**otto** eight
**ottobre** m October
**ottone** m brass
**otturatore** m shutter (in camera)
**otturazione** f filling (in tooth)
**ovatta** f cotton wool
**ovest** m west
**ovino(a): carni ovine** fpl lamb and mutton
**ovvio(a)** obvious
**ozio** m leisure

# P

**pacchetto** m pack; packet
**pacco** m package; parcel
**pace** f peace
**padella** f frying pan
**Padova** f Padua
**padre** m father
**padrino** m godfather
**padrona** f landlady
**padrone** m landlord
**paesaggio** m scenery; countryside
**paese** m country; land
**paesino** m village
**paga** f pay
**pagaia** f paddle (oar)
**pagamento** m payment; **pagamento alla consegna** cash on delivery; **pagamento anticipato** payment in advance
**pagare** to pay; to pay for
**pagina** f page
**paglia** f straw; **paglia e fieno** mixture of yellow and green tagliatelle
**pagliaccio** m clown
**pagnotta** f round loaf
**paio** m pair; **un paio di** a pair of; a couple of
**pala** f shovel

**palasport** m sports stadium
**palazzo** m building; palace; **palazzo comunale** town hall; **palazzo dei congressi** conference centre; **palazzo dello sport** sports stadium
**palco** m platform
**palcoscenico** m stage
**palestra** f gym(nasium)
**paletta** f dustpan
**palla** f ball
**pallacanestro** f basketball
**pallanuoto** f water polo
**pallavolo** f volleyball
**pallido(a)** pale
**pallone** m balloon; football
**pallottola** f bullet
**palma** f palm-tree
**palo** m pole; post
**palpebra** f eyelid
**palude** f swamp; bog
**panca** f bench
**pancetta** f bacon
**panciotto** m waistcoat
**pandoro** m type of sponge cake eaten at Christmas
**pane** m bread; loaf (of bread); **pane carrè** sandwich bread; **pane e coperto** cover charge; **pane integrale** wholemeal bread; **pan di Spagna** sponge; **pane di segale** rye bread
**panetteria** f bakery
**panettone** m light cake containing sultanas and crystallized fruit, traditionally eaten at Christmas
**panforte** m nougat-type delicacy from Siena
**pangrattato** m breadcrumbs
**paniere** m basket; hamper
**panificio** m bakery
**panino** m roll; **panino imbottito** sandwich; **panini caldi** hot rolls
**panna** f cream; **panna montata** whipped cream; **panna da cucina** ≈ double cream
**panno** m cloth

**pannocchia** f corn-on-the-cob
**pannolino** m nappy
**pantaloni** mpl trousers
**pantofola** f slipper
**panzarotto** m fried savoury turnover with a filling of mozzarella, bacon, egg and sometimes tomatoes and anchovies
**papa** m pope
**papà** m dad(dy)
**pappardelle** fpl wide strips of pasta; **pappardelle con la lepre** wide strips of pasta with spiced hare
**parabolico(a): antenna parabolica** satellite dish
**parabrezza** m windscreen
**paracadute** m parachute
**parafango** m mudguard
**paralume** m lampshade
**paraspruzzi** m mudguard
**paraurti** m bumper
**paravento** m screen (partition)
**parcheggiare** to park
**parcheggio** m car-park; **parcheggio custodito/incustodito** attended/unattended car-park
**parchimetro** m parking meter
**parco** m park; **parco demaniale** public park; **parco giochi bambini** children's play park; **parco marino** nature reserve for marine life
**parecchi(e)** several
**parente** m/f relation; relative; **parente stretto** next of kin
**parentesi** f bracket
**parere¹** to seem, appear
**parere²** m opinion
**parete** f wall
**pari: numero pari** even number
**Parigi** f Paris
**parlare** to talk; to speak
**parmigiano** m Parmesan: hard, tangy cheese often used in cooking
**parola** f word

**parrucca** f wig

**parrucchiere(a)** m/f hairdresser

**parte** f share; part; side; **d'altra parte** on the other hand

**partenza** f departure

**particolare** particular; m detail

**partire** to go; to leave

**partita** f match; game

**partito** m party (political)

**Pasqua** f Easter

**passaggio** m passage; gangway; **dare un passaggio a** to give a lift to; **passaggio a livello** level crossing; **passaggio pedonale** pedestrian crossing

**passaporto** m passport; **passaporto collettivo** group passport

**passare** to pass; to spend; to put through (on phone); **passare avanti** move forward

**passatempo** m interest; hobby

**passato** m past; **passato freddo di pomodoro** chilled tomato soup; **passato di patate/piselli** creamed potatoes/peas; **passato di verdura** cream of vegetable soup

**passato(a)** past; off (meat)

**passeggero(a)** m/f passenger

**passeggiare** to walk

**passeggiata** f walk; stroll; **passeggiata a mare** promenade

**passeggino** m pushchair

**passe-partout** m master key

**passera** f plaice

**passerella** f gangway

**passero** m sparrow

**passito** m sweet wine made with raisins

**passo** m pace; step; pass (in mountains); **passo carrabile** keep clear

**pasta** f pastry; pasta; dough; **pasta di acciughe** anchovy paste; **paste e ceci/fagioli** chick pea/bean and pasta soup; **pasta frolla** shortcrust pastry; **pasta integrale** wholemeal pasta; **pasta di mandorle** almond paste; **pasta sfoglia** puff pastry; **pasta all'uovo** egg pasta

**pastasciutta** f pasta served in a sauce, not in soup

**pastello** m crayon

**pasticceria** f cake shop

**pasticciere** m confectioner

**pasticcino** m petit four

**pasticcio** m muddle; pie (meat); **pasticcio di lasagne** wide strips of pasta in layers, with meat sauce, white sauce and cheese

**pastiglia** f tablet; pastille

**pasto** m meal; **prima dei/dopo i pasti** before/after meals

**pastore** m shepherd; minister (of religion)

**pastorizzato(a)** pasteurized

**pastoso(a): vino pastoso** mellow wine

**patata** f potato; **patate arrosto/al forno** roast/baked potatoes; **patate fritte** chips; **patate lesse/novelle/in padella/saltate** boiled/new/fried/sautéed potatoes

**patatine** fpl crisps

**pâté** m: **pâté di fegato** liver pâté

**patente** f licence; driving licence

**patrimonio** m estate; heritage

**patta** f flap

**pattinare** to skate

**pattino** m skate; **pattini a rotelle** roller skates

**pattumiera** f dustbin

**paura** f fear

**pausa** f pause; break

**pavimento** m floor

**paziente** patient

**pazienza** f patience

**pazzo(a)** mad

**peccato** m sin; **che peccato!** what a shame!

**pecora** f sheep

**pecorino** m hard, tangy sheep's-milk cheese

**pedaggio** m toll

**pedalò** m pedalo

**pedicure** m chiropodist

**pedone** m pedestrian; **pedoni sul lato opposto** pedestrians please use the other pavement

**peggio** worse

**peggiore** worse; worst

**pelati** mpl: **(pomodori) pelati** peeled tomatoes

**pelle** f skin; hide; leather; **pelle scamosciata** suede

**pelletterie** fpl leather goods

**pellicceria** f furrier's (shop); furs

**pelliccia** f fur coat; fur

**pellicola** f film (for camera)

**pelo** m hair; fur

**pena** f sentence; sorrow

**penale** f penalty clause

**pendenza** f slope

**pendere** to hang; to lean

**pendio** m hill; slope

**pendolare** m commuter

**penna** f pen; **penna stilografica** fountain pen

**pennarello** m felt-tip pen

**penne** fpl quill-shaped tubes of pasta; **penne all'arrabbiata** penne in a spicy sauce of tomatoes, mushrooms, bacon, chilli pepper, basil and garlic; **penne ai funghi** penne with mushrooms, parsley, cream, whisky and butter

**pennello** m brush; **pennello da barba** shaving brush

**pensare** to think

**pensiero** m thought

**pensionato(a)** m/f pensioner

**pensione** f boarding house; pension; **pensione completa** full board;

**mezza pensione** half board

**Pentecoste** f Whitsun; Whitsunday

**pentola** f pot; saucepan

**peoci** mpl mussels

**pepato(a)** peppery

**pepe** m pepper; **pepe bianco/nero** white/black pepper

**peperonata** f stew of peppers, aubergines, tomatoes, onion, garlic, oregano and basil

**peperoncino** m chilli pepper

**peperone** m pepper (capsicum); **peperone verde/rosso** green/red pepper; **peperoni ripieni** stuffed peppers

**per** for; per; in order to; **per le 4** by 4 o'clock; **3 metri per 3** 3 metres square

**pera** f pear

**percentuale** f percentage

**perché** why; because; in order that

**percorrenza** f: **biglietto con percorrenza superiore/inferiore a 100 chilometri** ticket for journeys of more than/less than 100 kilometres; **treno a lunga percorrenza** long-distance train

**percorrere** to travel; to cover

**percorribilità** f: **percorribilità strade** traffic information service

**percorso** m journey; route; **percorso panoramico** scenic route

**perdere** to lose; to miss (train); **perdere tempo** to waste one's time

**perdita** f leak; loss

**perdonare** to forgive

**pericolante** unsafe

**pericolo** m danger

**pericoloso(a)** dangerous

**periferia** f outskirts; suburbs

**perizia** f survey (of building)

**perla** f pearl; bead

**permanente** f perm; **permanente continua** parking restrictions still apply

**permanenza** f: **buona permanenza!** enjoy your stay!

**permesso** m permission; permit; **permesso di soggiorno** residence permit

**permettere** to permit

**pernice** f partridge

**pernottamento** m overnight stay

**pernottare** to stay the night

**perquisire** to search

**perquisizione** f: **sono previste perquisizioni personali** searches will be carried out

**persiana** f shutter

**persona** f person

**personale** m staff; personnel; **personale di sicurezza** security personnel

**pertinente** a relevant to

**pertosse** f whooping cough

**p.es.** e.g.

**pesante** heavy

**pesare** to weigh

**pesca** f angling; fishing; peach; **divieto di pesca, pesca vietata** no fishing; **pesche al vino rosso** peaches in red wine with cinnamon and sugar

**pescatore** m angler; fisherman

**pesce** m fish; **pesce persico** perch; **pesce spada** swordfish

**pescecane** m shark

**pescheria** f fishmonger's shop

**pescivendolo** m fishmonger

**peso** m weight; **peso a pieno carico** weight when fully loaded

**pessimo(a)** awful

**pesto** m: **pesto alla genovese** sauce made with fresh basil, pine kernels, garlic and cheese

**petardo** m banger

**petroliera** f oil tanker

**petrolio** m oil

**pettinare** to comb

**pettine** m comb; scallop

**petto** m breast; chest

**pezza** f patch; rag

**pezzo** m piece; cut (of meat); **pezzo di ricambio** spare (part)

**pezzuola** f cloth; rag

**piacere¹** to please

**piacere²** m enjoyment; pleasure; **piacere di conoscerla** pleased to meet you

**piacevole** pleasant

**pianerottolo** m landing (on stairs)

**pianeta** m planet

**piangere** to cry

**piano¹** slowly; quietly

**piano²** m floor; storey; plan; **al primo piano** on the first floor; **ai piani inferiori/superiori** on the lower/upper floors

**piano(a)** level

**pianobar** m bar offering musical entertainment

**pianta** f plant; sole (of foot); map (of town); plan

**piantare** to plant; to pitch

**pianterreno** m ground floor

**pianura** f plain

**piastra** f: **panini alla piastra** toasted sandwiches; **formaggio alla piastra** grilled cheese

**piastrella** f tile

**piattaforma** f platform

**piatti: piatti pronti/da farsi** prepared dishes/ dishes requiring preparation

**piattino** m saucer

**piatto** m dish; course; plate; **primo piatto** entrée

**piatto(a)** flat

**piazza** f square

**piazzale** m open square; service area

**piazzola** f: **piazzola (di sosta)** lay-by

**piccante** spicy; hot

**picchetto** m peg; picket; tent peg

**picchiare** to hit; to knock (*engine*)

**piccione** m pigeon

**picco** m peak; **a picco sul mare** rising straight from the sea

**piccolo(a)** little; small

**piccone** m pick; pickaxe

**piede** m foot; bottom (*of page, list*)

**piega** f crease; fold; pleat

**piegare** to fold; to bend

**pieno(a)** full; **il pieno, per favore!** fill it up! (*car*)

**pietra** f stone

**pietrina** f flint (*in lighter*)

**pigiama** m pyjamas

**pigro(a)** lazy

**pila** f battery (*for radio etc*)

**pilastro** m pillar

**pillola** f pill

**pineta** f pinewood

**pinne** fpl flippers

**pino** m pine

**pinoli** mpl pine kernels

**Pinot** m: **Pinot bianco** dry, aromatic white wine from north-east Italy; **Pinot grigio** dry, aromatic and full-bodied white wine from the same area as 'Pinot bianco'; **Pinot nero** dry, red wine with a fruity flavour, from the same area as the white Pinot

**pinze** fpl pliers

**pinzette** fpl tweezers

**pioggia** f rain

**piombo** m lead; **benzina senza piombo** unleaded petrol

**pioppo** m poplar

**piovere** to rain; **piove** it's raining

**pioviggine** f drizzle

**piovoso(a)** rainy; wet

**pipa** f pipe (*for smoking*)

**piroscafo** m steamer

**piscina** f swimming pool; **piscina comunale** public swimming pool

**piselli** mpl peas

**pista** f track; race track; **pista d'atterraggio** runway; **pista da ballo** dance floor; **pista di pattinaggio (su ghiaccio)** (ice-)skating rink; **pista per principianti** nursery slope; **pista da sci** ski run

**pistola** f gun; nozzle

**pittore** m painter

**pittoresco(a)** picturesque

**più** more; most; plus; **i più** most people; **in più** extra

**piuma** f feather; down

**piumino** m duvet; eiderdown; quilted jacket

**piuttosto** quite; fairly; rather

**pizza** f: **pizza alla diavola** pizza with spicy salami; **pizza margherita** pizza with tomato, mozzarella and oregano; **pizza napoletana** pizza with tomato, garlic and oregano; **pizza ai quattro formaggi** pizza with four kinds of cheese melted on top

**pizzaiola: alla pizzaiola** with tomato, garlic and oregano sauce

**pizzico** m pinch; sting

**pizzo** m lace

**placcato(a): placcato oro/argento** gold-/silver-plated

**platano** m plane (*tree*)

**platea** f stalls; **platea interi/ridotti** full-price/concessionary seats in the stalls

**plico** m parcel

**pneumatico** m tyre

**po'** see **poco(a)**

**pochi(e)** few

**poco(a)** little; not much; **un po'** a little; **fra poco** shortly

**poesia** f poem; poetry

**poggiatesta** m headrest

**poi** then

**poiché** because; since

**polenta** f sort of thick porridge made with maize flour; **polenta e osei** small birds, spit-roasted and served with polenta; **polenta e salsiccia** polenta with sausages

**politica** f policy; politics

**polizia** f police; **polizia ferroviaria** railway police; **polizia stradale** traffic police

**poliziotto** m policeman

**polizza** f policy; **polizza di assicurazione** insurance policy

**pollame** m thumb

**pollo** m chicken; **pollo alla diavola** grilled chicken, highly spiced

**polmone** m lung

**polmonite** f pneumonia

**polo** m polo; pole; terminal (*electricity*)

**polpa** f pulp; flesh; meat

**polpette** fpl meatballs

**polpettone** m meat loaf

**polpo** m octopus

**polsino** m cuff (*of shirt*)

**polso** m wrist

**poltrona** f armchair

**polvere** f dust; powder

**pomeriggio** m afternoon

**pomo** m doorknob

**pomodoro** m tomato

**pompa** f pump; **pompa di benzina** petrol pump

**pompelmo** m grapefruit

**pompiere** m fireman

**ponce** m punch (*drink*)

**ponte** m bridge; deck; **ponte a pedaggio** toll bridge; **fare il ponte** to make a long weekend of it

**pontile** m jetty

**popolo** m people

**porcellana** f china; porcelain

**porchetta** f roast suckling pig

**porpora** f purple

**porre** to put

**porro** m leek

**porta** f door; gate; goal;

**porta antipanico/di sicurezza** emergency exit

**portabagagli** m luggage rack; roof rack

**portabottiglie** m wine rack

**portacenere** m ashtray

**portachiavi** m key ring

**portafoglio** m wallet

**portale** m portal

**portaombrelli** m umbrella stand

**portare** to carry; to bring; to wear

**portasigarette** m cigarette case

**portata** f course; range; capacity; **fuori portata** out of reach

**portatile** portable

**portatore** m: **pagabile al portatore** payable to the bearer

**portauovo** m egg cup

**portavoce** m spokesman

**portellone posteriore** m tailgate

**porticciolo** m marina

**portico** m porch

**portiera** f door

**portiere** m porter (doorkeeper); janitor

**portineria** f caretaker's lodge

**porto** m port; harbour; **porto franco** carriage free; **porto fluviale** river port; **porto di scalo** port of call

**porzione** f portion; helping

**posare** to put down

**posate** fpl cutlery

**posologia** f dosage

**posporre** to postpone

**possedere** to own

**posta** f mail; stake; odds; **per posta aerea** by air mail; **posta raccomandata** registered mail; **fermo posta** poste restante

**postagiro** m post office giro

**Poste** fpl Post Office

**posteggio** m car park; **posteggio per tassì** taxi rank

**posteriore** rear; later

**postino** m postman

**posto** m place; position; job; seat; **posto di blocco** road block; border post; **posto riservato ad invalidi di guerra e del lavoro** seat reserved for disabled persons; **posto di soccorso** first-aid centre; **posto telefonico pubblico** public telephone; **posti in piedi** standing room; **posti a sedere** seating capacity; **posti prenotati** reserved seats

**potabile** drinking; drinkable; **acqua non potabile** this is not drinking water

**potente** powerful

**potenza** f power (of machine)

**potere**[1] to be able to; can

**potere**[2] m power; authority

**povero(a)** poor

**pozzanghera** f puddle; pool

**pozzo** m well

**pranzo** m lunch

**prassi** f normal procedure

**pratica** f practical experience; file

**pratico(a)** practical; handy

**preavviso** m advance notice; **soggetto a cambiamenti senza preavviso** subject to change without notice; **comunicazioni con preavviso** person-to-person calls

**precedente** previous; earlier

**precedenza** f right of way (on road); **dare la precedenza** to give way

**precipitarsi** to rush

**preciso(a)** precise; exact; accurate

**precotto(a)** ready-cooked

**predeterminare: predeterminare l'importo desiderato** select the amount required

**preferire** to prefer

**prefisso** m prefix; **prefisso (teleselettivo)** dialling code

**pregare** to pray; **si prega di chiudere la porta/non fumare** please close the door/do not smoke

**preghiera** f prayer

**prego** don't mention it!; after you!

**prelievo** m withdrawal; collection; blood sample; **prelievo gettoni e monete respinti** returned tokens and coins

**preludio** m overture

**pré-maman** m maternity dress

**premere** to push; to press

**premio** m bonus; premium; prize

**prendere** to take; to get; to catch

**prenotare** to book; to reserve

**prenotazione** f reservation; **prenotazione obbligatoria** seats must be booked

**preoccupato(a)** worried

**preparare** to prepare

**prepararsi** to get ready

**preparativi** mpl preparations

**presa** f socket; outlet; **presa di corrente** power point

**presbite** long-sighted

**presentare** to introduce

**presentarsi** to report; to check in (at airport)

**presentazione** f introduction; presentation

**preservativo** m sheath, condom

**preside** m/f headmaster; headmistress

**presidente** m president; chairman

**pressione** f pressure

**presso** near; care of

**prestare** to lend

**prestazione** f

performance; **prestazioni** services; **prestazioni ambulatoriali** outpatients' department

**prestigiatore** m conjuror

**prestito** m loan; **prendere in prestito** to borrow

**presto** early; soon; **faccia presto!** hurry up!

**prete** m priest

**prevendita** f: **biglietti in prevendita** tickets may be purchased in advance

**preventivo** m estimate

**previo(a): previa autorizzazione delle autorità competenti** upon authorization from the relevant authorities

**previsione** f forecast; **previsioni del tempo** weather forecast

**previsto(a): all'ora prevista** at the scheduled time; **come previsto** as expected

**prezioso(a)** precious

**prezzemolo** m parsley

**prezzo** m price; **prezzo del coperto** cover charge; **a prezzo di costo** at cost; **prezzo della corsa** fare; **prezzo fisso** set price; **prezzo di catalogo** list price; **prezzo al minuto** retail price; **prezzo d'ingresso** entrance fee

**prigione** f prison

**prigioniero(a)** m/f prisoner

**prima**[1] before; first; earlier

**prima**[2] première

**primato** m record

**primavera** f spring

**primo(a)** first; top; early; **prima classe** first class; **solo prima classe senza prenotazione** only first-class passengers may travel without a reserved seat

**principale** major; main

**principalmente** mainly

**principe** m prince

**principessa** f princess

**principiante** m/f beginner

**privato(a)** private;

personal

**privo(a) di** privo probable; likely

**procedimento** m procedure; process

**processo** m trial (in law); process

**prodotti** mpl produce; products

**prodotto** m product; commodity

**produrre** to produce

**produzione** f production; output; **gelati di produzione propria** our own ice cream

**professore** m professor; teacher (secondary school)

**professoressa** f teacher (secondary school)

**profondità** f depth

**profondo(a)** deep

**profumeria** f perfumery; perfume shop

**profumo** m scent; perfume

**progetto** m plan; project

**programma** m programme; syllabus; schedule; **fuori programma** supporting programme (at cinema)

**proibire** to ban; to prohibit

**proiettare** to show (film)

**proiettore** m headlight; floodlight; projector

**proiezione** f: **proiezioni cinematografiche** film shows

**promessa** f promise

**promettere** to promise

**promosso(a)** promoted; **essere promosso(a)** to pass (exam)

**pronostico** m forecast

**pronto(a)** ready; **pronto!** hello! (on telephone); **pronto intervento** emergency services; **pronto soccorso** first aid

**pronunciare** to pronounce

**proporre** to propose; to suggest

**proposito** m intention; **a proposito di** with regard

to

**proposta** f proposal; suggestion

**proprietà** f ownership; property; land

**proprietario(a)** m/f owner

**proprio** just; really

**proprio(a)** own

**proroga** f extension; deferment

**prosciutto** m ham; **prosciutto affumicato** smoked ham; **prosciutto crudo/cotto** raw/cooked ham; **prosciutto di Parma (con melone/fichi)** cured ham from Parma (with melon/figs)

**Prosecco** m dry, sweet white wine with a natural sparkle, from the Trieste area

**proseguimento** m: **volo con proseguimento per ...** flight with onward connection for ...

**proseguire** to continue

**prospettiva** f prospect; outlook

**prossimamente** coming soon

**prossimo(a)** next; **prossima apertura** opening soon

**proteggere** to protect; to guard

**prova** f proof; evidence; rehearsal; test

**provare** to prove; to try; to try on

**provenienza** f origin; **luogo di provenienza** place of origin

**provolone** m medium-hard white cheese

**provvedere a** to provide for

**provvisorio(a)** temporary

**provvista** f supply

**prudente** wise; careful

**prudere** to itch

**prugna** f plum

**prurito** m itch

**psichiatra** m/f psychiatrist

**psicologo(a)** m/f

psychologist
**PTP** *abbreviation of* **posto telefonico pubblico**
**pubblicare** to publish
**pubblicità** f publicity; advertising
**pubblico** m public; audience
**pubblico(a)** public
**pugilato** m boxing
**pugnale** m dagger
**pugno** m fist; punch
**pulire** to clean
**pulito(a)** clean
**pulitura** f: **pulitura a secco** dry cleaning
**pulizia** f cleaning
**pullman** m coach
**pulmino** m minibus
**pummarola** f: **spaghetti alla pummarola** spaghetti in tomato sauce
**pungere** to prick; to sting
**punire** to punish
**punizione** f punishment
**punta** f point; tip
**puntare** to point; to aim; **puntare su** to bet on
**punteggio** m score
**puntina** f drawing pin
**punto** m point; spot; stitch; full stop; **punto d'incontro** meeting place; **punto interrogativo** question mark; **punto di riferimento** landmark; **punto vendita** sales outlet
**puntualmente** on time
**puntura** f bite; sting
**pupazzo** m puppet
**purché** provided; providing
**purè** m purée; **purè di patate** mashed potatoes
**puro(a)** pure

## Q

**qua** here
**quaderno** m exercise book
**quadrato(a)** square
**quadretti: a quadretti** checked
**quadro** m picture; painting

**quaglia** f quail
**qualche** some; **qualche volta** sometimes
**qualcosa** something; anything
**qualcuno** somebody; anybody; **qualcun altro** somebody else
**quale** what; which; which one
**qualificato(a)** qualified
**qualsiasi** any
**quando** when; **di quando in quando** occasionally
**quanto(a)** how much; **quanti(e)** how many; **quanto a** as for
**quaranta** forty
**quarantena** f quarantine
**quartiere** m district; **quartiere popolare** working-class district
**quarto** m quarter; **un quarto d'ora** quarter of an hour
**quarto(a)** fourth; **la quarta (marcia)** top gear
**quasi** nearly; almost
**quattordici** fourteen
**quattro** four
**quei** those
**quel(la)** that
**quelli(e)** those
**quello(a)** that; **quello(a) che** what; the one who
**quercia** f oak
**questi(e)** these
**questione** f issue; question
**questo(a)** this; this one
**questura** f police headquarters; police force
**qui** here
**quindi** then; therefore
**quindici** fifteen
**quindicina di giorni** f fortnight
**quinto(a)** fifth
**quota** f subscription; quota; height; **quota d'iscrizione** enrolment fee; entry fee; membership fee; **quota di partecipazione** cost (of excursion *etc*); **quota per persona** amount per

person; **prendere/perdere quota** to gain/lose height (*plane*)
**quotazione** f: **quotazione dei cambi** exchange rates
**quotidiano** m daily (paper)
**quotidiano(a)** daily

## R

**rabarbaro** m rhubarb
**rabbia** f anger; rabies
**racchetta** f racket; bat; **racchetta da neve** snowshoe; **racchetta da sci** ski stick
**raccogliere** to gather; to collect; to pick up
**raccolta** f collection; **raccolta vetro** bottle bank
**raccolto** m crop; harvest
**raccomandare** to recommend
**raccontare** to tell (*story*)
**raccordo** m connection; slip road; **raccordo anulare** ring road
**raddoppiare** to double
**radersi** to shave
**radice** f root
**radiografia** f X-ray
**radiotelefono** m radiophone
**radunarsi** to gather
**raffermo(a)** stale
**raffica** f squall; gust
**raffineria** f refinery
**raffreddare** to cool; to chill (*wine, food*)
**raffreddore** m cold (*illness*); **raffreddore da fieno** hay fever
**ragazza** f girl; girlfriend; **ragazza squillo** call girl
**ragazzo** m boy; boyfriend
**raggio** m beam; ray
**raggiungere** to reach
**ragione** f reason
**ragioneria** f accountancy
**ragionevole** sensible; reasonable
**ragioniere** m accountant
**ragno** m spider

**ragù** m: **ragù (di carne)** meat sauce; **ragù vegetale** vegetable sauce

**RAI** f Italian State broadcasting company

**rallentare** to slow down or up

**rame** m copper

**rammendare** to darn

**ramo** m branch

**rana** f frog

**rango** m rank

**rapa** f turnip

**rapidamente** quickly

**rapido** m express train (for which supplement must be paid)

**rapido(a)** high-speed; quick

**rapire** to kidnap

**rapporto** m ratio; report; relationship; **rapporti sessuali** sexual intercourse

**rappresentante** m/f representative

**rappresentazione** f performance; production

**raro(a)** rare; scarce

**raso** m satin

**rasoio** m razor

**rassomigliare** to look like

**rastrello** m rake

**rata** f instalment

**ratto** m rat

**ravanello** m radish

**ravioli** mpl square cushions of pasta with meat or other filling; **ravioli panna e prosciutto** ravioli with cream and ham

**razza** f race; breed

**razzia** f raid

**razziale** racial

**razzo** m rocket

**re** m king

**reagire** to react

**reale** royal; real

**realizzare** to carry out; to realize (assets)

**realmente** really

**reazione** f reaction

**recapito** m address; delivery

**recarsi: recarsi alla cassa** pay at the cash desk

**recensione** f review

**recentemente** lately; recently

**recinto** m fence

**Recioto** m sparkling red wine from the Verona area

**recipiente** m container

**réclame** f advertisement

**reclamo** m complaint

**recluta** f recruit

**recupero** m: **recupero monete** returned coins

**redditizio(a)** profitable

**reddito** m income; yield

**redigere** to draw up (document)

**referenze** fpl reference (testimonial)

**regalare** to give (as a present); to give away

**regalo** m present, gift

**reggere** to support; to carry

**reggipetto, reggiseno** m bra

**regina** f queen

**regionale** regional; **(treno) regionale** local train

**regione** f region; district; area

**regista** m/f producer (of play); director (of film)

**registrare** to tape; to register; to record

**Regno Unito** m United Kingdom, U.K.

**regola** f rule

**regolamento** m regulation

**regolare¹** regular; steady

**regolare²** to regulate; to settle; to adjust

**relativo(a)** relevant; relative

**relazione** f relationship; report

**reliquia** f relic

**remare** to row (boat)

**remo** m oar

**rendere** to return; to render; to make; **rendersi conto di** to realize

**rendimento** m performance (of car); profitability; output

**rene** m kidney (of person)

**reparto** m department (in store); unit

**repellente** m insect repellent

**residenza** f residence

**residenziale** residential

**resistente** hardwearing; durable; tough

**resistenza** f resistance; strength

**resistere** to resist

**respingere** to reject

**respirare** to breathe

**respiratore** m breathing apparatus

**responsabile** responsible

**responsabilità** f responsibility; **responsabilità civile** civil liability

**restare** to stay; to remain; to be left

**restituire** to return

**restituzione** f return; repayment; **dietro restituzione dello scontrino** on presentation of the receipt

**resto** m remainder; change

**restringersi** to shrink

**restrizione** f restriction

**rete** f net; goal

**retro** m back; **vedi retro** P.T.O.

**retromarcia** f reverse (gear)

**revisione** f review; service (for car)

**rialzo** m upturn; rise

**rianimare** to revive

**rianimazione** f: **reparto rianimazione** intensive care unit

**riattaccare** to reattach; to hang up (telephone)

**ribasso** m fall (in price)

**ribes** m blackcurrant

**ricambio** m: **ricambi auto** car spares; **ricambi originali** car manufacturers' spare parts

**ricamo** m embroidery

**ricchezza** f wealth

**ricciolo** m curl

**ricciuto(a)** curly

**ricco(a)** wealthy; rich

**ricerca** f research

**ricetta** f prescription; recipe

**ricevere** to receive; to welcome; **si riceve solo per appuntamento** visits by appointment only

**ricevimento** m reception; reception desk

**ricevitore** m receiver (*phone*)

**ricevitoria** f Inland Revenue office; **ricevitoria del lotto** lottery office

**ricevuta** f receipt; **ricevuta di ritorno** acknowledgment of receipt

**ricezione** f reception

**richiesta** f request

**ricompensa** f reward

**riconoscere** ro recognize

**riconoscimento** m: **documento di riconoscimento** means of identification

**ricordare** to remember; to remind; **ricordarsi di** to remember

**ricordo** m souvenir; memory

**ricorrere a** to resort to

**ricotta** f soft white unsalted cheese

**ricuperare** to recover; to retrieve

**ridere** to laugh

**ridicolo(a)** ridiculous

**ridurre** to reduce

**riduzione** f reduction

**riempere** to fill; to fill in/out/up

**rientro** m return; return home

**rifare** to do again; to repair; **rifare i letti** to make the beds

**riferimento** m reference

**rifiutare** to refuse; to reject

**rifiuti** mpl rubbish; waste

**rifiuto** m refusal

**riflettere** to reflect; to think

**riflettore** m spotlight; floodlight

**rifornimento** m: **fare rifornimento (di benzina)** to fill up (*car*); **posto di rifornimento** filling station

**rifugio** m refuge; shelter

**rigido(a)** stiff

**riguardare** to concern

**riguardo** m care; respect; **riguardo a ...** as regards ...

**rilascio** m: **data di rilascio** date of issue

**rilassarsi** to relax

**rimandare** to send back; to postpone

**rimanere** to stay; to remain; to be left

**rimbalzare** to bounce

**rimborsare** to repay; to refund

**rimborso** m refund; **rimborso spese mediche a seguito infortunio** refund of medical expenses following an accident

**rimedio** m remedy

**rimescolare** to shuffle (*cards*); to stir

**rimessa** f remittance; garage

**rimettere** to put back; return; to remit; to postpone

**rimettersi** to recover

**rimorchio** m trailer; **a rimorchio** on tow

**rimozione** f: **divieto di parcheggio con zona rimozione** no parking: offenders' cars will be towed away; **rimozione forzata** illegally parked cars will be towed away

**rimpatrio** m repatriation

**rincrescere: mi rincresce che ...** I regret that ...

**rinforzare** to strengthen

**rinfreschi** mpl refreshments

**ringhiera** f rail; banister

**ringraziare** to thank

**rinnovare** to renew

**rinunce** fpl cancellations

**rinunciare** to give up

**rinviare** to send back; to postpone; to adjourn

**rinvio** m return; postponement; adjournment

**riparare** to mend; to repair

**riparazione** f repair; **riparazione gomme** tyre repairs

**ripassare** to revise

**ripetere** to repeat

**ripido(a)** abrupt; steep

**ripieno** m stuffing

**ripieno(a)** stuffed; filled

**riposarsi** to rest

**riposo** m rest

**riprendere** to take back; to resume; **riprendere i sensi** to come round

**risa** fpl laughter

**risalita** f: **impianti di risalita** ski lifts

**risarcimento** m compensation

**riscaldamento** m heating

**rischio** m risk; **il bagaglio viaggia a rischio e pericolo del partecipante** luggage is carried at owner's risk

**risciacquare** to rinse

**riscuotere** to collect; to cash

**riserva** f reserve; reservation; **riserva di caccia** game reserve; **riserva naturale** nature reserve

**riservare** to reserve

**riservato(a): riservato alle ambulanze** reserved for ambulances

**risi e bisi** m rice and peas cooked in chicken stock

**riso** m laugh; rice; **riso in bianco** boiled rice with butter; **riso alla greca** rice salad with olives

**risolvere** to solve; to work out

**risorse** fpl resources

**risotto** m dish of rice cooked in stock with various ingredients; **risotto ai funghi/alla marinara** risotto with mushrooms/

fish; **risotto alla milanese** risotto with saffron and Parmesan cheese; **risotto nero alla fiorentina** risotto with cuttlefish, garlic and white wine
**risparmiare** to save
**rispetto** *m* respect
**rispondere** to answer; to reply; to respond; **la compagnia non risponde di ...** the company cannot be held responsible for ...
**risposta** *f* reply; answer
**ristabilirsi** to recover
**ristorante** *m* restaurant
**ristorazione** *f*: **servizi di ristorazione** refreshments
**ristoro** *m*: **servizio ristoro** refreshments
**risultato** *m* result
**ritardare** to delay; to be late; to be slow (*clock, watch*)
**ritardo** *m* delay; **essere in ritardo** to be late
**ritenere** to hold back; to believe
**ritirare** to withdraw
**ritirata** *f* WC
**ritiro** *m* retirement; withdrawal; **ritiro bagagli** baggage claim
**ritmo** *m* rhythm
**ritorno** *m* return
**riunione** *f* meeting; conference
**riuscire** to succeed; to manage
**riva** *f* bank
**rivale** *m/f* rival
**rivedere** to see again; to revise
**rivendita** *f* resale; retailer's shop
**riviera** *f*: **la Riviera ligure** the Italian Riviera
**rivista** *f* magazine; revue
**roba** *f* stuff; belongings
**roccia** *f* rock
**rodare** to run in
**rognone** *m* kidney
**rollino** *m* spool
**romanzo** *m* novel
**rombo** *m* turbot; roar; rumble

**rompere** to break
**rompersi** to break
**rompicapo** *m* puzzle; worry
**rosa** pink; rose
**rossetto** *m* lipstick
**rosso(a)** red
**rosticceria** *f* shop selling roast meat and other prepared food
**rotaie** *fpl* rails
**rotocalco** *m* magazine
**rotolo** *m* roll
**rotonda** *f* roundabout
**rotondo(a)** round
**roulotte** *f* caravan
**rovesciare** to pour; to spill; to turn upside down; to turn over
**rovesciarsi** to spill; to overturn
**rovescio** *m* reverse side; wrong side
**rovina** *f* ruin
**rovinare** to wreck; to ruin
**rovine** *fpl* ruins
**rubare** to steal
**rubinetto** *m* tap
**rubino** *m* ruby
**rucola** *f* rocket (*vegetable*)
**rudemente** roughly
**ruga** *f* wrinkle
**ruggine** *f* rust
**rumore** *m* noise
**ruota** *f* wheel; **ruota di scorta** spare wheel
**ruscello** *m* stream
**ruvido(a)** rough; coarse

# S

**sabato** *m* Saturday
**sabbia** *f* sand
**sabbioso(a)** sandy
**sacchetto** *m* (small) bag
**sacco** *m* bag; sack; **sacco a pelo** sleeping bag
**saggio** *m* essay
**sala** *f* hall; auditorium; **sala d'aspetto** *or* **d'attesa** waiting room; airport lounge; **sala**

**cinematografica** cinema; **sala da gioco** gaming room; **sala giochi** games room; **sala di lettura** reading room; **sala operatoria** operating theatre; **sala TV** TV lounge; **sala di intrattenimento** reception rooms
**salame** *m* salami
**salario** *m* wage; wages
**salato(a)** salted; salty; savoury
**saldare** to settle (*bill*); to weld; **da saldare** to be paid
**saldi** *mpl* sales (*cheap prices*)
**saldo** *m* payment; balance
**sale** *m* salt; **sale fino** table salt; **sale grosso** cooking salt; **sali e tabacchi** tobacconist's shop
**saliera** *f* salt cellar
**salire** to rise; to go up; **salire a bordo (di)** to board
**saliscendi** *m* latch
**salita** *f* climb; slope; **in salita** uphill
**salmì** *m* game stewed in a rich brown sauce
**salmone** *m* salmon; **salmone affumicato** smoked salmon
**salone** *m* lounge; salon; **salone dell'automobile** motor show; **salone di bellezza** beauty salon; **salone di ritrovo** lounge
**salotto** *m* living room; sitting room
**salsa** *f* gravy; sauce; **salsa di pomodoro** tomato sauce; **salsa rubra** ketchup; **salsa tartara** tartare sauce; **salsa verde** sauce made with parsley, anchovy fillets, gherkins, potato, garlic and onion
**salsiccia** *f* sausage
**saltare** to jump; to explode; to blow (*fuse*)
**saltato(a)** sautéed
**saltimbocca** *m*:

**saltimbocca (alla romana)** veal escalopes with ham, sage and white wine

**salumeria** f delicatessen

**salumi** mpl cured pork meats

**salutare** to greet

**salute** f health

**saluto** m greeting; **distinti saluti** yours sincerely

**salvagente pedonale** m traffic island

**salvaguardia** f safeguard

**salvare** to save; to rescue

**salvataggio** m rescue

**salvia** f sage

**salvo** except; unless; **salvo imprevisti** barring accidents

**salvo(a)** safe

**sanato** m young calf

**sangue** m blood; **al sangue** rare (steak)

**sanguinaccio** m black pudding

**sanguinare** to bleed

**Sangiovese** m dry red table wine from Emilia-Romagna

**sanitari** mpl bathroom fittings

**sano(a)** healthy

**santo(a)** holy; m/f saint

**sanzioni** fpl sanctions

**sapere** to know; **sa di pesce** it tastes of fish

**sapone** m soap; **sapone da barba** shaving soap

**saponetta** f bar of soap

**sapore** m flavour; taste

**saporito(a)** tasty

**sarago** m bream

**Sardegna** f Sardinia

**sardella** f pilchard

**sarto** m tailor

**sartoria** f tailor's; dressmaker's

**sasso** m stone

**sbagliarsi** to make a mistake

**sbagliato(a)** incorrect; wrong

**sbaglio** m mistake

**sbalordire** to amaze

**sbandare** to swerve

**sbarcare** to land

**sbarco** m: **al momento dello sbarco** on landing

**sbarra** f bar

**sbarrare** to cross (cheque)

**sbattere** to slam; to whisk

**sbiadire** to fade

**sbornia** f drunkenness

**sbrigare: sbrigare le formalità** to deal with the formalities

**sbrinare** to defrost

**sbucciare** to peel

**sacchi** mpl chess

**scadenza** f expiry; **a lunga scadenza** long-term

**scadere** to expire

**scaduto(a)** out-of-date; expired

**scaffale** m shelf

**scaglia** f scale (of fish); flake

**scala** f scale; ladder; staircase; **scala mobile** escalator

**scaldabagno** m water heater

**scaldare** to warm

**scale** fpl stairs

**scalinata** f flight of steps

**scalino** m step

**scalo** m stopover; **scali intermedi** intermediate stops

**scaloppa** f: **scaloppa milanese** veal escalope fried in egg and breadcrumbs

**scaloppina** f veal escalope; **scaloppine al limone/al Marsala** veal escalopes in a lemon/Marsala sauce

**scalzo(a)** barefoot

**scamiciato** m pinafore dress

**scampi** mpl: **scampi ai ferri** grilled scampi; **code di scampi dorati e fritti** scampi tails, breaded and fried

**scampoli** mpl remnants

**scantinato** m cellar

**scapolo** m bachelor

**scappare** to escape

**scarafaggio** m beetle

**scaricare** to unload

**scarico(a)** flat (battery)

**scarpa** f shoe; **scarpe per la pioggia** waterproof shoes

**scarpette** fpl sneakers

**scarpone da sci** m ski boot

**scassinatore** m burglar

**scatola** f box; carton; **in scatola** tinned (food)

**scatolame** m tinned food; tins

**scattare** to take (photograph)

**scatto** m (telephone) unit

**scavare** to dig; to dig up

**scegliere** to choose

**scelta** f range; selection; choice

**scena** f scene

**scendere** to go down

**scheda** f slip (of paper); **vendita schede telefoniche** phonecards sold here

**scheggia** f splinter

**schermo** m screen

**scherzo** m joke

**schiacciare** to crush; to squash; to mash

**schiaffo** m smack

**schiantarsi** to shatter

**schiavo(a)** m/f slave

**schiena** f back

**schienale** m back (of chair); **mantenere lo schienale in posizione eretta** ensure your seat back is in the upright position

**schiuma** f foam

**schizzare** to splash

**sci** m ski; skiing; **sci accompagnato** skiing with instructors; **sci di fondo** cross-country skiing; **sci nautico** or **d'acqua** water-skiing

**scialle** m shawl; wrap

**scialuppa di salvataggio** f lifeboat

**sciare** to ski

**sciarpa** f scarf

**sciatore(trice)** m/f skier

**scienza** f science

**scienziato(a)** m/f scientist

**scimmia** f ape; monkey

**sciocchezze** fpl nonsense; rubbish

**sciogliere** to untie; to dissolve

**sciogliersi** to dissolve; to melt

**sciolto(a)** loose

**sciopero** m strike

**sciovia** f ski lift

**sciroppato(a): prugne/ciliegie sciroppate** plums/cherries in syrup

**sciroppo** m syrup; **sciroppo per la tosse** cough mixture

**sciupato(a)** ruined; spoilt; shop-soiled

**scivolare** to slip; to slide; to glide

**scodella** f bowl; basin

**scogliera** f cliff

**scoiattolo** m squirrel

**scolapiatti** m draining-board

**scolare** to drain

**scommessa** f bet

**scomodo(a)** uncomfortable; inconvenient

**scompartimento** m compartment

**sconfitta** f defeat

**sconosciuto(a)** unknown; m/f stranger

**scontabile: tariffa non scontabile** no discount on this rate

**sconto** m discount; **non si fanno sconti** no discounts given

**scontrino** m ticket; receipt; **esigete lo scontrino** ask for a receipt; **scontrino alla cassa** pay at the cash desk first and bring your receipt to the bar; **scontrino fiscale** receipt for tax purposes

**scontro** m collision; crash

**sconveniente** improper

**scopa** f broom; brush

**scoperto** m overdraft

**scopo** m aim; goal; purpose

**scoppiare** to burst; to explode

**scoppio** m explosion; bang

**scoprire** to discover; to find out; to uncover

**scorciatoia** f short cut

**scorcio** m glimpse; **scorcio panoramico** vista

**scorrere** to flow; to pour

**scortese** unkind; rude

**scossa** f shock

**scottarsi** to scald oneself

**scottatura** f burn; sunburn

**Scozia** f Scotland

**scozzese** Scottish

**scrittore(trice)** m/f writer

**scrittura** f writing

**scrivania** f desk

**scrivere** to write; to spell

**scultura** f sculpture

**scuola** f school; **scuola elementare** primary school; **scuola media** ≈ junior comprehensive school; **scuola (di) sci** ski school

**scuotere** to shake

**scuro(a)** dark

**scusa** f excuse

**scusare** to excuse

**scusarsi** to apologize

**sdraiarsi** to lie down

**sdrucciolevole** slippery

**se** if; whether

**sé** himself; herself; itself; oneself; themselves

**sebbene** though

**seccare** to dry; to annoy

**seccarsi** to dry up

**secchio** m pail; bucket

**secco(a)** dried; dry

**secolo** m century

**secondo(a)** second; according to; **di seconda mano** secondhand

**sedano** m celery

**sede** f seat; head office

**sedere**[1] m bottom

**sedere**[2] to sit, be seated

**sedersi** to sit down

**sedia** f chair; **sedia a rotelle** wheelchair; **sedia a sdraio** deckchair

**sedici** sixteen

**sedile** m bench; seat

**segale** f rye

**seggiolone** m highchair

**seggiovia** f chair-lift

**segnalazione** f: **segnalazioni guasti** reporting of faults

**segnale** m signal; road sign; **segnale di linea libera** dial(ling) tone; **un segnale acustico preannuncia l'avviamento del nastro** an acoustic signal precedes any movement of the conveyor belt

**segnaletica** f road signs; **segnaletica orizzontale in rifacimento** road markings being renewed

**segnare** to mark; to score (goal)

**segno** m sign; mark

**segretario(a)** m/f secretary

**segreteria** f secretary's office; **segreteria telefonica** answering service

**segreto(a)** secret

**seguente** following

**seguire** to follow; to continue

**sei** six

**sella** f saddle

**selvaggina** f game (hunting)

**selvaggio(a)** wild

**selvatico(a)** wild

**selz** m soda water

**semaforo** m traffic lights

**sembrare** to look; to seem

**seme** m seed; suit (cards)

**semifreddo** m chilled dessert made with ice cream

**seminario** m seminar; seminary

**seminterrato** m basement

**semola** f: **semola di grano duro** durum wheat

**semolino** m: **semolino al latte** semolina pudding

**semplice** plain; simple

**sempre** always; ever

**senape** f mustard

**seno** m breast

**sensibilità** f feeling

# senso

46

**senso** m sense; **strada a senso unico** one-way street
**sentiero** m path; footpath
**sentinella** f sentry
**sentire** to hear; to feel; to smell; to taste
**senza** without
**separare** to separate
**sepoltura** f burial
**seppia** f cuttlefish; **seppie in umido** stewed cuttlefish
**seppioline** fpl baby cuttlefish
**sera** f evening
**serata** f: **serata di gala** gala evening
**serbatoio** m tank; cistern
**serie** f series
**serio(a)** serious; reliable
**serpeggiante** winding
**serpente** m snake
**serra** f greenhouse
**serratura** f flock
**servire** to attend to; to serve; **servire a** to be of use; to be used for
**servizio** m service; service charge; report (in press); **servizi** facilities; bathroom; **in servizio** in use; on duty; **fuori servizio** out of order; off duty; **servizio di buffet** buffet service; **servizio interurbano/internazionale con prenotazione** booking service for long-distance/international calls; **servizio pubblico bus** public bus service; **servizio al tavolo** waiter/waitress service; **servizi igienici** bathroom fittings; **camera con servizi privati** room with private bathroom; **servizi di pubblica utilità** public facilities
**sessanta** sixty
**sesso** m sex
**sesto(a)** sixth
**seta** f silk
**setaccio** m sieve
**sete** f thirst; **avere sete** to be thirsty

**settanta** seventy
**sette** seven
**settembre** m September
**settentrionale** northern
**settimana** f week; **settimana bianca** week's skiing holiday
**settimanale** weekly
**settimo(a)** seventh
**severo(a)** harsh; strict
**sfinito(a)** worn out
**sfoderato(a)** unlined
**sfondo** m background
**sfortuna** f bad luck
**sfortunatamente** unfortunately
**sforzare** to force; **sforzarsi di** to struggle to
**sforzo** m effort
**sfuso(a)** in bulk; loose
**sgabello** m stool
**sganciarsi: sganciarsi adesso** let go of the bar now
**sgelare** to thaw
**sghiacciare** to de-ice
**sgombro** m mackerel
**sgonfio(a)** flat
**sgradevole** unpleasant
**sguardo** m look; glance
**si** himself; herself; oneself; each other; themselves
**sì** yes
**siccità** f drought
**Sicilia** f Sicily
**sicuramente** surely
**sicurezza** f safety; security
**sicuro(a)** safe; sure
**sidro** m cider
**siepe** f hedge
**sigaretta** f cigarette
**sigaro** m cigar
**significato** m meaning
**Signor** m Mr
**signora** f lady; madam; **Signora** Mrs
**signore** m gentleman; sir
**signorina** f young woman; miss
**silenzio** m silence
**simile** similar; alike
**simpatico(a)** pleasant; nice
**sinagoga** f synagogue
**sincero(a)** sincere
**sindacato** m syndicate;

trade union
**sindaco** m mayor
**sinfonia** f symphony
**singhiozzo** m sob; hiccup
**singola** f single room
**singolarmente** individually
**singolo(a)** single
**sinistra** f left; **a sinistra** on/to the left
**sinistro** m accident
**sinistro(a)** left
**sintomo** m symptom
**sirena** f siren
**sistema** m system
**sistemazione** f: **sistemazione alberghiera** hotel accommodation
**sito** m site
**skai**® m Leatherette®
**slacciare** to unfasten; to undo
**slavina** f snowslide
**slegare** to untie
**slip** m briefs
**slitta** f sledge; sleigh
**slittare** to slip; to skid
**slogare** to dislocate
**smacchiatore** m stain remover
**smagliatura** f ladder
**smalto** m nail polish, nail varnish; enamel
**smarrirsi** to lose one's way
**smarrito(a)** lost
**smeraldo** m emerald
**smettere** to stop; to cease
**smoking** m dinner jacket
**snello(a)** slim
**Soave** m dry white wine from the Verona area
**sobborgo** m suburb
**soccorso** m assistance; **soccorso pubblico di emergenza** emergency police service
**società** f society
**socio** m associate; member
**soddisfare** to satisfy
**sodo** hard; hard-boiled
**soffiare** to blow
**soffice** soft
**sofficini** mpl small savoury fritters
**soffitta** f loft; attic

soffitto *m* ceiling

soffrire to suffer

soggiorno *m* visit; stay; sitting room; **soggiorno balneare** stay at the seaside

sogliola *f* sole; **sogliola ai ferri** grilled sole; **sogliola alla mugnaia** sole lightly fried in butter with lemon juice and parsley

sogno *m* dream

solamente only

solare solare; **crema/olio solare** suntan cream/oil

solco *m* track; furrow

soldato *m* soldier

soldi *mpl* money

sole *m* sun; sunshine

soleggiato(a) sunny

solido(a) strong; solid; fast (*dye*)

solito(a) usual; **di solito** usually

sollevare to raise; to lift; to relieve

sollievo *m* relief

solo only

solo(a) alone; lonely

solubile soluble; **caffè solubile** instant coffee

somigliare a to be like; to look like

somma *f* sum

sommario *m* summary; outline

sommelier *m* wine waiter

sonnifero *m* sleeping pill

sonno *m* sleep

sono: **io sono** I am; **loro sono** they are

sontuoso(a) luxurious

sopportare to bear; to stand

soppressata *f* type of sausage

soppresso(a): **corsa soppressa nei giorni festivi** no service on holidays

sopra on; above; over; on top; **di sopra** upstairs

sopracciglio *m* eyebrow

soprattassa *f* surcharge

sopravvivere to survive

sordo(a) deaf

sorella *f* sister

sorgente *f* spring

sorgere to rise; to arise

sorpassare to overtake

sorpresa *f* surprise

sorridere to smile

sorriso *m* smile

sorvegliante *m/f* supervisor

sorvegliare to watch; to supervise

sospensione *f* adjournment; postponement; **sospensione voli (per avverse condizioni atmosferiche)** flights postponed (due to adverse weather conditions)

sospeso(a): **corsa sospesa** service cancelled

sospirare to sigh

sosta *f* stop; **divieto di sosta, sosta vietata** no waiting

sostanza *f* substance; stuff

sostanzioso(a) filling; nourishing

sostare: **vietato sostare nei passaggi di intercomunicazione** do not stand in the passageway

sostegno *m* backing; support

sostenere to support; to maintain

sostituire to substitute; to replace

sostitutivo(a): **servizio sostitutivo con autocorsa** back-up coach service

sottaceti *mpl* pickles

sottana *f* underskirt

sotterraneo(a) underground

sottile thin; fine; subtle

sotto underneath; under; below; **di sotto** downstairs

sottoesposto(a) underexposed

sottolineare to emphasize; to underline

sottopassaggio *m*

underpass

sottoporre to subject; to submit

sottosviluppato(a) underdeveloped

sottotitolo *m* subtitle

sottoveste *f* petticoat

sottrarre to subtract

sovraesposto(a) overexposed

sovvenzionare to subsidize

spaccio *m* shop; **spaccio di carni fresche** butcher's shop

spada *f* sword

spaghetti *mpl*: **spaghetti all'amatriciana** spaghetti in tomato sauce with garlic and Parmesan cheese; **spaghetti alla bolognese** spaghetti in a meat and tomato sauce; **spaghetti alla carbonara** spaghetti with bacon, eggs and Parmesan cheese; **spaghetti alla ciociara** spaghetti with black olives, tomatoes, peppers and cheese; **spaghetti al pomodoro** spaghetti in tomato sauce; **spaghetti alle vongole** spaghetti with clams

spago *m* string

spalla *f* shoulder

spallina *f* strap (*of dress etc*)

spalmare to spread

sparare to fire; to shoot

sparire to disappear

spartitraffico *m* central reservation

spaventare to frighten

spazio *m* space; room

spazzaneve *m* snowplough

spazzola *f* brush

spazzolino *m* brush; **spazzolino da denti** toothbrush

specchietto retrovisore *m* rear-view mirror

specchio *m* mirror

specializzato(a) skilled

specialmente especially

specie *f* kind

**specificare** to specify
**spedalità** f hospital admissions office; hospital expenses
**spedire** to send; to dispatch; to ship
**spegnere** to turn off; to put out
**spellarsi** to peel
**spendere** to spend
**spento(a)** off; out
**speranza** f hope
**sperare** to hope
**spesa** f expense; **fare la spesa** to go shopping
**spese** fpl expenditure; expenses; costs; **spese mediche** or **sanitarie** medical expenses; **spese di spedizione** postage
**spesso** often
**spesso(a)** thick
**spettacolo** m show; performance
**spezie** fpl spices
**spezzatino** m stew; **carni bianche in spezzatino** poultry stew
**spia** f spy; warning light; **con la spia spenta non selezionate** do not use when light is out
**spiacente** sorry
**spiacere = dispiacere**
**spiacevole** unpleasant
**spiaggia** f beach; shore; **spiaggia libera** public beach
**spicchio d'aglio** m clove of garlic
**spiccioli** mpl (small) change
**spiedino** m skewer; **spiedini di calamari** squid kebabs
**spiedo** m spit; **pollo allo spiedo** spit-roasted chicken
**spiegare** to explain; to unfold; to spread out
**spiegazione** f explanation; **spiegazione segni convenzionali** explanation of symbols
**spilla** f brooch
**spillo** m pin
**spina** f bone (of fish); plug

(electric); **spina dorsale** backbone; **togliere la spina** remove the plug
**spinaci** mpl spinach; **spinaci al burro** spinach in butter
**spingere** to push; **spingere i carrelli all'uscita** please leave trolleys at the exit
**splendere** to shine
**spogliarello** m striptease
**spogliarsi** to undress
**spogliatoio** m dressing room
**spolverare** to dust
**sporcizia** f dirt
**sporco(a)** dirty
**sporgersi: è pericoloso sporgersi** it is dangerous to lean out
**sport: sport invernali** mpl winter sports
**sportello** m counter, window; door (of car); **servizio sportelli automatici** automatic banking service
**sposa** f bride
**sposato(a)** married
**sposo** m bridegroom
**spostare** to move
**sprecare** to waste
**spremere** to squeeze
**spremuta** f fresh juice; **spremuta d'arancia/di limone/di pompelmo** fresh orange/lemon/grapefruit juice
**spruzzare** to spray
**spugna** f sponge
**spuma** f foam; fizzy drink; **spuma di tonno** tuna mousse
**spumante** sparkling
**spuntare** to trim (hair)
**spuntino** m snack
**sputare** to spit
**squadra** f team; squad; **squadra mobile** flying squad
**squillare** to ring
**S.r.l.** Ltd
**stabile** stable; firm; m building
**stabilimento** m factory; **stabilimento balneare**

bathing establishment
**stabilire** to establish
**staccarsi** to come off
**stadio** m stadium
**stagionato(a)** ripe; mature
**stagione** f season; **alta/bassa stagione** high/low season; **stagione di prosa** theatre season
**stagno¹** m tin
**stagno²** m pond
**stagnola** f tin foil
**stalla** f stable
**stampa** f print; press (newspapers, journalists)
**stampatello** m block letters
**stampigliatura** f: **non è valido senza la stampigliatura** not valid unless stamped
**stancarsi** to get tired
**stanco(a)** tired
**stanotte** tonight; last night
**stantio(a)** stale
**stanza** f room; **stanza da bagno** bathroom; **stanza doppia/a due letti** double/twin-bedded room; **stanza da letto** bedroom; **stanza matrimoniale** double room; **stanza degli ospiti** guest room; **stanza singola** single room
**stappare** to uncork; to uncap
**stare** to stay; to be; to fit; **stare per fare** to be about to do; **stare in piedi** to stand
**starnuto** m sneeze
**stasera** tonight
**Stati Uniti (d'America)** mpl United States (of America), US(A)
**stato** m state
**statura** f height
**stazione** f station; resort; **stazione autocorriere** coach station; **stazione balneare** seaside resort; **stazione base di partenza bus** bus departure point; **stazione marittima** seaside town; **stazione di**

**servizio** petrol station; **stazione termale** spa
**stecca** f splint; carton
**stella** f star
**stelo** m stem
**stendere** to stretch; to spread; to hang out; to lay down
**stendersi** to lie down
**sterlina** f sterling; pound
**sterzo** m steering wheel; steering
**stesso(a)** same; **io/lei** etc **stesso(a)** I myself/you yourself etc
**stile** m style
**stima** f estimate
**stinco** m shin
**stipendio** m salary
**stirare** to iron
**stirarsi** to strain (muscle); to stretch
**stitichezza** f constipation
**stitico(a)** constipated
**stivale** m boot
**stivalone di gomma** m wellington boot
**stoccafisso** m stockfish
**stoffa** f fabric
**stomaco** m stomach
**storia** f history; story
**storico(a)** historic(al)
**storione** m sturgeon
**storto(a)** crooked
**stoviglie** fpl crockery
**stracchino** m soft, creamy cheese
**stracciatella** f clear soup with eggs and cheese stirred in; vanilla-flavoured ice-cream with chocolate chips
**straccio** m rag; cloth
**stracotto** m beef stew
**strada** f road; street; **strada principale** main road; **strada secondaria** side road; side street; **strada sussidiaria** relief road; **strada statale** main road; **strada a doppia carreggiata** dual carriageway; **strada senza uscita** dead end
**straniero(a)** foreign;

overseas; m/f foreigner
**strano(a)** strange; odd
**straordinario(a)** extraordinary
**strappare** to tear; to rip; to pull off
**strapparsi** to rip; to split
**strappo** m tear
**strato** m layer
**stravagante** extravagant; odd
**strega** f witch
**stretto(a)** narrow; tight
**strillo** m scream
**stringa** f shoelace
**stringere** to squeeze; **stringere la mano** to shake hands
**striscia** f strip; stripe; streak
**strizzare** to wring
**strofinaccio** m duster; dishcloth
**strofinare** to rub
**strudel** m: **strudel di mele** apple strudel
**strumento** m instrument
**studiare** to study
**studio** m study; studio
**stufa** f stove
**stufato** m stew
**stufato(a)** braised
**stuoia** f meat
**stupore** m amazement
**stuzzicadenti** m toothpick
**stuzzichino** m appetizer
**su** on; onto; over; about; up
**sua** his; her; hers; its; your; yours
**sub(acqueo)** m skindiver
**subacqueo(a)** underwater
**subire** to suffer
**subito** at once
**succedere** to happen
**succhiotto** m dummy (baby's)
**succo** m juice; **succo di frutta** fruit juice; **succo di limone** lemon juice; **succo di pompelmo** grapefruit juice
**succoso(a)** juicy
**succursale** f branch
**sud** m south

**sudare** to sweat
**suddito(a)** m/f subject (person)
**sudicio(a)** filthy
**sudore** m sweat
**sue** his; her; hers; its; your; yours
**suggerimento** m suggestion
**sughero** m cork
**sugli** = **su** + **gli**
**sugo** m sauce; gravy; juice
**sui** = **su** + **i**
**suino(a): carni suine** fpl pork meats
**suo** his; her; hers; its; your; yours
**suocera** f mother-in-law
**suocero** m father-in-law
**suoi** his; her; hers; its; your; yours
**suola** f sole
**suolo** m ground; soil
**suonare** to ring; to play; to sound
**suono** m sound
**superare** to exceed; to pass; to get over; to overtake
**superficie** f surface
**superiore** upper; senior; superior
**supermercato** m supermarket
**supplementare** extra
**supplemento** m: **supplemento singola** supplement for single room; **supplemento rapido** supplement to be paid when travelling by rapido
**supplente** temporary; acting
**supporre** to suppose
**supposta** f suppository
**surgelato(a): prodotti surgelati** frozen foods
**surriscaldarsi** to overheat
**susina** f plum
**sussidio** m subsidy
**svago** m relaxation; pastime
**svaligiare** to rob
**svalutazione** f devaluation
**svantaggio** m disadvantage;

handicap
**sveglia** f alarm (clock)
**svegliare** to wake
**svegliarsi** to wake up
**sveglio(a)** awake; smart
**svelto(a)** quick
**svenire** to faint
**svestire** to undress
**svestirsi** to undress
**sviluppare** to develop
**sviluppo** m: **sviluppo rapido** fast developing service (photos); **sviluppo e stampa** developing and printing
**svincolo** m slip road
**svitare** to unscrew
**Svizzera** f Switzerland
**svizzero(a): (bistecca alla) svizzera** f ≈ beefburger
**svolta** f turn
**svuotare** to empty; to drain

# T

**T** ground floor; **T sali e tabacchi** tobacconist's (shop)
**tabaccaio(a)** m/f tobacconist
**tabaccheria** f tobacconist's (shop)
**tabacco** m tobacco; **tabacchi** tobacconist's (shop)
**tabella** f table (list)
**tabellone** m notice board
**tacchino** m turkey
**tacco** m heel; **tacchi a spillo** stiletto heels
**taccole** fpl mange-tout peas
**tachimetro** m speedometer
**tafano** m horsefly
**taglia** f size (of clothes); **taglie forti** larger sizes
**tagliare** to cut
**tagliarsi** to cut oneself
**tagliatelle** fpl flat strips of pasta
**taglierini** mpl thin soup noodles

**taglio** m cut
**tailleur** m (tailored) suit
**tailleur-pantalone** m trouser-suit
**tale** such
**taleggio** m mild, medium-hard cheese
**talloncino** m counterfoil
**tallone** m heel
**tamburo** m drum
**tampone assorbente** m tampon
**tanti(e)** so many
**tanto(a)** so much; so; **tanto(a) quanto(a)** as much/many as; **ogni tanto** now and then, now and again; **di tanto in tanto** from time to time
**tappa** f stop; stage
**tappare** to cork; to plug
**tappetino** m rug
**tappeto** m carpet
**tappezzare** to paper
**tappo** m top; cork; stopper; plug (for basin etc)
**tardi** late
**targa (d'immatricolazione)** f number plate
**tariffa** f tariff; rate; **tariffa doganale** customs tariff; **tariffa festiva** rate on holidays; **tariffa normale/ridotta** standard/reduced rate; **tariffa notturna** night rate; **tariffa ordinaria/a ore di punta** ordinary/peak rate
**tartufo** m truffle (fungus)
**tasca** f pocket
**tassa** f tax; **tassa d'ingresso** admission charge; **tassa di soggiorno** tourist tax; **tasse e percentuali di servizio** taxes and service charges
**tassì** m taxi
**tasso** m rate; **tasso di cambio** exchange rate; **tasso di interesse** interest rate
**tasto** m key
**tattica** f tactics
**tavola** f table; plank; board;

painting; **tavola calda** snack bar; **noleggio tavole** surfboards/windsurfing boards for hire; **tavola a vela** windsurfing board
**tavoletta** f bar (of chocolate)
**tazza** f cup
**te** you
**tè** m tea; **tè al limone/al latte** tea with lemon/milk; **tè freddo** iced tea; **tè alla menta** mint tea
**teatro** m theatre; drama
**tecnico(a)** technical; m/f technician
**tedesco(a)** German
**tegame** m (frying) pan; **patate in tegame** potatoes with peppers, onion, tomato and oregano
**tegola** f tile (on roof)
**teiera** f teapot
**tela** f cloth; canvas
**telaio** m chassis
**telecamera** f television camera
**Telecom Italia** f Italian telephone company
**telecronaca** f television report
**telefonare** to telephone
**telefonata** f phone-call; **telefonata a carico del destinatario** reversed charge call
**telefono** m telephone
**telegiornale** m television news
**teleobiettivo** m telephoto lens
**teleselezione** f S.T.D.
**televisione** f television
**televisore** m television (set)
**temere** to fear
**temperatura** f: **temperatura ambiente** room temperature; **temperatura di servizio:...** temperature for serving:...
**temperino** m penknife
**tempio** m temple (building)
**tempo** m weather; time
**temporale** m

thunderstorm

**tenda** f curtain; tent; **tenda canadese** ridge tent

**tendere** to stretch; to hold out; to tend

**tendina** f blind

**tenere** to keep; to hold; **tenere rigorosamente la destra** keep to the right

**tendina** f blind

**tenere** to keep; to hold; **tenere rigorosamente la destra** keep to the right

**tenero(a)** tender

**tenore** m: **tenore alcolico** alcohol content; **tenore di vita** standard of living

**tensione** f voltage tension

**tentare** to attempt; to tempt

**tentativo** m attempt

**tenuta** f estate (*property*)

**teppista** m vandal

**tergicristallo** m windscreen wiper

**terme** fpl thermal baths

**terminare** to end

**termine** m term

**terra** f ground; earth; soil; land; **a terra** ashore; **avere una gomma a terra** to have a flat tyre

**terrapieno** m embankment

**terrazza** f terrace

**terremoto** m earthquake

**terreno** m ground

**terzi** mpl third party

**terzo(a)** third

**teschio** m skull

**teso(a)** tight; tense

**tesoro** m treasure

**tessera** f (membership) card; pass; season ticket; **tessera di credito** credit card; **tessera nominativa** card with named user

**tessili** mpl textiles

**tessuto** m fabric; **tessuti e filati** textiles

**testa** f head

**testamento** m will

**testimone** m witness

**testimonianza** f evidence (*of witness*)

**testina** f: **testina di abbacchio/vitello** lamb's/calf's head

**testo** m text

**tettarella** f teat (*for bottle*); dummy

**tetto** m roof

**tettoia** f shelter

**Tevere** m Tiber

**TG** *abbreviation of* telegiornale

**ti** you; to you; yourself

**ticket** m prescription charge

**tifoso** m fan

**tigre** f tiger

**timballo** m mixture of meat, fish etc cooked in a mould lined with pastry or potato

**timbro** m (rubber) stamp

**timo** m thyme

**timone** m rudder

**tinca** f tench

**tinta** f dye

**tintoria** f dry-cleaner's

**tintura** f dye; rinse (*for hair*); **tintura di iodio** tincture of iodine

**tipo** m type

**tipografia** f typography

**tiramisù** m sponge cake soaked in coffee and filled with a kind of cream cheese mixed with eggs, sugar, whipped cream and sprinkled with chocolate

**tirare** to pull

**tiro** m: **tiro con l'arco** archery

**titoli** mpl stocks

**titolo** m headline; title; qualification

**toboga** m toboggan

**Tocai** m dry white wine from Friuli

**toccare** to touch; to feel; to handle; **tocca a Lei** it's your turn; **vietato toccare la merce (esposta)** do not handle the merchandise

**toeletta** f dressing-table; toilet

**togliere** to remove; to take away

**togliersi** to take off

**tomba** f grave; tomb

**tonfo** m splash; thud

**tonnellata** f ton

**tonno** m tuna

**tonsillite** f tonsillitis

**topo** m mouse

**torace** m chest

**torcere** to twist

**torcicollo** m stiff neck

**Torino** f Turin

**tornare** to return; to come/go back

**toro** m bull

**torre** f tower

**torrefazione** f coffee shop

**torrone** m nougat

**torta** f cake; tart; pie; **torta di gelato** ice-cream cake; **torta di riso** rice mould; **torta salata** savoury tart; **torta di uova e asparagi** egg and asparagus flan

**tortellini** mpl pasta rings filled with seasoned meat; **tortellini in brodo** tortellini in broth

**tortello** m pasta ring filled with spinach and cream cheese

**tortellone** m pasta ring filled with cheese, egg, parsley and cream cheese

**torto** m wrong; **aver torto** to be wrong

**Toscana** f Tuscany

**tosse** f cough

**tossicomane** m/f drug addict

**tostapane** m toaster

**tosti** mpl toasted sandwiches

**totip** m similar to football pools, but for horse-racing

**Totocalcio** m football pools

**tovaglia** f tablecloth

**tovagliolo** m napkin

**tra** between; among(st); in

**traccia** f trace; track

**tracciato** m: **posteggio limitatamente entro i tracciati** parking only within area indicated

**traduzione** *f* translation
**traghetto** *m* ferry
**traguardo** *m* finishing line
**trama** *f* plot
**tramezzino** *m* sandwich
**tramonto** *m* sunset
**trampolino** *m* diving-board
**tranne** except (for)
**tranquillante** *m* tranquillizer
**tranquillo(a)** quiet; calm; peaceful
**transito** *m*: **transito voli nazionali/internazionali** domestic/international transit passengers
**trapano** *m* drill
**trappola** *f* trap
**trapunta** *f* quilt
**trascorrere** to pass; to spend
**trasferibile** transferable
**trasferimento** *m* transfer
**trasferire** to transfer
**trasferirsi** to move
**trasgressore** *m*: **i trasgressori saranno assoggettati alla penalità di ...** offenders will be subject to a fine of ...
**trasloco** *m* move (*moving house*)
**trasmettere** to transmit; to broadcast
**trasmissione** *f* broadcast; transmission
**trasparente** transparent; clear
**traspirare** to perspire
**trasporto** *m* transport; **trasporto consentito con biglietto preacquistato** bus tickets must be purchased before boarding
**trasversale** *f*: **(strada) trasversale** side street
**trattamento** *m* treatment
**trattare** to treat; to handle
**trattative** *fpl* talks; negotiations
**trattenere** to keep back; to detain
**trattino** *m* dash; hyphen
**tratto** *m*: **tratto di linea interrotto per lavori** section of the line closed due to maintenance work
**trave** *f* beam
**traversata** *f* crossing; flight
**travestimento** *m* disguise
**tre** three
**treccia** *f* plait
**tredici** thirteen
**tremare** to shake
**treno** *m* train; **treno merci** goods train; **treno navetta** alpine train for the transport of cars and their passengers; **treno periodico** train which operates only during certain periods; **treni in partenza** train departures
**trenta** thirty
**tribù** *f* tribe
**tribunale** *m* court (*law*)
**triglia** *f* mullet
**trimestre** *m* term
**trinciare** to cut up
**trippa** *f* tripe
**triste** sad
**tritacarne** *m* mincer
**tritare** to mince; to chop
**trittico** *m* triptych
**tromba** *f* trumpet
**tronco** *m* trunk
**troppi(e)** too many
**troppo** too much; too
**troppo(a)** too much
**trota** *f* trout
**trovare** to find
**truccarsi** to make (oneself) up
**trucco** *m* make-up; trick
**truppa** *f* troop
**tu** you
**tua** your; yours
**tubo** *m* pipe; tube; **il tubo di scappamento** exhaust
**tue** your; yours
**tuffo** *m* dive; **vietati i tuffi** no diving
**tumulto** *m* riot
**tuo** your; yours
**tuoi** your; yours
**tuono** *m* thunder
**tuorlo** *m* yoke
**turista** *m/f* tourist
**turno** *m* turn; shift; **di turno** on duty; **chiuso per turno (di riposo) il lunedì** closed on Mondays
**tuta** *f* overall; suit (*astronaut, diver*); track suit
**tutore(trice)** *m/f* guardian
**tuttavia** nevertheless
**tutti(e)** all; everybody
**tutto** everything
**tutto(a)** all; **tutta la giornata** all day

# U

**ubbidire** to obey
**ubicazione** *f* location
**ubriaco(a)** drunk
**uccello** *m* bird
**uccidere** to kill
**ufficiale**[1] *m* officer; official
**ufficiale**[2] official
**ufficio** *m* bureau; office; service (*in church*); **ufficio informazioni** information office; **ufficio oggetti smarriti** lost property office; **ufficio del personale** personnel office; **ufficio postale** post office; **ufficio del registro** registry office; **ufficio turistico** tourist office
**ufficioso(a)** unofficial
**uguale** equal; even
**ultimo(a)** last
**umano(a)** human
**umidi** *mpl* stews
**umido(a)** wet, damp; **carne/pesce in umido** meat/fish stew
**umore** *m* mood
**un** a; an; one
**uncino** *m* hook
**undici** eleven
**unghia** *f* nail
**unguento** *m* ointment
**unico(a)** only; unique
**unire** to join; to unite; to connect
**unità sanitaria locale** *f* local health centre
**unito(a)** united; plain; self-coloured
**università** *f* university

**uno(a)** a; an; one; **l'un l'atro** one another
**uomo** m (pl **uomini**) man; **uomo d'affari** businessman
**uovo** m egg; **uovo al burro** egg fried in butter; **uovo in camicia/alla coque** poached/boiled egg; **uovo fritto/ripieno/sodo** fried/stuffed/hard-boiled egg; **uovo di Pasqua** Easter egg; **uova affogate** poached eggs; **uova in frittata** omelette; **uova strapazzate** scrambled eggs
**uragano** m hurricane
**urlo** m scream; howl
**urtare** to bump; to bump into
**usare** to use
**usato(a): auto usate** second-hand cars
**uscire** to come out; to go out; **vietato uscire dalla pista** follow the ski tracks
**uscita** f exit; **uscita operai** factory exit; **uscita di sicurezza** emergency exit; **uscita a vela** sailing trip
**uscite** fpl outgoings
**USL** abbreviation of **unità sanitaria locale**
**uso** m use
**utente** m/f user
**utero** m womb; uterus
**utile** useful
**utilitaria** f runabout
**uva** f grapes; **uva passa** currants; raisins; **uva spina** gooseberry

## V

**va: Lei va** you go; **lui va** he goes
**vacanza** f holiday(s)
**vacca** f cow
**vado** I go
**vagabondo(a)** m/f tramp
**vaglia** m postal order; money order; **vaglia estero** or **internazionale** international postal order
**vago(a)** vague
**vagone** m carriage; wagon; **vagone letto** sleeping car; **vagone ristorante** restaurant car
**vaiolo** m smallpox
**valanga** f avalanche
**valere** to be worth; to be valid; **vale la pena** it's worth it
**valico** m pass; **valico di confine** border crossing
**validare** to make valid
**valigeria** f leather goods; leather goods shop
**valigia** f suitcase
**valle** f valley; **a valle** downstream; downhill
**valore** m value
**Valpolicella** m light, dry red wine with a trace of bitterness
**valuta** f currency
**valutare** to value
**valvola** f valve
**valzer** m waltz
**vandalismo** m: **atti di vandalismo** acts of vandalism
**vaniglia** f vanilla
**vanno** they/you go
**vano** m room
**vantaggio** m benefit; advantage
**vantaggioso(a): a condizioni vantaggiose** on favourable terms
**vantarsi** to boast
**vapore** m steam
**variabile** variable; changeable
**variare** to vary
**varicella** f chicken pox
**vario(a)** various
**vasca da bagno** f bath
**vasellame** m crockery, china
**vaso** m vase; pot
**vassoio** m tray
**ve** before lo, la, li, le, ne = **vi**
**vecchio(a)** old
**vedere** to see: **non vedere l'ora di** to look forward to
**vedersi** to meet; to show
**vedova** f widow
**vedovo** m widower
**veduta** f view
**veicolo** m vehicle
**vela** f sail; sailing; **vela d'altura** ocean sailing
**veleno** m poison
**veliero** m sail(ing) boat
**velina** f tissue paper
**vellutato(a)** velvety
**velluto** m velvet; **velluto a coste** corduroy
**velo** m veil
**veloce** fast
**velocità** f speed
**vena** f vein
**venatura** f grain (in wood)
**vendemmia** f grape harvest, vintage
**vendere** to sell; **qui si vende ... ...** sold here
**vendita** f sale; **in vendita** on sale; **vendita al minuto** retail; **vendita promozionale** special offer; **vendita a rate** hire purchase; **vendita di realizzo per rinnovo locali** clearance sale due to refurbishing
**venerdì** m Friday; **venerdì santo** Good Friday
**Venezia** f Venice
**venire** to come
**ventaglio** m fan (folding)
**venti** twenty
**ventilatore** m fan; ventilator
**vento** m wind
**ventola** f fan
**ventuno** m twenty-one; pontoon
**veramente** really
**verbale** m minutes; record
**verde** green; **il rispetto del verde è affidato al senso civico dei cittadini** look after your town's parks and gardens; **benzina verde** unleaded petrol
**Verdicchio** m dry white wine from the Marche

**verdura** f vegetables

**Verduzzo** m dry white wine

**vergogna** f shame

**vergognarsi (di)** to be ashamed (of)

**verificare** to check

**verità** f truth

**verme** m worm

**vermicelli** mpl: **vermicelli alle vongole veraci** thin noodles with real clams

**vermut** m vermouth

**Vernaccia** m dry or sweet white wine

**vernice** f varnish; paint; **vernice fresca** wet paint

**vero(a)** true; real

**versamento** m payment; deposit

**versare** to pour; to deposit

**verso** toward(s)

**vertigine** f dizziness

**vescica** f bladder

**vescovo** m bishop

**vespa** f wasp

**vestaglia** f dressing gown

**veste** f dress

**vestiario** m wardrobe

**vestibolo** m hall

**vestire** to dress

**vestirsi** to dress (oneself)

**vestiti** mpl clothes

**vestito** m dress; suit (man's)

**vetrata** f glass door/window

**vetrina** f shop window

**vetro** m pane, glass

**vettura** f coach (of train)

**vi** you; to you; yourselves; each other; there; here

**via**[1] f street

**via**[2] via, by way of

**viadotto** m viaduct

**viaggiare** to travel

**viaggiatore** m traveller

**viaggio** m journey; trip; drive; **viaggi** travel; **buon viaggio!** enjoy your trip!; **viaggio di nozze** honeymoon; **viaggio organizzato** package holiday; **viaggi per**

**studenti** student travel

**viale** m avenue

**vicenda** f event; **a vicenda** in turn

**vicinato** m neighbourhood

**vicino** near; close by

**vicino(a)** m/f neighbour

**vicolo** m alley; lane; **vicolo cieco** dead end

**vietare** to forbid

**vietato(a): vietato fumare** no smoking; **vietato scendere** no exit

**vigile** m policeman; **vigili del fuoco** fire brigade; **vigile urbano** traffic warden

**vigilia** f ewe

**vigliacco** m coward

**vigna** f vineyard

**villaggio** m: **villaggio vacanze** holiday village

**villeggiante** m/f holidaymaker

**villeggiatura** f: **in villeggiatura** on holiday; **luogo di villeggiatura** holiday resort

**vimine** m wicker

**vincere** to win; to defeat

**vincitore(trice)** m/f winner

**vincolo** m: **senza alcun vincolo** without obligation

**vino** m wine; **vino bianco/rosso/rosato** or **rosé** white/red/rosé wine; **vino in lattina** can of wine; **vino novello di pronta beva** new wine, ready for drinking; **vini da pasto** table wines; **vini pregiati** quality wines; **vini da taglio** blending wines

**Vin Santo** m dessert wine, gold in colour, from Tuscany

**violenza** f violence

**violoncello** m cello

**viottolo** m lane

**vipera** f adder

**virare di bordo** to tack

**virgola** f comma; decimal point

**visiera** f visor; peak (of cap)

**visione** f vision; **cinema di**

**prima visione** cinema where new-release films are shown

**visita** f visit; medical examination; **visita guidata** guided tour; **visita in pullman** coach tour

**viso** m face

**visone** m mink

**vista** f eyesight; view; **camera con vista mare** room with sea view

**visto** m visa; **visto di ingresso/di transito** entry/transit visa

**visualizzatore** m: **nel visualizzatore si accenderà la lampadina rossa** the red light will show on the display

**vita** f life; waist; **vita notturna** night life

**vite** f vine; screw

**vitello** m veal; calf; **vitello tonnato** veal in tuna fish sauce, served cold

**vitigno** m vine

**vittima** f victim

**vivace** lively

**vivande** fpl food

**vivere** to live

**vivo(a)** live; alive

**viziare** to spoil (child)

**vocabolario** m vocabulary; dictionary

**voce** f voice; **ad alta voce** aloud

**voi** you

**volano** m badminton

**volante**[1] m steering wheel

**volante**[2] f flying squad

**volare** to fly

**volere** to want

**volo** m flight; **volo di linea** scheduled flight; **volo provenienza ...** flight from ...

**volpe** f fox

**volta** f time; **una volta** once

**voltare** to turn

**voltarsi** to turn round; to turn over

**vongola** f clam

**vortice** m whirlpool

**vostri(e)** your; yours
**vostro(a)** your; yours
**voto** m vote; mark (in school)
**vulcano** m volcano
**vuotare** to empty
**vuoto(a)** empty

# Z

**zabaione** m whipped egg yolks and sugar with Marsala wine
**zafferano** m saffron
**zaino** m rucksack
**zampa** f leg; paw; foot

**zampone** m pig's trotter stuffed with minced pork and spices
**zanzara** f mosquito
**zanzariera** f mosquito net
**zenzero** m ginger
**zia** f aunt(ie)
**zingaro** m gypsy
**zio** m uncle
**zitto(a)** quiet
**zolletta** f cube; lump
**zona** f zone; **zona pedonale** pedestrian precinct; **zona di produzione** area where produced; **zona residenziale** housing estate

**zoppo(a)** m/f cripple
**zucca** f pumpkin; marrow
**zuccheriera** f sugar bowl
**zucchero** m sugar
**zucchini** mpl courgettes; **zucchini in agrodolce** courgettes in a sweet and sour sauce; **zucchini in teglia** baked courgettes with onions and Parmesan cheese
**zuccotto** m ice-cream sponge
**zuppa** f soup; **zuppa di cipolle** onion soup; **zuppa di pesce** fish soup; **zuppa inglese** trifle